PRAISE FOR *THE EMMA LAROCQUE READER*

"This volume distills half a century of trenchant, eloquent, and deeply *lived* wisdom about Métis connectedness, colonial violence, and the enduring beauty of Indigenous voices. As we read her brilliant essays alongside her haunting and resonant poems, we are reminded on every page why Emma LaRocque is a legendary thinker, teacher, and artist."
  Warren Cariou, *Professor, Department of English, Theatre, Film & Media, University of Manitoba*

"A book well worth publishing, *The Emma LaRocque Reader* has interdisciplinary appeal. Scholars of feminism, of postcolonial and Indigenous studies, of Canadian political science, sociology, and other fields of critical scholarship will want to read this book and recommend it to their students. Activists will want to consult it, too. LaRocque has been an important voice over several decades. It is inspiring and informative to read her work over the decades and now."
  Joyce Green, *Professor Emerita (retired), Department of Politics and International Studies, University of Regina*

"Emma LaRocque, distinguished Métis poet, scholar, and essayist, has been quietly – and not so quietly! – dissecting the roots and architecture of our society with clarity, insight, and compassion for nearly five decades. In this magnificent collection of her writings across the fields of history, literature, decolonization, and resistance, the Cree-speaking Professor of Indigenous Studies is revealed as one of our most important critical thinkers, and a true national treasure. Read this book! It might just blow your mind! Her words have power, and they will continue to live. Fortunately for the nation, she is not finished with us yet…"
  Parker Duchemin, *Professor (retired), Departments of English and Canadian Studies, Carleton University*

"*The Emma LaRocque Reader* is a valuable contribution to scholarship and brings much-deserved attention to a neglected Indigenous intellectual. Elaine Coburn is to be praised as the material she has selected is carefully curated and will provide a very useful teaching resource for students of Indigenous, Canadian, and North American studies, especially those concerned with studying the evolution of Indigenous literatures over the past half-century. This book is a much-appreciated contribution to the field of Indigenous Studies in Canada and internationally."
  Deanna Reder, *Professor, Departments of Indigenous Studies and English, Simon Fraser University*

The Emma LaRocque Reader

On Being Human

EDITED BY ELAINE COBURN

FOREWORD BY ARMAND RUFFO

AFTERWORD BY EMMA LAROCQUE

UNIVERSITY OF TORONTO PRESS
Toronto Buffalo London

© University of Toronto Press 2025
Toronto Buffalo London
utppublishing.com

All rights reserved. No part of this publication may be reproduced, stored in or introduced into a retrieval system, or transmitted in any form or by any means (electronic, mechanical, photocopying, recording, or otherwise) without the prior written permission of both the copyright owner and the above publisher of this book.

ISBN 978-1-4875-6445-2 (cloth)   ISBN 978-1-4875-5189-6 (EPUB)
ISBN 978-1-4875-5188-9 (paper)   ISBN 978-1-4875-5190-2 (PDF)

Library and Archives Canada Cataloguing in Publication

Title: The Emma LaRocque reader : on being human / edited by Elaine Coburn ; foreword by Armand Ruffo ; afterword by Emma LaRocque.
Names: LaRocque, Emma, 1949– author | Coburn, Elaine, 1975– editor | Ruffo, Armand Garnet, writer of foreword
Description: Includes bibliographical references and index.
Identifiers: Canadiana (print) 20240490428 | Canadiana (ebook) 20240490703 | ISBN 9781487564452 (cloth) | ISBN 9781487551889 (paper) | ISBN 9781487551902 (PDF) | ISBN 9781487551896 (EPUB)
Subjects: LCSH: Racism – Canada. | LCSH: Sexism – Canada. | LCSH: Postcolonialism – Canada. | LCSH: Canada – Ethnic relations. | CSH: First Nations literature – History and criticism. | CSH: First Nations – Social conditions.
Classification: LCC E78.C2 L37 2025 | DDC 971.004/97 – dc23

Cover design: Mark Rutledge
Cover image courtesy of the author

Printed and bound by CPI Group (UK) Ltd, Croydon, CR0 4YY

We welcome comments and suggestions regarding any aspect of our publications – please feel free to contact us at news@utorontopress.com or visit us at utorontopress.com. Every effort has been made to contact copyright holders; in the event of an error or omission, please notify the publisher.

We wish to acknowledge the land on which the University of Toronto Press operates. This land is the traditional territory of the Wendat, the Anishnaabeg, the Haudenosaunee, the Métis, and the Mississaugas of the Credit First Nation.

University of Toronto Press acknowledges the financial support of the Government of Canada, the Canada Council for the Arts, and the Ontario Arts Council, an agency of the Government of Ontario, for its publishing activities.

Contents

Foreword vii
ARMAND RUFFO

Preface xi
ELAINE COBURN

Acknowledgments xiii
EMMA LAROCQUE

Acknowledgments for Permissions to Reprint xv
ELAINE COBURN

Introduction xix
ELAINE COBURN

1975 A Personal Essay on Poverty 3

1983 The Métis in English Canadian Literature 6

1988 On the Ethics of Publishing Historical Documents 14

1989 Racism Runs Through Canadian Society 19

1990 Preface: Here Are Our Voices: Who Will Hear? 23

1990 Geese (poem) 38

1990 Nostalgia (poem) 40

1990 "Progress" (poem) 41

1990 The Red in Winter (poem) 43

1990 Incongruence (poem) 44

1990 Loneliness (poem) 45

Contents

1990 Beggar (poem) 46

1990 Tides, Towns and Trains 47

1992 My Hometown Northern Canada South Africa (poem) 64

1993 Violence in Aboriginal Communities 69

1994 Long Way from Home (poem) 78

1996 The Colonization of a Native Woman Scholar 82

2001 Native Identity and the Métis: Otehpayimsuak Peoples 89

2001 From the Land to the Classroom 109

2004 When the "Wild West" Is Me 121

2006 Sweeping (poem) 136

2006 Sources of Inspiration: The Birth of
"For the Love of Words": Aboriginal Writers of Canada 137

2007 Métis and Feminist 139

2009 Reflections on Cultural Continuity
Through Aboriginal Women's Writings 158

2010 Native Writers Reconstruct: Pushing Paradigms 182

2013 For the Love of Place – Not Just
Any Place: Selected Métis Writings 205

2015 "Resist No Longer":
Reflections on Resistance Writing and Teaching 212

2015 Contemporary Métis Literature:
Resistance, Roots, Innovation 231

2016 Colonialism Lived 251

2017 Powerlines (poem) 259

2022 Wehsakehcha, Comics, Shakespeare and
the Dictionary 261

Afterword 265
EMMA LAROCQUE

References 275

Index 297

Foreword:
"For the Love of Words"

I first encountered Emma LaRocque's writing long before I met her in person. It was the late 1970s, and I was in Ottawa attending university and working for a national "Native"[1] organization. Perusing the office's collection of books, I happened to come across a slim volume called *Defeathering the Indian*[2] (1975; see an excerpt "A Personal Essay on Poverty" in this volume) tucked between other books by Indigenous activists writing at that time. I had read work by the Native American activist and scholar Vine Deloria Jr., but because there were precious few books by Indigenous authors in either bookstores or libraries, I was yet to encounter much of that kind of writing on this side of the border.[3] To say a light suddenly went on in reading Emma's book would not be an overstatement. Among the details about the author, the book told me that "Emma LaRocque, a Métis from northwestern Alberta, has drawn from her own experience and reading.... She has not been afraid to speak out forcefully and she skilfully uses her barbed wit." To this I can now add that as a highly regarded activist, intellectual, scholar, poet, and teacher, her influence and impact on the development of Indigenous literature and socio-political thought in Canada has been ongoing for some fifty years.

My next encounter with Emma's work was her seminal "1990 Preface: Here are our voices: who will hear?" (see chapter in this volume).

---

1 The term commonly used to refer to Indigenous peoples at the time.
2 An excerpt from *Defeathering the Indian* would be anthologized in Oxford University Press's *An Anthology of Native Literature in English* in 2013, and again in a revised edition in 2020.
3 I would also discover other political texts published in Canada, like Harold Cardinal's *The Unjust Society* (1969), George Manuel's *The Fourth World* (Manuel and Posluns 1974), and Howard Adam's *Prison of Grass* (1975).

viii   Foreword

Having her hand on the pulse of what was going on in "Indian Country"[4] and accordingly on a movement that would help foster profound change across Canada – the Indigenous literary movement – her essay was the first critical essay by an Indigenous scholar to encapsulate thematically what Indigenous literature was about. To read it today is to be amazed by her insight, which essentially gave scholars a structure to understand what was going on across the country. Though the essay speaks specifically of writing by Indigenous women, much of what she says is still applicable to all Indigenous writers. Suffice to say that her essay helped usher in what we call today Indigenous literary criticism. Other essays and poems followed, and over the years she has not been one to shy away from addressing Indigenous writers themselves. Her writing challenges us to see the larger human picture. How can we break through a myriad of stereotypes, she asks, when they have been so imbedded in the hearts and minds of the colonized? And contentiously in light of the "awards culture" that now dominates literature in Canada: have the literary qualities of Indigenous writing been overlooked by an emphasis on the anthropological and political dimensions?

Undoubtedly, despite setbacks, Indigenous peoples in Canada have made unimaginable gains over the last few decades. Compared to the 1970s when Emma (and I) took undergraduate degrees, the number of Indigenous people graduating these days from universities and colleges across the country has risen exponentially. Still, I remember that nascent period well. Those were heady days before the internet and virtual communication when a relatively small coterie of Indigenous writers, poets, and playwrights from across the country would meet – at first in cafes and bars and later in the 1990s at academic conferences – to discuss our writing and the growing field of Indigenous literature. The breakthrough coincided with Indigenous scholars and writers like Emma LaRocque entering the academia and pushing to open doors for Indigenous students and for the fields of "Native Studies" and "English" to include literary writing by Indigenous peoples.

Emma entered the academy at a time when she had to fight tirelessly for the inclusion of Indigenous space. And though a gentle soul, fight she did. Whether directly with administration, through her own pedagogical instruction, or through the development of curriculum, she brought the reality of Indigenous lives to the forefront at a time of wilful neglect and intolerance. And it was in her capacity as a professor at the University of

---

4 An inclusive term used by Indigenous peoples themselves to refer to their spaces and territories at large.

Manitoba that she brought us together by uniquely bringing literature and literary scholarship together. I am thinking now of the conference "For the Love of Words, Aboriginal Writers of Canada Conference" (see chapter "Sources of Inspiration: The Birth of 'For the Love of Words': Aboriginal Writers of Canada" in this volume) that she co-hosted along with the late Dr. Renate Eigenbrod in 2004. I remember it well because there were some much-admired female writers speaking at the conference, yet Emma could have easily and fittingly taken the stage. What struck me from my interactions with her during the proceedings, and elsewhere, is her intellect, generosity, and humility. It is a rare combination, and even rarer in a time of pervasive self-absorption, and in writing this foreword, it is my wish that readers think of the strength and character of the person behind the words.

Armand Garnet Ruffo
Kingston, February 2023

Preface

More than a decade ago, when I was still living in France, I asked Emma LaRocque if I could reprint her poem "Long Way from Home" (included in this volume) to open a symposium on Indigenous research for a journal I was editing. We never stopped emailing after that, exchanging bits of poems or photographs of flowers or talking about life in the academy.

If there is meaning to Emma's remark that "we are all potentially more than the sum of our colonial parts" (2010, 61) it may lie in such shared interests, despite the fact that we are from different generations and grew up in very different ways, precisely because of the unjust "sum of colonial parts" that make up Canada.

Somewhere along the way, in our conversations – often over email, sometimes by phone, occasionally by Zoom – it struck me that it would be a good idea to have a Reader of Emma's works, making it easier for others to read her nearly fifty years of writing, gathered together in one place.

Between the intention and the act, many more years transpired than I would have expected or liked! I am sure that Emma wondered if I would ever see the project through, but it was never for want of conviction, only too much to do. Here it is, at last, so that others can enjoy Emma's lively, direct writing in poetry and in prose, from the beginning of her writing to her most recent contributions, including a new Afterword for this volume.

In helping to make the book possible, I would like to thank Marianne Goetzke – Coburn and Av Verhaege for help to transform several chapters from books into manuscript form, which is meticulous labour. In addition, I would like to acknowledge the helpful work by Breanna Berry in tracking down some of Emma's early writing, which informed the introduction. I would like to thank Peter Kulchyski for his helpful critiques of an early version of the introduction. I am very grateful to Chris Trott, whose insights reflect a deep knowledge of LaRocque's oeuvre and person, and whose remarks improved the introduction (with all errors remaining my own). I am grateful to Armand Ruffo for his beautiful Foreword.

Thank you to editor Jodi Lewchuk at the University of Toronto Press for being enthusiastic about the project. This book was made possible by an internal grant from Glendon Campus, York University. And not least, much love to my family, especially Arthur, Marianne (above), William, and my spouse Matthieu, for making a happy home that allowed this work to be done, often (too) late into the evenings.

Finally, I am thankful for Ruthie, who shares my love of flowers and whose many delicious meals I heard about by email and by phone. Above all, thank you to Emma, one of the most remarkable people I have ever met.

Elaine Coburn
Toronto, January 2023

Acknowledgments

As scholars we usually work in solitude. We research and produce data and ideas. We write and submit papers for publication. While we may generate academic interest and feedback, we remain largely solitaire in our pursuits, especially in the writing process. Some of us may wonder where our efforts land. Who publishes us? Who reads us? Who understands our information, our questions, our argumentations, ideas, or theories? Who besides the academic community values scholarly writing? Reviews of our works – if we are fortunate enough to be reviewed – can be frustrating because the very nature of reviewing lends itself to works being abbreviated or downright misinterpreted.

Given this context I was very surprised to begin receiving emails from France, from a Dr. Elaine Coburn who expressed interest in my work. The more we corresponded the more I realized how much of my work she valued and truly understood. By "understood" I do not mean just comprehending the information or ideas, but that she understood the social and the intellectual basis and the context of why and what I write. Shortly after Elaine moved to York University she approached me with a proposal to collect my writings for the purpose of producing an "Emma LaRocque Reader"; I was not prepared for this proposal, and my initial response was a long hesitation. Of course, I was flattered, but I was also frightened! What if nobody reads it? But she persisted and my friends and colleagues were most encouraging, so I finally agreed. With the proviso that it would have a different title.

How do you properly or adequately thank a colleague – and now a friend – for such an honour? Elaine has done most of the work – she has researched, collected, and gleaned the University of Toronto Press to have it published. Elaine lives up to her principles in that she has consistently involved me with her choices of the works to be included. Sometimes she had to wait patiently for my replies. The project has taken longer than we anticipated, partly due to the pandemic and to our workloads. Elaine is a true scholar, and her erudition in many fields has thoroughly impressed me. Not only is she an academic but also has great appreciation for poetry and the arts in general. She is a determined advocate of human rights and at the same time has a generous spirit. What has been most important for me in this process is that she is not only a colleague but also a friend. Elaine, thank you – I am humbled and honoured.

I also thank those friends and colleagues who have enthusiastically supported the idea of this project. A special thanks to my friends and colleagues in Indigenous Studies Drs. Chris Trott and Peter Kulchyski, who both read Elaine's initial collection and provided helpful and thoughtful assessments and suggestions. I am also appreciative of Drs. Joyce Green, Jean Friesen, and Paul DePasquali for their steadfast friendship and encouragement. And to Armand Ruffo, a fellow intellectual and poet, for agreeing to write a Preface.

And always, a special thanks to Ruthie for her all her patience and the culture and beauty.

Emma LaRocque
Winnipeg, March 2023

Acknowledgments for Permissions to Reprint

Note: Permissions are listed in alphabetical order by name of the publisher.

Thank you to Emma LaRocque for permission to reprint all of the following works. This includes:

LaRocque, Emma. "A Personal Essay on Poverty." In *Defeathering the Indian*, edited by Emma LaRocque, 67–71. Agincourt: The Book Society of Canada Limited, 1975.

LaRocque, Emma. "Preface: Here Are Our Voices: Who Will Hear?" In *Writing the Circle: Native Women of Western Canada*, edited by Jeanne Perrault and Sylvia Vance, xv–xxx. Edmonton: NeWest Publishers Limited, 1990.

LaRocque, Emma. "Incongruence (Poem)." In *Writing the Circle: Native Women of Western Canada*, edited by Jeanne Perrault and Sylvia Vance, 138. Edmonton: NeWest Publishers Limited, 1990.

LaRocque, Emma. "Loneliness (Poem)." In *Writing the Circle: Native Women of Western Canada*, edited by Jeanne Perrault and Sylvia Vance, 142. Edmonton: NeWest Publishers Limited, 1990.

LaRocque, Emma. "The Beggar (Poem)." In *Writing the Circle: Native Women of Western Canada*, edited by Jeanne Perrault and Sylvia Vance, 142. Edmonton: NeWest Publishers Limited, 1990.

LaRocque, Emma. "Geese Over the City (Poem)." In *Our Bit of Truth: An Anthology of Canadian Native Literature*, edited by Agnes Grant. Winnipeg: Pemmican Publications, 1990.

LaRocque, Emma. "Racism Runs through Canadian Society." In *Racism in Canada*, edited by Ormand McKague, 73–6. Saskatoon: Fifth Street Publishers, 1991.

LaRocque, Emma. "When the Other Is Me: Native Writers Confronting Canadian Literature." In *Issues of the North*, Vol. 1, edited by J.

Oakes and R. Riewe, 115–34. Edmonton and Winnipeg: Canadian Circumpolar Institute and the Department of Human Ecology, University of Alberta and the Department of Native Studies, University of Manitoba, 1996.

LaRocque, Emma. "The Native Identity and the Metis: Otehpayimsuak Peoples." In *A Passion for Identity: Canadian Studies for the 21st Century*, edited by David Taras and B. Rasporich, 318–400. Scarborough, ON: Nelson Thomson Learning, 2001.

LaRocque, Emma. 2000. "From the Land to the Classroom: Broadening Aboriginal Epistemology." In *Pushing the Margins: Native and Northern Studies*, edited by Jill Oakes, et al., 112–24. Winnipeg: Native Studies Press.

LaRocque, Emma. "Powerlines (Poem)." *Prairiefire* 38, no. 1 (2017): 9–10.

LaRocque, Emma. "Wehsakehcha, Comics, Shakespeare and the Dictionary." *Shelf Portraits*, June 25, 2021. richlerlibrary.ca//shelf-portraits/wehsakehcha-comics-shakespeare-and-the-dictionary.

Thank you to *Border Crossings* for permission to reprint:

LaRocque, Emma. "My Hometown Northern Canada South Africa (Poem)." *Border Crossings* 11, no. 4 (December 1992): First Nations Art &Culture (#44): 98–9.

Thank you to the *Canadian Journal of Native Studies* for permission to reprint:

LaRocque, Emma. "The Metis in English Canadian Literature." *The Canadian Journal of Native Studies* 3, no. 1 (1983): 85–94.

Thank you to Fernwood Press for permission to reprint:

La Rocque, Emma. "Metis and Feminist." In *Making Space for Indigenous feminism*, edited by Joyce Green, 53–71. Halifax: Fernwood Press, 2007.

LaRocque, Emma. "Resist No Longer: Reflections on Resistance Writing and Teaching." In *More Will Sing Their Way to Freedom*, edited by Elaine Coburn, 5–23. Halifax: Fernwood, 2015.

Thank you to Johns Hopkins University Press for permission to reprint:

LaRocque, Emma. "Long Way from Home." In *Ariel*, Vol. 25, no. 1: 122–26. Johns Hopkins University Press and the University of Calgary, 1994. Online: https://journalhosting.ucalgary.ca/index.php/ariel/issue/view/2267

Permissions   xvii

Thank you to Oxford University Press for permission to reprint:

LaRocque, Emma. "Contemporary Metis Literature: Resistance,
    Roots, Innovation." In *The Oxford Handbook of Canadian Literature*,
    edited by Cynthia Sugars, 129–49. New York: Oxford University
    Press, 2016.

Thank you to the Privy Council Office of the Government of Canada for
permission to reprint:

LaRocque, Emma. "Violence in Aboriginal Communities." In *The
    Report of the Royal Commission on Aboriginal Peoples*, 72–89. Ottawa,
    1994. Permission granted by the Privy Council Office.© His Majesty
    the King in Right of Canada, 2024.

Thank you to *Studies in Canadian Literature* for permission to reprint:

LaRocque, Emma. "Sweeping (Poem)." *Studies in Canadian Literature*
    31, no. 1 (2006): 10.
LaRocque, Emma. "Afterword: Sources of Inspiration: The Birth of
    'For the Love of Words': Aboriginal Writers of Canada." *Studies in
    Canadian Literature*, 31, no. 1 (2006): 159–60.

Thank you to TouchWood Editions for permission to reprint:

LaRocque, Emma. "Colonialism Lived." *In This Together: Fifteen Stories
    of Truth and Reconciliation*, edited by Danielle Metcalfe-Chenail,
    133–44. Reprinted with permission of TouchWood Editions, 2016.
    touchwoodeditions.com.

Thank you to the University of British Columbia for permission to reprint:

LaRocque, Emma. "Nostalgia (Poem)." In *Native Writers and Cana-
    dian Writing*, edited by W.H. New, 132. Vancouver: University
    of British Columbia Press, 1990. All rights reserved by the
    Publisher.
LaRocque, Emma. "Progress (Poem)." In *Native Writers and Canadian
    Writing*, edited by W.H. New, 137. Vancouver: University of British
    Columbia Press, 1990. All rights reserved by the Publisher.
LaRocque, Emma. "The Red in Winter (Poem)." In *Native Writers and
    Canadian Writing*, edited by W.H. New, 136. Vancouver: Univer-
    sity of British Columbia Press, 1990. All rights reserved by the
    Publisher.

xviii   Permissions

Thank you to the University of Calgary Press for permission to reprint:

LaRocque, Emma. "When the 'Wild West' Is Me: Re-Viewing Cowboys and Indians." In *Challenging Frontiers: The Canadian West*,
   edited by Lorry W. Felske and Beverly Rasporich, 136–53. Calgary:
   University of Calgary Press, 2005. https://doi.org/10.1515/978155
   2383070-013.

Thank you to the University of Manitoba Press for permission to reprint:

LaRocque, Emma. "On the Ethics of Publishing Historical Documents."
   In *"The Orders of the Dreamed": George Nelson on Cree Northern Ojibwa
   Religion and Myth, 1823*, edited by Jennifer S.H. Brown and Roger
   Brightman, 199–203. Winnipeg: University of Manitoba Press, 1988.
LaRocque, Emma. "Tides, Towns and Trains." In *Living the Changes*,
   edited by Joan Turner, 76–90. Winnipeg: University of Manitoba
   Press, 1990.
LaRocque, Emma. "The Colonization of a Native Woman Scholar."
   In *Women of the First Nations: Power, Wisdom and Strength*, edited by
   Patricia Chuchryk and Christine Miller, 11–18. Winnipeg: Univer-
   sity of Manitoba Press, 1996.
LaRocque, Emma. "Reflections on Cultural Continuity through
   Aboriginal Women's Writings." In *Restoring the Balance: First
   Nations Women, Community, and Culture*, edited by Gail Guthrie
   Valaskis, Eric Guimond, and Madeleine Dion Stout, 149–74.
   Winnipeg: University of Manitoba Press, 2009.
LaRocque, Emma. "Pushing Paradigms: Native Writers Reconstruct."
   In *When the Other Is Me: Native Resistance Discourse, 1850–1990*,
   edited by Emma LaRocque, 146–60. Winnipeg: University of Mani-
   toba Press, 2010.
LaRocque, Emma. "For the Love of Place – Not Just Any Place:
   Selected Métis Writings." In *Place and Replace: Essays on Western
   Canada*, edited by Esyllt W. Jones, Adele Perry, and Leah Morton,
   179–85, Winnipeg: University of Manitoba Press, 2013.

Introduction

ELAINE COBURN

We were most assuredly "human," and how best to know this but by our uniqueness.

Emma LaRocque (2010, 155), *When the Other Is Me*

This book brings together the writing of Cree-speaking Métis scholar, human rights activist, feminist, and poet Emma LaRocque. It is motivated by the conviction that her work stands beside the contributions of Albert Memmi (1957), and Edward Said (1978), and others who offer critical insights into the struggle to be recognized as human in the dehumanizing context of colonialism. Her writings and poems are widely anthologized, and her second book, *When the Other Is Me*, published in 2010, is an award-winning contribution to critical history, gender, literary, Indigenous, and postcolonial studies. But these contributions are scattered across many different publications, making it difficult to appreciate her contributions as a whole. This reader brings together a selection of LaRocque's writing from a fifty-year period, inviting those unfamiliar with her scholarship and poetry to discover her unique, urgent voice. At the same time, the collection seeks to make her writing more easily available to those who know her work so that they may fully engage with the range and breadth of her insights.

The questions that LaRocque considers are at once specific and universal. What does it mean to be human? What does it mean to be human when you are dehumanized as an Indigenous person, in settler colonial states? How do colonial myths and realities distort the existential possibilities of colonized peoples? How do contemporary Indigenous persons, especially artists, create new ways of being, knowing, and doing, opening up Indigenous futures and transforming nations like Canada in the process? Through her scholarship and poetry, LaRocque asks such vital questions, challenging conventional histories of a major settler state – or the "re-settler" state, as LaRocque insists (2010, 7–8) – in Canada and in nations like Canada. At the same time, she offers insights into enduring questions about our human possibilities, despite and against the dehumanizing context of colonialism.

In LaRocque's writing, colonialism figures in its most visceral consequences, notably the special torment of racial shame that "makes us hate what and who we love" (2010, 121). At the same time, she insists on the resilience of Indigenous peoples, while critically celebrating the contributions of Indigenous writers who "rather brilliantly" (96) challenge colonial histories, racisms, and other "invader lies" (113). In writings gathered here together for the first time, LaRocque invites us, wherever we are situated within colonial relations, to listen and especially to *hear* theirs and her distinctive voices (see chapter "Preface: Here Are Our Voices – Who Will Hear?"). When we listen, LaRocque's writing and that of the Indigenous scholars and artists she champions, bring us to new understandings of the historical and contemporary context. In particular, her writing sheds important light on re-settler colonialisms and Indigenous peoples' determination to maintain their humanity against colonial violence.

Travelling Farther and Faster

Perhaps I have travelled farther and faster. It did not take half a lifetime, but barely a decade, for me to be flung across the ages, and across yawning chasms of experience.

(see chapter "Tides, Towns and Trains")

In her writing, LaRocque draws upon unique intellectual resources. As she observes, she has travelled "farther and faster" than most across time and experience. LaRocque was born in 1949 and grew up in a comfortable log cabin built by her father in northeastern Alberta, Canada. Later, attracted by "lights and lights" (2017, 6) but also pushed by the ever-present forces of colonial dispossession, LaRocque chose to go to high school in southern Alberta, far from her home. In the 1970s, she entered university, first in Alberta and then in the United States. After receiving a MA in Religion/Peace Studies in 1976, she came to the University of Manitoba to take up graduate studies in history. While still a student, LaRocque was asked to teach a summer course for the newly created "Native Studies" program, as Indigenous Studies was then called. She discovered her "niche," as she puts it, becoming one of few Indigenous university teachers and later, even

Introduction

xxi

rarer, an Indigenous woman professor. Surviving and challenging racisms and sexisms from both White and Indigenous colleagues, she was a vital force in the creation and development of what was then Native Studies at the University of Manitoba, in central Canada. During that time, LaRocque developed a body of writing that is paradoxically well-known and underappreciated, especially taken together as a whole.

Indeed, even among those who know and appreciate LaRocque's work, there is no overall appraisal of her scholarship. Instead, reflecting her wide-ranging contributions, LaRocque's scholarly writings have been read in distinct fields. Thus, literary and postcolonial theorists appreciate her deconstruction of what she terms "the civ/sav dichotomy" in colonial writings, while feminists have taken up her uncompromising defence of Indigenous women against both colonial and Indigenous patriarchal violence. Indigenous Studies embraces her nuanced critique of Indigenous literature as a form of resistance, while historians – or at least those attuned to colonial realities – have taken up her analyses of the "hero-ification" of White re-settlers and the narrow, misleading representations of Indigenous peoples in historical texts. Educators have learned from her perceptive critiques of the erasure, and when they are included, her deconstruction of the stereotyping of Indigenous peoples in elementary and university textbooks. If each contribution is important in its own right, I contend that new resonances and tensions become apparent when her decades of scholarly writing are brought together in one place, for the first time.

This introduction makes the argument for sustained critical engagement with LaRocque's writing over the last half-century; but a welcoming scholarly reception is more complicated, especially outside of postcolonial and Indigenous Studies. This is not because her work does not merit the attention. Rather, Indigenous intellectuals, perhaps especially Indigenous women scholars, have not always been taken seriously across academia in the ways that their work merits. If LaRocque's scholarship has been celebrated as transformative within Indigenous Studies, this has not always been true among broader academic or general publics.

This is unsurprising in a context in which Indigenous peoples have been excluded for centuries from universities and so from shaping scholarly inquiry, even if today there are "exciting and extensive changes ... underway" (LaRocque 2010, 71). As Cree and Saulteaux scholar Margaret Kovach observes about the history of universities in the national context:

> given that the first university in Canada, Laval University opened its doors
> in 1663 followed by the oldest English language university, the University

xxii   The Emma LaRocque Reader

of New Brunswick in 1785, one could interpret the integration of an Indigenous presence as constituting a short period of inclusion within a long history of exclusion. (Kovach et al. 2015, 23)

Indeed, in Canada, under an 1880 amendment to the *Indian Act*, those recognized by the Crown as "Status Indians" were forcibly "enfranchised" if they obtained a university degree – that is, they lost Indian Status.

This policy ended in 1960 and never applied to Métis people like LaRocque. Nonetheless, until recently, Indigenous peoples have not been recognized as valuable knowers from within the academy (see, for instance, Smith 1999; Battiste 2013), and even today, recognition remains precarious, partial, and contested. In a poem entitled "Long Way from Home" (see chapter "Long Way from Home"), LaRocque observes that in the university – with its hallways "pallored by/ivory coloured/thoughts" – the "ologists" name and claim Indigenous spiritual objects and stories for their own purposes:

they put Ama's moosebones behind glass
they tell savage stories
in anthropology Cree

For centuries, White expert authority in the university positioned Indigenous peoples as objects of knowledge but not as knowers, even of their own cultures. Against such histories, since the 1960s and especially the 1970s, Indigenous scholars have created spaces in and across the academy for their own knowledges, at least partly on their own terms (for an overview of Indigenous women's contributions since the 1970s, see Coburn 2020).

Half a century ago, LaRocque was one of a handful of Indigenous people bringing Indigenous knowledges into the university. As she recalls, "When I started teaching Native Canadian Lit – all the way back in the late 1970s – I was perhaps one of two or three professors in Canada teaching such a course" (LaRocque 2006, 11). Since then, what was then "Native Studies" and is now Indigenous Studies has grown, becoming a vast, interdisciplinary field with major conferences, like the North American Indigenous Studies Association meetings, attended by hundreds every year, a host of well-regarded journals, like *American Indian Quarterly*, the *Canadian Journal of Native Studies*, and *Wicazo Sa Review*, as well as tens of thousands of articles and hundreds of university press books (for an overview, see Hokowhitu et al. 2020). But

Introduction xxiii

such hard-fought changes do not mean that gendered colonial racisms have disappeared, including within the university. Instead, there are persistent differences in the appreciation of "mainstream" scholars over Indigenous intellectuals, like LaRocque.

Despite these challenges, in the current historical moment, LaRocque's insights may have special resonance, as Indigenous resistance movements challenge and change public and academic understandings of Indigenous peoples and their knowledges. Settler colonial states, including Aotearoa/New Zealand, Australia, Canada, and the United States, are among the most powerful nations in the world. Across them, Indigenous movements have joined an increasingly diverse, expansive Indigenous scholarship to robustly challenge the foundational myths on which settler colonial nations were built, refusing the identification of these countries' futures with White settlement and the disappearance of Indigenous peoples (e.g., Tully, Asch, and Borrows 2018). In Aotearoa/New Zealand, Māori presence in schools and public life is increasingly part of a bicultural Māori/Pakeha conception of New Zealand once claimed by the colonizers for themselves, alone (Smith 2000). In Australia, Aboriginal peoples whom the government formally declared "extinct" have insisted on their contemporary, vibrant presence, defying self-serving narratives about the inevitably vanishing Aboriginal, incompatible with the colonial present (Walter and Andersen 2013, 89; Allard-Tremblay and Coburn 2023, for an overview of the Vanishing Indian myth). Recently, in the United States, land defenders and water protectors at Standing Rock became worldwide symbols of Indigenous commitments to other-than-human kin and the lands, as they stand against a pipeline and seek to protect the waters that sustain all life (Estes 2019).

On lands now known as (or more precisely, claimed by) Canada, where LaRocque lives and continues to write, we are in the aftermath of the Idle No More movement of 2012. During "the winter we danced" (Kinonda-niimi Collective 2014) diverse Indigenous peoples participated in round dances in shopping malls and walked hundreds of kilometres in water walks, affirming their relationships to the land in defiance of federal legislation lifting protections on waterways and challenging ongoing colonial oppression. A few years later, in 2015, the national Truth and Reconciliation Commission (TRC) publicly documented the violence and abuses of the assimilationist residential school system for Status Indian children. Operational from 1880 to 1996, the aim of these schools was "to kill the Indian in the child." Accordingly, the colonial state separated Status Indian children from their family, their cultures, their languages, and the land. Many were subject to sexual and physical abuse, and more than 5,000 children died, as the TRC documents. In 2019, the Missing and Murdered Indigenous Women's Inquiry published its final Report, establishing that ongoing violence against Indigenous girls and women meets the United Nations' definition of genocide.

In this context, where Indigenous voices demand to be heard about the violence of the colonial past and its persistence into a still-colonial present, LaRocque's prose writing has much to say. Her scholarship documents Indigenous resistance and broadens concerns beyond the residential school system to describe what it means to suffer the abuses of the public school system, from her own vantage point "as a public school survivor" (see chapter "Afterword"). She speaks out consistently and forcefully against violence against Indigenous women, and she takes care to unpack the backlash that Indigenous people face whenever they seek to raise concerns about the injustices they face (see chapter "Racism Runs Through Canadian Society").

Reaching beyond the current moment, LaRocque's work, gathered here, describes the dynamics that shape Indigenous–re-settler relationships beginning with the colonial invasion by Europeans more than five hundred years ago. She recounts stories of colonial invasion and dispossession, but she insists that neither the Indigenous past nor the Indigenous present is exhausted by genocide and violence. Rather, LaRocque's work celebrates creative expression by Indigenous writers and poets – voices that in their contemporary exploration of human existence are as unique and rich as any other literary tradition.

Finally, the edited collection here is informed, throughout, by LaRocque's vantage point as a Plains Cree–speaking Métis woman, as someone who grew up with a close connection to the land, later moving and adapting to an urban lifestyle. As LaRocque observes, in her lifetime, she has therefore travelled "farther and faster" than most, from her small family cabin, nurtured by parents whose livelihood was land-based, to her current role as a university professor. The consequence is a range of unusually clear-eyed analyses of our age, not least a devastating critique of the comfortable mythologies that persist about the historical foundations and present day of settler colonial nations. As LaRocque describes, the violence of the settler colonial project is not abstract, but about everyday *experience* (2010, 100). At the same time, LaRocque insists that Indigenous peoples and settlers alike are irreducible to the violence of colonial relationships. As she insists, "we are all potentially more than the sum of our colonial parts" (2010, 61), and so her writing is meant to speak to all of us.

Introduction   xxv

Growing Up Métis

LaRocque was in born into a Cree-speaking Métis people in the mid-twentieth century near Lac La Biche, which is about 222 kilometres northwest of Edmonton, in what is now called Western Canada. As LaRocque explains, if the historical origins of the Métis are in the relationships between White re-settlers and Indigenous women, by the mid-1700s, the Métis were "more than the sum of White and Indian mix" (see chapter "Native Identity and the Métis: Otehpayimsuak Peoples"). By the early 1800s, "(t)he Red River Métis were culturally distinct, geographically concentrated and politically and militarily organized [people]" (see chapter "Native Identity and the Métis: Otehpayimsuak Peoples"), both a people and a polity. As LaRocque describes:

> Cree-Métis peoples ... of course, originate from both Europeans and Indians during the fur-trade era, but over time formed their own ethnicity (i.e., Métis marrying Métis) with a culture blended, yet distinct from both groups. Although these people were excluded from the *Indian Act* and treaties,[1] they were and remain primarily connected to *Nehiyawewak* (Cree speaking people), who themselves speak or grew up with *Nehiyawewin* (Cree language). Most were raised with parents, kin and communities whose cultural lifestyles were intimately connected with the land and with other Aboriginal people. (see chapter "Reflections on Cultural Continuity Through Aboriginal Women's Writings"; italics in original)

This Cree-speaking Red River Métis people and culture, sustained through relationships with kin and with land, is the family and culture into which LaRocque was born. Yet the Métis remained unrecognized by the colonial state as Indigenous peoples until the Constitution Act of 1982.

Indeed, even today, there are persistent misconceptions about what it means to be "Métis." Too often, the term is misunderstood, used to describe any person with "mixed" White and Indigenous ancestry (see also Andersen 2014; Gaudry 2018). Rather than being recognized as a distinct people, with a specific history and culture, being Métis is conflated with "métissage" and then taken up as a politically potent,

---

1 In Canada, the *Indian Act* of 1876 legally designates and legislates some people as "Indians" under the Crown. The Act provides Status Indian peoples with some distinct rights, but historically placed important restrictions on Indigenous peoples' movements, religious practices, and until 1960, the right to vote.

xxvi The Emma LaRocque Reader

hybridized symbol, naturalizing White national belonging through literal "mixing" with Indigenous – native – blood. As LaRocque observes, these misconceptions have consequences for Métis rights to their own lands. Hybridity confounded with Métisness erases the distinctive claims of the Métis people. Many political theorists and lay actors:

> ma(k)e no distinctions between individuals who are half-white/half-Indian, and those Métis Nation peoples of western Canada who formed a distinct ethnic culture and community. The more recent post-colonial emphasis on hybridity or border-crossing, useful concepts in some contexts, can serve to further obscure Métis national identity and culture and, in turn, Métis land and resource entitlements. (see chapter "For the Love of Place – Not Just Any Place: Selected Métis Writings")

In this supposedly postcolonial but actually re-settler colonial narrative, the Métis people disappear into a nativized White population, "as if they had no history, no cultures, no life worth mentioning" (2010, 83) – and hence no rights to their own lands.

Although there is significant confusion around what "Métis-ness" signifies today, ironically the nineteenth-century Métis leader Louis Riel is nevertheless well-known among Canadian publics, even recently becoming the hero of a graphic novel (Brown 2021). As a young man, Riel led the Métis against the colonial state in the unsuccessful Red River Resistance of 1869–70, and then, after a period in exile in Montana, he once more led the Métis in the Northwest Resistance of 1885. Riel lost both of these armed battles for Métis land and nationhood; he was hanged by colonial authorities for treason in 1885, aged forty-one, a "traitor" for defending his own lands against the colonial invading forces. The dramatic and tragic circumstances of his life may explain the national fascination with Riel. And yet, as LaRocque observes, Riel was not representative of all Métis people, but something of an anomaly: urban, French-speaking and formally educated, while in contrast, the Cree-speaking Métis were land-based hunters and traders (see chapter "Native Identity and the Métis: Otehpayimsuak Peoples").

For LaRocque's father, or Bapa,[2] born at the turn of the twentieth century, the colonial dispossession that Riel fought against – but lost –

---

2 As LaRocque explains, "'Ama' and 'Bapa' were/are our family terms for my mother and father." In using these affectionate names in her writing, she invites the reader to see her father within this loving family relationship.

Introduction   xxvii

profoundly marked his existence. As LaRocque remembers, "Bapa was a hard-working man forced by colonial history to raise his family in a road allowance section of land he never got to own" (see chapter "For the Love of Place – Not Just Any Place: Selected Métis Writings"). This fate was so common that the Métis became widely known as the "Road Allowance people" (Campbell 1995), so-called because they were restricted to living on the "allowance" lands set aside on either side of the future railway, from which they could be evicted at any time. This original dispossession was followed by others that have successively marked LaRocque's family life. As late as the 1950s, the northern Métis, including LaRocque's father, lost their traplines when "the province simply declared their trapping area a bombing range" (see chapter "Native Identity and the Métis: Otehpayimsuak Peoples"). Her father and other family members moved one hundred miles north seasonally to accommodate schooling at Lac La Biche, but in the 1960s that land was bulldozed and LaRocque "watched [as] my uncle's backyard [was] turned into a man-made lake" (see chapter "Native Identity and the Métis: Otehpayimsuak Peoples").

In the broader public imaginary, the violence of these waves of colonial dispossession is transformed into the comfortable stereotype of the Métis as nomad. As LaRocque explains, however romantically portrayed in popular culture, this narrative masks much more than it reveals:

> Many Métis – not all, but altogether too many – have been forced in some way or other to leave their special places. In this sense, there is some truth to the image of the Métis as prairie gypsies, but this should be seen as a consequence of displacement – not as a cultural or individual trait to be romanticized. The sad fact is that many Métis cannot come back to their places of origin due to urban and industrial encroachments, or outright dispossession by either federal or provincial laws and actions. (see chapter "For the Love of Place – Not Just Any Place: Selected Métis Writings")

When they could, the Métis of LaRocque's father's generation continued to live on the land; this was not only a deeply felt attachment, but a way of life that they loved and by which they could sustain their livelihood.

For LaRocque and her family, like other northern Métis, "land represented identity, culture, self-sufficiency, and independence. Landedness also meant family, home life, kin, and community"

xxviii   The Emma LaRocque Reader

(see chapter "For the Love of Place – Not Just Any Place: Selected Métis Writings"). As LaRocque recalls, "My father used to say we are nothing without land. Rarely did my gentle father make such categorical pronouncements" (see chapter "For the Love of Place – Not Just Any Place: Selected Métis Writings"). Despite this attachment, the colonial state has not honoured Métis relationships with the land, instead forcing the Métis into a peripatetic existence. For LaRocque's father's generation, survival demanded a life divided, combining subsistence living with waged labour on other peoples' land. As LaRocque describes, her parents and others in her community:

> continued to live off the land by hunting, trapping, fishing, gardening or picking berries and roots wherever possible [but t]hey supplemented their land-based resourcefulness with wage labour wherever they could: working the sugar beet fields, cutting and selling wood, picking rocks, stooking hay, picking and selling blueberries and seneca roots, sewing and so forth. (see chapter "Native Identity and the Métis: Otehpayimsuak Peoples")

Despite this resourcefulness, many of the Road Allowance People, lived in "dire poverty" (LaRocque 1985), succumbing to a range of diseases, including tuberculosis, "(m)any of my relatives among them," as LaRocque soberly reports.

This is the experience of colonialism that shaped the Métis people, from Louis Riel's failed military battles against colonial dispossession to LaRocque's family's containment on Road Allowance lands to subsequent displacements, up to the 1950s, 1960s, and 1970s, from much-loved lands. Her father's generation lived from a combination of land-based practises and wage labour in town. Despite these forced conditions, LaRocque explains, most Métis developed homes and hamlets from which they travelled to their satellite camps during hunting and trapping seasons or to work sites. These were tough conditions, however, with the Métis living on the margins of their own lands, forced into poverty and weakened by poverty-related illnesses. This is the context that shaped LaRocque's life and scholarship, so that her experiences inform her analysis. In this way, her story is part of an Indigenous tradition of "resistance writing" that refuses the colonial erasure of distinctive Indigenous, here Métis, histories and present (see chapter "'Resist No Longer': Reflections on Resistance Writing and Teaching").

Introduction   xxix

"When We Were the Other"

Despite the many hardships that the Métis, including her father and mother, survived, LaRocque's childhood holds warm memories. In recalling her early years, she describes a Métis culture and family at once practical and richly imaginative, self-sufficient but not without wonder:

> I was born into a world of people whose roots of pride, independence, industriousness and skills go back to the Red River Métis, back to the Cree. I was born into a world of magic, where seeing and hearing ghosts was a routine occurrence, where the angry Pehehsoo (thunder-bird) could be appeased by a four-directional pipe chant, where the spirits danced in the sky on clear night and where tents shook for people to heal. (see chapter, "Tides, Town and Trains")

But LaRocque warns against any romantic idealization of her childhood, insisting, "I was not born into a garden of Hiawathian paradise. Our own humanness and the effects of European colonization were very much with us" (see chapter "Tides, Town and Trains"). Within her own community, as well as among the White people of the Town, there were those "whom we feared. Violence stalked among us" (see chapter "Tides, Town and Trains").

The discovery of the self as the "Other," outside of the bounds of the human, was the lesson of life in Town. LaRocque describes her experiences of "ugly bigotry" (1985, 36) in stark terms. As she recalls, "when I was about 10 years old, I was sipping pop and reading a comic book in a café when a fat, red-faced, old white man approached me, flung a quarter in my direction and slurred, 'wanna go for a ride, little squaw?'" (1985, 36). Her parents were not spared similar treatment. Leaving a café one evening, as her mother and father prepared to take a taxi cab:

> An officer darted out of the dark, collared my mother and growled 'you wanna go in?' My mother, who spoke only Cree, blurted 'yeh', upon which the officers unceremoniously plunked her into the paddywagon and sped off. She told us they then threw cold water on her in her cell. (1985, 36–7)

LaRocque's scholarly writing looks unflinchingly at such hatreds. About her own, sometimes brutal encounters with racism, LaRocque states simply, "One never forgets" (1985, 36). Characteristically, she does not stop there, but defines and analyses institutional and personal racisms in Canada, not least through stereotyping, calling on Canadians to have "the foresight, the compassion, and the courage" to confront and challenge the racisms that are part of our histories and present (see chapter "Racism Runs Through Canadian Society").

As a child, for LaRocque, the public school in town was no refuge from racism. Although by now the genocidal intent and horrors of the residential schools for Status Indians are well known (MacDonald 2019; Starblanket 2018), public schools like the one LaRocque attended were often not much better. In recalling the lesson of White superiority she learned at school, LaRocque turns to the words of another Indigenous woman writer, Alice Lee:

> the/year i turned six i began school i wanted to learn to read/the first day i learned that the teachers are white the/children are white in my new book Dick Jane and Sally are/white i learned new words at recess squaw mother dirty half-/ breed fucking indian i hope i know how to read soon i already/know my colours. (Lee quoted in LaRocque 2010, 8)

Despite speaking English as a second language and a curriculum that routinely portrayed Indigenous peoples as historical relics and gruesome savages, LaRocque excelled, surprising teachers, many of whom were coldly resigned to the failure of Indigenous students (1975, 43). Then finally, from grades seven through nine, LaRocque had the support and attention of a teacher, at a different school, who was "humane, sensitive and attentive" (1975, 43). This could not compensate for the hatreds LaRocque survived daily, in the curriculum as much as in violent relationships in the Town, but this teacher's care was essential to her decision to continue in school.

"Discovery in Leaps and Bounds"

After completing high school, when she boarded with a Mennonite family, LaRocque was briefly employed as a ward-clerk in a hospital and then as a counsellor for juvenile criminal offenders in summer camp. She subsequently enrolled in the Education Faculty at Camrose Lutheran College in Alberta. She recalls her learning there as a "time of discovery in leaps and bounds" (LaRocque 1975, xi), although she observes that the slow recovery of her Indigenous heritage and pride in that heritage was not without its own pains, not least given her growing "anger and bitterness against oppression" (xi). After graduating in 1971, she became a journalist and then assistant editor for the Alberta Native Communications Society (ANCS).

In cooperation with the ANCS and the Alberta School Broadcasts (1975, xii), she developed educational radio programs specifically for Indigenous audiences.

Later, LaRocque enrolled as an undergraduate at Goshen College in Indiana, from which she graduated with a BA just a year and a half later, in 1973. Two years after her undergraduate degree, when she was twenty-five years old, she published her first book *Defeathering the Indian* (1975; see an excerpt "A Personal Essay on Poverty" in this volume). There LaRocque argued that in the Canadian classroom, "history which is truthful to the Native experience has yet to be learned" (1975, 4); her book was written for anyone teaching Indigenous children or, as she insisted, anyone teaching "*about* Native people" (4, italics in original). In particular, LaRocque critiqued teachers who equated Indigenous culture with "ancient artefacts" and promised that her analyses would help the educational system "to move beyond this frozen image" (4) of indigeneity. Short chapters conceptualize the distinction between Indigenous heritage and contemporary Indigenous cultures, deconstruct stereotypes in the media and in the classroom, and suggest ways forward that neither "delete" the histories of diverse Indigenous peoples, nor demean them as nothing more than poverty-stricken "social problems."

The overall aim of *Defeathering the Indian* is to challenge stereotypes, deconstructing both the "noble red men and the savage" (1975, 32): the former the "perfect primitive," stoic, nature-loving, wise and the latter his "sinister shadow" (33), sullen, hostile, and violent. Anticipating her subsequent writings, LaRocque (1975) observes:

> Neither the noble red man nor the savage Indian myth says much about Indians as human beings, people who are capable of 'the good, the bad and the ugly.' People who can laugh, cry, hate and love. People who have dreams, aspirations, and hopes. People, like the rest of humanity, who are facing *and* adapting to change. (43–4; italics in original)

While writing *Defeathering the Indian*, LaRocque began and then, in 1976, completed a master's degree in peace studies from the Associated Mennonite Seminaries in Indiana, funded through a Rockefeller scholarship. She then took a second master's degree in history in 1980 at the University of Manitoba and finally, a PhD in English/history in interdisciplinary studies, in 1999, also from the University of Manitoba.

But long before completing her PhD, LaRocque began teaching at the University of Manitoba. In the 1970s, while still a MA student, she was a key actor in developing the Native Studies program (now Indigenous

Studies), shaping the curriculum in ways that resonate into the present. Among her contributions, she introduced the teaching of Indigenous feminisms at a time when this was not always a welcome effort. The White students she taught were often more comfortable with descriptions of Indigenous women's difficult social conditions than with Indigenous feminisms, perhaps because the former reinforced images of Indigenous women as sexually available victims of White violence, but not actors fighting back against patriarchy and violence. In a familiar critique, some Indigenous male students who had some power over LaRocque's working life through their teaching evaluations – argued that raising issues of gender inequalities in Indigenous societies amounted to "airing dirty laundry in public" (see chapter "Métis and Feminist"). Nor did she always find support from deans' offices, department chairs, or colleagues.

Despite such efforts to silence her Métis feminist voice, LaRocque persisted in telling her "exact-speaking" truths (LaRocque 2010, 29), as she sees them. Unusually in a context in which many Indigenous women rejected feminism as a white women's political agenda, irrelevant to their own struggles (e.g., Monture-Angus 1995, 20; but see Green 2007, 2017), LaRocque directly and explicitly critiqued patriarchy and sexism, whether rooted in colonial paternalisms and Christian fundamentalisms or in supposedly "authentic" pre-colonial Indigenous traditions, including rigid ceremonial mandates demanding stereotypical gender conformity. As she writes:

> Historically, there is overwhelming evidence that Indigenous women's roles have been largely limited to the domestic sphere. In popular discourse as well as in some academic works, much of this has been explained as indicating "balance" or complementarity between genders, and "honour" and "respect" for women. But what is meant by "honour" and "balance"? Does honour translate into equality and empowerment in all areas of women's lives, including, for example, in decision-making in the body politic? (see chapter "Métis and Feminist")[3]

Nor is LaRocque shy about describing how her own and her mother's lives were shaped by patriarchy, in both its colonial and Indigenous

---

3 Elsewhere, LaRocque recognizes the diversity of women's roles across different Indigenous cultures (see chapter "Métis and Feminist"). What remains consistent is that women's empowerment remains her measure in all cases, whether assessing colonial or Indigenous patriarchal practices and norms.

variants. She consistently denounces violence against Indigenous women, and indeed, any restrictions on self-determining expression by Indigenous women, writing with some exasperation, for instance, that "we [Indigenous women] continue to be stereotyped as some Mother-Earthy mass of battered bodies" (see chapter "Métis and Feminist"). From a very young age, she rejected more apparently benign gender-stereotypical roles, a future in which she would "attend to household chores and eventually ... become someone's wife" (see chapter "Tides, Towns and Trains"). This was the role that her mother had played but did not necessarily embrace. Instead, LaRocque forged her life in the academy, now more – if unevenly – hospitable to her Indigenous feminist insights.

Troubling Paradigms

Among LaRocque's contributions as a scholar is her literary criticism of Indigenous writers. In her view, Indigenous writing – "history, biography, social commentaries, essays" (2010, 120) but also poetry and literature – has been and is one site where Indigenous people have sought to deconstruct dehumanizing colonial hate literature, while reconstructing their own histories and stories. In early Indigenous literature, especially, such reconstruction often meant a degree of romantic idealization of Indigenous cultures.

In her engagement with Indigenous literature, characteristically, LaRocque does not simply champion Indigenous writers.[4] Rather, she points to the ways that Indigenous literature does not always escape colonial stereotypes, due to internalized colonialism (Memmi 1957). "[B]efore we can trouble paradigms," she insists, "we must sift through colonial debris, much of which sits in the hearts and minds of the colonized" (2010, 120). LaRocque therefore critiques Indigenous writers who, perhaps unconsciously, reproduce noble savage stereotypes about wise nature-loving Indigenous persons, warning that "taken to extremes, cultural romanticization can lead to fundamentalism, even jingoism" (2010, 137). Similarly, she rejects portrayals, by both colonial and Native writers, that demand and insist upon an absolute Indigenous Otherness, asking, "Whose interest does it serve that we be different? Are we that different?" (2010, 137).

---

4 With regret, LaRocque observes that "White Canadian reviewers, perhaps afraid to offend our presumed cultural sensibilities, have been reluctant to touch our works. *We* are reluctant to criticize each other" (LaRocque 2006, 12–13; italics in original).

But LaRocque emphasizes that this is not a general rejection of Indigenous writing that is "contrapuntally" romantic (LaRocque 2010, 11–13).[5] Beyond valuing devalued Indigenous cultures, the interest in any particular romantic literature by Indigenous writers lies in the skill of the writer. LaRocque is quick to appreciate the "romantic *and* resistant" (2010, 132, italics added) poetry of Chief Dan George, Rita Joe, and George Copway, among others. Further, LaRocque insists that not all romanticisms are equal: there is a difference between writing romantically about the land from the stereotypes of the noble savage and writing from deep, close relationships with specific lands. The lyrical qualities of her own prose are fully in evidence, as she explains:

> As Métis from northern Alberta, my family does not legally own the land I grew up on, but the land, if it belongs to anyone, belongs to my Plains Cree-Métis ancestors and family. My bones have known this land long before [the Canadian province of] Alberta was born. My younger brother has lovingly tended to this land since the passing of our parents. There is a blueberry patch there that I especially love; when I go there I experience that particular land; I hear it speaking with the luminosity of blueberries in September sun embraced in sunlit green of gently waving poplar leaves. And I remember too why bears and panthers still prowl through my dreams. (2010, 136)

And she concludes with a reminder of both the romantic and existential qualities of the land: "The land feeds us, sings to us, gives us light – but it also steals us away from this earth. The land does teach us about life and death" (2010, 136).

From LaRocque's perspective, what matters is engaging with Indigenous literature as *literature*. Too often, she laments, the literary qualities of Indigenous writing have been overlooked, with an emphasis instead on the anthropological and political dimensions. Against such social

---

5 LaRocque borrows from Said's (1993, 66–7) concept of "contrapuntal" reading, where he argues that colonial texts must be analysed from the standpoint of the colonized to be understood in their full complexity. As LaRocque emphasizes, however, she takes up Said's idea in her own way to "use the concept somewhat from the other way around; that is, I read Aboriginal resistance to Canadian textual techniques of mastery as contrapuntal" (LaRocque 2010, 11). If Said's aim is to offer counter-readings, from the vantage point of the colonized, to illuminate colonial texts in new ways, LaRocque's aim is to contrapuntally highlight the rich "experience and insight, epistemologies and arguments" of Indigenous scholars and writers, as sources of "theoretical possibility" (LaRocque 2010, 12), including (and perhaps especially) with respect to colonial misrepresentations.

scientific readings, she asks, "is a poem about loneliness or lost love or death a matter of ethnology?" (2006, 12). Her own intervention invites us to be attentive to and to "analyze and theorize imagination, beauty, and play of words, which is the stuff of Aboriginal reflection, satire, novels, novellas, plays, and poetry" (see chapter "Sources of Inspiration: The Birth of 'For the Love of Words': Aboriginal Writers of Canada").

This means refusing tendencies to understand Indigenous writers as cultural avatars, as typologies of a different kind of indigeneity. Literary criticism of Indigenous writers must, she insists, "be human centred and fluid ... [about] trends and tasks in motion rather than [about] traits or cultural grids" (2010, 159). This may be especially important, she writes, as more and more Indigenous people live in cities and develop their own understandings of Indigenous cultures – irreducible to ossified, stereotypical representations of indigeneity – in a changing world:

> Native intellectuals do have a rich romantic tradition, but it is clear not all romanticization in Native writing is made from the same stuff. Further, it may become increasingly alien for younger, strictly urban generations to relate to cultural signs and practices that have normally depended on land-based knowledges. However, we cannot submit to any ossification. Obviously ... we are challenged to revise ideas of cultural change and continuity if we hope to step out of Hiawatha's shadow. Native peoples are living lives as Natives in a contemporary world. (2010, 157)

LaRocque suggests that artists play a particularly important role, not simply in living, but in living in meaningfully ways that matter not just for the moment but more enduringly. In the opening address at a conference on Indigenous (then "Aboriginal") literatures, she puts her views about the importance of artists and writers to Indigenous cultural continuities and to meaningful life, *tout court*, this way:

> What will last, I think, is what the human spirit creates. To live life creating is a vocation. Much of that vocation belongs to the artists in our cultures. I believe it is the weavers, bakers, carvers, painters, gardeners, songmakers, storymakers, the dramatists and dream speakers, the orators – and yes, the writers – who fashion for us shapes, forms, and colours to express the rivers of yearnings in the human soul. The human spirit creates, not only in an effort to find meaning in our existence, but also to bring meaning into being. The very act of human creation brings meaning, and this we call culture. I believe it is the artists, the writers, who will pass on the torch of vibrant Aboriginal cultures to the next generations. (2006, 11–12)

This affirmation is arguably characteristic of a certain existentialist gesture in LaRocque's writings. She never denies the weight of colonial history upon the present, but she does reject what she understands as naïve – and often dangerous – romantic idealizations of Indigenous societies, past and present. Instead LaRocque insists on human life "in all its dimensions, complexity and even contradictions" (2010, 169) and the ways in which every society and every human being carries within them "the good, the bad and the ugly" – but also the possibility of meaning-making.

The Places My Soul Has Been Scorched

LaRocque's own contributions are wide-ranging. To appreciate the depth and scope of her contributions, we might turn to the words of the Black studies geographer Katherine McKittrick, who observes:

> [The] well-known history in the Americas, of white masculine European mappings, explorations, conquests, is interlaced with a different sense of place, those populations and their attendant geographies that are concealed by what might be called rational spatial colonization and domination: the profitable erasure and objectification of subaltern subjectivities, stories, and lands. (McKittrick 2006, x).

In multiple ways, LaRocque's writings participate in this elaboration of a "different sense of place" in settler colonial contexts, purposefully erased, but nonetheless still enduring and present. She shares a distinctive voice to tell new stories about Métis history, colonial hatreds and stereotypes in school curriculums and popular cultures, and Indigenous entanglements with dehumanizing colonial imagery. She reminds us that Indigenous writers, as artists, create a literature that, at its best, is not simply contrapuntally romantic but resistant to colonial dehumanization.

This has not been easy. Even the apparently banal fact of writing in English has often been painful. As LaRocque describes, in characteristically vivid prose, "English is like an ideological onion whose stinging layers of racism and sexism must be peeled away before it can be fully enjoyed" (see chapter "Preface: Hear Are Our Voices – Who Will Hear?"). Elsewhere, she observes "resistance can wear out a person. My bones know the places where my soul has been scorched" (see chapter "Tides, Towns and Trains"). Despite this scorching, she has refused to be silenced. Over nearly half a century she has created a body of writing with relevance for contemporary literary theorists, feminists, historians, educators, and all those interested in the settler colonial state and Indigenous resistance.

But this is not only a book for scholars and specialists of Indigenous studies or histories. Emma LaRocque's writings tell us a great deal about racisms, survival, and existential yearnings for meaning, in a voice at once unique and universally human.

THE EMMA LAROCQUE READER

1975

A Personal Essay on Poverty

Liberalism has made much of poverty in our last decade. Statistics on poverty have been flying around from all directions. And as I mentioned before, Native people have been closely associated with it; so closely in fact that some very significant questions have been bypassed.

What is poverty anyway? Is it the failure to reach beyond that magical Poverty Line established by the Economic Council of Canada? Or is it "relative to the living standard the rest of society enjoys"? And more important, what is so sacred about what the majority enjoys?

To me it seems obvious that poverty is relative all right; but not necessarily relative to the wealth of the majority, but rather to one's own perceptions of his material possessions.

My two brothers, one sister and I grew up in a one-roomed but well managed log cabin. Many of our clothes were handsewn by my very resourceful mother. All our wooden furniture (two beds, one table, a cupboard, several night stands, three chairs and a bench) was put together by my practical father. Our diet consisted of a large variety of wild meats, berries, bannock, potatoes, some vegetables and herbal teas and so on, all of which were usually cooked with originality and imagination.

At the age of nine, against my father's perceptive advice, I howled my way into school. He knew only too well that sooner or later I would come home with new desires. As predicted, a few months later I wanted juicy red apples, oranges, bananas, trembling jello, bread and even red-and-white striped toothpaste! Once, my father teasingly wondered what I could possibly do with toothpaste and brush because my teeth were all falling out! Toothless or not, I found the pictures at school powerfully suggestive.

Other school pictures also played with my mind. I saw Dick, Jane and Sally's suburban home and their grandparent's expansive and, oh, so clean farm. Not for a long time was I to appreciate my home again.

The point is, I had been perfectly content to sleep on the floor, eat rabbit stew and read and play cards by kerosene lamp until my perceptions were swayed at school. Neither had I suffered spiritual want. I had been spellbound by my mother's ability to narrate Cree legends and enriched by my father's dreams, until the teacher outlawed Cree and made fun of dreams.

From then on I existed in poverty; not with reference to our log cabin, our food and our small wood-stove as compared to the brick schoolhouse, its food and its huge, coal-burning pot-belly stove, but because I was persuaded by my teacher's propaganda and the pictures.[1] The teacher's authoritarianism, coupled with his failure to reinforce whatever world we came from, effectively weakened our respect for our parents.

Still, there is more to poverty than its relativity. Even if I had believed in my home and its simple beauties, it is true that I had no money. And without that commodity, eventually I could not be mobile. And to be immobile in any society is to be quite choiceless. It is at this point that equal opportunity becomes meaningless.

It is psychologically cathartic to know that one has a choice with his existence. Ultimately, poverty in the North American context is not having enough money to choose among alternatives. Poverty exacts its toll on people not always because of a mere lack of material possessions, but often because of choicelessness.

Today, there are hundreds of urban dwellers who are suffering from "cabinitis". Come Friday afternoon there is a mass and speedy exodus to the "simple" life of their cabins. These people are often happy there because they are there by choice. They feel a sense of self-direction. People may be "culturally deprived" perhaps only in that they are deprived of choice. In this sense then, most of us are "culturally deprived" in some area because most of us cannot choose everything we want out of life.

Now I live in a city, and I often see children playing on concrete, at artificial playgrounds and in overcrowded parks or swimming pools. I always feel a profound sense of sadness that these children cannot have what I had as a child. No spruce branch from which to master a Tarzanian swing. No soft moss to land on if you fall. No moonlight rendezvous beside a creek, watching a beaver tirelessly build his dam. No place to build an honest-to-goodness, creaking, but functioning, ferris

---

1 It must be said that this teacher meant well. He was by nature a disciplinarian but not malicious. Apparently, he sincerely believed that his ways were for the good of the Native children.

A Personal Essay on Poverty

[*sic*] wheel! No pond or lake or river to try out a selfmade raft, row boat or canoe. Or to skinny-dip in. No green space to just run and run and run. No wooded meadow in which to lie and sleepily feel akin to the lethargic clouds. No crocuses, wild roses, tiger lilies or bluebells to sniff.

Cultural deprivation?

Yes, we must work towards equal opportunity for all. We must help people reach a sense of self-direction and mobility. We must lift people to the place of choice. But we cannot, we must not, dictate what people should choose.

1983

The Métis in English
Canadian Literature

Before we can proceed with a discussion of the Métis in English Canadian literature we must understand the traditional interpretation of Indian history, namely, that the Indians were, and in many cases are still, classified as savage, and the Europeans and their descendants as civilized.

To be sure, all kinds of theories, debates and controversies have abounded since 1492 about the nature of the Indian. Still, no matter how divergent the views, how fiercely fought the controversies, there were common beliefs about the Indian. Whether in a colonial, imperial, and/or missionary position ... the "Whiteman", whether Roman Catholic or Protestant, believed in a cultural hierarchy through which humanity moved from savagery, through barbarity to civilization. The Whiteman's belief in "civilization" and its antithesis "savagery" was perhaps the most central and certainly the most persistent idea throughout the centuries (LaRocque 1978, 6–7).

If the belief in cultural hierarchy has survived, so has its ethnocentric basis. For those who classified humanity into a step ladder structure were not only invariably European (or of European origin) but they just as invariably measured civilization by their standard (LaRocque 1978, 10).

One of the results of ethnocentrism was the "double-standard" way in which Indian vices and virtues were judged. That is, the same traits/behaviour may be equally evident in both White and Indian peoples, but the "civilizer" would judge them according to the levels of stratification (LaRocque 1978). For example, the "civilizers" commonly believed that there was a distinction between civilized and savage warfare. It was assumed that civilized warfare was rational, directed and essentially non-violent, whereas savage warfare was irrational, aimless and "bloody"! American ethnohistorian

Francis Jennings (1975) performs academic surgery on this as well as other accompanying beliefs that go towards maintaining what he calls the "cultural myth" of civilization "locked in battle with savagery".

Other American writers have begun to examine this dichotomy of civilization/savagery that has been the framework through which Indian-White encounters have been judged. These include Bernard Sheehan, Robert Berkhofer, R.H. Pearce, and Wilcomb Washburn. In Canada, James Walker (1971) lists numerous Canadian historians who present an "incomplete and contradictory" image of Indians, but does not question the dichotomy itself. And in 1981, Leslie Monkman published *A Native Heritage: Images of the Indian in English-Canadian Literature*, but neither does Monkman examine the notions of civilization versus savagery per se.

In an unpublished mini-thesis footnoted below, I deal more extensively with what I call the "civ/sav" interpretation, and frankly, I view it as simplistic, ethnocentric and of little scientific value. The scientific value lies in that the writing says more about the writers than it says about the Indian people.

Although a growing number of authors are beginning to comment on this "civ/sav" dichotomy, very few have actually rejected it. As already noted Francis Jennings (1975) does dismantle with careful documentation what he calls the "cultural myth" of civilization/savagery. Still, this cultural myth is a very prevalent and deeply rooted *weltanschauung*, really – a *weltanschauung* that has been equally imposed on the Métis history, as well as on the literary characterization of the halfbreed or Métis.

In historical writing the theme persists that in the halfbreed/Métis peoples lies this dichotomy between savagery and civilization. The popular interpretation of the Riel Rebellions is that it was "the clash between primitive and civilized peoples". G.F. Stanley (1936) assessed this supposed clash in graphic and categorical terms. In interpreting the events surrounding Rupert's Land and the North-West, Stanley declares:

> Again and again, in different places and in different ways…. The European, conscious of his material superiority is only too contemptuous of the savage, intolerant of his helplessness, ignorant of his mental processes and impatient at his slow assimilation of civilization. The savage, centuries behind in mental and economic development, cannot readily adapt himself to meet the new conditions. (194)

8 The Emma LaRocque Reader

In an article "The Canadian Métis" (1950), W.L. Morton succinctly stated a similar position:

> In the Red River colony civilization and barbarism met and mingled.... This admixture of civilized life and barbaric, this conjunction of settled and roving ways, indeed occurred in the very persons of the half-breed population of Red River and the West.
>
> The result was a society quaint and unique, in which were reconciled the savagery of the Indian and the culture of Europe. (3)

More recently, two Métis authors, D. Bruce Sealey and Antoine S. Lussier (1975) echo Stanley and Morton in their interpretation of Métis history. In exploring the causes of the Riel Rebellions, they believe that Stanley, author of *The Birth of Western Canada and Louis Riel* (1936), "perhaps explained it best when he described the confrontation as one of civilization facing the frontier." The authors continue:

> The Métis people were interested in the survival of their way of life and feared progress. They wished to be left alone to live their own lives in a world set apart. Because the Métis attempted to halt the inevitable encroachment of civilization, the Red River Insurrection was doomed to fail. (Sealey and Lussier 1975, 75)

Such a promulgation of the civ/sav scheme has resulted in the distortion and obscurity of facts. For example, the unexamined acceptance of the myth that the Métis dispersed from the Red River because they were afraid of progress, and that they "preferred the excitement of the chase", as Stanley (1936) put it, has obscured the fact that the majority of the Métis were systematically coerced from their land – their land which was not only a vast prairie full of buffalo, but also of settlements and farming strips. They dispersed because a new order was imposed upon them, and that new order was not some romantic and mythic notion of "progress" or the "inevitability of civilization", but rather involved insensitive surveyors, unscrupulous land speculators, a deaf Ottawa, administrative delays and even outright deception, a new language and the British Colonel, Garnet Wolseley.[1]

---

1 The recent research by the Manitoba Métis Federation Land Commission has exploded the myth that the Métis foolishly lost their land scrips, and voluntarily left the Red River area. These findings are available in the *Final Report of the Manitoba Métis Land Commission For the Fiscal Year 1979–80*, submitted to the Canadian Joint Committee of Cabinet on Métis and Non-Status Indian Land Claims, April 18, 1980.

The Métis in English Canadian Literature

Further, it makes no historical sense to argue that the Métis were inherently afraid of new things or "progress", because their very life-style involved being in the "thick of things"! They were, after all, in the heart of the continent playing active, if not leading roles in commerce, transportation, food supplies and linguistics!

The issue for the Métis, as it was for the Indian, was not some great, psycho-societal, static conflict between a supposed savagery versus civilization, but rather colonization and eventual powerlessness.

The conventional dichotomy of civ/sav is a cultural myth, a propa-ganda, if you will, that has served to rationalize the invasion of Native peoples. We must demythologize this myth, and as we do, we gain a truer picture of what really happened to the Métis, and hence, a truer picture of Canada.

One wonders whether the historians borrowed from the novelists, or vice-versa because Canadian novelists have as a rule, used halfbreed/ Métis characters to illustrate the civ/sav point of view.

One of Ralph Connor's minor characters in *The Foreigner* (1909) is a Scot-Cree halfbreed whose name is Mackenzie. Mackenzie is a joe-boy and boozing partner to Jack French, a love-sick English bachelor. A teenage boy Kalman, the "foreigner", comes to stay with these two men. In one scene Kalman tries to dispossess Mackenzie of his whisky bottle; Mackenzie goes through a transformation:

> The change in Mackenzie was immediate and appalling. His smiling face became transformed with fury, his black eyes gleamed with the cunning malignity of the savage, he shed his soft Scotch voice with his genial man-ner, the very movements of his body became those of his Cree progenitors. Uttering hoarse guttural cries, with the quick crouching run of the Indian on the trail of his foe, he chased Kalman.... There was something so fiend-ishly terrifying in the glimpses that Kalman caught of his face now and then that the boy was seized with an overpowering dread ...

After some more chasing French finally appears and as master shouts at Mackenzie: "Give me that gun, you dog", and:

> Mackenzie hesitated but only for a moment, and without a word sur-rendered the gun, the fiendish rage fading out of his face, the aboriginal blood lust dying in his eyes like the snuffing out of a candle. In a few brief moments he became once more a civilized man ... (223–34)

Within Mackenzie is the unresolvable tension between the supposed savagery of the Indian and the supposed civilagery of the European.

The descriptions of the halfbreed/Métis character are classic. In *Blue Pete: Rebel* (Allan 1940), Blue Pete is a halfbreed who helps out the Mounties in rounding up a murderous cattle rustler. Unlike Mackenzie, Blue Pete is nobody's joe-boy; he is tough, reckless and opportunistic. He hates the Indians about as much as he disdains the Mounties. But like Mackenzie, Blue Pete is driven by the opposing forces within him. When he encountered the Indians:

> ... his white blood was forgotten. Against Indians he fought as an Indian until the moment of crisis. His Indian blood gave him cunning, animal instincts, and a certain amount of ruthlessness.... But always at the last moment his relentlessness was tempered by the white blood in him. (Allan 1940, 108)

Gilbert Parker, a nineteenth century novelist who presented Indians as victims of their "savage" passions, produced a novel *Pierre and His People* (1894) in which Parker cannot seem to make up his mind whether Pierre is an Indian or a Frenchman. Some traits in Pierre are delineated as "The Indian in him" (3, 5), while at other times Pierre is simply described as the "French-man".

The point to be made is that neither Pierre, Blue Pete nor Mackenzie have integrated personalities. Nor do they represent the Métis people at all. They are really frontier-type cowboys who happen to be part Indian – and that part is what provides the conflict within themselves and in their relationships with others. These characters are not presented as a people or as individuals in their own right, but are literary inventions in the service of the authors' cultural myths.

Even in modern novels, the Métis or halfbreeds, are used as vehicles to convey the authors' messages. The characters are usually steeped in squalor, despair and sexual promiscuity, presumably to symbolize the cultural and contemporary death of the Indian, not even the Métis!

Mort Forer's *The Humback* (1969) unfolds a horror tale of tragedy and babies. Toinette, the central character, lives in a northeastern Métis settlement called the Humback. In it, or even out of it, the Métis are dull, depressed and dying. Toinette endures by replacing her dead children and relatives with more babies. After a relentless series of tragedies, Toinette takes up with an old man Joshua, a sort of a community stud, and in the end philosophizes that "Kids is good..., what the hell can we do here at the Humback after we cut the wood, except make kids" (315). Joshua agrees and adds, "Everytime something dies ... there should be something to take its place. There is nothing better than people. Nothing. People are everything."

The Métis in English Canadian Literature   11

Forer may cling to the biological ability to make babies as some desperate symbol of endurance, but the novel itself says nothing of the Métis' spiritual and cultural endurance.

André Tom Macgregor (1976) by Betty Wilson is an award-winning novel about a Métis young man who comes from a northeastern Alberta Métis community – a community much like the Humback, in which almost everybody drags around in a stupor from too much booze and sex. But André is an exception; besides being very good looking and sexually irresistible, he is very intelligent. After a few hair-raising escapades in Edmonton, he will survive and make it in "the whiteman's world".

In order for André to be the romantic and almost tragic hero that he is, Wilson imagines his family and community to be revolting. When André's parents come to visit him and his pregnant, White wife Dolly (caricatured as White trash), Dolly is repelled:

> There, crowded behind Andre, were a couple she had often seen in Fish Lake. She couldn't have named them, but she had always thought of them as 'dirty Indians'. She had seen the woman poking with a stick through reeking garbage in the town dump. Once she had seen the man, drunk, and disgustingly sick at the back of the hotel. Now they examined her with opaque, black eyes set in heavy, expressionless faces. Her stomach nearly rebelled at the reek of their smoke tanned moccasins. (157)

Overall, the conversations are sterile and predictable; the plot and characters lack authenticity. One truly wonders why and how this novel won the "Search-For-A-New-Alberta-Novelist" award as well as the Hudson's Bay Company's Beaver Award!

Totally different in content, style, mood and substance is Rudy Wiebe's *The Scorched-Wood People* (1977). It is an epic novel exuding noble thoughts, heroic conflicts and great men. Somewhat loose with historical details (for being an historical novel), Wiebe weaves a moving and inspiring tale about Riel and [Gabriel] Dumont. But the story is also about Wiebe and his theological struggles about the universality of Christ, about justice, and about the ability of people to keep faith, to maintain community.

George Woodcock in a recent article (1982) argues that Wiebe is not an historical novelist as much as he is an historical moralist, and that:

> *The Scorched-Wood People* is an invention of its author, and the Métis are there, as they were in *Peace Shall Destroy Many* (Wiebe 1962), to pose a recurrent Wiebe theme, which is the relationship between spirit and community. (Woodcock 1982, 13)

As to Woodcock himself, I think he is so concerned about making the "earthy" Dumont a hero that he almost goes to the other extreme, namely, that he does not take Riel's struggles as seriously as he perhaps should.

The one author whose Métis characters seem plausible and human is Margaret Laurence. In her Manawaka series (*The Stone Angel* 1974; *A Jest of God* 1966; *The Fire-Dwellers* 1969; *A Bird in the House* 1970; *The Diviners* 1974), the Métis family of Jules Tonnerre "becomes the focus of suffering and death, acceptance and endurance that are integrally related to the experience of each of Laurence's heroines" (Monkman 1981, 57).

It is interesting to note that with each narrative, the Tonnerre members edge closer into town, into the consciousness of White society. Finally, in *The Diviners* the Métis do not merely serve as the uncomfortable mirrors to White society, but Jules Tonnerre enters Morag Gunn and her world. Jules embodies pain and anger, yet finds a way to accept his fate, thus maintaining his dignity. He becomes the standard by which Morag measures her pain, her White background and finally learns to "divine freedom out of suffering" (Laurence 1974, 64).

Margaret Laurence is a great writer and all her characters exude authenticity, and from the White perspective her Métis characters are believable. But even in Laurence's work, the Métis are incomplete. They are still portrayed as dying, though nobly; and they are still portrayed as the more passionate, more sexual and the more unrestrained peoples as opposed to the puritanical strictures of White society. This theme is really a carry-over from the civ/sav dichotomy.

Finally, you may ask, in exasperation, "What on earth are you looking for? What do you consider to be authentic?" Authenticity is that undefinable phenomenon in literature – you know it when it is there, and you know it when it isn't. I cannot define it – so let me end by relating an experience.

I do not read Maria Campbell's *Halfbreed* – I experience it. I read that book in one sitting – and I laughed, I cried, I loved, I raged. I knew those legends she had heard; I knew the blueberry picking, the dancing. I knew about being so scared of ghosts one couldn't piss in the dark! And I knew about the hardships: the prejudice, the struggle for food, for acceptance, for political recognition. I knew about the people – their humour, their gossipings, their foibles; and their generosity, intelligence, industriousness and finally, their frustrations.

Maria told a story, her story. She did not use the Métis as a vehicle for a worldview, a doctrine or even as a social protest. She simply told a story, and because it is authentic, it is my story too. Not in every detail of course, but detail is not the ultimate criteria of authenticity; the mood, the spirit and ethos in *Halfbreed* is what makes it our story.

I envision a time when Canadian historians will reflect our humanity: our failures as well as our achievements, our despairs as well as our dreams, our deaths as well as our endurance – at face value, not within the dichotomy of civilization versus savagery. And I envision a time when Canadian fiction writers will reflect our human foibles as well as our great potentials. In short, I envision a time when Canadian writers will reflect both the unique and the universal in us, both the blessings and the burdens of that undefinable phenomenon in life known as the human condition.

1988

On the Ethics of Publishing Historical Documents

When I first read George Nelson's journal,[1] I reacted to it in much the same way I have reacted to a host of fur trade journals, missionary writings, and other "original" sources on Indians. Like these sources, the Nelson journal raises layers of issues, ranging from the "mild" problem of inaccurate ethnography to the very grave problem of entrenched ethnocentrism, not only in the primary sources but in subsequent scholarly works as well. As these problems are finally being exposed and challenged, especially by the growing number of concerned scholars, native and non-native alike, questions are being raised regarding ethics and objectivity in scholarship. The members of the Board of Manitoba Studies in Native History faced such challenges when they considered this manuscript for publication.

First, the problem of ethnocentrism. This problem is so immense, so all-embracing, so far-reaching, yet so typical that it is extremely difficult to attempt to respond, especially in a few pages! Whatever particular merits there are in Nelson's journal, it is, in the final analysis, informed by a Eurocentric perception of Indian life. It is written within a framework I have come to call "the dichotomy of civilization versus savagery" which is pervasive in scholarly and popular literature on native peoples (see chapter "The Métis in English Canadian Literature").

---

1 Nelson was an Anglo-American fur trader who "stands out for his interest in the life and ways of the natives he encountered" (Brown and Brightman 1988, 3). The opening of the edited collection that includes LaRocque's contribution explains that "Nelson's papers are comprised of two major groups of materials: the manuscripts written during his fur trade service, and a body of reminiscences written between 1825 and about 1851, from two to twenty-eight or more years after he left the northwest". (3). Elaine Coburn – editor's note.

There have been many theories and controversies since 1492 about the nature of the Indian. But the most persistent and common belief has been the European idea that humanity moved from the depths of savagery to the heights of civilization. This belief in cultural hierarchy is ethnocentric in its basis for, historically, Europeans categorized themselves as "the civilized" and the Indians as the "savages." "Civilization," and its antithesis "savagery," was (and still is) invariably measured by white European standards. The underlying assumption was that, as savages, Indians could not be as developed, organized, or ordered as Europeans, and from this has come a cluster of ideas, images, and terminology that has set Indians apart in an inferior status. This dichotomy of white civilization and Indian savagery has resulted in gross distortions about Indians in literature, historiography, and ethnography.

The Nelson manuscript may be praised for its attempts at fairness and its ethnographic detail. Given his era, Nelson is remarkably open-minded and seems to have been genuinely interested in presenting correct information. He also criticized his own society, albeit from a primitivist perspective. As to the information it contains, the journal is both marvellous and problematic. It is marvellous in that the information regarding the shaking tent ceremonies (which Nelson reduces to "conjuring") is largely consistent with what is generally known about these ceremonies. Yet, it is precisely at this point that Nelson reveals his quintessential Eurocentrism: because the "civilized" Nelson views Indian culture as "savage," he judges, belittles, and thereby reduces the rich, intricate, and multi-faceted aspects of Indian world views, religions, and mythologies to "witchcraft," "sorcery," "conjuring," "shamanism," and so forth. In doing so, Nelson typifies the double standard inherent in structuring white "civilization" as a diametric opposite to Indian "savagery." In fact, what really happens from such a "civ/sav" dichotomy is a double standard by which white and Indian virtues and vices are judged. That is, the same traits or behaviours (good or bad) or organizational systems may be evident equally in white and Indian peoples and cultures, but whites, no matter how bad or good, are always civilized, and Indians are always savage. To be sure, offending whites are freely criticized, but the condemnation is never extended to all whites. On the other hand, all Indian behaviour is deemed savage, and an Indian exhibiting "civilized" or Christian characteristics is seen as an exception. Indians are judged as a sub-genus to the white to the point that even "acceptable" Indian ways have to be set apart or used as a castigation of white civilization. Hence, the Noble Savage of primitivist construct.

In this framework Indian life cannot be judged at face value; it is scaled then according to the civ/sav stratification. Savagery is seen as a psychosocietal, static condition – the antithesis of the highest human condition, civilization. Even in warfare, the "civilizers" made a clear-cut distinction between a supposed civilized and savage warfare. American ethnohistorian Francis Jennings notes the assumption that civilized warfare is rational, purposeful, and essentially non-violent, whereas savage warfare is irrational, aimless, and bloodthirsty (Jennings 1976). As Hollywood has so plainly presented it: cowboys "scout," Indians "lurk"; cowboys "battle," Indians "massacre" (LaRocque 1975).

Similarly, tendentious words and classifications are used to describe Indian forms of religio-mythic expressions. For example, white Christians "worship" and "pray"; Indians engage in "ceremony" or "ritual" and "conjure." Yet, when the biased definitions are put aside, Indians and whites are doing essentially the same things: both are entertaining notions of the supernatural. Scientifically, it can be said that both are in the arena of "magic"; that is, both believe in the possibilities of "an extra-ordinary power or influence seemingly from a supernatural source." But because Indians are supposedly within the confines of a savage state, they remain "superstitious" while civilized Europeans have "great religions."

The implication here is radical. Our larger scholarly task is not merely to sort out ethnographic detail (though, heaven knows, this too is very important since Indian ethnography has been mutilated by so many well-meaning scholars!), but also to accept native thought and organization as of equal worth to European thought while acknowledging the differences. For this to take place, we must dismantle the civilization/ savagery dichotomy which is rooted so deeply in Euro-white cultural myth. This will entail dismantling traditional and judgmental thought and classification. It will mean the elimination of terms such as "sorcery," "conjuring," "witchcraft," and "primitive." In short, we must overturn the ethnocentrism inherent in Western thought and scholarship concerning notions of development, order, organization, and society.

What then is the worth of this manuscript? The editorial board of this series, led by the native members, struggled through a number of concerns. It is true that this manuscript does make, with qualifications, a substantial contribution toward a greater understanding of Indian life and thought in the 1800s. But because of the cumulative effect of biased (and often racist) scholarship on native peoples, this journal, if read in ignorance with an ethnocentric bias, might contribute to a further defamation and belittlement of native life and thought. We chose to publish it, to open it to scrutiny. But manuscripts such as this should raise questions regarding ethics and balance in scholarship. Must we

On the Ethics of Publishing Historical Documents 17

print everything we find in the archives? What happens when it is anti-Indian? Would we publish anti-semitic documents or material that defames another ethnic group? Many original sources contain such inflammatory material on Indians that they qualify as hate literature. The portrayal of Indians has ranged from that of inhuman, flesh-eating, cruel, howling savages (in portions of the Jesuit Relations) to that of "poor blind unfortunate creatures" in Nelson's journal. And what about the perpetuation of demeaning images of women? This journal in spots refers to "sluts" or "bitches." While it is not immediately clear what Nelson meant by these references, I am not comfortable with the overall presentation of women in this manuscript. Yet, we continue to publish and to use these sources in the name of scholarship. Such questions must be faced whenever the wider circulation of an "original source" is contemplated.

That these primary documents have contained deplorable material on native peoples seems to have largely escaped the eyes of most scholars. The insistent focus on culture and anthropology has served to distract or dilute the uncomfortable issues inherent in much of the literature on native peoples. But how far can we take such "scholarship"? Wherein lies our responsibility to combat slander, pornography, racism, hate, or plain ignorance in literature? It happens that, comparatively speaking, the Nelson journal is moderate in its approach to native peoples, but it is still constructed around the civilization (Christian)/savagery dichotomy with its tendentious terminology and classifications. Do we risk, one more time, perpetuating this framework? In exchange for what? A few more morsels of raw ethnography to satisfy our unsatiated intellectual appetites? Yet, what else do we have? We are faced with the task of extricating "truth" from sources immersed in murky ambiguity, at best.

Finally, apart from the all-encompassing issue of the civ/sav framework, how may Nelson's cultural contribution be assessed? Very briefly, what amazes me about this manuscript is that my Plains-Cree Métis community in northeastern Alberta was still living and reciting in the 1950s and 1960s essentially the same religion, legends, and myths discussed in the manuscript! This shows me that a lot of cultural knowledge is extant in native community and that scholars of native culture are not solely dependent on the problematic original sources; that cultural information can be received and tested against the living knowledge of many native persons. There is now a growing number of native scholars and they may best be able to synthesize living knowledge of their culture with research in academic disciplines.

On the issue of culture itself, I would caution that, while Nelson has a good grasp of some of the central Algonquian beliefs and myths, he is limited by his lack of comprehensive, contextual, and regional knowledge of Cree and Ojibwa languages, legends, myths, and religion(s). While Nelson understood the literal meaning of many words, he missed the nuances in translating Indian words, phrases, myths, personae, and concepts into English.

To Nelson's credit, he does try to compare the Indian world view and stories with those of others around the world. He did sense, even with his prejudices, that there is a universality in Indian myths and legends as well as in Indian religions. Here, a comparative literary perspective on mythology and symbolism may be useful, including motifs of good and bad twin sets, male-female tension/balance, male-female symbolism, the flood or catastrophe, the creator or transformer (re-creator), the "trickster" (a mirror to society, to human foibles), and the good-evil deity(ies). It is important that in our quest for specific ethnographic details we not isolate the Indian Weltanschauung from other universal human motifs.

Nelson clearly struggled within himself on matters related to the apparent power of Indian thought and beliefs. What was obscure to him was that the architecture of his struggle was framed by his engagement in the Western dichotomization of white "civilization" over Indian "savagery."

1989

Racism Runs Through
Canadian Society

In the summer of 1976, I was coming home to Canada after having finished graduate studies in Indiana. As I crossed the Emerson border, I turned the car radio on to [the] CBC [Canadian Broadcasting Corporation]. The programme was on racism and a broadcaster declared: "There is racism in Canada!" Expecting that the discussion would be about Canada's treatment of Native peoples, I was disappointed that the discussion of racism in Canada was limited to black-white conflict, as is so often the case. I was disappointed because as a Native person and as an educator I knew racism on many levels and had long wanted Canada to address this disquieting issue.

Since 1976, there have been a host of incidents throughout Canada which indicates that racism against Native peoples is rampant. While more reports are filtering into the press, these are just the tip of the iceberg.

Every day, Natives encounter some form of personal prejudice or institutional violence. This comes not only from the proverbial "redneck" but from high and influential places in society – from judges, journalists, doctors, businesses, teachers and politicians. It is not surprising that one consistent message being brought before the Aboriginal Justice Inquiry is the horrifying degree to which Native peoples are being subjected to racism throughout Canadian society.

Clearly there is a problem which is distressing enough, but what is even more discouraging is the widespread lack of awareness of the history and nature of racism against Native peoples.

Racism is discrimination based on the belief that one, or a group, is innately superior to another. Racism may be expressed individually or institutionally. It is especially important to understand that racism against Native (Indian, Inuit and Métis) peoples is embedded in Canadian institutions. For example, there is racism in the school system which can be traced back to the Euro-Canadian interpretation of history, an interpretation that has been uncritically transmitted in the education system. Historically, Europeans categorized themselves as the "civilized" and Indians as the "savages." The underlying assumption was that, as "savages", Indians were at the bottom of human development and from this has come a complex of images, terminology and policies that has set Indians apart and as inferior. Such an unscientific belief was and is racist because it sets up whites as superior and non-white as inferior.

The civilization/savagery framework of perception is steeped in Western tradition and literature and continues to be perpetuated by many historians, many textbooks, and many teachers. In this sense, there is institutionalized racism in the school system. Much writing (historical and literary) contains such degrading and dehumanizing material on Indian peoples that it qualifies as hate literature. In short, Indians have been called every name under the sun and their histories have in effect been falsified.

Racism, in this sense, is not personal or "intentional." An individual teacher may like a Native child but to the degree that he/she transmits the above material (embedded in the curriculum), he/she is passing on racism. In other words, institutionalized racism conditions students to have racist views towards Indians.

The effect on non-Native students is ignorance, fear and possible hatred of Native peoples. The effect on Native children is self-rejection. The net effect on society is the stereotyping, mistrust, and mistreatment of Native peoples.

Stereotypes have an important function in the maintenance of racism. Between 1500 and 1800 A.D. the stereotype of Indians as savage served to justify the dispossession of Indian lands. The dispossession and its legacy have created a powerful-powerless relationship between white and Native peoples. In order to maintain this power structure, new stereotypes of Native peoples have been created, as the need has arisen.

There seems to be a need to deny that racism exists. There are many denial mechanisms such as stereotyping, blaming the victim, and backlashing. An area of growing concern for me is the very common practice of blaming Native peoples for their socioeconomic conditions. Blaming "forgets" that racism has also been institutionalized in government policies of assimilation, paternalism and the historical and continuing confiscation of Native lands and resources. These policies have had a devastating impact on Native peoples but the fallout has been explained away as stemming from "cultural differences". In turn "cultural differences" are reduced to stereotypes such as "Indians can't or won't adjust" to city life. In other words, Indian "culture" rather than colonialism or racism, is blamed for whatever has happened to Native peoples. Recent outbursts on "Main Street Indians" are examples of this process of stereotyping-to-blame.

Related to the politics of racism is the game of playing "backlash." As more Natives have spoken out against racism and injustice, there has been a growing backlash against us. As part of the backlash, Native peoples have been, among other things, branded as "prejudiced", "angry" or "blaming whites"!

I recently experienced such a backlash when I made a presentation at the Dakota Collegiate Institute. A Glenlawn student accused me of being "prejudiced against white people." The student's comments and the fact that they were highlighted disturbed me (*Native Professor's Racism Speech Draws Mixed Response*, Free Press, 9 March).

But the student does provide an excellent example of what so many others are doing. In effect, the student is labelling and psychologizing. To call Natives "angry" is to imply that there is something emotionally wrong with them and they therefore do not have to be taken seriously. To call a Native speaker "prejudiced" is to label and to try and discredit his/her integrity. Resorting to these below-the-belt tactics is an attempt to neutralize and to sidestep the uncomfortable truths inherent in any honest discussion on racism.

In response to the charge of being prejudiced it must be emphasized that racism is a particular prejudice that legitimizes an unequal relationship. In other words, racism is political; it facilitates and justifies socioeconomic mobility for one group at the expense of the other. In this sense, it is not possible for the oppressed to be "prejudiced" against the oppressor because there is no power base from which to act our "prejudice" (which is often meant to be synonymous with discrimination or racism). While there may be mutual dislike, there is no such thing as a mutual discrimination in an unequal relationship.

One of the great Canadian myths is that there are always two sides to a story, therefore there must be two sides to prejudice. Another myth is that we are all equal. In real life where there is systemic inequality, there are no two sides. For instance, would this student charge South African blacks with prejudice or argue that there are two sides to apartheid?

The student also said: "Two wrongs don't make a right." This is also a backlash tactic which tries to put the moral onus on the oppressed to bear the oppressor with a grin. This is the classic expectation that minority peoples should be "bigger" than their oppressors. At best, such ill-formed thinking, which tries to pass as some sort of philosophy or ethic, is self-serving.

Again, would this student say to anti-apartheid groups: "Two wrongs don't make a right"? The depth to which racism against Native peoples is accepted as a norm is revealed in the Canadian contradiction: when peoples around the world speak out against racism in a manner stronger than I or other Native persons have done, they have been accorded heroic stature; we, on the other hand, are often maligned and censured! Indeed, the censorship and discreditation of Native voices are very profound. For example, it has been my observation that audiences will believe a white professor over a Native one when both are dealing with the very same subject and data, or a judge will believe white witnesses over Native ones, or a white scholar is assumed to be objective while a Native one is "biased." The accusation that Natives are prejudiced or biased comes in part from the ideology that only whites are objective and only they can create objective standards of measurement. This process is self-perpetuating but it is outrageous.

Since when is a person prejudiced for exposing racism and injustice? Since when is one prejudiced or wrong for believing in freedom, in justice and in equality? Since when is a Canadian prejudiced for advocating the ideals of the Canadian charter of human rights? In what way are we blaming whites when we are merely pointing to a history of racism, a history that is documentable many times over?

"If Canadians are disturbed or shocked by revelations of racism in their society, that is as it should be. If they are surprised or puzzled by it however, *that* demonstrates an abysmal lack of awareness – undoubtedly fostered by our education systems – of the less creditable aspects of Canadian history" (Hill 1977, 7[1]). The question is: do Canadians have the foresight, the compassion, and the courage to confront these "less creditable aspects of Canadian history?" I hope so, for we will all deal with much more pain if we cannot deal with the cancer of racism.

---

1 I regret that I was unable to locate the original source from which this quote is drawn – Elaine Coburn, editor's note.

1990

Preface or Here Are Our
Voices – Who Will Hear?

To be a Native writer of some consciousness is to be in a lonely place. Happily, our isolation is about to come apart at the seams. This collection, which represents some fifty voices and has already engendered much discussion, is one of a growing number of anthologies reflecting nothing short of a revolution in Native literature.

To discuss Native literature is to tangle with a myriad of issues: voicelessness, accessibility, stereotypes, appropriation, ghettoization, linguistic, cultural, sexual, and colonial roots of experience, and, therefore, of self-expression – all issues that bang at the door of conventional notions about Canada and about literature.

It was not too long ago that Native peoples were referred to as voiceless, even wordless, sometimes with the association of these with illiteracy. But were Indian and Métis voiceless? And what did it mean to be classified as illiterate? To be sure, many Natives were illiterate up to the 1970s, even into the 1990s, due to the unconscionable failure of the Canadian education system to impart to Native youth basic reading and writing skills. And illiteracy does render people voiceless in the life of a country that revolves around the printed word. But what other nuances may be found in these terms? Did it mean Native peoples spoke no words? And since illiteracy is often associated with lack of literature, even lack of intelligence, did it imply that Native peoples were bereft of literature or of knowledge?

In contrast to the inane stereotype of the Indian as soundless, we know from the vast storehouse of our oral traditions that Aboriginal peoples were peoples of words. Many words. Amazing words. Cultivated words. They were neither wordless nor illiterate in the context of their linguistic and cultural roots. The issue is not that Native peoples were ever wordless but that, in Canada, their words were literally and politically negated.

24 The Emma LaRocque Reader

It is now well known that Indian and Métis children in residential or public schools were not allowed to speak their Native languages. What is perhaps less well known are all the ways our words have been usurped, belittled, distorted, and blockaded in Canadian culture. Whether we spoke or wrote in Cree or in English, we had very little access to mainline communication systems.

Literature is political in that its linguistic and ideological transmission is defined and determined by those in power. This is why Shakespeare rather than Wisakehcha is classified as "classical" in our school curriculums. And, of course, the written word is advanced as superior to the spoken word. Oral traditions have been dismissed as savage or primitive folklore. Such dismissal has been based on the self-serving colonial cultural myth that Europeans (and descendants thereof) were/ are more developed ("civilized") than Aboriginal peoples ("savage"). So arrogant is this myth and so arrogantly held has this myth been that, except for Christian or scholarly purposes, the colonizers have not bothered to learn Aboriginal languages. To this day, inept and ideologically informed translations of legends or myths are infantilizing Aboriginal literatures.

Power politics in literature is also evident in the decisions of publishers and in audience reception. For example, around the time we were being described as "voiceless," hundreds of us were actually articulating our colonized conditions throughout Canada. Much of this articulation came in the form of speech, but it also came in the form of writing, for there were already a number of very fine Native writers by the later 1960s to the mid-1970s. But rarely were these writers approached or included in the existing literatures of those times. Publishers, including editors and journalists, turned to white authors to speak on our behalf. Just two examples: in *Native Peoples in Canadian Literature* (Mowat 1975), the majority of authors are white, including Hugh Dempsey, Rudy Wiebe, Emily Carr, Al Purdy, and George Ryga; in *Many Voices: An Anthology of Contemporary Indian Poetry* (Day and Bowering 1977), there are four poets, one of which is Cam Hubert, whose identities are put in such a way that it is difficult to tell whether they are "Indian poets" or not.

The interplay between audience reception and publishing cannot be minimized. As one of those earlier Native writers, I experienced and studied what may be called the Native-voice/white-audience dynamic. The interactions were often poignant. On another level, we were again rendered voiceless no matter how articulate we were. Apparently unable to understand or accept the truth of our experiences and perceptions, many white audiences, journalists, and critics resorted to racist techniques of psychologically labelling and blaming us. We were psychologized as "bitter," which was equated with emotional incapacitation, and once thus dismissed we did not have to be taken seriously.

We were branded as "biased," as if whites were not! Sometimes, we were even unabashedly charged with lying. The innocence and goodness of white Canada was stridently defended: How could all this oppression happen? How could police, priests, and teachers be so awful?

Our anger, legitimate as it was and is, was exaggerated as "militant" and used as an excuse not to hear us. There was little comprehension of an articulate anger reflecting an awakening and a call to liberation, not a psychological problem to be defused in a therapist's room.

Influenced by uncomprehending critics and audiences, publishers controlled the type of material that was published. It is no surprise that whatever Native protest literature was produced from authors like Harold Cardinal (1969), Howard Adams (1989 [1975]), George Manuel (Manuel and Posluns 1974), Duke Redbird (1980), Wilfred Pelletier (1971), or Waubageshig (1970) was short-lived. In direct contrast to the hailing given "Black protest literature" as a new genre by white American intellectuals, Canadian critics accused us of "blustering and bludgeoning society." Basically, we were directed just to tell our "stories" (and the more tragic the better) not, in a manner reminiscent of archival descriptions reflecting earlier colonial attitudes, to be so "arrogant" or so daring as to analyze or to call on Canadian society for its injustices.

From about the mid-1970s, there was a noticeable turn to soft-sell Native literature. Personal narratives, autobiographies, children's stories, legends, interviews with elders, cultural tidbits, and "I remember" sorts of materials were encouraged. Here, I must hasten to say that it isn't the Native efforts I am criticizing; given all the suppression, misinformation, and stereotypes that exist, we can never speak enough or do enough correction or debunking. It is the white Canadian response to and use of this literature I am addressing.

Even soft-sell literature has been misunderstood and abused. I recall reading an incoherent review of Beatrice Culleton's moving allegory *Spirit of the White Bison* (1985) with the general accusation that "minorities" were "strangling in their own roots" (*Winnipeg Free Press*, 10 August 1986)! Maria Campbell's *Halfbreed* (1973) and Culleton's *In Search of April Raintree* (1983) have been reduced, at times, to grist

26 The Emma LaRocque Reader

for social workers rather than being treated as the powerful mirrors to Canadian society that they are.

Actually, much of Native writing, whether blunt or subtle, is protest literature in that it speaks to the processes of our colonization: dispossession, objectification, marginalization, and that constant struggle for cultural survival expressed in the movement for structural and psychological self-determination. Ruby Slipperjack's gentle and wonderfully written novel *Honour the Sun* (1987) and even Chief Dan George's (1974) Hiawathian prose reflect protest.

Native writers have been creating new genres in Canadian English literature, but this fact has been largely missed by readers and critics. For example, the more overt protest books of the 1970s often combined their sharp analyses of society with wit, humour, poetry, history, anthropology, and/or personal reflections. Authors turned to facts of biography to humanize the much dehumanized "Indian." Instead of being read as new genres, they were attacked as biased and parochial. Few bookstores, libraries, or professors knew what to do with Native writing that crossed or integrated well-defined genres, styles, or schools. Native writing soon got thrown into one pot variously called "Native Literature" or "Native Studies."

I have viewed such hashing of our writing with considerable ambivalence. On one hand, Native literature has become a new genre, and Native studies has certainly become a well-respected field of study in the university. On the other hand, categorizing literature on the basis of ethnicity, gender, or politics raises the spectre of ghettoization. While one must be supportive of both Native literature and Native studies, one must be concerned about ghettoization because of its effects on Native writers and writing.

The lumping of our writing under the category "Native" means that our discussion of issues and ideas that are universally applicable may not reach the general public. For example, an analysis of the Canadian school system by a Native author is rarely placed under "education" or "sociology" or "social issues." The poetry and poetic prose in much of the writing of the 1970s is rarely, if ever, placed under poetry or literature proper. And what about Native writers who do not write about Native themes? What about Native women writers who do not write specifically or only about women, and so get excluded from "women's writing" shelves?

Perhaps the ugliest effect of ghettoization is that it raises doubts in the deeps of a writer. Is our writing published because we are good writers or because we are Native? Of course, we may never know, judging from the contradictory responses from editors and publishers. I will never forget a new Winnipeg magazine of poetry returning my poems with a rejection slip that read, "Not Indian enough"! And several years ago, a major literary journal chose a poem (out of perhaps twenty) because, I believe, it has one Cree word at the end. Indeed, one of the editors even suggested that my poems were not authentic because they played too much with words. I do wish I could recall her exact words, since they were quite stunning in their implications – especially since I worry that my poems do not have enough "word play."

Occasionally, I collect my poems, along with my courage, and take them to a reputable poet with the request that he or she critique my works strictly on their poetic merits, not on the basis of my ethnicity or gender. I take some consolation from the fact that there are many white people who get published not necessarily because they are good writers but more because they have access to the publishing world. And that Native writers choose to explore Native themes does not mean they are incompetent. After all, most white writers deal with white issues or characters, but no one thinks of this as either parochial or ghettoized.

Still, the ramifications of ghettoization are unsettling. Generally, the Canadian intellectual establishment has disregarded Native writing. Such disregard reveals a profound Canadian contradiction: even as Native voices are silenced, the writings and movements of other oppressed peoples around the world are saluted. Yet, a study of Albert Memmi's (1957) portrait of the colonizer and the colonized in Tunisia reveals a striking similarity to the faces of the colonizer and the colonized of Canada. Indeed, the very resistance of the Native's use of the colonizer's language is consistent with this portrait.

So is the belittlement and stereotyping of Native cultures. Canadian society has not understood that earlier Native writing styles have reflected a holistic way of seeing and placing space and time that produced a sense of integration with the variant aspects of life. This has been confused with the misguided notions of Indian culture (still prevalent today), notions that portray Indians as having taken no direct control over their environment, their children, their urges, their resources, their art, their thoughts, or their knowledge. A presentation that blurs Indians with their landscape only serves to de-culturalize them. In fact, Indians were multifaceted and cultivated peoples who acknowledged and practised a host of distinctions, yet maintained a functional connectedness between parts. And despite the disintegrative forces on Native cultures, many of us grew up with a holistic rather than an atomistic or discrete *Weltanschauung*.

There are numerous Native peoples yet who live or carry this world view. And every Native author of my generation or older has tried, in philosophy and in praxis (in the blending of genres), to teach our audiences our way of seeing and naming our worlds. It appears we have not been received. Superficial, even flaky, conceptions and objectifications of Indian culture have muted the deeper, life-sustaining currents of cultural continuity.

It must also be understood that Native writers have a dialectical relationship to the English (or French) language. Not only do we have to learn English, we must then deal with its ideology. To a Native woman, English is like an ideological onion whose stinging layers of racism and sexism must be peeled away before it can be fully enjoyed.

A word must be said about words. Native readers and writers do not look at English words the same way as non-Natives may, for we have certain associations with a host of them. It is difficult to accept the following terms as neutral: savage, primitive, pagan, medicine man, shaman, warrior, squaw, redskin, hostile, civilization, developed, progress, the national interest, bitter, angry, happy hunting grounds, brave, buck, redman, chief, tribe, or even Indian. These are just a few of the string of epithets that have been pejoratively used to *specifically* indicate the ranking of Indian peoples as inferior to Europeans, thus to perpetuate their dehumanization. This is why I often use a lot of quotation marks even though standard editorial practice discourages it. Then, there is the challenge of wanting to use soul language, which for me is Cree, but having to explain it with a running bracketed glossary is distracting. This is made even more difficult by the fact that there is no standard way to spell Cree words in English. Kokom, which can be spelled in at least five different ways, is just such an example. We may also disagree with what is aesthetically pleasing. We may prefer Basil Johnston or Louise Erdrich over Stephen Leacock. We may bring our oratorical backgrounds to our writing and not see it as a weakness. What is at work is the power struggle between the oral and the written, between the Native in us and the English. And even though we know the English language well, we may sometimes pay little attention to its logic – perhaps we will always feel a bit rebellious about it all. For, it must be said, that perhaps the height of cheekiness in a colonizer is to steal your language, withhold his from you as long as he can, then turn around and demand that you speak or write better than he does. And when you do, he accuses you of "uppityness" or inauthenticity.

The Native intellectual struggle to maintain our cultural integrity at these profound levels is perhaps most severely tested within the confines of scholarship and scholarly writing. Some of us de-colonizing Native scholars are challenging existing conventions in research methodology, notions of objectivity, and writing styles. So far, there has been little comprehension on the part of our colleagues. The academic world may be the hardest nut to crack. Long-standing conventions hold that objectivity must necessarily entail the separation of the "word" from the "self." As a scholar, I am expected to remain aloof from my words; I am expected to not speak in my own voice. But I am a Native woman writer/scholar engaged in this exciting evolution/revolution of Native thought and action. My primary socialization is rooted in the oral literatures of the Plains Cree Métis, which does not separate the word from the self and certainly knows the difference between atowkehwin (stories of legendary bent or sacred origin) and achimowin (factual and objective accounts). Further, there is ample evidence in the study of justification literature for the argument that objectivity can be a self-serving tool of those accustomed to managing history. This is not to mention my feminist understanding of the use of the English language. So, as an integrated person, I choose to use my own voice whether I am writing history or whether I am writing poetry. I may not always speak in my own voice, but when I do I experience no disconnection between my "self" and my footnotes.

With respect to scholarship and Native literature, many professors still turn to Rudy Wiebe (1977), George Ryga (1970), Robert Kroetsch (1973), or [W.P.] Kinsella (1977) when discussing Native themes. Yet, there are numerous Native authors available. To list just a few more (at the risk of offending many, and in addition to the ones referred to already): George Kenny (*Indians Don't Cry* 1977), Sarain Stump (*And There Is My People Sleeping* 1970), Marty Dunn (*Red On White: The Biography of Duke Redbird* 1971), Basil Johnston (*Moosemeat and Wild Rice* 1978), Jeanette Armstrong (*Slash* 1985), Lee Maracle (*I am Woman* 1988), Linda Griffiths and Maria Campbell (*The Book of Jessica* 1989), Beth Cuthand (*Voices in the Waterfall* 1989), Jane Willis (*Geneish: An Indian Girlhood* 1973), Tomson Highway (*The Rez Sisters* 1987), Arthur Shilling (*The Ojibway Dream: Faces of my People* 1986), Rita Joe (*Song of Eskasoni: More Poems of Rita Joe* 1988). This is not to mention a number of older compilations of Native essays and poetry. And now there is such a spate of new Native writers (in a wild variety of anthologies and special features) that I cannot keep up with them. There are new poets, short story writers, novelists, and playwrights. There are also new autobiographies, protest literature, children's literature, and more recollections of legends, myths, and earlier times. Even as I write this preface, I have received three different calls for submissions to Native women's anthologies. So, it cannot be said that we have been wordless from lack of skill or effort. Yet, we have been silenced in numerous and ingenious ways. In effect, we have been censored.

For the last two decades, we have been faced with the weary task of having to educate our audiences before we could even begin dialoguing with them! Our energies have been derailed from purely creative pursuits. Many speakers and writers have been cornered into the hapless role of apologists, incessant (and very patient) explainers, and overnight experts on all things Native. And in response to the negation and falsification of our histories and cultures, some have been pushed to cultural romanticism, even perhaps cultural self-righteousness. But, incidentally, nobody on earth has ever romanticized their culture to such mythic proportions (cowboys moving west and killing Indians being equated with moral and human progress) as white North Americans.

A sentence in Marlene NourbeSe Philip's delightful article, "The Disappearing Debate: Or how the discussion of racism has been taken over by the censorship issue" (*This Magazine* July–August 1989)[1], gripped me: "No work is in any full practical sense produced unless it is also received." If Native writers have felt like they have been speaking into a vacuum, it is because we have. Neither the white nor the Native audience has received us. If white audiences have largely misunderstood us, Native audiences have been virtually non-existent. Linguistic, cultural, geographic, and social distances fostered by colonial forces have prevented the development of a broadly based Native intellectual community. And those few of us who have been around for a while do not speak with each other as much as we speak to audiences. This has been due, in part, to unavoidable political and economic circumstances.

The lonely echoes of our own words have been amplified by a strange but perhaps predictable colonial phenomenon: white intellectual judgement and shunning of Native intellectuals. The dearth of Native intellectual voices and artists in the media and in Canadian creative pursuits makes one wonder if the media is aware of our existence. Or are they avoiding us? Or is our invisibility an indication of the extent to which we are ghettoized?

The most distressing thing I have observed is the assumed estrangement between Native intellectuals from "the real people." How it is that white rather than Native intellectuals can better speak for the "real Natives" remains a puzzle. But the following is a typical, if bizarre, scenario: when white journalists "discover" an "articulate" or "bright"

---

1 This essay may be found in the following collection: Philip, M. NourbeSe. "The Disappearing Debate: Or, How the Discussion of Racism Has Been Taken Over by the Censorship Issue. In *Blank: Essays and Interviews*, 99–110. Canada: BookThug, 2017 – Elaine Coburn, editor's note.

Native, they proceed to judge her as an intellectual, then bypass her in their liberal search for the grassroots.

In 1985, Métis writers, including myself, were unearthed. One incident remains for my memoirs: a CBC radio journalist from Regina called for cultural sorts of information. After regaling him (about bears, blueberries, fiddles, ghosts, and things) for about an hour, it somehow dawned on him he was speaking to a professor. He abruptly ended his interview with this request: "Could you tell me where I could find a *real* Métis storyteller?"

During the first Constitutional Conference on Self-Government, Barbara Frum interviewed a white sociologist who off-handedly accused "the Native intellectual elite" of "leading their people down the garden path." (He was from Regina too.) Perhaps because there is no Native intellectual elite, Barbara couldn't find one to interview. Seriously, I know there have not been a vast number of us intellectuals and/or writers around and I know perhaps we do not hustle for the spotlight as much as we should, but we are around. And there are more of us every day.

More seriously, we are not alienated from our roots. Society has made sure of that. And unlike many white intellectuals, we were not born into our stations in life. This is another reason why our selves are not (yet) separated from our words. To be exceptionalized is but another rung on the ghettoization ladder.

It is against this backdrop of keeping us voiceless that a movement against the appropriation of Aboriginal literatures has been born. There is absolutely no question but that radical intellectual surgery is required in the existing literatures on Aboriginal peoples. There are not enough superlatives in English to say how deeply Aboriginal peoples' worlds have been falsified in white North American literary traditions and popular culture. I, for one, have long been calling for the dismantling of racist thought and language in scholarly and popular works. Again, recently, I addressed my fellow scholars in an essay on the ethics of publishing those historical documents that qualify as hate literature against Indian and Métis peoples (see chapter "On the Ethics of Publishing Historical Documents"). Some missionary and fur trade journals, even some standard Canadian history books, would qualify as hate literature, even under the most stringent court requirements. But who will go to court against this hate literature? Who will face charges for falsifying Aboriginal histories? For that essay, I have received some thoughtful reviews. But several reviewers have dismissed my legitimate and scholastically sound concerns with the accusation that I am into "censorship."

32   The Emma LaRocque Reader

Ironically, these silly charges came at a time (early 1990) when I was contemplating my continued involvement with this anthology, which was catapulted into the appropriation controversy because several Native women have felt that white editorship of Native women's literature constitutes appropriation. There is an obvious need for clarification and debate on the definition, direction, representation, and strategy of this issue. For now, I will simply submit that the editors of this anthology have not appropriated this literature; instead, they have facilitated its possibilities and transmission. They outline their work and approach in their prefatory comments. If I thought appropriation was involved, I would have removed my materials. For the record, however, I would not have tried to stop the publishing process.

But I do call on *all* writers of consciousness to address the continuing dehumanization of Indians as grunting and bloodthirsty savages in the cowboy and Indian movies and comic books, both of which are amply available on late night shows, VCRs, or comic book stands. All must challenge the exploitation of Indian motifs in the media and marketplace. How, I have wondered so many times, is it possible in our era of supposed awareness about "minority rights" that there are still teams called Washington Redskins, Cleveland Indians, Atlanta Braves (hasn't anyone seen their jerseys?), or Edmonton Eskimos? Then there are the archival materials protected as historical documents no matter what racist and inflammatory language they carry. And what could we ever do with the fathomless well of novels that qualify as hate literature but are also protected as classics in our libraries and schools? Then, there are those individual authors who presume to speak from the Native point of view, though this to me is a grey area, depending on how it is done. For instance, I value Cam Hubert's short story "Dreamspeaker" (1981) while, on the other hand, David Williams's *The Burning Wood* (1975), Betty Wilson's *Andre Tom Macgregor* (1975), and Mort Forer's *The Humback* (1969), among many others, would have been better left unwritten. Even so, I have my students read these books for critical purposes. All of this and more needs urgent attention. But what kind and degree of attention? And where might we begin? And since racism informs so much of mainstream literature, surely the onus cannot be on Native writers to address it all. Natives cannot be the only ones responsible for confronting racism and hate literature of this magnitude. Colonized peoples often end up cleaning up the debris colonizers have left – can we refuse to do it this time? That we are raising our voices provocatively (see, for example, Lenore Keeshig-Tobias's important article "Stop Stealing Native Stories" in *The Globe and Mail*, 26 January 1990) should not be used as an excuse to further ignore us or to wash one's hands from the responsibility of fighting racism with respect to Native peoples in literature (and everywhere else, for that matter).

Appropriation is one of many issues that should be addressed by white or Native anthologists of Native literature. The irony is that, after reading this manuscript for purposes of writing the preface, I wanted more editorial changes, particularly with several pieces because they may, however unconsciously, perpetuate stereotypes. After all, much of my life has been spent "defeathering" stereotypes (LaRocque 1975). But my concern (and it is legitimate) is one among many other considerations here. Even though I can rhetorically ask, "What good is the democratization of voice if it is one more avenue for the transmission of stereotypes?", I am painfully aware of the long history of suppressing Native voices, especially women's voices, and I am as anxious as anyone to help facilitate their/our expression. What a bizarre situation to be in: to know so well the nooks and crannies of colonization that this "knowing" threatens to stand in the way of other voices. Happily, this dilemma was resolved for me because, in the main, this anthology carries many good and worthy words.

And I do care about the quality of writing within the Native community. I do believe in such a thing as literary excellence (albeit dialectical as discussed above) in the tradition of the Cree who were known as Nehiyawak, The Exact Speaking People (although in some dialects it could refer to People of Four Directions). It is in keeping with the spirit of our original cultures to produce excellence in the contemporary context. Accordingly, I do call for an "exact" articulation of our humanity and our oppressed conditions in the advancement of our liberation.

Native peoples, however, are still making a transition from oral to written literatures, from aboriginal to foreign languages. This is both a gift and a challenge. It is a gift to know more than one language, more than one culture. It is a challenge to be able to fly with "the gift," given the colonial state of affairs in our country. But this is 1990. To speak, read, and write in English is the birthright of contemporary Native peoples. It may be said that linguistic "appropriation" can go both ways. My first language is Plains Cree. My parents were forced to allow me to go to school where I was forced to learn English. In due time, I have "appropriated" this language without abandoning my Cree. I have sought to master this language so that it would no longer master me.

Colonization works itself out in unpredictable ways. The fact is that English is the new Native language, literally and politically. English is the common language of Aboriginal peoples. It is English that is serving to raise the political consciousness in our community; it is English that is serving to de-colonize and to unite Aboriginal peoples. Personally, I see much poetic justice in this process.

To be sure, we must attend to the task of "recreating the enemy's language," as Native American poet Joy Harjo put it (at a Native Women Speaker Series in 1989 at the University of Manitoba). This does take some skill, but our survival, as always, depends on skill. Native writers, like all writers everywhere, must have access to and must avail themselves of good and conscious editing and editors. To that end, then, we can make a distinction between editing as craft and editing as ideology. We must make room for the advancement of skill.

Native writers face a monumental but purposeful task: that of giving voice to a people's journey that spans centuries, a journey that at once says so much about white Canada. Alanis Obomsawin, Abenaki filmmaker, singer, and poet from Quebec, in explaining the purpose of her films, said:

> The basic purpose is for our people to have a voice. To be heard is the important thing, no matter what it is we're talking about.... And that we have a lot to offer our society. But we also have to look at the bad stuff, and what has happened to us, and why.... We cannot do this without going through the past, and watching ourselves and analyzing ourselves, because we're carrying a pain that is 400 years old. We don't carry just our everyday pain. We're carrying the pain of our fathers, our mothers, our grandfathers, our grandmothers – it's part of this land." (Alioff and Levine 1987, 13)

Much of that 400-year-old pain has been expressed in the war of words against us. And to that, we are pressed to explain, to debunk, and to dismantle. To the war of ways against us, we are moved to retrieve, redefine, and reconcile our scattered pieces. To the voices of despair among us and in us, we are challenged to dream new visions to bring hope for the future.

We are the keepers of time. We must know the places of invasion in our histories and in ourselves so that we may illumine the paths of those who cannot see or who do not know. Because our pain is a "part of this land," we are also the Uncomfortable Mirrors to Canadian society. And few can look at the glaring reflections our mirrors provide. "My knee is so badly wounded no one will look at it/The pus of the past oozes from every pore/ ... Anger is my crutch/I hold myself upright with it" writes Native American poet Chrystos (1988).

Finally, we cannot be cast as voices of the past, or even of the present. As writers, we are seekers of truth. We are called to transcend our own prejudices and politics, even our centuries-old pain, so that we can do what writers must do – tell the truth about the human condition. In this task, we cannot spare our own human make-up, which, however, must be done with an awareness of the social dimensions influencing it.

This anthology gives voice to Native women, and these women, in unexpected ways, tell the truth about this land, about the oppressor, and about the oppressed in us all. Ideologists will find this wonderfully democratic collection puzzling. It is clear that Native women are not in any uniform stage of political consciousness (but whose "consciousness"?), either about the oppression of Natives or of women. Nor are they at a uniform level of ability. Both are to be expected, because the tidal waves of colonization have hit Native communities at different times in different ways over a span of five centuries. This is not to mention that Aboriginal peoples are also *different* from each other, quite apart from European influences. Represented here are women of different languages, religions, cultures, generations, educational levels, and personal circumstances.

There is a range of movement in theme and style that reflects the transitional nature of contemporary Native consciousness and writing from oral to written, from ambiguity to clarity, from hesitation to self-assertion, from internalization of stereotypes to an articulation of our colonial experience, and from romanticization to quiet criticism of "our people" and "our culture" (a hint of what is to come). Some themes unique to a people dispossessed stand out: a haunting and hounding sense of loss that drives one to reminisce. "I remember," many of us write, "I remember."

The poignancy of "taking on" the historical millstone of keeping our ancestors' memories alive comes through in our unsettling dreams and visions. "It's with terror, sometimes/That I hear them calling me" wrote Sarain Stump (1970). Then there is the plodding through the maze of identity crises that come from the political burdens and contradictions of our times. Questions of religion, traditionalism, modernism, racially mixed ancestries or offspring, mixed marriages, or feminism all pull at our loyalties.

There is the loneliness that comes from so many places: forced separation from one's children or parents, emotional and intellectual isolation, the experiencing of daily indecencies inherent in a racist society, the grieving that follows death.

Nor is there any escape from having to live in the eye of the storm – a storm one cannot tangibly touch or immediately give voice to, but still it is there. Always there. Like Pakak, the "thousand year companion" who "pierced my heart" with his "socket eyes" (Halfe 1993, 79). And *forever* trying to remove the speck of self-doubt from one's eyes, and the boulder of arrogance from the whites of others' eyes.

So we share our humanity – over and over again. We share our dreams, our fears, our loves, our hates, our mourning for the dying of the Grandmother, our culture, the Mother, our land, the Children, our future.

Themes specific to Native women are, of course, here: birthing children, nurturing, sense of vulnerability, fear of violence, wife battering, and sexual assault. And there is some allusion to the developing tensions between male-defined traditions at variance with the women's spirituality, suffering, and perceptions. There is eloquence in the humour, wit, and gentle chiding employed on self and others on issues such as loss of innocence, sexism, hypocrisy, personal foibles, sexuality, and even betrayal.

Finally, a word must be said about the theme of the spectrum of betrayal that permeates these writings. There is betrayal that a child feels about being sent to a hospital, a residential school, or fostering. There is the priestly betrayal of a child in the confessional (Higgins 1993, 87–108), of a teenager in "the black sedan" (Barton 1993, 9). There is the beastly betrayal in the policeman's frenzied raping of a six-year-old child, left alone in the woods during the traitorous treaty days, a story that must be set in a Hiawathian garden to accent the profound loss of innocence (Gladue 1993, 62–74). There is "the man in the shadows" who must be "masked" yet (Chisaakay 1993, 31). There is betrayal by men who jump into children's beds in their own home (Lee 1993, 153).

The metaphorical layers of betrayal are just as damning, and infinitely more difficult to say: Where were the grandmothers, the mothers, the fathers, the brothers, the "warriors"? Why did they not protect? Too, there is the disloyalty of kin and community in looking the other way, even blaming. And what more can one say about the betrayal of "cold-stone Canada" (see chapter "My Hometown Northern Canada South Africa") for creating the conditions, then abandoning the oppressed to the oppressed, and to snake priests and yellow-striped sons of ... Her Majesty?

To these devastations of war-time proportions, and to all the other indignities available in our society, women here write with such subtlety and restraint, it brought a hammer to my guts and stinging water to my eyes. And with some amazement, I notice a remarkable lack of despair. Or rage.

No one can read these words and say they cannot understand – there is no mystification here. No longer can our words be discarded

"as irrelevant as Native poetry" (*The Globe and Mail* 16 November 1985[2]).
Nor should Native women's writing form a new body of ghettoized literature. Both white and Native communities are implicated; both are invited to hear.

Aiy Aiy my sisters for writing with such honesty and courage. Aiy Aiy Jeanne and Sylvia for "sweating" this through. Our loneliness has been lifted.

Aiy Aiy I offer you this poem:

Brown Sister
O my beautiful brown sister
your eyes are deep pools of pain
your face is prematurely lined
your Soul of Sorrow
is the Sorrow of Every Woman
Every Native
My beautiful brown sister
I know you
I know you
you heal me
you sweep sweetgrass over
the scars of my Exile

---

2 I regret that I was unable to locate the original source from which this quote is drawn – Elaine Coburn, editor's note.

1990

Geese over the City

In the city
one awakes to the sound
of man-made mobility
    coughing motors,
    clanging truck boxes,
    wailing sirens,
    tire screeches.
There are treadmarks on my soul.
But this morning - day
Very early -
Even before the sun
made it through the October grey --
I heard the Geese.
       The Geese
          The Geese ---
            and in my half-sleep
                 I jumped up,
             ready to run out and see
            Their V-formation
         as was the tradition
       of the great northern Cree
But sounds of some shifting gears
made me stop
and aware that
the obstinate elm leaves,
electric wires
and too tall buildings

would not let me see,
　　　　let me see,
　　　　　let me see –
　　　　　　so I fell back to sleep,
　　　　　　　no, to reverie
　　　　　　　　I saw a little log-shack
　　　　　　　　　full of family faces
　　　　　　　　　　　all embraced
　　　　　　　　　by a tangle tussle
　　　　　　　　　of green-gold laces
　　　　　　　　And I smelled
　　　　　　　the racy fragrance
　　　　　　of a widowed willow – leaf
　　　　　etched with the earth
　　　　broken birch branch
　　　and damp dew
ahh
Twice more
The Geese
went over the city
making me sad
that I could not see
making me happy
that I could see
there was much Cree in me
despite
town height.

1990

Nostalgia

Where does it go
the log-cabins,
woodstoves and rabbit soup
we know
in our eight year old hearts?

I tried to hold it
with my Minolta
As Sapp stills it
with paint and brush

I ran out of film,
and Sapp out of brushes.

1990

"Progress"

Earth poet
So busy
weaving
      magic
into words

so busy
placing
      patterns
quilting
      stars
so busy
making
      the sun
dance
so busy
singing
      your songs
in circles
so busy
tipping
      moons
in dreams

Earth poet
so busy

touching
        the land
      scape
mad modern man
must take me
look at
cool steep spires
stealing earth and sun
       dance.

1990

The Red in Winter

The blushing river the Cree called her
She wears no rouge today
She speaks no Cree
I ask her about her other lifetimes
beneath her white mask.

1990

Incongruence

A verdant, crooked path
So earth-soft
Framed by ash and poplar
Surprised by red berries
waving from the undergrowth
Enveloped by a warm, cerulean sky
Your beauty knives through me
as a cold snap in October.
I should be holding hands
With my lover
I should be picking berries
With my mother.

1990

Loneliness

Ah Loneliness,
How would I know
Who I am
Without you?

1990

The Beggar

i met a boozed-up, begging Indian
on the proverbial mainstreet
ten years ago
when i had no money
i would have fed him
today
i slinked off
in my unfaded blue jeans
harry rosen plaids
and turquoise rings.

then
i stole a poem.

1990

Tides, Towns and Trains

Where and how do I tell the story of the many worlds my mother and I have travelled? How does one tell a post-modern society that one has traversed centuries in half a lifetime?

While I have undergone some "predictable" stages in the four decades of my life, my journey has been more than the "passages" of life described by Sheehy (1977). Because I was born into a world quite different in race, culture, political and socio-economic status from the "ordinary" Canadian, there has always been an "un-ordinary" and multi-dimensional aspect to my life and, therefore, to my thinking. For me, there have been no road maps; there have been few role models. There have been days when I have felt that I was in some space and time warp. And, indeed, in some ways I have been. At the age of 20, I could identify with Chief Dan George who, in his seventies, poeticized:

> Was it only yesterday that men sailed around the moon...? You and I marvel that man should travel so far and so fast.... Yet, if they have travelled far then I have travelled farther ... and if they have travelled fast, then I faster ... for I was born a thousand years ago.... But within the span of half a lifetime I was flung across the ages to the culture of the atom bomb ... (George 1970, 184)

If Chief Dan George travelled far and fast – as indeed he and my parents did – then perhaps I have travelled farther and faster. It did not take half a lifetime, but barely a decade, for me to be flung across the ages, and across yawning chasms of experience between my world and the world of Town.[1]

---

1 *Town* is spelled with an initial capital letter throughout when used metaphorically. My birthplace was only six miles from Lac La Biche, which my family referred to as "town." Town, for me, came to have a metaphorical meaning, a point of uneasy contact between our land-based life and the Town's urban, industrial and profit-based culture, with its condescending attitudes towards Aboriginal ways.

I was born in the morning in the dawn of 1949 in a one-roomed, kerosene-lit log cabin, into a small family in the small Métis community of Big Bay, Alberta, near the town of Lac La Biche. I was born into a world of people whose roots of pride, independence, industriousness and skills go back to the Red River Métis, back to the Cree. I was born into a world of magic, where seeing and hearing ghosts was a routine occurrence, where the angry Pehehsoo (thunderbird) could be appeased by a four-directional pipe chant, where the spirits danced in the sky on clear nights, and where tents shook for people to heal. When my mother brought home from town a comic book of Henry Wadsworth Longfellow's *Hiawatha*, which I later learned was a "classic," I could identify with its world. The magic and natural world of *Hiawatha* was my world too!

Yet I was not born into a garden of Hiawathian paradise. Our own humanness and the effects of European colonization were very much with us. Even as we lived off the land, we also lived off the railroad, and by fighting forest fires, and picking rocks and sugar beets in the "deep south" of Alberta. Even as we ate moose, trout and berries, we also ate canned Spork, sardines and white sugar. Even as my grandmother's lover shook tents in the ancient ceremony of the Cree, we were kissing the Stations of the Cross in the annual pilgrimages of the Roman Catholic Church. And even as my mother chased away Pehehsoo, soon after I entered school I was lecturing her about the physics of thunder and lightning. And even as my father spoke of smelling the swooping night-spirit dancers, I lectured him about the gaseous flickers of aurora borealis. Even as we chanted to drums, jigged to fiddles and laughed, we were also crying, hurting and burying grandparents, aunts, uncles, brothers and sisters who were felled by tuberculosis (T.B.) and other diseases. And even as we generously shared foods and other kindnesses with each other, there were those amongst us whom we feared. And there were those from Town whom we feared. Violence stalked among us.

I was born into a complex community that was open to natural change but that simultaneously experienced forced change. Change was not and is not new to Indian and Métis culture. The issue is to differentiate between change that is imposed and change that comes from free choice. And change that is forced is oppression. Oppression over time, such as that of the colonizing of Native[2] peoples in Canada, has had

---

2 *Native* is an umbrella term for the Indian, Inuit and Métis of Canada. (The Métis of the 1950s to the 1970s were often subsumed under the term *non-status Indian*.) See my fuller discussion of the Native's dialectical relationship to the English language in my preface to Jeanne Perreault and Sylvia Vance, eds., *Native Women of Western Canada: Writing the Circle – An Anthology* (see chapter "Preface – Here Are Our Voices – Who Will Hear?").

various and varying effects on different generations. I believe changes came slower for my parents than for me, but my parents experienced changes that were more directly forced upon them by Canadian society, especially in regard to their children and schooling. It may be harder to unravel the effects of changes that were at once forced and at once sought after. Schooling was forced on me too, yet I actually fought my parents in order to go to school. At the time, I did not know that school was an institution of colonization invading and disturbing the way of life of my family, my community, my ancestors. Nor could I have anticipated the school's denigration of Native peoples, which was to affect my self-image profoundly. And what could I make of the violence by white and Native alike in the playground as well as in the classroom?

Even though I soon hated school, I idealized learning, and unknown to me I internalized much of what Métis author Howard Adams (1989 [1975]) calls the "white ideal." Early in my childhood I quite consciously rejected the roles expected of me by my family and community, namely, to attend to household chores and eventually to become someone's wife. So, I kept on going to school. I kept on going. And I kept on going.

My going to school presented numerous complications for my family. Living off the land was a family affair. Parents and children were engaged in the various activities associated with trapping, hunting, working on the railroad, fire fighting, gardening, processing food and animal hides, sewing clothing, making tools, cooking, healing, fishing, berry picking, creating and recreating, the sum of which formed a well-integrated, functioning culture. Our culture cut across all seasons and some geography. However, in the early 1950s, forced schooling and governmental confiscation of Métis trap lines in the northeastern area intercepted the seasons, geography and rhythm of our culture and, hence, our family life. My parents had to juggle between a land-based lifestyle, which was available to us only at Chard (a little whistle-stop on the Northern Alberta Railroad[3] [NAR]), and a lifestyle that could accommodate school, which was available only in the Lac La Biche area. The distance between Chard and Lac La Biche was only 100 miles numerically speaking, but it seemed much greater, because we were crossing more than the muskeg. But we managed. My mother stayed at our home near town so we children could go to school, and my father shared a trap line with my favourite uncle and worked seasonally for

---

3 The Northern Alberta Railroad was a line that ran from Edmonton through Lac La Biche, Big Bay, Chard and Anzac to Fort McMurray.

the NAR at Chard. My father came home regularly every two to six weeks, and we joined him in Chard whenever school was out.

Chard was our haven. At Chard we had our second cabin (the first one being at Big Bay) just a few yards from the railroad. On the rail line between Lac La Biche and Fort McMurray there were Métis hamlets about every 20 to 25 miles. Métis men worked as section hands for the NAR and the women worked tirelessly at home.[4] I have many fond memories of our numerous family trips on the train, going back and forth between town and Chard. I learned to play poker from the best on those train trips!

Just prior to my reaching grade seven, we learned about a dormitory that was opening at Anzac, between Chard and Fort McMurray, for Métis children whose parents lived along the NAR line. We would board at the dorm and go to a public school nearby.[5] To get to Anzac, we would board the train, stay for two weeks and then come home for a weekend. I had no idea what this place would be like; I only knew I had to get away from the town school. And just as I had demanded to go to school in the first place, I pushed my parents to let us go to Anzac Dorm. Even now it hurts me to think of the loneliness, the powerlessness and the emptiness my parents must have felt, watching us moving away from them.

At the tender age of 13, I boarded the old NAR train on my way to Anzac. For more than a decade I was to board that train over and over again on my way somewhere in pursuit of "higher" education. For more than a decade I was to visit my parents only for short periods whenever economically possible, and then to take that train again away from them. It was never without enormous heartache. I still remember standing at the back of the coach waving goodbye to my mother as she

---

4 The role of women changed somewhat, depending on the type of work men did. When the men trapped, the division of labour along gender lines was minimal, with women enjoying greater flexibility; when men were wage-earners, women played traditional roles with respect to housekeeping.

5 As a rule, Métis children did not go to residential schools, which were federally operated for Treaty Indians. Treaty Indians are defined by the Indian Act. Many Canadians of Native ancestry have been excluded by this act and do not have the same rights to education and health services. The Anzac Dorm was not a "residential school," as the term is traditionally used with reference to Treaty Indians. It was a dormitory centrally located to accommodate Métis children who lived along the NAR rail line. Most of these hamlets had no schools. Anzac Dorm was provincially funded by the Northland School Division and it was operated by a group of Mennonites through their Voluntary Services Programme. The dormitory was not a school – it was a place where Métis children lived while they attended a public school nearby.

stood on the tracks waving back. I would watch her until the steel ribbons blurred together by the distance and by my tears. I knew she was crying too. And I remember the joy of arriving. The train could not go fast enough (and it could not – it barely mustered 20 miles per hour). Finally, we would creak and rumble into Chard. My parents would be standing by their cabin, waiting, hoping. When they could determine it was really me coming towards them, my mother would break into a little jog, hesitating, then running, to greet me. And she always had such delicious food ready for me. All too soon there would be the devastating pain of leaving them again. I remember it all, still, as if it were yesterday.

Each time I took that train away from them I was not only leaving a family and a place I loved so much, I was leaving a culture, a familiar way of life, for a world that was, initially, foreign, frightening and, at times, excruciatingly lonely. With each train ride the distance between my two worlds grew, not only in miles but in ways that no words in English could ever adequately describe. What kind of a society forces families into such heartbreaking, no-win situations?

The overused and flimsy phrase, "cultural differences," comes nowhere near describing the tidal waves of changes that I, my family, and my ancestors have undergone. The real difference between Native peoples and other Canadian people is no longer cultural so much as it is political. Native cultures have been inextricably related to lands and resources; Euro-Canadian culture continues to invade these lands and resources, pulling the ground from under Native cultures, creating a power/powerless relationship that generates results immensely more profound than mere cultural differences could ever create. To speak of cultural differences as if there is a balance of power is to hide the truth of colonization.

The history of colonizing Native peoples in Canada may best be understood as the ebb and flow of an ocean. There was the initial tidal wave of the fur traders, missionaries and disease. The nature of this wave was such that Indian peoples could, for at least two centuries, stem, redirect, even dam the intermittent tides. Then there was the crushing wave of Confederation and "the national dream" – the building of the railway. Already weakened by disease, demoralization and the growing loss of economic independence, western Native peoples could not withstand this rush. Indians were forced into treaties, residential schools and reserves. Métis were forced out of the Red River area and left landless and marginalized throughout the prairie provinces. Remarkably, both Indians and Métis endured, and even regrouped, when they were left largely to themselves during the low tide between 1890 and the 1950s.

The third tidal wave, which continues to affect my generation, took place soon after World War II. This wave was the modernization movement, in which various white agencies seemed driven to whip Indian and Métis into white, middle-class, "ordinary" Canadians. This is the wave in which governments confiscated or restricted the trapping, hunting and fishing areas and resources that Native peoples loved and used. This is the wave that forced families between town schools and trap lines.[6] This is the wave in which police unabashedly picked up the most vulnerable Native people from Town streets, and in which social workers began "scooping" children away from their homes (see Johnston 1983). This is the wave that made our village crouch when townsmen came, sometimes striking with brutal rapacity. This is the wave in which disorientation, grief, fear and internalized rage grew among us.

And this is the wave I was born into, a wave that has haunted my heart and influenced my research and understanding of the human being as the oppressed and as the oppressor. The late 1940s to the 1960s was the tidal wave of the town – in which, like headlights of a car in the night coming closer and closer, the town loomed larger and larger. It was not just one town; it could be any town, anywhere in Canada. Town consisted of "white" people who spoke English with various accents: French, Anglo-Saxon, Ukrainian, Syrian, Chinese. To us, they were all white and they owned and ran everything. Restaurants. Stores. Offices. Schools. Churches. Hospitals. Rooming houses. Barrooms. Jails. And even the very corners of the streets we walked on. In Cree, we called them *ooh-gu-mow-wuk* (the governing ones).

Going to town was a major event, for in the 1950s we went only occasionally. For me, it was almost always a very unpleasant experience. *Ooh-gu-mow-wuk* stared and glared at us. Sometimes they called us names, like "squaws" and "bucks." Sometimes they yelled at us, "Go back home, dirty Indians."[7] And sometimes, my parents stayed to visit with their friends and relatives on the streets, in secret wine circles, or in barrooms because they had no access to the recreational and tourist facilities in town. We, the children, waited in movie houses, looked at comic books in cafes, or, if late into the night, waited vigilantly in hotel lobbies. Sometimes fights in barrooms spilled out onto the street – then, to be sure, there were the police. In the 1950s, there were few fights for

---

6 A comparable story is to be found in Shkilnyk (1985).

7 They cared not whether we were Métis or Indian – we were all tar-feathered in the same way. There are profound cultural, linguistic, historical, legislative and regional differences among Native peoples, yet the pattern of generalizing them persists.

Tides, Towns and Trains

there was little excessive drinking – but there would still be the police. Many times I saw police roughing up and/or picking up Native people, among them my uncles, my aunties, and even my mother. Years later I was to learn, with horror, that there were times when the police picked up defenceless women just to assault them!

If we did not go to town, the Town came to us. The presence of the priests is a good example. Wherever the Métis went, the priests went. They carried their portable god and confessionals. Priests functioned as catechism enforcers, baptizers, and buriers of the dead. I do not have any happy memories of priests. I remember them as austere-looking, authoritarian men with big dark beards who dressed in black. They taught an extremely simplistic version of heaven and purgatory, as if they were afraid we would fathom the contradictions of theology. They would pop in unexpectedly once or twice a year demanding confession, while my mother scurried to feed them. I especially remember one priest who, holding hands with my 15-year-old cousin, led her into the woods. I asked my mother why he carried such a big flashlight in the front of his pants! In retrospect, I wonder why no one stopped that priest.

For all the times and ways priests controlled Métis' lives from the Red River days up to the 1950s, their presence is almost nil today in the Lac La Biche area. When my family needed spiritual support and nurturing friendship during my mother's eight-month illness in 1981, no priest or other Roman Catholic representative ever came to us or stood by us. The priest who performed my mother's last rites and burial was and is a complete stranger to me and my family. Other friends and caring people stood by us, knowing the sorrow of the passing of seasons, and the sorrow of my gentle father, my brothers, my sister and I, and of the grandchildren.

Town brought disease. Throughout the first half of this century, thousands of Native people were felled by T.B. My community did not escape. People with advanced T.B. were shipped off to Edmonton, and often their bodies were shipped back. We had no money. We spoke no English. Edmonton may as well have been Russia, it was that inaccessible to us. Even the town hospital was inaccessible. It was only in the late 1950s that municipal health workers discovered our hamlet (which is only six miles from town) and started to immunize children against T.B. and polio. By the time I was 10 years old, I had lost more relatives and neighbours than an average white person will ever lose in a lifetime. What emotional and ideological havoc all these deaths must have wreaked on us. What questions and doubts the medicine people must have had about their knowledge and their Cree and Christian gods. We, the survivors, walk in grief for much of our lives. There are ever new diseases that stalk our communities.

Then there were the storekeepers in town, and Town storekeepers in each hamlet. Storekeepers probably had the greatest power of any whites who had a connection with us. They acted as post office workers, bankers, translators, and managers of our family allowance, old age pension and pay cheques. In the 1950s and much of the 1960s, there was no social assistance, but the storekeepers acted in the manner of welfare agents. They kept the accounts, doling out credits against debits. They determined the price of goods, furs and berries. They watched us like hawks when we shopped in their aisles.

In this era, Native people, including my parents, never fought back. They tolerated the stares, the dehumanization, the violence, the price-fixing. One time, I challenged the books of an old-timer, a storekeeper who was always very friendly, accepting of, and dependent on his Native customers. He was buying blueberries from us and his arithmetic did not match mine. I exposed the discrepancy and made him pay us the correct amount, but my parents were mortified – not at him, but at me! "*Keyam, keyam*," they ordered me. *Keyam* means, among other things, let it be – don't rock the boat. Don't question. Don't challenge.

My parents were reflecting centuries of colonial conditioning: fear and obey *ooh-gu-mow-wuk*. The flip side of this can be found in missionary and fur-trade journals in which colonizing Europeans assumed governing positions and considered any Native expression of independence or resistance as "haughty," "impetuous" or "arrogant."

Quite early in childhood, I became aware of the serious gaps between the world I was born into and the world of the Town with which we had to deal. It is not surprising that a large part of my life has been focussed upon trying to understand and build bridges of communication between these two worlds. For me, formal education finally formed the channel through which I could articulate my many worlds. I must say, however, that who and what I am today has been despite, not because of, the school system.

From grade one onwards my student life has been filled with discomfort, loneliness and anger. Before I knew about racism in Canada, I experienced shame and alienation from teachers and textbooks that portrayed Indians as backward savages. And of course, the Cowboy and Indian movies and the attitudes of Town did not help. Yet I knew that there was absolutely no connection between such biased portrayals and the consummate humanity of my parents, brothers and sister, my *nokom* (grandmother), my aunts and uncles. But what does a child do when she knows from a place that had not yet been "documented"?

Later, as I pursued "higher" education I soon discovered that university textbooks presented Indian and Métis peoples in as distorted and insulting ways as the elementary texts had done. The racist theme of the myth of Indian savagery was ever-present. Indian culture was described as "primitive" and "simple," Indian society as static (LaRocque 1993a). And of course I knew that there was nothing simple or static about the world my parents or I grew up in. Today, as an historian, I document what I have always known.

As I said earlier, my going to school presented numerous complications for my family. It also presented problems for me. The deeper I moved into the education system and into the white world, the more I found myself encountering conflict: with my family, with my new white friends and acquaintances, within myself. The longer I stayed in school, the less my family knew me. The more I knew white people, the more I became aware of their profound lack of knowledge or appreciation of my background.

Throughout my elementary and high school years I heard many racist comments. Travelling in buses or trains, sitting in classrooms or in cafes, I would hear comments about "Indians" wafting mean and dirty. There was nowhere I could go, nowhere I could be, without hearing words about "Indians." Stupid words. Incredibly insulting words. It was as if Canadian whites were given some divine injunction to prattle incessantly about "the Indian problem," as they put it. I became aware that I was part of a group that was "open season" for anyone's misjudgments and slurs.

As a child, I never spoke up in classrooms or in playgrounds. As an adolescent, I felt shame and confusion. But in my late teens, I began to speak out. I began to talk back to teachers, missionaries, farmers, bus drivers, train conductors, cab drivers. To those whites I considered friends, I made special attempts to explain. Years later I came to understand that, like many Native individuals before me, I had been forced into the position of being an apologist for "my people."[8]

At the age of 19, I started what has become my career: the university. In several classes, but mostly from reading on my own, I learned about colonization, racism, slavery and poverty. I read Harold Cardinal's (1969) *The Unjust Society*, and could identify with nearly every page. Finally a Native person had articulated what I had been experiencing!

---

8 I use the word *apologist* in the literary sense – of explaining, speaking and writing in defence of. I do not mean it in the sense of apologizing.

I came to understand that our economic poverty and marginalization, our landlessness and our fragmentation, and all the hostility and stereotyping around us were neither accidental nor isolated, nor were they due to some "cultural difference" or innate deficiency in us. Racism and injustice, deeply entrenched in all major institutions, tore our communities apart and broke people down. This oppression was rooted in a racial, religious and patriarchal ideology that claimed that whites were civilized and their manifest destiny was to enslave Blacks and overtake Indians, both of whom were considered savage. In Canada, racism was and is the foundation and the justification for colonization.

Institutionalized oppression was an earth-shaking concept for me. For years I, like my parents before me, had been conditioned to fear and obey *ooh-gu-mow-wuk* and to *keyam*. All our lives, priests preached the acceptance of one's "station" in life; evangelicals preached personal sin as the cause of all grief. My parents explained disease and misfortune as a manifestation of "bad medicine." Life was a matter of fate and personal stupidity. In addition to all this, I was indoctrinated in grades seven to nine by well-meaning Mennonites at Anzac Dorm; I was taught to adopt the Beatitudinal posture of meekness and of forgiveness and prayer for those who would devastate us. At the Prairie Bible Institute in southern Alberta (where I took grades 10 to 12), I was brainwashed never to question, never to challenge. There, medieval rules were equated with godliness. And on our town streets, Pentecostals yelled: "Prayer moves mountains," and "take it all to Jesus."

I was born into a whirlpool of *keyams* and karmas. But I was born asking. I was born, as poet Joy Harjo writes, "with eyes that can never close" (1983, 73). Even when blindness struck me in my early teens, I saw – at home and in Town – what no one wanted to see. As a child, in the safety of my own home, I asked and challenged incessantly. In elementary school, terrified of my peers and teachers, I was cowed into deadening silence. As a vulnerable teenager, desperately in need of a framework to live by, I clung to religions that had simplistic "answers" to life.

Discovering earth-shaking concepts usually changes a person. Moving away from the concept of the "personal" to the "sociological" was, for me, a revolution. Learning that poverty and other problems in my community were due to some traceable oppressive processes was for me liberation from shame and confusion. I became politicized. What was more, I was politicizing on at least two fronts: as a Native and as a woman. The early stages of decolonization entail much anger. I was as angry about the subjugation of female persons in my hamlet, and in my town, and in churches, as I was about the oppression of Native people. I was shedding innocence and layers of myths, leaving patriarchal and paternalistic "friends." I was taking on new theories, pushing past boundaries. I soon found myself confronting people who made sexist or racist remarks. I lectured to my family and relatives, on one hand about racism in Town, and on the other about sexism and the sexual offenders in our communities and towns. I was explaining issues to whomever would listen and, incidentally, even educating professors along the way.

Clearly embarrassed, my family tolerated me. My other relatives avoided me. My real friends said little. The "ordinary Canadian" whites reacted with disbelief, defensiveness and shock. I had become the Uncomfortable Mirror. What no one understood was that I was in a revolution of many layers and there is little that is comfortable or "quiet" in such a revolution. I also soon discovered that there is nothing easy about trying to educate either the oppressed or the oppressor. Nor is there anything particularly angelic about either group. Both are afraid of self-inspection and change. The familiar is safer than the unknown.

Meanwhile, I pursued life at top speed as only a healthy person in her twenties can do. Quite by accident, I got into journalism, writing and lecturing. At the age of 20, I had a major essay published in a college paper and republished in a Native newspaper. At 21, I found myself lecturing to an audience of 2,000 at a church conference in the United States of America. At 23, I travelled across the United States, visiting Choctaw, Sioux and Navajo reservations. Feeling like John Steinbeck (1962) "in search of America", I experienced that hot, sticky summer as one of tremendous personal growth. At 24, I became a published author. Because my book, *Defeathering the Indian* (LaRocque 1975), was (and is) categorized as a curriculum guide, it was never widely advertised. Even so, it was given considerable media and public attention. This initially flattered me, but I soon found myself retreating.

Something about the pace of my process frightened me, and much about public reaction frustrated me. I went back to university and, after receiving two master's degrees (in religion/peace studies and in history), I began a teaching career in Native studies at the University of Manitoba. I have been teaching there since 1977. I have pursued scholarship and teaching with the same incisive passion and exuberance I've explored my different worlds. And here too, I've found myself confronted with many contradictions, ironies and resistance. For what does a Native woman scholar do when she has had to "master" the very authors and materials that have always left her with the knowledge that they "see," but they do not see?

How incredulous I was to read the fathers of anthropology, psychology, socialism, sociology, history, political science and the great religions, and discover that much of their theories on human development are premised on patriarchal, ethnocentric and ill-formed notions about so-called "primitive people."

In the same vein, how maddening it has been for me to read "classics" such as *The Plains Cree* in which David G. Mandelbaum (1978) essentially chops Cree culture into disparate pieces of "primitive" tools. Equally maddening are the assorted manuals for nurses, police and teachers for "Native awareness days," which reduce Indian culture into a pathetic list of seven or so traits.

How enraging it was to hear a colleague in history describe Indians as having a "hand-to-mouth" existence. What could a white, middle-class, male urbanite know about the nuances and genius of being Native living in and off the land? Reading "classics" and an assortment of biased archival materials, he formed his eclipsed view of Indian existence. Like so many others, he assumed the authority of white authors, passing it on as fact.

How eerie it has been to referee and comment on a problematic missionary journal of the 1820s, describing, among other things, the shaking-tent ceremony, and to know that my grandfather performed the ceremony and my father was healed through it (see chapter "On the Ethics of Publishing Historical Materials"). My friends still participate in such ceremonies. What could I say to those white colleagues who treat this as a remarkable archival find?

Sometimes, my feelings of being flung across the ages are highlighted in the most memorable of ways. In the summer of 1977, my mother and niece came from Alberta to visit me. In so many ways, it was a very important visit. It was the first time Mom, a woman who had travelled centuries in her lifetime, had had the opportunity to travel miles from her home, the first time to come to my world. Unknown to us, it was the last time she would travel in full health; in but a few years she would embark on that journey of no return.

Among many good memories I have of this visit, one incident stands out. We visited the Manitoba Museum of "Man" and Nature, where there was a display of a northern Native campsite and its attendant cultural tools. In an instant, Mom recognized everything, and her whole person beamed. With great animation, she began to identify each tool and to explain its usage. She described, for example, how specific moose bones had to be shaped and honed with precision so that moose hides could be scraped without damage. She went on at great length in Cree to detail the technologies of her world. My niece and I stared at her

Tides, Towns and Trains

in wonder and in pride. At times white audiences formed around us. I found myself interpreting to them parts of my mother's impressive lecture.

Besides the fact that we rediscovered my mother as the great orator, educator and walking encyclopaedia of culture that she was, the significance of this episode is how poignantly it illustrates the gaps in experience and knowledge between academic perception and Native reality. What academics and other members of white society have filed away as "artefact" or "historic," my mother (and all our family members, for that matter) knew and used in everyday life. My mother, who did not ever have the opportunity to read English, experienced the museum display as an affirmation of her living culture. She would have been astonished and amused had she been able to read the descriptions, which dated the materials as prehistoric.

I was not amused. I have walked, feeling cold and lonely, in Canada's archives, libraries, cathedrals, martyr's shrines, museums and forts that venerate priests and settlers at the awful expense of Indian and Métis peoples.[9] I have cringed each time I come upon an historic site, a tourist shop, or Parks Canada's pale plaques. I have noted that at every important juncture and place in my life or in my family's life, our culture and perceptions have been either chronologically misplaced, fragmented, belittled, infantilized, denied or disagreed with by the vast majority of non-Native Canadians representing all walks of life. I should say, though, that particularly in history and anthropology, academic perceptions and language have changed dramatically since the mid-1970s. I believe that the development of Native studies as a discipline in a number of universities has influenced the changes. However, the positive and intellectually exciting changes that have taken place in some scholarly circles have not yet touched the public or the media. By and large, the public and the media have continued to indulge in outdated views and hackneyed stereotypes about Native peoples.

Stereotypes are created by those in power in order to maintain their position in society. Stereotypes about Indians abound in archival and contemporary materials, and have been repeated over a span of four centuries. We have all been shaped to view, and therefore to treat, "Indians" in a distorted way. In fact, stereotyping is so prevalent that I, as

---

9 The term *settler*, associated with Europeans, is often juxtaposed with the term nomadic, which is associated with Indians. In fact, Indians had settlements and were certainly rooted to their lands. Was it not nomadic Europeans who tried to unsettle aboriginal peoples from their lands?

a Native and as a woman, have often felt it was not safe to walk our streets, to ride in taxis or trains, to go to a hospital or to meet a police officer alone. I have not felt safe in my own community. I do not say these things lightly. There are hair-raising examples of how far racism and sexism has been carried. For example, the image of the sexually loose "squaw" renders all Native girls and women vulnerable to gross sexual, physical and/or verbal violence. Hollywood's portrayal of the good cowboy on guard against lurking savages renders all Native persons vulnerable to white fear and hatred.

Given that our violence-crazed cellulose culture feeds on the degradation of women and of Indians, it is conceivable that Betty Helen Osborne was savagely murdered because she, a "squaw," had dared to resist white male sexual attacks.[10] In the minds of the "good boys who did bad things,"[11] it is not the place of "squaws" to resist white power, especially power snakily connected to male ego.

Similarly, it is conceivable that J.J. Harper's death in Winnipeg was triggered by cowboy-conditioned reflexes.[12] A male Indian in the dark is perceived as dangerous and aggressive, especially if he dares to talk back or to tussle with the powers that be. The tradition of seeing Natives who resist as rebellious and out of their place goes far back in history. The arrogance of oppressors is, of course, universal.

We know that the oppressor can be conditioned to be callous and inhuman by the very dehumanizing stereotypes he creates. Over time the oppressed internalize these stereotypes. What may happen to Native boys and men who, along with being exposed to pornography, internalize the view that Native girls and women are "squaws"? What may happen to Native persons who grow up with comics, textbooks and movies that objectify Indians as wild and violent? The phenomenal growth of violence in Native communities in which females of all ages are the most obvious victims is an indication of what is happening.

And what may happen to a society that tolerates all this racism and layers of sexism? I believe such a society becomes inured to injustice, evil and dehumanization. The recent hero-ification of sexual "offenders" as

---

10 The story of Betty Helen Osborne of The Pas, Manitoba, can be found in Priest (1989).

11 The phrase is from George Ryga, *The Ecstasy of Rita Joe*, recorded by Ann Mortifee and Chief Dan George (Vancouver: Jabula Records, n.d.).

12 The Aboriginal Justice Inquiry was established 1988 in response to the 1987 trial of two men for the 1971 murder of Helen Betty Osborne and the 1988 shooting death of J.J. Harper following an encounter with a Winnipeg police officer." See the Aboriginal Justice Implementation Commission Final Report (Government of Manitoba 2001). Elaine Coburn – editor's note.

"victims" is a stunning example of how low our valuation of human dignity has plummeted. And in the case of Natives attacking Natives, it is a form of racism for Canadian lawyers, judges, doctors, nurses, therapists, child welfare workers, and other social-service workers, to be passive and silent while the oppressed oppress the oppressed.

I know there are many of us from all walks of life who care. I know, too, that those of us who have raised these unwieldy and painful issues risk censureship. Neither white nor Native Canadians seem ready to deal with racism or sexism.

Only recently have I begun to discuss violence, especially sexual violence, in my classes and in my public presentations. I have been stunned at the speed with which I have been labelled, lied about and psychologized. But again, I can no longer be silent. I come from a long line of silenced women who have been victimized, as if war had been declared on their persons. My *nokom*, my mother, my aunties and my sisters of many colours across this land have been victims of violence. All kinds of violence. Perpetrated by all kinds of boys (yes, boys) and men. From grandfathers, stepfathers, fathers, brothers, cousins, sons and nephews, and strangers. From peddlers to priests and police. From poor men on Main Street to rich men in business suits. There is also violence by and between women that must be addressed.

But where is the outrage? Who grieved and raged for that fostered 14-year-old Indian teenager who was raped 17 times at Lac Brochet, her place of origin?[13] I was rendered speechless when a prominent woman in government sat in my living room during elections and actually tried to justify the actions of those rapists. I believe she thought she was showing openness about "cultural differences." The members of original Native cultures considered rape shameful and unmanly. Besides, at what cost do we accept or excuse human behaviour in the name of "culture"?

I have seen enough. I have heard enough. I have read enough about the human condition (including some very naive and irresponsibly liberal criminology studies by white, middle-class men who dearly know not what they write). I know enough not to entertain naive or bleeding-heart notions about the nature of man, whether he is the oppressor or the oppressed: at the bottom is the woman or the girl.

---

13 This is a horrible story of an Indian child who was initially "scooped" from a hospital by social service agents when she was a baby. Then when she was 14, she was forced to come back to her place of origin, where she was violated. See, for example: *Winnipeg Free Press*, October 13, 1988; January 12, 1989; February 17, 1989; February 25, 1989.

Recently I was invited to address a federal Human Rights Commission "hearing" on the place of minority women in society. I raised the issue of violence and suggested that the commission work towards persuading the United Nations to list rape as a crime against humanity. A number of the commissioners were clearly uncomfortable. After all, had they not asked me to speak (softly, apparently) on racism and "cultural differences"? Were they surprised to hear that violence/oppression of women is not a "cultural difference" but a universal human illness? And why is it that a problem global in scope continues to be called "deviant" by so many sociologists?

Later it came to my attention that at a dinner hosted by the Human Rights Commission, one of the commissioners labelled me "radical." For two decades now I have been chasing down and debunking stereotypes. I have learned that for every image I have "defeathered," another one has popped up. Once I was "disadvantaged"; now I dare to be a "radical." Should not a human rights officer know all the ingenious ways whites psychologize Natives, and men censure women? This is the nature and function of stereotypes: as long as a power struggle exists between peoples or between the sexes there will be new convenient stereotypes for those in power.

Stereotyping, labelling, blaming, denying, censuring or psychologizing are all patterned responses in a colonial or patriarchal society (see chapter "Racism Runs Through Canadian Society"). Just as Native people are the Uncomfortable Mirrors for white Canadians, conscious women are the thorns in the flesh in a sexist society. And just as very few people want to see the underbelly of Canada, fewer still care to look into the caves of men.

It has not been easy to be framed an uncomfortable mirror. It is not easy to hear about "the Indian problem" everywhere one goes, or to see stereotypes almost everywhere one looks. It tests my patience to be baited, excessively challenged or branded. I have had to live with the echoes of my own words, even the echoes of my research and analyses, because no one could receive them. This disheartening and lonely place is exacerbated by the fact that there are not many Native writers or scholars with whom to share.

Educating for change is exciting but exacting. While preservers of tradition and the status quo can assume authority simply from their positions, seekers of change must always "prove themselves." And resistance can wear out a person. My bones know the places where my soul has been scorched.

So sometimes, just sometimes, I do wish I could stay with the fence-sitting side of Canada. I wish I could teach only statistics so that my students would stay sleepy, or simply tell jokes so that my audiences would keep on laughing. Sometimes I wish I could "tone down" the fire in my voice that aggravates those who want to hear a demure Indian princess. Could I write poetry without politics? And why do I not dress more traditionally? At times, I wish I could "live and let live," tolerate the moral majority, accept everybody and, as some have chided, "understand that we mean well, we are all human, be accepting, be bigger than us." I wish I could be satisfied with mediocrity and, of course, sincerity. I wish I could be happy just being nice, being with my nice friends talking about nice things, going to board meetings and church or believing in karma. If only I did not expect so much from others, or from myself. I wish I could believe in feasibility studies, inquiries, conference resolutions and royal assents. Maybe I could be a yuppie, or even an "ordinary" Canadian. I know my bones would like this very much. I wish I could dance for Wisakehcha with my eyes closed.[14] I wish I could say *keyam*.

But I was born asking, and with eyes that can never close. The real wishing I do entails the transformation of people and of society. But how shall we transform the oppressed and the oppressor? And upon whose shoulders, whose consciousness does the task of transformation fall? I cannot trust ideological formulas. And I cannot be satisfied with conformity. I have known the shadows. I have heard the voices crying in the night. I have seen the sleeping. I know

> the sorrow of the poor
> the sorrow of woman
> the sorrow of Native
> the sorrow of the earth
> the world that is with me
> in me
> of me.   (LaRocque 1993, 148)

I have been flung across the ages – and I have been the one to take the train, to ride the tides, to learn English, to cross the chasms. But who will know my world, my mother, my Cree?

---

14 This is in reference to a Cree legend where Wisakehcha, the central "trickster," invites ducks to a dance, but the ducks had to have their eyes closed so that Wisakehcha could pounce on them for his dinner!

1992

My Hometown Northern Canada
South Africa

How did they get so rich?
How did we get so poor?
My hometown Northern Canada South Africa
How did you get so rich?

We were not always poor
How did they get
our blueberry meadows
our spruce and willow groves
our sun clean streams
and blue sky lakes?
How did they get
Their mansions on the lake
Their cobbled circle drives
with marbled heads of lions on their iron gates

How did they get so rich?
How did we get so poor?

One sad spring
when my mother my Cree-cultured Ama
was dying
Or was it
the sad summer
when my father my tall gentle Bapa
was dying
I stood on the edge
of that blue sky lake
to say goodbye

My Hometown Northern Canada South Africa   65

to something
so definitive
no words in Cree
no words in Métis
no words in that colonial language
no words
could ever say

I looked at my hometown
no longer a child afraid
of stares and stone-throwing words
no longer a child
made ashamed
of smoked northern pike
bannock on blueberry sauce
sprinkled with Cree

I looked at my hometown
Gripping my small brown hands
on the hard posts of those
white iron gates
looking at the lions
with an even glare

How did they get so rich?
How did we get so poor?

How did our blueberry meadows
Turn to pasture for "Mr" Syke's cows?
How did our spruce and willow groves
turn to "Mr" Therien's General Store?
How did our aspen covered hills
Turn to levelled sandpiles
for gas pipelines
just behind my Nokum's backyard?
How did our moss-green trails
down to the beaver creek
turn to cutlines
for power lines?
How did the dancing poplar leaves
Fall before their golden time?
How did my Nokum's sons and daughters

and their sons and daughters
and their sons and daughters
Fall before their seasons?
How did my auntie Julia die?
When she was 19 she was found dead
under a pile of sawdust
long after it happened
She was last seen with a whiteman
sometime in World War II they said
There was no investigation
Not even 16 years later

Now did my Nokum lose her grandchildren
that she so carefully housed in her loghouse
made long by her widower sons?
Was it really about
a child stealing a chocolate bar from
Therien's Store?
Or was it about The Town
Stealing children to make us white
Taking Uncle Ezear's Lillian Linda Violet
Taking Uncle Alex's Lottie Robert
all they had left
after T.B. stole their mothers
in far away places of death

How did my uncles Alex and Ezear die?
Singing sad songs on the railroad tracks
on their way home from Town
2 a.m. in the morning
Was it really by the train as the RCMP said?

When did my mother and her sisters
Catherine, Agnes, Louisa and Mary
stop singing
those haunting songs in Cree
about lost loves and aching
to find their way home?
When did they lose the songs
those songs in their steps
Wasn't it when the Priests the Police
and all those Home and Town good boys doing bad things

My Hometown Northern Canada South Africa 67

came
No one talks about it
My Nokum and her daughters
Singing sad songs on the railroad tracks
on their way home from Town
2 a.m. in the morning

How did we put away Pehehsoo,
and Pahkak?
When did we stop laughing with Wesakehcha?
When did we cross ourselves
to pray to Joseph and the Virgin Mary?
How did we stop speaking Cree
How did we stop being free?

How did they get so rich?
How did we get so poor?

How did my Bapa and Ama's brothers
Alex, Ezear and Victor
and my aunties' husbands Stuart and Moise
lose their traplines?
Was it really for the Cold War planes
Or was it for one of those cold marbled lions?
And what war
takes my brothers' traplines today?
Some say to save the lions

My hometown Northern Canada South Africa
making marble out of lions
making headstones out of earth
turning the earth on
Nokum's sons and daughters
and their sons and daughters
and their sons and daughters
turning Nokum
into a bag lady
before she died in the Town ditch

How did they get all the stones?
Those stones in their fireplaces,
Those stones around their necks,

The boulders in the whites
of their eyes,
Those stony stares,
How did they get the marbled stones in their hearts?

I look at you
My hometown Northern Canada South Africa
I look at you
no longer a child afraid
of stony stares
and rockhard words
no longer a child
made ashamed
of my Cree
dipped in cranberry sauce
giggling with Wesakehcha
I look at the paper head-dresses
you got from Hollywood
for your Pow Wow Days
Trying to feel at home
in your postcard tourist ways
Giggling with Wesakehcha
I look at the turquoise
in your stones
I look at your lions
with an even glare
Even in my dreams I see

But still
I look
From the inside out
Gripping my still brown hands
on the hardposts
of White Iron Gates

My hometown coldstone Canada South Africa

1993

Violence in Aboriginal Communities

The issue of domestic violence in First Nations and Métis communities is one that demands urgent study and action. There is every indication that violence has escalated dramatically. For example, studies show that among Indians "the single most important group of health problems in terms of both mortality and morbidity is accidents and violence" (Young 1988, 54). The goal of this paper is not to comment on family violence generally, though it does require further comment. This paper will focus on family violence as it affects Aboriginal women, teenagers and children. And since much family violence involves sexual assault, special attention is given to sexual violence within the Aboriginal community.

While domestic or family violence clearly affects all members within a family, the most obvious victims are women and children. A 1989 study by the Ontario Native Women's Association reported that 8 out of 10 Aboriginal women were abused. While this study focussed on northern Ontario, it is statistically representative of other communities across the country. There is growing documentation that Aboriginal female adults, adolescents and children are experiencing abuse, battering and/ or sexual assault to a staggering degree. A 1987 report by the Child Protection Centre of Winnipeg stated that there is "an apparent epidemic of child sexual abuse on reserves". And just recently, it was reported by the press that on one reserve in Manitoba, 30 adults were charged with having sexually abused 50 persons, many of them children.

Since it is considerably more difficult to get precise statistics on Métis people, it is virtually impossible to say with any exactness the extent of sexual violence in Métis families or communities. However, as more victims are beginning to report, there is every indication that violence, including sexual violence, is just as problematic, just as extensive as on reserves. In November 1992, the Women of the Métis Nation of Alberta

70   The Emma LaRocque Reader

organized an historic conference near Edmonton dealing specifically
with sexual violence against Métis women. The interest shown by Métis
women from across Canada was overwhelming. The stories shared by
the 150 or so conference participants indicated that Métis women, no
less than Indian women from reserves, have been suffering enormously –
and silently – from violence, including rape and child sexual abuse.

In accordance with the request by the Royal Commission, this paper
will address the following: (1) women's perspectives on factors that
generate and perpetuate domestic violence and (2) strategies proposed
to reduce and eliminate violence. Barriers to implementing these strategies are implied within this discussion.

I understand that the Royal Commission wants policy recommenda-
tions more than an extensive analysis of violence. However, I believe
it is of value to take some time to think about the possible reasons for
violence against women. Not only is analysis an inherently indispensable tool in working toward proposed solutions, but it is also part of the
educational process we all need in order to address this horrific issue
with comprehension and compassion.

Naturally, this paper cannot and does not propose to look at all
possible reasons for family or sexual violence. There are a number of
works that provide useful but fairly standard views on sexual violence,
especially in regard to treatment and to 'offenders' (Martens, Daily,
and Hodgson 1988; Government of Manitoba 1991). I wish to provide
additional perspectives, some of which may disagree with commonly
held beliefs about the nature of sexual violence and the reaction to
'offenders'.

Colonization

Colonization refers to that process of encroachment and subsequent
subjugation of Aboriginal peoples since the arrival of Europeans. From
the Aboriginal perspective, it refers to loss of lands, resources, and self-
direction and to the severe disturbance of cultural ways and values.
Colonization has taken its toll on *all* Aboriginal peoples, but it has taken
perhaps its greatest toll on women. Prior to colonization, Aboriginal
women enjoyed comparative honour, equality and even political power
in a way European women did not at the same time in history. We can
trace the diminishing status of Aboriginal women with the progres-
sion of colonialism. Many, if not the majority, of Aboriginal cultures
were originally matriarchal or semi-matriarchal. European patriarchy
was initially imposed upon Aboriginal societies in Canada through the
fur trade, missionary Christianity and government policies. Because of

Violence in Aboriginal Communities

white intrusion, the matriarchal character of Aboriginal spiritual, economic, kinship, and political institutions was drastically altered.

Racism, Sexism, and the Problem of Internalization

Colonization and racism go hand in hand. Racism has provided justification for the subjugation of Aboriginal peoples. While all Aboriginal people are subjected to racism, women further suffer from sexism. Racism breeds hatred of Aboriginal peoples; sexism breeds hatred of women. For Aboriginal women, racism and sexism constitute a package experience. We cannot speak of sexual violence without at once addressing the effects of racism/sexism. Sexual violence is related to racism in that racism sets up or strengthens a situation where Aboriginal women are viewed and treated as sex objects. The objectification of women perpetuates sexual violence. Aboriginal women have been objectified not only as women but also as Indian women. The term used to indicate this double objectification was and is 'squaw'.

A complex of white North American cultural myths, as expressed in literature and popular culture, has perpetuated racist/sexist stereotypes about Aboriginal women. A direct relationship between racist/sexist stereotypes and violence can be seen, for example, in the dehumanizing portrayal of Aboriginal women as 'squaws', which renders all Aboriginal female persons vulnerable to physical, verbal and sexual violence.

One of the many consequences of racism is that, over time racial stereotypes and societal rejection may be internalized by the colonized group. The internalization process is one of the most problematic legacies of long-term colonization.

It is not well understood, but it is certainly indicated by various oppressed or minority groups in North America. Many Black, Chicano and Aboriginal writers have pointed to this problem. Understanding the complex workings of the internalization process may be the key to the beginnings of understanding the behaviour of the oppressed and the oppressive in our communities.

In his book *Prison of Grass* (1975), Howard Adams referred to the problem of "internalization". By this he meant that as a result of disintegrative processes inherent in colonization, Aboriginal peoples have subconsciously judged themselves against the standards of white society, often adopting what he called the White Ideal. Part of this process entails "internalizing" or believing – swallowing the standards, judgements, expectations and portrayals of the dominant white world. Many other Aboriginal writers have pointed to the causes and consequences of having struggled with externally imposed images about themselves and the policies that resulted from them. The result was/is often shame and rejection not only of the self but also of the similar other, i.e., other Aboriginal people.

A lot has changed within the Aboriginal community since Adams wrote *Prison of Grass* (1975). A lot more Aboriginal people are aware of the whys and wherefores of their position in Canadian society. As more Aboriginal people grow in political awareness, they are less prone to judge themselves or act by outside standards. However, the damage has been extensive, and the problem of internalization does still exist. It is still of value to study how Aboriginal internalization of racist/sexist stereotypes may be at work in the area of violence.

One of the central questions we need to address is this: we know there has been violence by white men against Aboriginal women, but what do we make of the violence by Aboriginal men against Aboriginal women and children?

Too often the standard answer or reason given is that Aboriginal "offenders" were themselves abused and/or victims of society. There is no question that this answer may be partly true for some of the abusers, especially the young. However, it is hardly a complete answer and certainly should not be treated as the only or final answer to this problem.

There are indications of violence against women in Aboriginal societies prior to European contact. Many early European observations as well as original Indian legends (e.g., Wehsehkehcha stories) point to the pre-existence of male violence against women. It should not be assumed that matriarchies necessarily prevented men from exhibiting oppressive behaviour toward women. There were individuals who acted against the best ideals of their cultures. Even today, all the emphasis on Mother Earth has not translated into full equality and safety of women.

There is little question, however, that European invasion exacerbated whatever the extent, nature or potential violence there was in original cultures. Neither is there much question that Aboriginal men have internalized white male devaluation of women. As one scholar observes:

> Deprived of their ancestral roles ... men began to move into areas that had previously been the province of women, adopting some of the white attitudes toward women and treating them as inferiors rather than equals.[1]

---

1 Dexter Fisher (1980, 13).

How might this internalization work with respect to violence generally and sexual violence specifically? Consider this: what happens to Aboriginal males who are exposed not only to pornography but also to the racist/sexist views of the "Indian" male as a violent "savage" and the Aboriginal female as a debased, sexually loose "squaw"?

Pornography in popular culture is affecting sexual attitudes and behaviour within Aboriginal communities. And [given] the lengthy and unrestricted mass media projection and objectification of 'Indians' as violence-crazed savages, the problem of internalization should come as no surprise.

But it is disturbing. Aboriginal internalization of racist/macho views of Aboriginal men and women has contributed to violence generally and to sexual abuse specifically.

Defence of Offenders Perpetuates Violence

It is difficult to say whether there is more sexual violence in Aboriginal communities than in white ones, for we know that sexual assault is also prevalent in white homes and neighbourhoods. But I don't think we should defend either community in this regard. Rather, we should expend our energies in showing categorical disapproval appropriate to the crime and seeking solutions to what is an intolerable situation.

I have been troubled by a number of things relevant to the discussion on sexual violence. It is distressing to observe apathy by both Aboriginal and non-Aboriginal populations concerning sexual violence. The Aboriginal leadership, in particular, must be called on to address this issue. Nor should the general public or governments walk away. The onus for change cannot rest solely on Aboriginal shoulders. White people in positions of power must share the burdens of finding answers, as they have been part of the problems.

I have also been concerned about the popularity of offering "cultural differences" as an explanation for sexual violence. When the horrifying story of the Lac Brochet teenager came out in the late 1980s, I was stunned by comments and attempted explanations around me. The numerous males who had attacked this 14-year-old girl (who had been repatriated against her will in the name of "culture" to [begin] with) were being defended with tortured and distorted notions of Aboriginal culture.

Erroneous cultural explanations have created enormous confusion in many people and on many issues. Besides the problem of typecasting Aboriginal cultures into a static list of "traits", 500 years of colonial history are being whitewashed into mere "cultural differences".

Social conditions arising from societal negligence and policies have been explained away as "cultural". Problems having to do with racism and sexism have been blamed on Aboriginal culture. When cultural justifications are used on behalf of the sexually violent, we are seeing a gross distortion of the notion of culture and of Aboriginal peoples. Men assault; cultures do not. Rape and violence against women were met with quick justice in original cultures. And if there is any culture that condones the oppression of women, it should be confronted to change. But sexual violence should never be associated with Aboriginal culture! It is an insult to healthy, functioning Aboriginal cultures to suggest so! Would one entertain using "racial differences" as an explanation for sexual assaults? Is it any less racist to resort to 'cultural' ones?

As long as offenders are defended in the name of culture, they will continue to avoid taking any personal responsibility for their actions. And this will only perpetuate the problem.

Equally troubling in the defence of offenders is popular advancement of the notion that men rape or assault because they were abused or are victims of society themselves. The implication is that as "victims", rapists and child molesters are not responsible for their actions and that therefore they should not be punished – or, if punished, "rehabilitation" and their "victimization" must take precedence over any consideration of the suffering or devastation they wreak on the real victims! Political oppression does not preclude the mandate to live with personal and moral responsibility within human communities. And if individuals are not capable of personal responsibility and moral choices (the things that make us human), then they are not fit for normal societal engagement and should be treated accordingly.

Obstacles Facing Real Victims

And what do victims of sexual assault face within Aboriginal and mainstream communities? The following is a brief but realistic scenario. Aboriginal victims face obstacles that come with all small communities. There is a lack of privacy. Fear of further humiliation through community gossip and fear of ostracism and intimidation from supporters of the perpetrator may all be at work. Often a Victim is confronted with disbelief, anger, and family denial or betrayal. Secrecy is expected and enforced. There is, in effect, censorship against those who would report sexual assault or even other forms of violence.

But if a victim does proceed with reporting, who will want to hear? And if she goes out of the community, she faces racism/sexism in the form of judgement, indifference or disbelief. Many non-Aboriginals

Violence in Aboriginal Communities 75

in positions of social service or power either have little knowledge of what circumstances confront the victim, or they do not take complainants seriously. The stereotype that Aboriginal women are sexually promiscuous is still quite prevalent. Also, in many communities women cannot trust policemen since some policemen, especially in previous generations, were also doing the attacking! This is not to mention that the entire process of reporting is itself a formidable challenge.

If the victim goes as far as the courts, a whole new set of problems emerges. It is well-known that even for white middle-class women, rape trials are torturous, with no guarantee of justice at the end of it all. If only 10 percent of white women report sexual assault, then considerably less than 10 percent of Aboriginal victims report. And of course, the conviction rate is dismal.

The other problem, a problem I believe perpetuates sexual violence, is the fact that the courts are wantonly lenient with regard to sentencing. As a rule, thieves and minor drug dealers receive way stiffer penalties than do child molesters, rapists or even rapist-murderers! This in itself is a chilling message regarding societal devaluation of human dignity. Many Aboriginal communities have expressed concern that courts are especially lenient with Aboriginal offenders who assault other Aboriginal people. The easy parole system, along with lenient sentencing, further sets up Aboriginal victims.

If the victim succeeds in sending her assailant to prison, she may expect quick retaliation. Sexual offenders may come out of prison within three weeks, perhaps six months. These men usually go straight back to their small settlements and proceed to wreak further violence and intimidation.

When all is said and done, what of the victim? Where is the help for her? Where is the concern for *her* rehabilitation?

The whole judicial process reflects privileged, white male definitions and experience. It also reflects tremendous naïvete – naïvete often found in white liberal social workers, criminologists and justices. These lenient sentences are consistent with the growing heroification of rapists and child molesters as 'victims'. Today there is persistent sympathy for sexual offenders with little, if any, corresponding concern for the real victims. It is a bizarre situation!

Questions About the Causes of Sexual Violence

Given the popularity of presenting rapists as victims, and given that such a notion has not in any way resolved the problem – and in fact may be perpetuating sexual violence – is it not time for new and hard questions here? While it is sociologically apparent that poverty and marginalization can play havoc in a community, it is difficult to accept without question that being a so-called victim causes one to be a victimizer. If that were true, millions of women would take to victimizing. Further, if poor social conditions necessarily breed "offenders", this raises more questions than it answers. Why, when the chips are down, do men turn on women and children? What are we saying here about the nature of man? What are we saying of Aboriginal men – that when conditions of oppression, poverty or abuse exist, they cannot think of anything else but to turn on innocent women and children? And this should then be met with sympathy? And what about the other statistics – what about all the poor men and abused men who do not turn to violence?

Sexual violence is global and universal. Men of all backgrounds, cultures, classes and economic status assault women. Indeed, history is replete with examples of rich, powerful and privileged men who abused women and children. This suggests that the origin of sexual violence is considerably more disturbing than we might like to admit. Maybe it is not as mysterious as we make it out to be.

Most adults who violate others do so from a place of awareness and choice. As one article on child sexual abuse, written by a group of concerned Aboriginal women, states: "Offenders are aware of what they are doing and they know it is wrong" (Aboriginal Women's Council of Saskatchewan 1989/90, 90). I believe sexual violence is best explained by sexism and misogyny, which are nurtured in our society. North American popular culture feeds off the objectification and degradation of women. Women are presented as sexual playthings who must conform to male needs. Stereotypes of female sexuality are concocted as a rationalization for violence. It is about male maintenance of power, but it is a conscious and deliberate form of power, not one that is necessarily caused by "abuse" or other traumas. Obviously power brings all sorts of advantages. It has been in the interests of men to keep women down. Society supports all this with its tolerance of violence against women. The criminal justice system reflects its bias through its laws and judgements.

Rape in any culture and by any standards is warfare against women. And the degree to which any community tolerates sexual violence is an indication of concurrence in this warfare against women.

The point is, we may never know for certain what exactly causes sexual violence. But whether we know or not, we should never use any "explanation" – be it psychological, personal or political – as absolution for the offender. We should never justify or tolerate sexual violence. The criminal justice system must do its duty and serve 'justice' not only because justice is essential to a victim's healing, but also because a message must be given that sexual violence is insupportable. Justice and concern for rehabilitation must not be seen as mutually exclusive.

The other point, and perhaps more to the point, is why all this concern with finding reasons or explanations for what causes men to be rapists and child molesters? Given that we may never know, should we not turn our attention to the real victims?

1994

Long Way from Home

I've walked these hallways
a long time now
hallways held up by
stale smoke
thoughts

I've walked these hallways
a long time now
hallways pallored by
ivory-coloured
thoughts

I've walked these hallways
for a long time now
hallways without windows
no way to feel the wind
no way to touch the earth
no way to see

I've walked these hallways
a long time now
every September closed doors
stand at attention
like soldiers
guarding fellow inmates
guarding footnotes
guarding biases

as I walk by

Long Way from Home

I do my footnotes so well
nobody knows where I come from
hallways without sun
the ologists can't see
they count mainstreet
bodies behind bars
they put Ama's moosebones
behind glass
they tell savage stories
in anthropology Cree

My fellow inmates
they paste us prehistoric
standing in front of us
as if I am not there too
as if I wouldn't know
what they think they show
showing what they don't know
they don't know what they show
they take my Cree for their PhD's
like Le Bank
as my Bapa would say
they take our money for their pay

When I first came to these hallways
I was young and dreaming
to make a difference
thinking truth

With footnotes pen paper
chalk blackboard
I tried to put faces
behind cigar store glazes
I tried to put names
behind the stats
of us brown people
us
us brown people
in jails
in offices
in graveyards
in livingrooms

but to them it was
just Native biases

I've walked these hallways
a long time now
hallways hallowed by
ivory-towered
bents

way too long now
hallways whitewashed with
committee meetings memos
promotion procedures
as fair as war
pitting brown against colonized brown
choosing pretend Indians

When I first came to these hallways
I was young and dreaming
to make a difference

but only time has passed
taking my Ama and Bapa
my Nhisis my Nokom
my blueberry hills

I've walked these hallways
a long time now
I wanna go home now
I'm tired of thinking for others
who don't wanna hear anyways

I wanna go home now
I want to see the evening stars
get together for a dance
the northern light way
like Ama's red river jig
I want to see the sun rise
hot orange pink
like Bapa's daybreak fire

no one could see the morning come
as my Bapa

Long Way from Home

no one could scurry in the stars
as my Ama

I wanna go home now
but where is home now?

I do my footnotes so well
nobody knows where I come from
my relatives think
I've made it
they don't know
how long I've walked these hallways
my feet hurt
at 43
I wanna play hookey
but I can't
I have credit cards to pay
footnotes to colonize
My relatives think
I've made it
they don't know
who all owns me
they won't lend me money
from their UIC's
my relatives laugh.

Oh I did my footnotes so well
nobody knows where I come from

I've walked these hallways
with them a long time now
and still they don't see
the earth gives eyes
injustice gives rage
now I'm standing here
prehistoric and all
pulling out their fenceposts of civilization
one by one
calling names in Cree
bringing down their mooneow hills
in English too
this is home now

1996

The Colonization of
a Native Woman Scholar

The history of Canada is a history of the colonization of Aboriginal peoples. Colonization is a pervasive structural and psychological relationship between the colonizer and the colonized and is ultimately reflected in the dominant institutions, policies, histories, and literatures of occupying powers. Yet, it is only recently that Canadian scholars from a variety of fields have begun to situate the Native/white relationship within this context of dominance-subjugation.[1] There is ample room in Canadian scholarship for macroscopic explorations of the dynamics of oppression. In other words, we must seek to understand what happens to a country that has existed under the forces of colonial history over such an extended period of time. We must seek to recognize the faces of both the colonizer and the colonized,[2] as they appear in society and in the academic community. We must become aware of the functions of power and racism, its effects on the Native population, and the significance of resistance.

---

1 There are fine works from various fields on the colonization of Canadian Native peoples. They include E. Palmer Patterson, *The Canadian Indian Since 1500* (1972); Mel Watkins, *Dene Nation, Colony Within* (1977); Thomas R. Berger, *Northern Frontier, Northern Homeland* (1977); Hugh and Karmel McCullum, *This Land Is Not for Sale* (1975); Anastasia M. Shkilnyk, *A Poison Stronger Than Love* (1985); Dara Culhane Speck, *An Error in Judgement* (1987); A.D. Fisher, "A Colonial Education System: Historical Changes and Schooling in Fort Chipewyan" (1981). Many more conventional studies have not placed the Native experience into any cohesive theoretical framework; instead, the emphasis has been on "the impact of" the white man, his tools, his religion, and his diseases, and so forth. Fur-trade volumes, in particular, are replete with "impact" notions and items.

2 I am suggesting, of course, that as Canadian peoples, both Native and non-Native, we may find ourselves, our respective experiences, mirrored in Albert Memmi's *The Colonizer and the Colonized* (1957).

The Colonization of a Native Woman Scholar

Colonization has taken its toll on all Native peoples, but perhaps it has taken its greatest toll on women. While all Natives experience racism, Native women suffer from sexism as well. Racism and sexism[3] found in the colonial process have served to dramatically undermine the place and value of women in Aboriginal cultures, leaving us vulnerable both within and outside of our communities. Not only have Native women been subjected to violence in both white and Native societies, but we have also been subjected to patriarchal policies that have dispossessed us of our inherited rights, lands, identities, and families. Native women continue to experience discrimination through the Indian Act, inadequate representation in Native and mainstream organizations, lack of official representation in self-government discussions, under-and/or unequal employment, and ghettoization of the educated Native woman, for example.[4] The tentacles of colonization are not only extant today, but may also be multiplying and encircling Native peoples in ever-tighter grips of landlessness and marginalization, hence, of anger, anomie, and violence, in which women are the more obvious victims.

The effects of colonization, then, have been far-reaching, and numerous issues remain to be examined, not the least of which is how colonization affects men and women differently.[5] As a long-standing scholar in Native studies, I especially wish to bring to this discussion some of my reflections about what confronts those of us who are not only Native and women but are also intellectuals and researchers caught within the confines of ideologically rooted, Western-based canons, standards, and notions of objectivity

---

3 Racism and sexism together result in powerful personal and structural expressions in any society, but they are clearly exacerbated under colonial conditions. However, it should be noted that sexism, in particular, did not derive solely from European culture or colonization. As alluded to throughout this paper, there are indications of pre-existing patriarchy and sexism within Aboriginal cultures.

4 For a more detailed discussion on patriarchy, see my article, "Racism/Sexism and Its Effects on Native Women" (LaRocque 1989). See also: Joyce Green, "Constitutionalising the Patriarchy: Aboriginal Women and Aboriginal Government" (1993); Gail Stacey-Moore, "In Our Own Voice: Aboriginal Women Demand Justice" (1993).

5 Further study is required on how colonization affects men and women differently. Diane Bell, a critical anthropologist, has pointed out that, while mainstream scholars have begun to "develop more and more sophisticated models of colonial relations, … they have, for the most part, paid scant attention to the different impact of colonial practises on men and women," which has led to creating "a niche for the consolidation of male power; … the most consistent outcome appears to be that while men assume the political spokesperson role, the women run the welfare structures" (1989, 6).

84 The Emma LaRocque Reader

and research.[6] We are in extraordinary circumstances: not only do we study and teach colonial history, but we also walk in its shadow on a daily basis ourselves. What do we do with our knowledge as well as with the practises of power in our lives, even in places of higher learning?

I find it impossible to study colonial history, literature, and popular cultural productions featuring Native peoples, particularly women, without addressing the social and ethical ramifications of such study. To study any kind of human violation is, *ipso facto*, to be engaged in ethical matters. And we must respond – as scholars, as men and women, Native and white alike. These destructive attitudes, unabashed biases, policies, and violence that we footnote cannot be mere intellectual or scholarly exercises. They do affect Native peoples, real human lives. I believe there is a direct relationship between racist/sexist stereotypes and violence against Native women and girls.[7] The dehumanizing portrayal of the "squaw" and the over-sexualization of Native females such as in Walt Disney's *Pocahontas* surely render all Native female persons vulnerable. Moreover, these stereotypes have had a profound impact on the self-images of Native men and women, respectively, and on their relationships with each other.[8]

In addition to the questions of the social purpose of our knowledge, we are confronted in scholarship with having to deal with Western-controlled education, language, cultural production, and history. For example, classically colonial archival and academic descriptions and data about Natives' tools, physical features, "rituals," or geography have been equated with objectivity,[9] while Native-based data has been subsumed under subjectivity. Native scholars, particularly

---

6 On the issue of non-Western intellectuals confronting Western hegemonic canonical assumptions in post-colonial writing, see: Barbara Harlow, *Resistance Literature* (1987); Ashcroft, Griffiths, and Tiffin, *The Empire Writes Back* (1989); and Peter Hitchcock, *The Dialogics of the Oppressed* (1992).

7 For a more detailed discussion on violence against Native women, see chapter, "Violence in Aboriginal Communities." See also the Aboriginal Justice Inquiry of Manitoba, Government of Manitoba (1991); and the report, *Breaking Free: A Proposal for Change to Aboriginal Family Violence,* Ontario Native Women's Association (1989).

8 Native men and women have experienced and reacted to colonial influences quite differently. This is particularly evident with respect to gender roles and stereotypes. For further comment on this, see my article: "Racism/Sexism and Its Effects on Native Women" (1990); and see chapter "Violence in Aboriginal Communities."

9 There is an air of detachment to these descriptions, and it is this imperial aloofness that has been mistaken for objectivity. For a brilliant analysis of "textual strategies of domination" through European descriptions of Native ethnography that give "an appearance of impartiality," see Parker Duchemin, "'A Parcel of Whelps': Alexander Mackenzie among the Indians" (1990).

those of us who are decolonized and/or feminist, have been accused of "speaking in our own voices," which is taken as "being biased" or doing something less than "substantive" or "pure" research. Not only are such accusations glaringly ironic given the degree of bias, inflammatory language, and barely concealed racism evident in much of early Canadian historical and literary writing on Native peoples,[10] but they are also adversarial. Native scholars' contribution to contemporary scholarship is significant, for, in a sense, we bring "the other half" of Canada into light. Not only do we offer new ways of seeing and saying things, but we also provide new directions and fresh methodologies to cross-cultural research; we broaden the empirical and theoretical bases of numerous disciplines, and we pose new questions to old and tired traditions. And often, we live with many anomalies. If we serve as "informants" to our non-Native colleagues, for example, about growing up within a land-based culture (e.g., on a trap line), our colleagues would include such information as part of their scholarly presentations; it would authenticate their research. Yet, if we use the very same information with a direct reference to our cultural backgrounds, it would be met, at best, with scepticism, and, at worst, with charges of parochialism because we would have spoken in "our own voices."

Clearly, the tension in the colonizer/colonized dichotomy has not escaped the academic community, and much work needs to be done to acknowledge the dialectics of colonization in Canadian scholarship. And I, as a Native woman, am compelled to pursue and express my scholarship quite differently from the way my non-Native counterparts do. I do this by maintaining orality in writing, taking an interdisciplinary approach to genre, calling for ethical re/considerations (not to be confused with "censorship") in the archiving of hate material, and openly (rather than covertly) referring to "voice" within academic studies. My use of "voice," for example, is a textual resistance technique. It should not be assumed, as it so often is, that using "voice" means "making a personal statement," which is then dichotomized from "academic studies." Native scholars and writers are demonstrating that "voice" can be, must be, used within academic studies not only as an expression of cultural integrity but also as an attempt to begin to balance the legacy of dehumanization and bias entrenched in Canadian studies about Native peoples. Colleagues, publishers, editors, and readers

---

10 For a discussion on inflammatory language that should qualify as hate literature, see chapter "On the Ethics of Publishing Historical Documents."

86 The Emma LaRocque Reader

of academic material need especially to acquaint themselves with the political nature of the English language, Western history, and other hegemonic canons of scholarly and editorial practises and criticism before they are in a position to appreciate what should most appropriately be understood as "Native resistance scholarship."[11] There is no basis for assuming that Native intellectuals are somehow more predisposed to bias than are white intellectuals.

The growing body of international literature on "post-colonial voices" as expressed by non-Western scholars and writers should serve as an instructive reminder that Native scholars and writers in Canada are part of this non-Western international community. This is not to say that the colonial experience is "in the past" for Canadian Native peoples; rather, it is to say that we are responding within the post-colonial intellectual context. As Ashcroft, Griffiths, and Tiffin (1989) put it, we are emerging "in our present form out of the experience of colonization" and asserting ourselves "by foregrounding the tension" with the colonial power by writing or talking back to "the empire."[12] We are challenging our non-Native colleagues to throw off "the weight of antiquity" with respect to hegemonic canonical assumptions, which continue "to dominate cultural production in much of the post-colonial world."[13] We are challenging them to re-evaluate their colonial frameworks of interpretation, their conclusions and portrayals, not to mention their tendencies of excluding from their footnotes scholars who are Native.[14]

There are many and varied layers of "colonial" practises in current Canadian scholarship. Of interest is the less than judicious treatment of the Native women writers who contributed to *Writing the Circle* (Perrault and Vance 1993) by some critics who, among other things, exclude the theories, criticisms, creativity, and experience of these

---

11 For a more detailed discussion, but in the context of literary treatment of Aboriginal themes and writers see chapter "Preface, or Here Are Our Voices – Who Will Hear?"; see chapter "When the Other Is Me: Native Writers Confronting Canadian Literature."

12 Ashcroft, Griffiths, and Tiffin, *The Empire Writes Back* (1989, 2).

13 Ibid., 7.

14 Non-Native scholars are increasingly using Native sources that they, however, reformulate or discount as ethnographic or personal accounts; there has been a persistent tendency on the part of white intellectuals to disregard Native scholars and other intellectuals, apparently assuming that they cannot be "of the people," or cannot be "objective." Either way, Native-based scholarship is put in a no-win situation.

women.[15] A number of critical responses have based their theories about Native women writers on such small, repetitive, and highly selective samples[16] that it does raise troubling issues of exclusion especially to those of us (both male and female) who are at once scholars, critics, and/or creative writers. We do present complexities in that we are crossing cultures, disciplines, and genres, and we obviously do not fit into conventional categories or ideological formulas. But we have been writing and footnoting at least as early as the 1970s, and our combined backgrounds of scholarship and marginalization as well as critical and/or creative works do model what is at the very heart of post-colonial discourse. It remains that as scholars we are all challenged to cross borders and to seek greater understanding. Western-based assumptions (including feminist, deconstructionist, and/or "post-colonial" discourse) can no longer claim exclusive rights to the ways and means of academic methodology and insight.

The challenge is, finally, to ourselves as Native women caught within the burdens and contradictions of colonial history. We are being asked to confront some of our own traditions at a time when there seems to be a great need for a recall of traditions to help us retain our identities as Aboriginal people. But there is no choice – as women we must be circumspect in our recall of tradition. We must ask ourselves whether and to what extent tradition is liberating to us as women. We must ask

---

15 See, for example, Hartmut Lutz, "Confronting Cultural Imperialism: First Nations People Are Combating Continued Cultural Theft" (1995). Lutz's article is wide-ranging but, in the context of discussing "Stolen Stories" (141–2), he lists *Writing the Circle* (Perrault and Vance 1993) as one of the works criticized (led by two Native women) for "cultural appropriation"; he then goes on to claim that "most Native writers support" the debate without making clear whether, by *debate*, he means the broad topic of cultural appropriation or the small controversy surrounding *Writing the Circle*. Lutz bases his conclusion on an extremely small representation, quite mysteriously (and uncharacteristically, as he usually treats Native literatures and writes with depth and scope) overlooking the theoretical ramifications of the fifty or so Native women writers involved in the production of *Writing the Circle*. For a similarly perplexing treatment of *Writing the Circle*, see also Julia Emberley, *Thresholds of Difference: Feminist Critique, Native Women's Writings, Postcolonial Theory* (1993).

16 Attention has been poured repeatedly and almost exclusively on three or four Native women writers in most "Native issues" publication specials or literary conferences over the last five years. See, for example, articles by Agnes Grant, Noel Elizabeth Currie, Margery Fee, and Barbara Godard in W.H. New, eds., *Native Writers and Canadian Literature* (1990). I should emphasize that my comment is not intended to focus on the Native writers upon whom attention is lavished but on the literary and academic critics who persistently neglect to study the other several dozen or so Native writers in Canada.

ourselves wherein lies (lie) our source(s) of empowerment. We know enough about human history that we cannot assume that all Aboriginal traditions universally respected and honoured women. (And is "respect" and "honour" all that we can ask for?) It should not be assumed, even in those original societies that were structured along matriarchal lines, that matriarchies necessarily prevented men from oppressing women. There are indications of male violence and sexism in some Aboriginal societies prior to European contact[17] and certainly after contact. But, at the same time, culture is not immutable, and tradition cannot be expected to be always of value or relevant in our times. As Native women, we are faced with very difficult and painful choices, but, nonetheless, we are challenged to change, create, and embrace "traditions" consistent with contemporary and international human rights standards.

Sadly, there are insidious notions within our own communities that we as Native women should be "unobtrusive, soft-spoken and quiet," and that we should not assume elected leadership, which is taken to mean "acting like men." The "traditional Indian woman" is still often expected to act and dress like an ornamental Pocahontas/"Indian Princess." But who should our models be? How should we maintain the traditions we value without adhering to stereotype or compromising our full humanity? If one must look to the past for models and heroes, we might do well to take a second look at Pocahontas. The irony is that the real Pocahontas was neither unobtrusive nor quiet. Quite the contrary: she was in fact revolutionary – for the wrong cause, but revolutionary nonetheless!

If we wish to act on history rather than be acted on, we can ill afford to be silent or stay content in the shadows of our male contemporaries. Speaking directly to the exclusion of women's experience and the analysis of this exclusion, Joyce Green (1993), a Native doctoral student in political science at the University of Alberta, writes: "So much of women's experience has been classified as nondata. So much of women's analysis as women has been ignored by the academy and by the activists. The consequence is male-gendered theoretical and epistemological development that is presented as authentic reflection of the human condition.... But knowledge is dynamic, and there is nothing preventing the incorporation of new female and Aboriginal ways of knowing."

History demands of us to assume our dignity, our equality, and our humanity. We must not move towards the future with anything less. Nor can we pursue scholarship in any other way.

---

17 Many early European observations as well as original Indian legends (e.g., Cree Wehsehkehcha stories I grew up with) point to pre-contact existence of male violence and sexism against women.

2001

Native Identity and the Métis: Otehpayimsuak Peoples

Introduction: Halfbreed and Métis Peoples

There have been a number of odd definitions of "Métis." Several years ago I read in a college report that the Métis are neither Indian nor Inuit. There was no further explanation. Even the Royal Commission on Aboriginal Peoples (RCAP) begins its chapter on the Métis by defining them more in terms of who they are not instead of who they are: "Métis are distinct Aboriginal peoples, neither First Nations or Inuit" (1996, 199). They have also been defined as "half white, half Indian" persons, or "halfbreeds." More often, people who have some combination of both White and Indian ancestry are lumped together into the category "Métis." Others make a distinction between those Métis whose origin can be traced back to the Red River and those "Métis" who are of mixed Indian and non-Indian ancestry with no direct links to the Red River Métis. Métis have also been described as people "between two worlds" (Harrison 1985)[1] who lack a core culture with distinct cultural markers

---

1 In part reflecting her sources, many of whom seem equally confused, Julia D. Harrison (1985) in *Métis: People Between Two Worlds*, seems unable to make sense of those Métis who "have a clear sense of their own identity as they individually define it," yet "see themselves as a distinctive people" (15). Métis identity is based on much more than individual definitions, or individuals caught between two worlds. It is true that the Métis have suffered marginality, but as repeatedly established, the marginality is in large part due to the persistent refusal by society and governments to accept the Métis as a cohesive indigenous-based distinctive ethnic group.

90   The Emma LaRocque Reader

(Sawchuk 1978).[2] But all these descriptions are either misleading or inadequate as Métis and Halfbreed histories and identities cannot be so easily generalized or fused together. It is only recently that scholars and perhaps politicians have begun to recognize that Métis peoples are an Aboriginally-based ethnic group who are more than the sum of White and Indian mix.

There is much misunderstanding and misperception about Aboriginal peoples generally, but there is even a much greater and more widespread confusion about Métis people. Stereotypes, politics and government policies have contributed much to the confusion. Misrepresentation in colonialist narratives and subsequent cultural popular productions have almost totally negated Métis presence in North America, both in terms of Métis ethnicity and of Métis significance in historical and cultural roles. Although various archival sources throughout the 1700s and 1800s commented on the growing numbers of Métis communities scattered along trade routes in the Old Northwest (Peterson and Brown 1985), as a rule, Métis peoples were treated not as ethnic collectivities but as unpredictable "halfbreed" individuals without a community who could either be romanticized or demonized, depending on the needs of fictionalists and historians (see chapter "The Métis in English Canadian Literature"). And even though the Red River Métis were acknowledged as a "population," they and their leader Riel were dismissed as confused, volatile half savages who embodied presumed conflicting forces of "civilization" and "savagery" (Stanley 1936; Morton 1950).[3]

Such Eurocentric interpretations of history were popular until about the 1970s when some scholars began to review Native/White relations in Canada. Since about the 1980s and in response to the commemoration of Riel's political death in 1885, there has been a growing recognition

---

2 Sawchuk argued that the Manitoba Métis were less a "culture bearing" unit with distinct cultural markers than a reformulated politically-determined group (1978, 10). In response to this limited vision of Métis ethnicity I wrote a playful review "Conversations on Métis Identity," *Prairie Fire* 7, no. 1 (Spring 1986): 19–24. Certainly, political consciousness has played an important role in strengthening contemporary Métis identity, and the ebb and flow of cultural expression does change from generation to generation, but just as certainly, Métis peoples have always had strong cultural identities. Sawchuk was confused between peoples of Métis Nation backgrounds and those who appropriated Métis identity. Sawchuk has since broadened his understanding of the Métis in subsequent works.
3 Echoing G.F. Stanley's thesis (1936), W.L. Morton declared: "This admixture of civilized life and barbaric ... indeed occurred in the very persons of the half-breed population of Red River and the West" (1950, 2).

Native Identity and the Métis

that the western Métis, particularly those of Red River ancestry, are a culturally distinct ethnic group. Today, this group refers to themselves as Métis Nation peoples. However, there are many different Métis communities across Canada, and not all of them originate in Red River. The Royal Commission on Aboriginal Peoples (RCAP) makes a distinction between the "Métis Nation" (of Red River origins) and the "other Métis" such as eastern and Labradorian Métis. It is not clear whether RCAP recognizes that in the prairie provinces and the northern territories, there were also "other Métis" ethnic groups who developed independently of Red River. It is not surprising that, given the differences among Métis peoples, some Métis groups object to the universal application of the term "Métis." In 1984 the Métis National Council proposed using upper case M to refer to those Métis "originally of mixed ancestry who evolved into a distinct indigenous people," specifically those in western Canada who were dispossessed by Canadian governments in the late 1870s on, and small m "Métis" for all the other persons of mixed ancestry (Peterson and Brown 1985, 6). Peoples of Métis Nation origins argue that the term "Métis" belongs to them and its generalized application serves to obscure their distinct identity.

There has especially been much confusion in the lumping together of any persons or peoples with any "Indian" in them as "Métis," no matter their generational, historical or cultural differences. Perhaps the term "Halfbreed" has added to the confusion. It was often used as a self-designation by most Métis groups throughout the 1800s, whether they were of Anglosaxon-Indian or of French/Cree ancestry, or whether they were from James Bay, Red River, Batoche or Lac La Biche areas. Some Métis still prefer to identify themselves as "Halfbreed." Prior to the *Canadian Constitution* of 1982, the federal government used the hyphenated "Half-Breed" especially in the context of the scrip and land grant programmes in western Canada.[4] There are of course, first generation peoples who are "half white and half Indian" or are "part Indian" in their family history, but it is not the case that all such peoples are necessarily or automatically Métis, ethnically speaking. The fact is, there may be no historical or cultural connection between those persons who

---

4 For example, in the aftermath of the Métis Resistance movements, the federal government set up *scrip* for Half-Breed Heads of Families, and after 1885, the Half-Breed Land Grants Commission. In 1935 the province of Alberta set up the Half-Breed Commission, later known as the Ewing Commission. For a good overview of official attitudes reflected in these various programmes, see Sawchuk and Sawchuk et al. (1981), *Métis Land Rights in Alberta: A Political History*.

have a "mixed" ancestry consisting of Indian and non-Indian, and those peoples of a distinctly Métis ethnicity whose roots go back to the Fur Trade alliances between European and Indian traders, but over time married within their own group from which grew a distinctly Métis peoplehood or ethnicity. Such peoples and communities developed throughout North America and Canada. They are not "half white, half Indian" or people in-between cultures, they are a distinct ethnic group with undisputed Aboriginal connections and identity (RCAP 1996).

The Royal Commission on Aboriginal Peoples (1996) attempts to clarify the situation by focussing on culture as an objective criteria by which the Métis can be identified:

> It is primarily culture that sets the Métis apart from other Aboriginal peoples. Many Canadians have mixed Aboriginal/non-Aboriginal ancestry, but that does not make them Métis or even Aboriginal. Some of them identify themselves as First Nations persons or Inuit, some as Métis and some as non-Aboriginal. What distinguishes Métis people from everyone else is that they associate themselves with a culture that is distinctly Métis. (202)

While this may be helpful in considerable ways, for example, in the recognition that Métis have a distinct culture, it certainly does not answer everything. The phrase "associate themselves" can be problematic as anyone can "associate themselves with a culture" that is Métis. Further, ethnic identity is more than about "association," especially when such an association is purely self-declared rather than historically and culturally rooted. Anthropologists and sociologists generally make distinctions between peoples based on objective cultural markers. In addition to political consciousness which is an important aspect of contemporary identity, Métis Nation peoples do have such cultural markers which form a foundation to their identity.

Métis Ethnicity

In an attempt to clarify the matter of the Métis as a distinct Aboriginal culture in Canada, I will here briefly trace the development of Métis ethnicity and will refer to my family and community history. The emergence of Halfbreed and later Métis peoples is directly related to the commercial partnerships between European men and the Original societies. Relationships between European men and Indian women facilitated trade through kinship between the two worlds. In areas of languages, geography, foods, clothing, medicines, transportation and other technologies, not to mention cross-cultural diplomacy, the significance of Indian women in these circumstances and relationships cannot be overemphasized as they provided companionship, knowledge and skills to the European men (Van Kirk 1980). They also inculcated their Halfbreed children with Aboriginal values and lifeskills.

From these early relationships grew families who in time became Halfbreed peoples, some segments of which eventually became Red River Métis peoples whose descendants of western Canada now identify themselves as The Métis Nation. In order to best understand this development, it may be useful to look at the various components of identity such as biology, culture and endogamy (marriage within own's own group), the combination of which can create a new ethnic group. Naturally, all human beings begin by biological processes: Halfbreed peoples are the result of two different "racial" groups. Generally speaking, by the 1600s, there were Halfbreed individuals everywhere there was significant contact between Indians and Europeans. All humans, no matter their racial ancestry, are born into human cultural groups. Initially, Halfbreed children were usually raised by their mother's cultural group, that is, by Aboriginal cultures. Over time, as the population of Halfbreed persons grew, Halfbreed individuals began to marry other Halfbreed persons. The practise of endogamy is a very common tendency among humans. As more and more Halfbreed peoples practised endogamy, it became possible to develop communities of people who really were no longer "half white, half Indian," but an entirely new ethnic group. Such peoples were/are of Métis-Métis ancestry.[5] As this new unified population grew, they began to develop a culture which we may call Métis. Such a culture was at once unique and yet one that naturally blended both Indian and European cultures.

By the mid-1700s, a number of White travellers began to notice and comment on this group of Métis populations and communities who were quite distinct from both Indians and Europeans. Such Métis communities were acknowledged throughout the Great Lakes and the Ohio Valley. These peoples were identifiable in terms of family connections, occupational identification, dress, speech (usually tri-lingual, and

---

5 For example, both of my parents were Métis and all four of my grandparents were Métis, and three of my great grandparents were Métis. My family is not at all atypical in western Canada. It would be ludicrous to describe such a family or community of people as "half white, half Indian."

94 The Emma LaRocque Reader

eventually Michif),[6] recreation and geographic location (Peterson and Brown 1985). Many towns and cities throughout North America got their beginnings as early Métis settlements or trading towns.

Some scholars (Peterson and Brown 1985) theorize that social and economic networks linked the Old Northwest (Great Lakes/Ohio Valley) with the Far Northwest (Red River/Rupertsland). They believe that the cultural and national development of the Red River Métis was related to the early sense of cultural distinctiveness of the Old Northwest Métis.

"Métis" is a French word that simply means "a person of mixed ancestry." It is not clear when Halfbreed peoples were first called "Métis," and more importantly, when they first called themselves "Métis." We do know that French/Indian Halfbreeds in Red River called themselves "Métis" in the early 1800s, but it is not a term that was widely used by anyone until about the 1970s when contemporary Métis organizations were established. We also know that other Halfbreed peoples preferred to call themselves "Halfbreed," especially in James Bay and in areas now known as Saskatchewan, Alberta and the Northwest Territories. We also know that Anglosaxon/Indian Halfbreed peoples referred to themselves as Halfbreed in Red River.

The complexity of Métis origins and history has been obscured because much of the focus has gone to the Red River Métis. The French-connected Métis of southern Manitoba gained attention partly because of the fact that the Red River community, unlike many other Halfbreed-concentrated communities in North America, developed not only cultural distinctiveness but a strong sense of nationalism. The Red River Métis were culturally distinct, geographically concentrated and politically and militarily organized. Throughout the 1800s the Métis did not hesitate to protect their interests by a show of force, whether against the Sioux or against the Hudson's Bay Company. In 1869, in the face of imposing Confederation, they were prepared to defend their culture and their homelands, a fact that caught John A. McDonald with his eastern prejudices of "half castes" off-guard. Unfortunately for the Métis

---

6 RCAP describes Michif as a "unique language that blends components of French and Aboriginal language." For an overview of issues surrounding the development of Michif see "What is Michif? Language in the Métis tradition" by John C. Crawford (1985) in Peterson and Brown. The use and extent of Michif varies among Métis of Red River origins. In my family we put French prefixes and suffixes to many of our Cree words but I did not learn of "Michif" until I came to Winnipeg where some Métis have a conversational knowledge of Michif. I have noted differences in Michif depending whether the speaker is French or Cree in linguistic orientation.

people, and in no small measure due to the prejudices of the times, their Provisional Government, under the leadership of Riel, fell.

I read these events in Red River as a people's resistance to colonial incursion and prefer to call it the First Métis Resistance, but of course, it was Riel who caught the imagination of scholars and artists. So much so that it was long assumed by historians that when Riel died the people died with him. But in fact, the Métis as a cultural group never died and they have certainly refused to disappear. They did, however, suffer great losses and dispersal. About 83% of the Red River Métis lost their lands due to various administrative and legal manoeuvres of both the federal and Manitoba governments throughout the 1870s. Dispirited and systematically dispossessed, a great many of these Métis moved out of their homelands, a movement which has been characterized as an "involuntary exodus" (Sprague 1980). The majority moved west and northwest, creating new communities all along the way and/or joining other existing Halfbreed communities of the Northwest. The Second Métis Resistance better known by non-Native Canadians as the 1885 Northwest Rebellion produced much the same results for the Métis as the Red River Resistance: marginalization and landlessness. They had neither treaty rights nor private property. And after 1885 the Métis became, and perhaps continue to be, Canada's "forgotten people" (Sealey and Lussier 1975). Their expertise, skills and ways of life (largely land-based: hunting, trading, fishing, some farming) which had sustained the commercial flow between east and west, north and south, Indian and white, became irrelevant in a new Canada bent on white settlement, agriculture and urban and industrial "development."

Legislative Discrimination and Métis Identity

The Canadian government has not been kind to the Métis. Its history of dismissing and dispossessing Métis peoples has greatly contributed to the confusion about the Métis. Not only has the Canadian government consistently refused to recognize the Métis as a distinct ethnic group, it has consistently divorced the Métis from their Indian or Aboriginal roots. Generally, Aboriginal peoples refers to those peoples whose ancestors and whose cultural, social and racial attributes can be identified as Aboriginal. Until recently, most Aboriginal peoples of Canada have been known as "Indians," a term inherited from Columbus and later defined by colonial legislation. In Canada, the first statutory definition of who was an Indian was enacted in 1850 and with the establishment of the *Indian Act* (1876), the term "Indian" became a legal definition. The problem with the *Indian Act* is that it was/is not all inclusive. The *Indian Act* has created Aboriginal sub-groups and identities with unequal rights. Not only did it exclude the Inuit[7] and the Métis from being considered "Indian," it created a legal loophole known as Enfranchisement by which Status Indians would lose their Status. Enfranchisement created a new group: the Non-Status Indians.

Enfranchisement was a legal process by which Status Indians lost or gave up both the 'benefits and burdens' of the *Indian Act*. "Benefits," or "rights" as is interpreted by Indians, include such things as reserved lands, health care and schooling within specified terms. "Burdens" means that the *Indian Act* has had total control of Indian peoples in areas of identity, religious practices, education, fiscal development and expropriation of lands. It is only since the 1970s that Status and Treaty Indians have begun to pry apart this control. Many Indian people gave up their Status as a way of getting away from this totalitarianism as well as accessing what mainstream Canadians assumed to be basic rights such as the federal vote, public schools, joining the army or simply being able to go into Liquor Commission premises. In the 1900–1950s era, many Indian agents coaxed Indians to give up their status; often, the Indian people did not understand the full implications of doing so, for example, enfranchised Indians had to leave their reserves as well as other interests in reserve communities. There was also involuntary enfranchisement. For example, under Section 12(1) (b) of the *Indian Act* Indian women (and their children) lost their status if they married any man who was not legally a Status Indian. Indian women also automatically lost their status if their Status husbands enfranchised voluntarily or not. Between 1876 and 1985 approximately 25,000 Indians directly lost their status, not counting the descendants who also automatically became Non-Status (Frideres 1998). Enfranchised Indians became classified as Non-Status Indians.

Non-Status is not to be confused with either Non-Treaty Status Indians or the Métis. Non-Status is a legal not a racial designation, however, there is now a complex connection between Non-Status and various Métis/Métis communities. When Indians lost their Status, most of them had to move out of their reserves and since they were not welcomed by Canadian society, many moved into Métis communities, especially to those Métis communities located close to reserves. Also, many Indians and Métis were related to each other so it was not surprising that many Non-Status Indian people joined the Métis. Over time in some

---

7 In *re Eskimo 1939*, the Supreme Court of Canada held that the Inuit were "Indian" within the meaning of section 91(24) of the BNA Act. The Métis have not been so considered, an issue taken up by RCAP.

Native Identity and the Métis

communities it has become virtually impossible to make a distinction between Non-Status Indians and Métis as some Métis may also be legally Non-Status, and some Non-Status may be racially and culturally Métis.

Nor has Bill C-31 clarified the identity situation. Bill C-31 amended the *Indian Act* with respect to Indian status and band membership and became effective April 17, 1985. Although Bill C-31 ended sexual discrimination and provided a mechanism for Non-Status to re-apply for Status, it clouded the issue of membership with complex and confusing eligibility rules. Many say Bill C-31 has become as contentious, unfair and divisive as the old 12(1) (b) of the *Indian Act*. In any event, Bill C-31 has had quite an impact on both Indian and Métis populations. By 1996, 99,710 Non-status peoples, many of whom had considered themselves Métis, had been reinstated as Status (Frideres 1998). This of course means that the Métis population has been substantially reduced.

Métis as Distinct Aboriginal Cultures

The Canadian government has also failed to protect or advance the Métis as a distinct Aboriginal culture with legitimate land rights. Section 12 of the *Indian Act* excluded any person who "has received or has been allotted Half-breed lands or money scrip" which generally referred to those Métis in the Prairie Provinces who "chose" scrip under the Half-breed Scrip Commission terms as an alternative to treaties. "Scrip" was a voucher which could have either money or land value and was given to "eligible" Métis individuals on a raffle-like basis. As noted above, the Métis suffered massive land loss from the Red River area in the 1870s, and again in the Northwest areas in the 1880s largely through legalese, and the unsubtle maladministration of the scrip system (Sawchuk and Sawchuk 1981; Sprague 1988; Chartrand 1991; RCAP 1996).

Some continue to believe that the Canadian government acted properly and whatever losses the Métis suffered were due to their primitive passions, poor leadership and fear of "progress." Frankly, I find such accusations incredulous in the face of overwhelming documentation that the Canadian governments aggressively facilitated White settlement of western Canada.[8] The vast majority of the Red River and

---

8 Earlier scholars and more recently Flanagan (1983), have blamed the Métis for losing their lands, and have justified Government actions with the Eurocentric myth that the Indian-related Métis feared and resisted "progress" by "rebelling" and then retreating to "the chase." White expansionism is here associated with Manifest Destiny, that is, that as a "civilization" Eurocanadians had some inherent moral and racial right to dispossess Aboriginal peoples whom they predetermined as "primitive" or "savage."

98 The Emma LaRocque Reader

Northwest Métis who lost their homelands (or lots as in Red River) were land-based Cree (and/or Michif) speaking hunters and traders who found John A. McDonald's schemes, bureaucracy and legalese as culturally foreign as Plains Cree leader Big Bear found treaties and reserves to be. It is important not to confuse these Cree-Métis with the French-speaking, eastern educated, urbanized Riel. In an effort to secure homelands for the Métis, Riel did lose his life, but he was in many respects an anomaly, both in cultural orientation and education.

But despite the losses, the dispersals, and the prejudices experienced by the Métis, they were and remain survivors. They continued to live off the land by hunting, trapping, fishing, gardening or picking berries and roots wherever possible. They supplemented their land-based resourcefulness with wage labour wherever they could: working the sugar beet fields, cutting and selling wood, picking rocks, stooking hay, picking and selling blueberries and seneca roots, sewing and so forth. Many Métis, especially during the Depression, became gypsy-like labourers, moving from place to place on horse-drawn wagons, looking for work. The women and children would frequently stay in one place, usually small Métis hamlets, while the men mobilized in search of work. Throughout Canada's history, Métis have been the labouring backbone of this country, serving first as portaging and fur packing *coureur de bois*, defining the buffalo industry with their organization and technologies, then on to building railroad lines and roads, clearing fields for farmers or fighting fire for the forestry. Today countless Métis continue to form part of the modern labouring class that sustains this country.

After the dispersals, most Métis were forced to become "Road Allowance people" (Campbell 1973, 8[9]). Through assorted federal and provincial legislations which facilitated immigration, agriculture and industrialization with its Westernized concepts of land improvements, Métis were legally rendered "squatters" on the very homesteads and homelands they had possessed (both in the sense of Aboriginal use and occupancy or through *scrip*). As "squatters" such Métis were forced onto unsurveyed Crown lands or "road allowance" strips of land. In these places scattered throughout north-central and northern areas of the prairie provinces, they developed all-Métis hamlets and retained much of their culture. Left largely to themselves, they were able to

---

9 This appears to be a reference to Campbell's 1973 book, *Halfbreed*. Later, in 1995, Campbell authored *Stories of the Road Allowance People* – Elaine Coburn, editor's note.

Native Identity and the Métis

retain their Cree and/or Michif language, their freedom and their love of land as well as their worldviews. They were, however, extremely poor and often confronted with deadly epidemics such as tuberculosis or influenza. They were also extremely vulnerable to repeated neocolonial incursions. From the late 1880s to about the 1970s, such Métis remained marginalized from Canadian cultural and economic life. For example, in Alberta, formal education was generally inaccessible for the northern Métis until the mid-1950s when they began to trickle into public schools. Because Métis were/are not "Indian" under the terms of the *Indian Act*, most Métis could not attend residential schools. But even if they could, it is doubtful that Métis parents would have allowed their children to go to these schools for many Métis of my parents' generation viewed schools, residential or public, as a threat to their cultural integrity.

Most Métis in the western provinces represent the blending of the Red River and locally developed Northwest Métis, and our great grandfathers and mothers ended up on road allowance strips of lands. For generations now, very little has changed for such Métis in regards to land ownership. Many Métis do not own the lands they live on and use for traditional pursuits. Alberta is the only province in Canada that did actually set aside lands for 12 Métis settlements (only 8 are in existence; 4 were rescinded at various times) in 1938 through the *Métis Betterment Act*. Pressured by Métis leaders, the Alberta Government established the Ewing Commission in 1934 to study social conditions facing the Métis. Although the Métis Settlements began essentially as patronizing welfare schemes to assist the destitute Métis, they did at the time provide a landbase for several thousand Métis, and since the late 1980s the people have gained some control in terms of governance, lands and resources. Today there are about 5,500 Métis (Dickason 1992, 364) in the settlements or "colonies" as they were called.

The Royal Commission on Aboriginal Peoples takes these settlements as possible models for Métis self-government. But the majority of Métis did not get into these settlements because either they did not know about them or they were afraid. My father, who was born before the Province of Alberta, explained to me that many northern Métis were afraid that these Settlements were reserves, and that the people would become politically and geographically confined like their Status Indian friends and kin. Métis such as my parents and grandparents whose ancestors were free traders, were proud and protective of their freedom and independence. In fact, in Cree they were known as *Otehpayimsuak*, the independent and self-reliant ones. Geographical and agricultural restrictions conflicted with their hunting, trapping or fishing. Reserves

100   The Emma LaRocque Reader

and residential schools were anethema[10] to *Sagaweenuak*, or bush people, as we also called ourselves. Not surprisingly, we were among the numerous Métis communities throughout central and northern Alberta who did not get into these settlements. My community of people owned no land, and to this day, we own no land. We were able only to rent acreages or traplines.

My father used to say that we are nothing without land. He represented a generation of people who associated their identities inextricably with the land. Our linguistic, epistemological and economic way of life was nurtured by the ecology, seasons and spirit of the land. To use more familiar phraseology, I come from a Métis peoples whose primary culture throughout much of the 1900s was traditionally land-based, that is, Cree-speaking (with some forms of Michif) hunters, trappers, fishermen and women, berry and root pickers as well as gardeners. In summers, men turned to wage labour for railroads, forestry and farmers. Because we did not have geographically contained or legally protected land bases, my parents' generation had to practise their hunting and trapping in creative ways. In practical terms this meant, for example, that my parents leased and lived on an acre of land where they built a cabin. This cabin was situated so that we could be bussed to school. Our everyday family life took place in this cabin. For hunting and trapping, Métis men (families could not go during school seasons) had to travel considerable distances to satellite campsites inside their traplines which were leased from provincial Natural Resources departments. But long before the province of Alberta was born, long before Confederation was born, my paternal and maternal Plains and Woodlands Cree/ Métis ancestors filled these lands, if not by population, by indigenous use and love of the land. Like other Métis, my parents knew every nook and crannie of those lands ranging several hundred miles.

Such Métis communities existed throughout northern Alberta, and in fact, throughout the northern parts of most provinces. But little has been known about such communities because much of the research or interest about the Métis has been about Riel and Red River. And in Alberta, the Métis Settlements have overshadowed the unpropertied northern

---

10 In this respect, I am frankly puzzled to read in Dickason, in the context of counting federal land "allotments" to Aboriginal peoples, that "Alberta, with only ninety-six reserves (eight of which are Métis settlements) has by far the highest allotment" (Dickason 1992, 325). This is incorrect on two counts: the Métis Settlements are provincial not federal arrangements, and they are not reserves. Elsewhere in the textbook, Dickason provides a fine summary of the Settlements.

Native Identity and the Métis

Métis. Yet it is these unpropertied but traditionally land-based peoples whose lives have changed most dramatically due to waves of urban and industrial encroachments which really began to overrun the Métis in the post-war years. In an era when the Métis were most defenceless in terms of representation, literacy or familiarity with mainstream bureaucracy and legislation, provinces and industries went about assuming ownership of lands and traplines upon which the people depended. There was no protection for these Métis' way of life. For example, in the early 1950s people in my hamlet lost their traplines when the province simply declared their trapping area a bombing range. Within a decade later many families were forced to accept social welfare to feed their children. Some people even lost their own backyards as various industrial urban aggressions impinged on our communities. Needless to say, all this, among other socio-economic injuries, had a very demoralizing effect on the people.

Many Métis including my father refused to take any social assistance. My parents had to make difficult decisions in order to be able to keep practising their independent way of life. They moved (or commuted by train to accommodate the school schedule) 100 miles further north where my father found stable seasonal (summer) work for the Northern Alberta Railways (N.A.R.) and trapped with my uncle in the winters. There were self-sufficient Cree-Métis communities strung all along the N.A.R. line which stretched from Lac La Biche to Fort McMurray. But by the 1960s, oil and gas companies were everywhere bulldozing over campsites and traplines with their huge machines. They may as well have been army tanks for they destroyed hunting areas and so dispossessed the Métis as effectively as any army would. There I watched my uncle's backyard turned into a man-made lake (reasons for which remain unknown to us). By the 1980s, neither traplines nor trapping was available or feasible for most Métis in these areas. The Métis youth faced an untenable situation: they could no longer make a viable living based on an indigenous relationship with the land, yet were ill equipped to enter mainstream culture on any equal footing. Public schools which we attended hammered us with assimilation policies just as effectively as residential schools battered Status Indian children. The accumulative effect of all these pressures turned our worlds into socio-cultural war zones.

To put it mildly, the results have been heart-breaking. Forced to make a new world for ourselves, many of us had to leave families and homes we loved, especially if we wanted to pursue education beyond grade school. Those who stayed faced their own difficulties. But whether we moved or stayed, few survived unscathed and many became lost

102 The Emma LaRocque Reader

or actually died in the chaos of urban and industrial invasion that has come with neo-colonialism. Such industrial aggressions have been rationalized as progress by so-called Developed Nations. In this country, particularly since the World Wars, both the governments and society have been aggressively whipping Native peoples into "modernization." There is powerful evidence that forced modernization batters and disorients Indigenous peoples even as it is dispossessing them.[11] Whatever awareness there is about this process in Canada has been largely focussed on Status Indians who have experienced forced relocation.[12] There has hardly been any notice taken about all the cultural stress and dispossession the unpropertied Métis have endured. Nor is there any notice that federal and provincial governments continue to allow industries to overtake lands that properly belong to *Sagaweenoo-Apeetowgoosanak*, or Métis bush peoples.

What has happened in the area I come from is not an atypical example of what happens to contemporary Métis generations when the unprotected lands upon which their parents depended are no longer meaningfully accessible to them. Given the array of assaults the Indigenous-based Métis have sustained, it should come as no surprise that many Métis communities throughout western and eastern Canada are disappearing or fragmenting, and this does have implications for Métis identity. There is a direct connection between cultural erosion and lack of legal protection for lands upon which these Métis cultures and communities were built.

However, cultural erosion does not mean cultural amnesia. The relationship between dispossession and cultural survival is of course a complex discussion, a discussion that demands much greater attention than I can give it here. Dispossessed peoples do not necessarily forget or abandon their languages, beliefs, traditions, values, arts and skills, not

---

11 Most aboriginal communities have been battered and/or dispossessed by urban and industrial aggressions. For an excellent overview (though there are only oblique references on the Métis) see Geoffrey York, *The Dispossessed: Life and Death in Native Canada* (1990). See also Boyce Richardson, ed., *Drumbeat* (1989). For more personal observations on "modernization" see my autobiographical essay (see chapter "Tides, Towns and Trains").

12 Shkilnyk (1985) in *Poison Stronger Than Love* locates forced relocation in 1963 (ostensibly to accommodate the Native people's access to the modern amenities of a nearby town) as the source for the social disintegration of an Ojibwe community in northern Ontario. Shkilnyk provides a disturbing but intelligent and compassionate portrait of a traditional peoples who suffered "collective trauma" (xvi) as a consequence of forced modernization (capped with industrial poisoning in 1970).

Native Identity and the Métis

to mention the human connections, all of which weave into a people's culture. This fact is now better appreciated by modern anthropology but the old stereotypes that "natives" are stone-age primitives unable to cope with "civilization" or "progress" have long served colonial interests. There is nothing inherently moribund about Aboriginal cultures. And certainly for Métis peoples, and to the extent we have had choices, we have always integrated various components of Indigenous and Canadian cultures. What needs to be understood is the interplay between forced change and change which can be seen as "normal" in any given culture. There is no question but that Métis peoples have undergone various phases of forced change throughout the last century, yet they have also engaged in cultural exchange as vibrant peoples who were often at the forefront of innovation prior to Confederation's takeover of western Aboriginal lands. It is perhaps more difficult to discern all the cultural spaces from which Métis (and other Aboriginal peoples) have freely acted. It is true of course that colonization continues to impact negatively on Aboriginal cultures and persons, particularly in the area of lands and resources, but it is just as true that Aboriginal peoples are not cardboard caricatures without cultural elasticity or political agency.

What is remarkable is that despite the relentless pressures the Métis have suffered, many of us managed to build some sense of cultural continuity meaningful to us, whether in places of origin or in the cities. We still know ourselves in Cree as *Apeetowgoosanak* or "Half-sons." Our traditions and cultural expressions remain uniquely Métis. Our legends and ghost stories, our Cree chants or Red River jigs, our humour and temperament, the embroidery in our moccasins or pillow cases, as well as our protocols for familial and social behaviour remain distinctly Métis. We do have our own beliefs and practises which reflect our syncretistic religion (Cree/Roman Catholic) and language (forms of Michif), as well as our integrated approach to lands and technology. And both individuality and social responsibility are still highly valued.

I found it surprising that RCAP restricted its assessment of "cultural loss" of the Métis to "traditional Aboriginal activities" that are "cultural, spiritual, ceremonial or recreational in nature" (1996, 214–15). By "Aboriginal" RCAP here really means "Indian," and reflects the common tendency to evaluate the Métis in terms of Indian traditions (often associated with and confined to elders and pow-wows). Elders and pow-wows were not familiar to many Métis until about the 1970s. What is not well understood is that there were and are cultural differences between Indian and Métis peoples, a point Maria Campbell made in her book *Halfbreed* (1973). Some of these differences may be more subtle than others, but were the Métis properly assessed in terms

104   The Emma LaRocque Reader

of Métis traditions, the profile on cultural loss or retention would come
out quite differently.

Nonetheless, while it is true that the Métis are a remarkably resilient
peoples and will continue to forge and re-forge their identities meaningful to them, they have sustained heavy cultural damage with respect
to land-based traditions. Not only is a certain way of life ultimately
lost but so are the resources upon which a new life could be developed. And unpropertied people become marginalized, dispirited and
often fall into a cycle of poverty. As peoples whose core culture has been
the blending of two distinct societies, it is not "progress" or change or
any technological developments per se that the Métis have feared, it is
choicelessness that has always come with colonization. Even though we
may optimistically believe that culture is what people do together and
as such is dynamic and portable, dispossessed peoples do become landless and can only respond within certain parameters. With respect to
being able to carry on in our places of origin, my brother is an example
of how many Métis struggle heroically to maintain their *sagaweenuak*
independence by combining land-based resources with wage-labour.
But my brother's remaining and tiny land base is diminishing before
his eyes as provincial and global corporations, not to mention, animal
rights politics, are still encroaching upon these lands and his way of life.

Métis must take active steps to prevent cultural erosion that comes
from lack of legal protection for their lands and cultures. RCAP takes
the position that the federal government has a legal and moral mandate
to assist the Métis in the rebuilding and retaining of their identity. RCAP
recommends that the federal government must end legal discrimination against the Métis with respect to Aboriginal rights and homelands,
and take remedial action in areas of cultural redevelopment.

While the Canadian Constitution (1982) included the Métis as one of
the Aboriginal peoples, many issues on Métis land rights and identity
remain unresolved. In Manitoba, legal and historical debate continues
concerning Métis lands arising from the Manitoba Act 1870, Sections 31
and 32. In Alberta, some 50–70,000 Métis do not live in the Settlements
and many remain as landless and marginalized as the vast majority
of Métis across Canada.[13] The federal government has persisted in its

---

13 It is impossible to get precise figures for Métis populations. In 1981, the Métis
    Association of Alberta provided an estimate of 75,000 Métis in Alberta, with 3400
    in the Métis Settlements. RCAP uses the 1991 Aboriginal Peoples Survey figure of
    56,310 who identified as Métis in Alberta. Dickason (1992) provides an estimate of
    55,000 who live off the settlements. Taking into account these discrepancies, I have
    used a range of 50–70,000 Métis who live outside of Métis Settlements.

Native Identity and the Métis   105

refusal to recognize the Métis as "Indian" under the terms of section 91(24) of the *Constitution Act, 1867*, a refusal which is tantamount to withholding Aboriginal rights from the Métis. But Métis peoples have held to the view that they are Aboriginal, ancestrally, culturally and now constitutionally, and should qualify for land claims on the basis of Aboriginal rights. RCAP concurs:

> The refusal by the Government of Canada to treat Métis as full-fledged Aboriginal people covered by section 91(24) of the constitution is the most basic form of government discrimination. Until that discriminatory practice has been changed, no other remedial measures can be as effective as they should be. (219–20)

In this context the Status Indian adoption of the term "First Nations" (which excludes the Métis) is unfortunate because it has resulted in disconnecting the Métis from their Aboriginality as the media and the public increasingly make a terminological distinction between "Aboriginal" or "Native" and "Métis." It would appear that this is convenient for the provincial and federal governments; the further removed the Métis are from their Aboriginality, the less pressure for governments to address Métis land and resource claims.

But Métis are Aboriginal and in fact it is this that contributes to the complexity of Métis identities. While scholars generally restrict and divide differences among the Métis to their Anglosaxon or Francophone origins, Métis cultural differences are more than equally determined by connections to different Aboriginal cultures. For example, that the Métis of Labrador are different from the Métis of Red River or the Métis from British Columbia speaks to the many cultural differences among Indigenous peoples whose cultural stamp on various Métis ethnicities is considerable. At point of European arrival, there were perhaps several hundred different Original cultures consisting of about 11 linguistic families representing about 50 different languages (Dickason 1992). There were great diversities among the Original cultures ranging from the fishing coastal peoples along the Atlantic and Pacific, the great hunters of the Boreal Forest and of the Plains, the Iroquoian farmers of the Woodlands, or the tundra peoples of the Arctic. It is estimated that there were about 500,000 to a possible 2,000,000 Original peoples when Europeans arrived (Dickason 1992). Not only was there intermarriage between various Original peoples, undoubtedly, giving rise to many Aboriginal peoples of 'mixed ancestry,' but each locality where there was significant contact between European and Indian peoples generated their own Halfbreed peoples who then developed their own distinct Métis identities. Of course, not all such communities survived but as we do more research we will uncover more such histories.

There are of course, historical and cultural differences among the Métis. As the Royal Commission on Aboriginal Peoples discovered, there are many such communities throughout Canada outside the prairie provinces, for example, in British Columbia, Ontario, Labrador or Nunavut. There are also regional differences among the Métis Nation peoples. That we are able to trace our roots to Red River does not mean that we are necessarily the same. There are, for example, some fundamental differences between French-connected Métis of southern Manitoba and Cree-oriented Métis of northern Alberta, or even of northern Manitoba. Some of the differences include linguistics, lifestyles and worldviews as well as experience and education. A Métis who grew up speaking French Michif with a Roman Catholic religion in an urban area is different from a Métis who grew up speaking Cree Michif with an Aboriginal epistemology in a bush or rural setting. There are also persons who can clearly trace their family histories to the Red River Fur Trading systems but who were not raised in a Métis culture. Then there are those whose one parent is Métis, the other not. The 'other' may be Salish, Stoney, Micmac, Irish, Ukrainian, Black or Asian, and so forth. There are still those who are "half white, half Indian" and do adopt Métis values and communities and remain strong supporters of the Métis. To what extent these peoples of various origins have a rightful claim to Métis identity with Aboriginal rights remains to be sorted out. In the words of historian Olive Dickason: "… the many backgrounds of individuals of mixed ancestry has complicated the matter of identity for the Métis" (Dickason 1992, 365).

That there are cultural differences, some even substantial, among the Métis does not mean that the Métis lack distinct cultural markers. It only means that they reflect their many origins and levels of political awareness. Scholars have been slow to sort out these differences. The public has been singularly unable to fathom the fact of these differences among the Métis. In their minds, the word "Métis" represents a hodge podge in which is thrown any person who claims some Indianness, no matter how remote or questionable. It appears this has been inversely convenient for various parties. On one hand, employers such as the civil service, universities or even Métis organizations can fulfil human rights mandates to hire "minority" or "Aboriginal" staff by hiring anyone who claims Métisness but can confirm little, if any, such background or identity. On the other hand, provincial and federal governments continue to deny or contest Métis claims to Aboriginal rights

Native Identity and the Métis

based on the confusion surrounding Métis identity! Both the public and politicians have failed to respect the Métis Nation peoples as a distinct Aboriginal group. For these reasons the Métis Nation peoples have emphasized their distinctive and Aboriginally-based ethnicity among a peoples with such a complex history.

Conclusion

How to maintain an ethnic identity in the face of imposed change and/ or legislation is a challenge for any group. For the Métis, it has been particularly taxing. Peoples usually maintain their identity through "enclavic factors" such as a) geographical concentration or isolation; b) language retention; c) shared lifestyles and so on. Different histories and ethnicities, government policies, industrial encroachment, urbanization and lack of legally protected Métis homelands continue to threaten Métis identity (or identities). Still, despite all odds, the Métis continue to survive as a distinct ethnic group with strong Aboriginal ties in terms of kinship, language, land use and spirituality. The racial and cultural connection is indisputable. Depending on terms of reference estimates on Métis/Métis populations range from about 500,000 to over one million (Frideres 1998).

The Métis Nation community is often put in an awkward position of having to make a distinction between itself and non-Métis persons (presumably of mixed ancestry) who pass themselves as Métis. There are those who appropriate Métis identity in an attempt to secure employment or services and rights that should properly go to Métis peoples. In an attempt to address these concerns, Métis organizations have established criteria for membership which usually requires community confirmation or documented evidence of one's Métis ancestry. This is particularly important for purposes of identifying the Métis population entitled to Métis-specific land grants or Aboriginal rights. Within the context of self-government negotiations, a Métis Nation controlled national registry was proposed by the Métis National Council (MNC) during the Charlottetown deliberations. MNC defined "Métis" as "(a) ... an Aboriginal person who self-identifies as Métis, who is distinct from Indian and Inuit and is a descendant of those Métis who received or were entitled to receive land grants and/or scrip under the provisions of the *Manitoba Act, 1870,* or the *Dominion Lands Act* ..." and "Métis Nation" as the "community of persons in subsection a) and persons of Aboriginal descent who are accepted by that community" (RCAP 1996, 377).

For those who insist that anyone should have the right to become "Métis" merely by self-declaration is engaging in colonial imposition.

108 The Emma LaRocque Reader

If Aboriginal self-government or the actualization of land grants and Aboriginal Rights is to mean anything for the Métis, they must have the right to define and determine their constituencies. Such rights are not disregarded for Status Indians or for many other Canadian groups. This is not an issue of discrimination on the part of the Métis, it is simply an attempt to ensure that Aboriginal and other rights flow properly to them. They also wish to clarify anthropological and historical factual differences about their ethnicity. Naturally, the Métis are interested in maintaining their identity in much the same way that any other ethnic or cultural group, for example, the Blackfoot, the Mohawks, the Ukrainians, the English or the French, is working to maintain its identity. The Métis Nation peoples make no claim to racial or ethnic purity or cultural superiority; if anything, they have been open and generous to numerous individuals of many backgrounds who have come to their doors claiming kinship. But poor history and generalized terminology has long resulted in the obscuration of Métis identity as well as legislative and sociological discrimination with respect to their Aboriginality, land and resource rights. Although some scholars have rightly pointed out there are 'many roads to Red River' (Peterson and Brown 1985), that is, the Métis/Métis have many origins, clearly, there are substantial cultural and historical differences among peoples and persons who claim "some Indian" in them. The generalized notion and usage of the term "Métis" remains a question of some contention within Métis communities. Perhaps the Métis Nation peoples should adopt a different name, say, *Otempayimsuak*, for their identity in order to foreground the point: that they are an indigenous-based distinctive ethnic group who have constitutional, historical, cultural and moral claims to Aboriginal rights. To be unique among many remains an important emotional, psychological and spiritual fact among human groups. *Otempayimsuak* Métis are no different. They simply want recognition that they are indeed an ethnic group with a distinct culture whose rights and roots go back to the very bones of this land.

2001

From the Land to the Classroom:
Broadening Epistemology

As an Aboriginal scholar who has long worked within the university system and liberal arts programme, I have been taking keen interest in recent but rapidly growing research and debate on Indigenous "traditional ecological knowledge" (TEK). So far, much of the discussion revolves around Traditional Knowledge (TK) with respect to environmental concerns and resource management, with some attempts to clarify the relationship between western science and TK. As a researcher in Canadian historiography and contemporary Native literature, I am interested in the fact that there is now finally some concession by western scientists and researchers that Aboriginal peoples' knowledge, both in fundamentals and practise, is coherent and valuable. Though this may be cause for some celebration for those of us who have long advanced or modelled such a view, certain characterizations of "traditional ecological knowledge" indicate the limited extent to which Aboriginal knowledge is applied. This paper will generate thoughts on broadening the application of critical Aboriginal epistemology.

There are a number of challenges which confront those of us who are applying Aboriginal epistemology in areas of study or teaching which concentrate on what may be called, for lack of more appropriate terminology, pure intellectual work rather than field research. In addition to the philosophical demands of combining Western and Aboriginal epistemologies, certain associations of "traditional knowledge" with field research and the Aboriginal "community" are posing political problems for Aboriginal scholars. I begin with prevailing notions of "traditional knowledge".

Defining Traditional Knowledge

TK is largely profiled as "holistic" land-based knowledge transmitted by the elders through oral Native language and praxis (Colorado 1988; Johnson 1992; Stevenson 1992; Berkes 1993; Gadgil et al. 1993; Emery

110 The Emma LaRocque Reader

and Associates 1997; Simpson 1999). Hoare et al. (1993) provide a fairly typical definition of "indigenous knowledge" as:

> [T]he culmination of generations of experience and insight passed down through oral tradition. This knowledge was holistic in nature incorporating spiritual, ecological, human and social experiences into one understanding of Native peoples' place in the universe. (48)

Hoare et al. (1993) note that TK is "built on observation, experience and reflection, while its teachings are grounded in the natural world" (48). Invariably, attempts to define TK has led to valuative comparisons between Traditional Ecological Knowledge (TEK) and Western Science (Colorado 1988; Johnson 1992; Berkes 1993).

While we can appreciate that these are attempts to clarify and even validate "traditional" knowledge, there are some potential problems and stereotypes with these treatments. With respect to Aboriginal peoples in the United States and Canada, stereotypic images of "the Indian" (Berkhofer 1978; Doxtator 1992; Francis 1992; LaRocque 1999) have informed many of the notions associated with "traditional knowledge". For example, for lack of more precise translations, or research, we have in modern times generalized Native cultures as "intuitive", "spiritual", "qualitative", "moral" and "holistic" but these are descriptions subject to oversimplification, particularly in treatments which trait-list Western and Native cultural characteristics (Stevenson 1992; Berkes 1993; Emery and Associates 1997). Charting Native cultural traits in juxtaposition to Western ones has become deeply embedded in current social and even academic thinking. I have long had serious concerns with this and have recently called for its re-examination in criminal justice applications (see chapter "The Colonization of a Native Woman Scholar", LaRocque 1997), and in literary criticism of contemporary Native literature (LaRocque 1999), Such a re-examination is needed in TK studies but I do not go into a detailed analysis here.

Of course, understanding and treatment of TK is rapidly expanding. Researchers continue to discover that the holistic world view is by no means simple or merely mystical. Aboriginal practitioners of the land do pay exquisite attention to detail (Warry 1990; Ryan and Robinson 1996; Reimer 1993; McDonald et al. 1997), and their spirituality is intrinsic to strategic applications of cultural knowledge with respect to resource use (Ridington 1982; Feit 1986; Colorado 1988; Johnson 1992). It is just that they have used a different 'language' in these developments.

From the Land to the Classroom   111

There is certainly a growing appreciation that Native knowledge systems are way more sophisticated, coherent and systematic than heretofore recognized (Colorado 1988; Johnson 1992; Berkes and Henley 1997; McDonald et al. 1997; Simpson 1999). The extent to which Indigenous cultures and peoples of the Americas have contributed to world knowledge, not to mention, to European prosperity, is explored, for example, by anthropologist Weatherford (1988). There is also growing concession that Western Science needs the Aboriginal perspective, approach and knowledge (Knudtson and Suzuki 1992; Gadgil et al. 1993). Nonetheless, it remains that Aboriginal knowledge is still largely limited to 'traditional' and ecological knowledge.

Grounding Aboriginal Knowledge

With some exception (Colorado 1988; Johnson 1992; Stevenson 1992; Simpson 1999), TK theorists have, by inference, treated 'traditional' knowledge not only as the sum total of Aboriginal knowledge but as dying. Indeed, some have pointed to a 'crisis of knowledge' as elders are passing away. Within a certain context, perhaps such concerns may be valid. "It is undoubtedly true that some erosion of TEK has taken place. However, both the research of social scientists and indigenous peoples themselves confirm the continued vitality of their cultures and note that TEK is changing or evolving rather than dying" (Johnson 1992, 4). But the call to urgently retrieve and record TEK is reminiscent of the 'Vanishing Indian' line of thought, a well-travelled theme of the perpetually dying Indian (Francis 1992). This is the view which confines Native peoples and cultures to the typologized static 'traditional' culture (a view challenged in LaRocque 1975). In contrast, Western culture is somehow inherently progressive. By definition, Native culture is condemned to die since anything it does is 'traditional', while, by definition, western culture can never die since anything it does constitutes 'progress'. This line of thinking continues to plague not only the study but the very identity of contemporary Native peoples.

In so far as Aboriginal world view is tied to the land and its resources, its basis and collection of knowledge is fundamentally tied to the land. This quite literally grounds Aboriginal knowledge. While this should provide some explanation to non-Native Canadians why it is that the land base is so vital to Aboriginal peoples (the significance of space and place cannot be overemphasized here), it does present us with some significant problems. The implications should be unsettling: if Aboriginal knowledge is confined to non-industrial use of land or language, 'tradition' and 'elders' obviously, it is condemned to limited use and a

112   The Emma LaRocque Reader

certain demise! Questions arise as to the wider application and life span of Aboriginal knowledge.

What room is there for contemporary Aboriginal knowledge in all this? This question demands much greater attention than I can give it here. There are many important issues bearing on realities of colonization and decolonization as well as notions of change and tradition within Aboriginal thinking and practise. The fact of change in Aboriginal cultures is a complex thing. Native peoples have experienced forced change through colonization, yet at different times and phases, they have engaged in cultural exchange as peoples with an evolving culture. While it is possible to trace various colonial forces such as the Indian Act, residential schools, and so forth, it is more difficult to discern all the crucial cultural spaces from which Native peoples have freely acted. The fact is, Native knowledge is being transmitted from generation to generation in Native cultures. Aside from the problem of defining 'eldership', it is not only 'elders' who do the teaching in Native homes and communities. Consequently, it is not only 'elders' who have 'traditional' knowledge. Many younger people also have 'traditional' knowledge in terms of their relationships to ecology and in terms of their world views, languages, and land-based expertise.

But is this all there is to Aboriginal knowledge, that is, that it can only be practised 'traditionally' on the land, whether 500 years ago or today? What about all the knowledge and experience gained over the last 500 years? What about Native persons who live modern lives both on the land or in cities? For example, my brother who is in his early 40s not only knows, practises and lives a land-based (Cree-Métis) way of life, he also knows and practises contemporary languages and skills. He has not suffered from cultural dislocation in his process of translating ancient knowledge into contemporary meaning. Then there are those who live in cities and have jobs such as teaching in mainstream Canadian classrooms. We practise contemporary languages and skills, yet carry within us and continue to transmit our languages, oral literatures and land-based ways. Many of us also have close connections to the land or to those in our communities who chose to stay and keep on living off the land (as much as is feasible). Like my brother, we too are translating traditional knowledge into contemporary meaning without suffering any necessary cultural dislocation.

Among other things, if Native peoples have not moved into industrial centres, the industrial has long moved into their worlds. As one who grew up in the bush (with all that this implies in terms of ecological cultural knowledge and practise) complete with gardens, clocks, radios, steel tools, trains, towns and schools. I often feel a time-warp

From the Land to the Classroom

when reading about 'traditional knowledge'. For the most part, as their parents before them, my parents and their generation of hunters and trappers integrated non-industrial and industrial worlds quite comfortably, as long as they had a resource base and choice to exercise their cultural knowledge. In many respects, ideas on 'traditional knowledge' today are both primitivist and eclipsed, perpetuating a static version of Aboriginal cultures and peoples. This is not to mention that Native identity today cannot be confined to those with linguistic and/or land connections. Those of us who were privileged to have grown up immersed in a Native language in a land-based lifestyle are challenged to open our minds and hearts to a whole new generation of 'Aboriginals'.

Re/Constructing Aboriginal Knowledge

We face challenges we have not even thought about in our attempts to re/construct Aboriginal knowledge meaningful in today's realities. We must avoid portraying Aboriginal cultures and knowledge in that fixed romanticized sense of the treatment. The surest way to freeze any culture is to package it in a formulaic container of traits. The ossification of Native cultures is a real concern to those of us who must struggle to get a hearing as contemporary Native peoples, both on the lands and in the classrooms. There is every historical and anthropological evidence Aboriginal cultures of the Americas were and are dynamic (Weatherford 1988; Dickason 1992; Morrison and Wilson 1995). What will keep Aboriginal knowledge vibrant and meaningful is our ability to translate it into contemporary terms from generation to generation.

Colonization has disturbed Native cultural development and decolonization will enable Native cultures and peoples to carry on into future generations. As long as Native peoples have self-determination and as long as they have the ground and means of "doing things together" (Puxley 1977, 111), they have the potential to exercise and translate 'old' Native science into meaningful modern terms. Our ground of knowledge and experience must include our contemporary realities. We must recover that which is dynamic and inherently portable in Aboriginal epistemologies. Even though Native peoples have suffered from colonial shock, they have displayed remarkable cultural resilience. My idea of colonial shock is perhaps best understood as a response to 'collective trauma' (Shkilnyk 1985) experienced under sustained colonial assaults. For far too long such trauma has been mistaken or whitewashed as mere culture shock, suggesting that there was something innately weak about 'traditional' cultures. It is imperative we locate the root of the issue in our discussions of Native cultural changes and responses.

The Emma LaRocque Reader

Adaptive strategies should not be mistaken for total assimilation. I believe the greatest strength of the Aboriginal weltanschauung is its ethical basis (Deloria 1973; Cardinal 1977; Colorado 1988; Sioui 1996[1]). Native knowledge is informed by an ethical and spiritual basis which is intimately linked with Aboriginal people's relationship with each other, and with the land and its resources.

The ethical basis and the ethos of Aboriginal epistemologies have sustained cultural survival. The more obvious ways we 'carry' our cultures are through our languages, upbringing and training, but we also carry our world views in infinitely subtle ways. All these ways are expressed in our contemporary epistemologies. This means that our bases and approaches to knowledge, and to the gathering, use and dissemination or teaching of knowledge may be quite different from Western conventions. These differences though are much more complex, profound and potentially reconstructive than any cultural typologies which have become current in comparisons between Aboriginal and Western ways of knowing. Equally, it must be emphasized that though our epistemological bases may be 'different, both systems require "thoughtful and systematic observation" (Johnson 1992, 3), and "rigour, reliability and validity" (Colorado 1988, 51). There are important meeting points between Western and Aboriginal systems, if only they were not clouded by political inequalities.

Much like my parents but in a different context, of course, I have integrated western and Aboriginal knowledge systems. But I did always have a language to frame what I have modelled as a contemporary Native educator. The relatively recent surge of interest and research on TK has been an affirming addition to my work of revisiting Aboriginal and colonial languages in a post-colonial world. Throughout the years, I have come to identify and 'name' key elements of both Aboriginality and coloniality in the way that I teach and pursue knowledge and research. A post-colonial Aboriginal epistemology necessarily entails deconstruction and reconstruction. For Aboriginal scholars, it has meant, among other things, dismantling stereotypes and uncovering the covert but dominant narrative in western scholarship. For me, this has entailed actually modelling the use of overt voice. I not only teach students to become critically aware of the numerous techniques of impartiality in western history and literature, I do not remain distant or alienated from both my research and my community of origin. As a

---

1 LaRocque is likely referring to Sioui (1992) –Elaine Coburn, editor's note.

matter of principle, I have avoided aloofness and mystification of English (both often mistaken for objectivity and height of scholarship) in the classroom or in my writing. And of course, the Native perspective and experience necessarily provides the hub in the wheel of our teaching in the field of Native Studies. In ways beyond words, we have been advancing the legitimation of Indigenous knowledge.

TK and Native Studies

But there is a marked difference between the ways our knowledge is received and the ways 'traditional knowledge' provided by 'elders' is being received. The characterization of TK has created a hierarchy (not to mention, a stereotype) of Aboriginal knowledge with 'elders and traditional knowledge' on top and academic and contemporary knowledge on the bottom. How TK is conceived and prioritized does not always or universally bring happy results to either Native Studies or to Native scholars.

In a number of respects, 'Native Studies' is currently in the process of being segregated. It is an irony that as appreciation for 'traditional' knowledge is gaining, the process is marginalizing Aboriginal scholarship to TEK, PAR [Participatory Action Research], linguistics and legends, spirituality and healing and 'community'. This does not bode well for Aboriginal scholars who do not adopt a language identified with 'traditional knowledge', or whose work is centrally intellectual and whose disciplines are in the arts and humanities. Such scholars may find their perspectives and work questioned. They may be criticized for not having an 'Aboriginal' perspective, making them vulnerable to politically-motivated opinion and ideological control.

There is also the new political pressure for scholars to have their research and findings go through scrutiny and authentication by Aboriginal communities. I note that university funding agencies are moving in this direction as well. I fully support Native control of cultural knowledge and resources for those engaged in field research in Native territories. Because unequal power relations exist between western scientists/agencies and communities, Native peoples have every reason to be vigilant in protecting their lands as well as their cultural and intellectual properties. Ethical guidelines for responsible research are being developed (Colorado 1988; Berkes 1993; Masuzumi and Quirk 1993; Reimer 1993; Carpenter 1993; Inuit Tapirisat of Canada 1993; Flaherty 1994; Oakes and Riewe 1996). However, I worry about the direction universities are moving concerning the application of community control in our classrooms, research and even staffing. For example, I am concerned about extending 'community' control into our hiring policies and practises in departments or programmes having to do with 'Native Studies'. Over the last several years, most university and college ads for teaching or administrative jobs in Native-focussed academic programmes and departments stipulate that a successful candidate must have some kind of community connection or expertise. Often, the ads require that community expertise must include fund-raising capabilities. I view such requirements as part of putting pressure on Native academics and Native communities to provide their own funding or do their own fund-raising for programmes that are within universities! This neatly takes financial responsibility away from universities in the guise of community support but I do not see mainstream scholars being made to do their own fund-raising for their departments. In what way is this being supportive to Native scholars who should be free to teach and pursue knowledge without having to expend time and energy around funding? The biggest concern I have, though, centres around notions and uses of 'community' which is placing an extra 'burden of proof' on Native candidates. This is especially true for those who do not do field or 'traditional' work but are otherwise perfectly qualified academics. Add to this the fact that the majority of field and TEK researchers are not Native.

The notion of 'community' is quite amorphous and certainly vulnerable to political manipulation. There are so many different cultural and interest groups within the four different Native umbrella groups (Status, non-Status, Métis, Inuit) that some measure of community identification and accountability must be put in place in our hiring procedures. Further, 'community' is increasingly limited to 'traditional knowledge', elders and spirituality, even though the Native population is culturally diverse, and increasingly young, English-speaking and urbanized (Dickason 1992; Frideres 1998). If community opinion is going to be used as a major consideration in university hiring, then we must be very clear and careful as to who and what we define as 'community'. Obviously, there are jobs which should require community expertise but should this be so in *academic-based* university departments especially within the liberal arts faculties? This question takes on a sombre significance when we see that mainstream university departments such as history, sociology, psychology, political science, English, and so forth, do not place an extra dimension of community responsibility or authentication on their scholars for their teaching positions. To put it more starkly, are mainstream non-Aboriginal scholars made to go to *their* (non-Aboriginal or 'White") communities for permission and cultural validation in order to qualify for teaching and/or administrative jobs, research grants or promotions?

The 'community' situation that faces Native academics is not the same as what faces most other Canadian intellectuals. Most Native scholars of my generation were not born into their stations, and so we as "engaged researchers" tend to identify ourselves as part of "the community", not estranged from it in the way mainstream intellectuals often are (see chapter "Preface – Here Are Our Voices – Who Will Hear?" 1990; LaRocque 1999). To make us prove our "communitability" is redundant. But education is a two-edged sword for Native peoples. The irony is that my generation of Native scholars entered universities without community support. Even today Native scholarly knowledge is neither understood nor given the same respect as other kinds (traditional, elders) of knowledge in many Native communities. But as more First Nation, Métis and Inuit students enter universities, Aboriginal scholarship will take on greater significance.

What responsibilities (and to whom) do Native scholars have? Are they to be treated as mere mouthpieces of "community" needs or belief systems? Scholars in Native Studies have "an extra-ordinary mandate" (as our Native Studies mission statement states) to reflect sensitivity to Native perspectives and experiences, and I have long advanced such a mandate, however, it cannot mean subjecting scholars to ideological or political control, or to evaluations outside of university protocol. Aboriginal scholars must have as much academic freedom and as fair treatment as our non-Aboriginal colleagues. Scholarship directs us to aspire for "that critical and relatively independent spirit of analysis and judgement ought to be the intellectual's contribution" (Said 1996, 86).

Aboriginal Scholarship and the University Classroom

The effects of colonization on both white and Native scholars and scholarship in Canada is barely beginning to be investigated but it is clear that colonization affects our respective pursuits of research and theory as well as our pedagogies and ranking in academia. It is still largely the case that the "globalization of knowledge and Western culture constantly reaffirms the West's view of itself as the centre of legitimate knowledge, the arbiter of what counts as knowledge and the source of 'civilized' knowledge" (Smith 1999, 63). My observation and experience is that the university community including students, colleagues and administration has not known how to respond to or even recognize Aboriginal pedagogies within western systems, especially those which combine cultural ethos with critical analysis. Although this is in the process of changing, especially within Native Studies, we do still face resistance in the way our knowledge base and cultural information as well as our decolonized methodologies are received (see chapter, "Preface: Here Are Our Voices – Who Will Hear?", Acoose 1995; Monture-Angus 1995; Smith 1999; Green 2000).

Our teaching faces extra-ordinary challenges as well, especially for those of us engaging more in critical intellectual work than in cultural portraiture. Because we serve fairly disparate (in culture, colonial experience, economic status, educational heritage and system facilitation) student communities, and therefore, expectations, we are vulnerable to multi-pronged criticisms. Native students may require and demand culturally-appropriate pedagogies. Recently, in a class of Native adults, a number of students assuming the role of 'elders' challenged me concerning the basis of knowledge, and by implication, academic evaluation. We had an engaging discussion on legitimation of knowledge. How do we really deal with the western hegemonic canons which have a direct bearing on scholarship refashioned by non-western experience? Is academia willing to make any real changes to accommodate different knowledge systems?

Politics enters our classrooms as well when students (both Native and Non-Native) deeply conditioned to assume the universality and objectivity of the western narrative, do not or will not understand the political nature of history, representation and epistemology. In the context of teaching English literature from a non-western view, Mukherjee (1994) reports similar experiences in her classrooms. Stereotypes about 'traditional knowledge' and how this is expected to function in 'Native Studies' or in Native instructors have played no small role in this. Schools and society have failed to prepare most students for critical and cross-cultural or multi-racial education. While White students may react to a critical treatment of Canadian history or popular culture, Native students may feel threatened by critical treatment of gender roles or spirituality, for instance. Some students may not recognize or accept Aboriginal epistemology when Aboriginal scholars use 'voice', encourage group work, encourage multidisciplinary and interdisciplinary research and perspectives, provide documentation on colonization or insist on academic excellence. Such students may resort to techniques of backlash by accusing us of bias or even reverse discrimination in their evaluations. Most evaluations in universities are based on standardized western notions and expectations. Such evaluations fail to take into account cross-cultural or multi-racial realities in classrooms. There are no evaluations. For that matter, there are no critically-appropriate types of evaluations. As a number of post-colonial scholars have pointed out (Ashcroft, Griffiths, and Tiffin 1995), there is little, if any, systemic support for non-western critical pedagogies in

From the Land to the Classroom

universities. We are directed through "sanctioned ways of writing" and "publishing in the right places" (Mukherjee 1994, xiii), and I would add, we are evaluated through sanctioned ways of thinking and teaching. Standardization, then, has direct implications in our promotions and ranking (Mukherjee 1994; Christian 1995).

Conclusion

The onus is often put on Aboriginal scholars to 'prove' themselves within (and now outside of) the academic community. After 25 years, we must now ask some tough questions in return. What have mainstream universities learned from Aboriginal scholars over the last 25 years? What have they done to not only accommodate but actually facilitate both Native Studies and Native scholars and/or scholarship? How many unsegregated Native Studies departments are there across Canada? How many Native instructors and administrators are there in these departments? How many graduate programmes are there in these departments? How many Native instructors have tenured faculty ranking consistent with their publications, years of teaching, intellectual output and Aboriginal knowledge-base? Why do we not recognize Aboriginal intellectuals who not only bring western academic excellence but equally, Aboriginal epistemological excellence? We give degrees to those who fulfil western-defined programmes but there are no symbols or avenues of legitimation for those Native individuals who not only go through rigorous academic training in western scholarship but also bring with them Aboriginal ethos and knowledge systems into the classrooms. This part of our expertise is taken for granted. There are no increments for this knowledge, neither in pay nor promotions. There are some exceptions. For example, Native linguists, lawyers and Elders are gaining facilitation in academic systems.

In large part, the advancement of TK has taken place within the context of decolonization. In order for me to practise decolonization, I have had to create a discourse built on all my intellectual heritages. Resistance scholarship and the contemporization of Aboriginal epistemology is a complex topic. In the context of Native resistance literature, I treat the discussion in some interdisciplinary (History/English) depth in my recently completed dissertation: *Native Writers Resisting Colonizing Practices in Canadian Historiography and Literature* (LaRocque 1999). As resistance Native scholars we have both a cultural and colonial experience from which to build our discourse, and this does take us to the cutting edge of what is circumscribed as 'scholarly' or as 'traditional'. The task is to create a space and place to be able to enter into the particular discourse of western thought and format without having to internalize its coloniality or to defy our personal and cultural selves. How we integrate these worlds within scholarship remains a tug of war but it is an issue about which Native scholars are in the process of forging. It is within the context of challenging the assumptions, methodologies and uses of western 'science' that traditional Aboriginal knowledge has been 'discovered' and in some fields, increasingly validated. Our contemporary Aboriginal epistemologies and educators also need to be validated. It remains for universities to recognize, in theory and in practise, our unique and substantially original contributions.

2004

When the "Wild West" Is Me:
Re-Viewing Cowboys and Indians

BILL CODY (by an old comrade)
You bet I know him Pardner, he ain't no circus fraud.
He's Western born and Western bred, if he has been late abroad;
I knew him in the days way back, beyond Missouri's flow.
When the country round was nothing but a huge Wild Western Show.
When the injuns were as thick as fleas, and the man who ventured through
The sand hills of Nebraska had to fight the hostile Sioux;
These were hot times, I tell you; and we all remember still
The days when Cody was a scout, and all the men knew Bill.

1895, as quoted in Doxtator (1992)

We did not think of the great open plains, the beautiful rolling hills, and wind-ing streams with tangled growth, as 'wild.' Only to the white man was nature a 'wilderness' and only to him was the land 'infested with 'wild' animals and 'savage' people. To us it was tame.... Not until the hairy man from the east came ... was it 'wild' for us. When the very animals of the forest began flee-ing from his approach, then it was that for us the 'Wild West' began. Luther Standing Bear (1933)

It was the Indian of the white man's imagination rather than the Indian of histori-cal fact who finally became dominant in English-American literature. This fact has had a long-range effect upon the Indian image ... LaRocque (1975)

Canadians are conflicted in their attitudes toward Indians. And we will con-tinue to be so long as the Indian remains imaginary. Non-Native Canadians can hardly hope to work out a successful relationship with Native people who exist largely in fantasy. Chief Thunderthud did not prepare us to be equal partners with Native people.... The distance ... between fantasy and reality,

122   The Emma LaRocque Reader

is the distance between Indian and Native. It is also the distance non-Native Canadians must travel before we can come to terms with the imaginary Indian, which means coming to terms with ourselves as North Americans.
Daniel Francis (1992)

What does a Plains Cree-Métis child think or feel when she sees and hears for the first time a typical Cowboy/Indian movie thundering across a huge silver screen? To best appreciate this question, I begin by providing a sociological snippet of a typical Métis child growing up in a Métis community in northern Alberta in the 1950s or 1960s. Such a child would have grown up in a cabin situated on a meadowy hill surrounded by poplars and pines. This is a time and setting where Métis life was grounded and nurtured by the land. People went about their lives: preparing foods, sewing clothing, repairing or inventing tools for fishing, hunting, trapping or tanning, picking seneca roots, picking berries, picking rocks, fighting fires, working on the railroads, and so forth. Skilled and extraordinarily resourceful on the land, these self-sufficient and independent people worked hard and laughed easily. They loved to chant in Cree, recite Wesehkehcha legends, tell tall tales, play the fiddle and dance. They also knew the angst and the anguish that comes with illness or death, often losing loved ones to tuberculosis. They learned how to survive bitter winters, as well as knowing how to celebrate the harvesting of resources. These people were by no means Hiawathan. Some were materialistic and profane, others more spiritual. Some were fatuous, some were prudent. Some were mean, mendacious, angry, and selfish. Many others were unpretentious, unobtrusive, open, generous, and kind. The point is that they were just a community of humans. Then came the jangle of Cowboys and Indians on screen.

How well I remember my first Cowboy/Indian movie. I was riveted, revolted, and terrified. I was perhaps eight years old. I do not remember the name of the movie; I only remember "the Indians": grotesque, wild-eyed, lurking creatures with painted bodies and hideous faces, tomahawks on hand, howling and whooping, crouching like animals across the screen, preying on beautiful white people on their way west to bring law and order. Like everyone else in the audience, both white and Native, I cheered for the beautiful people and I hated "the Indians." Little did I know that White North American society had dubbed us "Indians" – until I entered school (at the age of nine), where I again had to confront the Ignoble Savage in textbooks. Here, from grade one to university, I was to learn the "heroic point of view" (Duchemin 1990, 54) which situated the North American landscape as a moral battlefield between White Civilization and Indian Savagery in which the Cowboys were in moral combat against "the Indians." If my beloved Ama and Bapa, the consummate human beings that they were, were "Indians," and these inhumane gruesome creatures on screen were also "Indians," how was I to feel or make sense of it all? My attempts to reconcile the dissonance between my world and the "Imaginary Indian" (Francis 1992, 224) undoubtedly led to my career as a writer and a scholar.

The history of imagining and subsequently imaging 'the Indian' as 'wild' and 'savage' runs long and deep in White North America's intellectual and cultural productions. Rooted in pre-Columbian European mythology (Honour 1975; Berkhofer 1978; Dickason 1992), re-designed and intensified by colonial expansionist interests, the invention of the "Indian" now continues as a requisite constituent of White North American popular culture. Caricatured as wild and savage, the "Indian" remains as a cultural signpost from which has come a self-perpetuating Indian image industry (Doxtator 1992; Francis 1992). Indian motifs with stock themes of good and evil, of light and darkness, of the "primitive" or the "savage" in "man" have served and continue to serve mainstream art and entertainment. And of course, much of western intellectual development is founded on racial notions of Civilization encountering Savagism (Pearce 1965; Jennings 1975). Indeed, there is very little in western scholarship that does not base itself in some kind of cultural evolutionary theory, with European-originated cultural markers still serving as the standard bearers of civilization and human "development" (LaRocque 1999). In traditional Canadian historiography, Native/White relations have been treated within a framework of interpretation I have come to dub as the "civ/sav dichotomy" (LaRocque 1983). In Wild West terms, the Cowboy represented the Civilage (my term) and the Indian the Savage.

I first experienced the Wild West with its shrieking savage on screen in the late 1950s. If my experience was isolated and time-confined, perhaps we could treat it as atypical and not worthy of much comment or scholarly pursuit. However, my experience was neither isolated nor limited to a bygone era. Cowboy/Indian movies remain current. And as I will show, their impact on both Native and non-Native audiences was and remains extensive and profound. While in some specialized scholarly and literary circles the use of the Indian is increasingly enlightened, in pulp fiction and many other cultural productions, the dehumanization of "the Indian" is continuing at a fairly frenetic pace. I emphasize dehumanization because the media and the marketplace, especially Hollywood, have continued to produce horrific images of savagery located as "Indian" in origin.

Hollywood is churning out a relentless array of remakes (*The Last of the Mohicans*, *Pocahontas*) and new takes (*Dances with Wolves*, *Black Robe*, *Legends of the Fall*, *The Scarlet Letter*, *Squanto*, *Indian in my Cupboard*), depicting "Indians" in the tradition of captivity narratives and Buffalo Bill's Wild West Shows (Berkhofer 1978; Francis 1992).

In many ways these new movies are worse than the old-fashioned, openly racist Cowboy and Indian "dusters" because these new ones use very seductive and devious techniques to fool audiences into thinking they are watching objectively produced real Indians in real history. Often, a strand of the Noble Savage is woven in by accenting the loyalty, bravery, or stoicism of a befeathered but defeated warrior/chief. The Noble Savage construct (about which I shall say more) has served White American cultural productions well. The more modern twist has an elder/prophetic figure who not only communes with nature and spirits but can also dissect cowboy duplicity. Other techniques include exhibiting ragged pieces of Indian "culture," having "real" "Indians" performing the savage acts, tossing in white violence or presenting an aura of cross-cultural tolerance. Referring to cultural customs, however distorted, gives the audience a false sense of authenticity which, as we shall see, is an essential even if confused requirement for modern audiences. Making some whites perform equally gruesome acts of violence (*Soldier Blue*, *Little Big Man*, *Dances with Wolves*) or having some Indians or one white maverick presented as more human or noble than others (*Little Big Man*, *Dances with Wolves*) gives the audience a false sense of fairness and objectivity in the treatment of "Indians" in movies. Confusing history with Hollywood (*Black Robe*, *The Last of the Mohicans*, *Squanto*, *Tecumseh*), or putting, say, 1868 at the beginning of a John Ford/John Wayne western (*The Searchers*, *The Rio Grande*) has the effect of oversimplifying a complex colonial encounter ridden with communication, political, and cross-cultural problems. And racist/sexist images are made more palatable, especially in their effects on children, by using animation or cartoon/mascot genres (*Pocahontas*, *An Indian in my Cupboard*, *Man in the House*).

Movies set in contemporary times are particularly disturbing. In *Legends of the Fall*, Tristan (Brad Pitt) is a white savage cut loose on the fields of World War I. Among other things, there are close-up pictures of him ritualistically fondling his dead brother's heart, which he has cut out to bring back to America. One of his fearsome techniques is sneaking up on enemy soldiers, whose scalps he takes. Tristan grew up with Indians, servants to his family, Indians who taught him legends and visions.

Portrayed as wild and fierce as his nemesis the bear, with which he has a lifelong spiritual connection, there is every inference Tristan has "gone Indian."

In *Clearcut*, Arthur (Graham Greene) is a contemporary Native man whose band loses a land claim to a pulp mill. He abducts the pulp mill owner and his band's legal counsel and takes them to an isolated area where he essentially turns into a "savage," tormenting and torturing his terrorized white hostages. Here again, the prevailing image is that of Indian savagery, even if interspersed with witty truths that Arthur utters.

The overwhelming lingering imagery in all these movies is still that of Indian savagery and primitivism no matter how variously plotted or how "sympathetic" to the Indian cause. Or how noble the protagonists may be. *Pocahontas* is no exception. While this animated film does romanticize its main Indian characters, even blurring the grandmother spirit with the tree, it clings to the savagery theme by having the encroaching shipload of Englishmen, whether through song or directed comments, incessantly refer to "savages" – and they were not referring to themselves. And this is not to mention the gross over-sexualization of the Pocahontas figure as she sensuously slides (or crouches) from verdant tree to verdant tree, showing her voluptuous cleavage and gleaming thighs. This brown Barbie-doll presentation is all the more offensive given that, in historical fact, Pocahontas was a Powhatan child about twelve years of age when she presumably saved John Smith, an Englishman squatting on Powhatan land, from execution (Green 1975; Tilton 1994).

The fact remains that there is little historical objectivity or validity to any of these images, despite the occasional touch of nobility. They were produced to provide inferior but "action-filled" entertainment, but more importantly, they reflect the Manifest Destiny doctrine – a long-standing belief by the majority of mainstream North Americans that America belongs to the "Anglo-Saxon race." In the chilling words of a group of frontiersmen during the violent days between aggressive White American expansionists and the resisting Plains Indians of the 1800s: "The rich and beautiful valleys of Wyoming are destined for the occupancy and sustenance of the Anglo-Saxon race…. The same inscrutable Arbiter that decreed the downfall of Rome has pronounced the doom of extinction upon the red men of America" (Brown 1970, 184). In the tradition of the Buffalo Bill's Wild West Shows, Hollywood put in motion the hero-ification of the Cowboy, moving west and killing Indians being equated with moral, cultural, and racial progress. And while it is true that there were violent confrontations between White and Native Americans, they were neither as violent, as frequent or as Indian-instigated as portrayed in movies (O'Connor 1980). The

126 The Emma LaRocque Reader

"Western" tradition, which really began with sensationalized captivity narratives and has continued through pulp fiction and movies, was developed in part to address White American needs for a national culture (Pearce 1965). But the undercurrent to such cultural development was to justify White hegemony in the Americas (Jennings 1976).

Although mainstream Canadians have worked out (and are still working out) their trek west quite differently than Americans with respect to Aboriginal peoples, they have nonetheless espoused much of the western heroism and frontierism abundant in American history and popular culture. There is an intimate connection between racism and the Wild West/frontier thesis. In other words, Cowboy/Indian movies are one significant aspect of institutionalized racism.

There are serious conflictual situations between White and Native Canadians, and institutionalized racism is not an insignificant contributing factor. According to Canadian sociologist James Frideres, there is unmistakeable evidence which "reveals that racism widely distorts the attitudes toward Aboriginal people" (Frideres 1998, 10). Perhaps it is a "chicken-and-egg" dilemma, for it can be argued that distorted attitudes contribute to or entrench racism, and clearly, Cowboy/Indian movies widely distort the attitudes toward Aboriginal peoples. Such attitudes result in a domino effect of related attitudes: "[W]hether blatantly or covertly, most Canadians still believe that Aboriginals are inferior; as a result, these people believe that there is a sound, rational basis for discrimination against Aboriginals at both the individual and institutional level" (Frideres 1998, 10). Frideres highlights biased Canadian historical treatment of Native peoples as an institutionalized expression of racism: "To legitimize its power, the dominant groups must reconstruct social history whenever necessary ... today, most Canadians continue to associate 'savage' and 'heinous' behaviour with Canadian Aboriginals" (Frideres 1998, 12).

It is certainly not surprising that Euro-Canadians would associate "savage" with Native peoples given the constant exposure of this view from all major mainstream cultural institutions, including archival, historical, literary, and popular sources. In particular, the gross (and often graphic) misrepresentations of "the Indian" in the media and the marketplace, especially through the powerful medium of motion pictures, have affirmed and re-affirmed Euro-Canadian prejudices. The power of graphic presentation is incalculable. The impact technology has on us in its ability to bring two-dimensional material to 3-D is inestimable. Through movement, sound, and colour, the historical glorification of the European colonial enterprise, much of it already expressed in the cardboard comics and textbooks most of us Canadians grew up with, is made even more "real" through the experiencing of contemporary techniques of motion pictures. Looking at still photography is impressive enough; looking at John Ford's larger-than-life savages in the full splendour of technology's sound and fury is terrifyingly awesome.

There is also the power of repetition. Hilger, in *The American Indian in Film*, points out that "[t]he repetition of these techniques through each historical period is what really impresses the fictional Indian on the minds of audiences" (Hilger 1986, 4). "Westerns" are scripted tall tales in celluloid, but because Hollywood has bombarded the public with hundreds, if not thousands of Cowboy/Indian type movies, the image of the "Indian" as a crazed, bloodthirsty *"Wilder Mann"* terrorizing good and innocent white people has become more real in the minds of the public than any *real* Native peoples as human beings. What sticks in the collective mind is the theme of Indian savagism "inevitably" yielding to white civilization as it advances west (or to the frontier).

To be called a savage is to be called non-human. In the words of ethnohistorian Francis Jennings: "To call a man savage is to warrant his death and to leave him unknown and unmourned" (Jennings 1976, 12). Berkhofer traces "the image behind the terminology" to an ancient German legend of the *Wilder Mann*. Such a wild man "was a hairy, naked, club-wielding child of nature who existed halfway between humanity and animality," one who lived "a life of bestial self-fulfilment, directed by instinct, and ignorant of God and morality ... and degraded of origin" (Berkhofer 1978, 13). In any context, civilization means being more "human," and savagery less than human. As historian Olive Dickason explains, "to be savage meant to be living according to nature, in a manner 'closer to that of wild animals than to that of man.' The beast far outweighed the innocent" (Dickason 1992, 63–4).

For both Native and non-Native audiences, the accumulative effect of all this dehumanization, distortion, infantilization, and falsification of Aboriginal persons, histories, and cultures has been far-reaching. As noted above, when it comes to the Indian image, audiences cannot tell the difference between fantasy and reality. As Robert Berkhofer in *The White Man's Indian* (1978) has established, the "Indian" is a white man's invention, and is a classic example of the social construction of reality. This then has profound political, cultural, social, and even scholarly implications for Native/White relations. To the extent historians, novelists and Hollywood control and perpetuate the Wild West myth, Non-Native peoples remain conditioned to see through "stereotypic eyes" (Pakes 1985), that is, to see "the Indian" and not Native peoples. And the space between the imaginary concept "Indian" and the actual peoples who are Native, is, in the words of Daniel Francis, "The distance ...

128 The Emma LaRocque Reader

between fantasy and reality" (Francis 1992, 224). Native peoples remain stereotyped, objectified, and alienated.

Besides the fact that indigenous peoples of the Americas lost their lives in the millions (Jennings 1976), there are other long-lasting grave consequences here: children, both Native and Non-Native, internalize the White Man's heroic point of view. As most contemporary Native writers, fictionalists and non-fictionalists alike, have indicated, Native children can grow up confused and ashamed of their racial and cultural heritage (Campbell 1973; Adams 1975; LaRocque 1975; Culleton 1983; Armstrong 1985; Paul 1993). In the words of Métis historian and critic Howard Adams:

> I knew that whites were looking at me through their racial stereotypes ... it made me feel stripped of all humanity and decency, and left me with nothing but my Indianness, which at the time I did not value.... Not only did my sense of inferiority become inflamed, but I came to hate myself for the image I could see in their eyes. Everywhere white supremacy surrounded me. Even in solitary silence, I felt the word 'savage' deep in my soul. (Adams 1975, 16)

The Micmac poet Rita Joe has simply declared, "I am not/What they portray me/I am civilized" (Joe 1978, 10). The characterization of Native peoples as savage has not only caused pain and aggravation to Native peoples, but it continues to affect their political and social standing in society. Not only do they remain largely marginalized and poor, they continue to lose the ground of their cultural existence, their lands and resources. In no small way, this is so because Non-Native children, whose ways of seeing "Indians" have been informed by stereotypes, grow up to be Canadian adults in positions of influence. They can be teachers, historians, filmmakers, and novelists, or the judges and politicians who will and who have ruled against Aboriginal land rights or self-government on the Frontier/Wild West premise that "Indians" were only a handful of savages who "roamed" rather than "used" the "virgin" land. A contemporary case in point is the Supreme Court of British Columbia's 1991 ruling against the Gitskan and Wet'suwet'en peoples on old European biases. Quoting Thomas Hobbes, who in the eighteenth century imagined that the "natives" lived "nasty, brutish and short" lives, Chief Justice Allan McEachern ruled that Aboriginal peoples had been too savage to now qualify for land rights! He dismissed their testimonies regarding their indigenous relationship to the land as mere romanticization! Too savage or too noble, either way Aboriginal peoples are boxed in and censored. Although this ruling was overturned in 1997, on a number of fronts Canadian Native peoples continue to struggle with the Frontier/Wild West constructs in the Canadian courts – and most everywhere else in society.

No stone is left unturned in the reification of the colonial enterprise. In the United States of America, John Quincy Adams' rhetorical question, "What is the right of a huntsman to the forest of a 1000 miles over which he has accidentally ranged in quest of prey?" (Rogin 1975, 6), was and remains a classical note of self-exoneration in pursuit of Native lands. And now in the recent movie *Amistad* this same Indian-hating John Quincy Adams is being whitewashed as a freedom fighter for enslaved Africans! It is no exaggeration to say that White North American culture rests on the fantastic and obviously very powerful hero-ification of the White Man which is quintessentially expressed in the Frontier/Wild West cultural and constitutional productions.

Perhaps for non-Native producers of the Wild West myth, whether through sanctioned text or mass production, presenting "the Indian" as savage is so common as to appear unimagined or benign. However, given its impact on our perspectives and politics, we must raise questions about its longevity and its utility. Its very persistence must make us wonder what it is that this image (and its offshoots) serve. While its *raison d'être* is fairly transparent, namely, that the Ignoble Savage has served both justification and commercial purposes for the dominant culture, there is yet another aspect to the on-going misrepresentation of "the Indian."

Re-viewing the role assigned the "Indian" in the Wild West complex is not complete without some attention to the other half of the savage, the noble half. I am referring, of course, to the Noble Savage. This Hiawathian version has faded in and out of popularity throughout the last five centuries, depending on the political circumstances of the colonizers and the colonized. In my grade school years, I was introduced to Longfellow's *Hiawatha* through the colourful "Classics" comic books my mother gave to me. While Hiawatha's ability to talk to deer, Nanabozho, and assorted apparitions impressed me, it by no means compared to the intensity of the howling savage on screen. I saw and read a lot more of the frontiersmen's savage than I ever saw of the poetic Hiawatha. Overall, my generation of Native writers were exposed much less to the Noble Savage, although it has been steadily gaining in popularity since the "greening of America" movements of the 1960s. In fact, the Noble Savage construct has had and continues to have an extensive and powerful impact on our respective psyches and cultures, and merits its own study. Perhaps it is easier to see or understand how the plain old savage dehumanizes and impairs relationships

130   The Emma LaRocque Reader

between Native and non-Native peoples. But we should not underestimate the complex of difficulties the Noble Savage presents us. Being blurred with the landscape should not be taken as a compliment. There are many and layered issues involved. Here, I provide a brief assessment of its connection to Cowboys and Indians, particularly its role in the making of the authentic Indian. It is in the Noble Savage that contemporary White and Native generations locate their search for the authentic Indian.

Europeans and their descendants have always been looking for the authentic Indian. Besides looking for monsters, Europeans were also looking for the perfect primitive basking in primordial bliss. They found both, of course, because they expected and created both. The search for the authentic Indian goes back to Europe's primitivist tradition and has found its niche in the invention of the Noble Savage. Of course, Europeans and their American descendants had to first destroy the Ignoble Savage so that they could move into the Americas safely. And once "safely dead and historically past" (Berkhofer 1978, 90), the menacing savage or the *Wilder Mann* could be transformed into a more innocent undomesticated primitive living in proverbial harmony with nature, unconstrained by convention. The ennoblement of the wild man (or woman) depended on the extent to which he or she defended or died for the European. Longfellow's Hiawatha faded into the western sunset to make way for God's favoured son, the White Man. However, and unlike [Jean-Jacques] Rousseau's *bon sauvage*, White North America's Hiawatha was not a critic of society, as he represented cultural appropriation and affirmation for the colonizer's art. In other words, the Savage could become Noble only after its destruction, and what remained of "the Indian" could gain sympathy, but only if he remained the Vanishing Indian. As a Vanishing Indian he could become and has remained both a cultural marker and a cultural commodity.

In the 1800s, many painters and photographers, Edward Curtis among them, ensconced themselves into history by capturing "a record of their [Indian] culture before it died away" (Francis 1992, 53). "Capturing" meant inventing. People like Curtis and other well-known artists, such as George Catlin and Paul Kane, doctored their pictures to convey what they became famous for, images of Indians "unspoiled" by White culture. As Berkhofer points out, "Most romantic of all was the impression of the Indian as rapidly passing away before the onslaught of civilization" (Berkhofer 1978, 88). Creating an Indian unspoiled by contact, especially one who was passing from history, meant turning to a well-worn tradition, the Noble Savage. In effect, the artists recycled what they and their audiences wanted – and expected.

But despite centuries of expecting the "Indian" to vanish, the Indian has not. Nor have the *real* Native people. But the ever-vanishing romanticized "Indian" is now propagated as the only pure expression of Indianness, the only "authentic" Indian. And what is it that will mark a Native as authentic? Essentially, a layered but predictable configuration of "cultural difference" has emerged out of this process. Fused together as one are the largely stereotyped notions of Indian culture and "tradition," the ingredient that gives Indian culture authenticity. Apparently – and as can be gleaned from a variety of schools, programmes, and the arts – the marks of cultural authenticity revolve around certain notions of customs, legends, linguistics, ceremonies, and the environment. And central to this is the current sacralization of elders, whose function it is to impart wisdom and advance "healing" through spirituality and "forgiveness." One can take from this that political action or decolonization is discouraged. There are even certain expectations about physical appearance, consisting usually of chiselled cheeks, leathery brown face, long, flowing or braided hair complete with material objects commonly associated as "Indian." In other words, Hiawatha has become the authentic Indian.

But "authenticity" in legendary form exacts a deadly price, for the Noble Savage can exist only in a timeless vacuum. If the Indian did not vanish physically, he had to remain culturally and chronologically motionless. As such, he can only be primitive, with "traditions" and "traits," rather than fully human with a contemporary culture or history. The moment the Indian steps out of timelessness, that is, comes into focus as a real cultural or historical figure, he or she is deemed assimilated or non-Indian. As Francis explains, "Indians were defined in relation to the past and in contradistinction to White society. To the degree that they changed, they were perceived to become less Indian" (Francis 1992, 39). Not uncoincidentally, most popular productions continue to portray the caricatured Plains Indian of the 1800s; rarely do we see any convincing treatment of contemporary and diverse Aboriginal life. While westerners have assumed their culture is dynamic and endlessly progressive, they have invented a Native whose culture is moribund and whose history is fixed. In a certain sense, in being relegated to a primitive past, the Indian is perpetually vanishing. The dominant culture requires a Vanishing Indian, for as the Cowboy expression goes, "the only good Indian is a dead Indian" (Brown 1970, 166).

To say the least, the socio-cultural effects and political ramifications of this version of the ever-dying but the only "real" Indian are chilling – and powerful. They leave "natives" culturally embalmed and irrelevant, and they certainly leave each Aboriginal generation vulnerable to

132   The Emma LaRocque Reader

the twists and turns of colonial machinations. Even a famous poet like
Pauline Johnson, a Mohawk/English, essentially Victorian "lady," was
forced to assume an Indian Princess persona during her poetry recitations. Her British-Canadian audience demanded that the "Indian," if
alive, must remain a cultural curio. Nor was this limited to performers
or individuals. In 1899, at Treaty Number Eight negotiations, Charles
Mair, poet and secretary to the Half-Breed Scrip Commission, expressed
surprise and dismay to find "commonplace men" instead of "the pic-
turesque Red Man" (Francis 1992, 4). Mair wrote:

> One was prepared, in this wild region of forest, to behold some savage
> types of men; indeed, I craved to renew the vanished scenes of old. But
> alas! One beheld, instead, men with well-washed unpainted faces, and
> combed and common hair; men in suits of ordinary store-clothes.... One
> felt disappointed, even defrauded. (Francis 1992, 3–4)

We continue to feel the pressure of being judged against the White
Man's "authentic" Indian. There is tremendous pressure today for all
Native artists and intellectuals, including Native scholars and scholarship, not only to produce elder-validated and "culturally different"
material, but even to look authentic and different! It is not surprising we continue to have "warriors," shamans, and Indian princesses.
But what of those of us who cannot, or will not present ourselves in
stereotypical ways? As a frequent guest lecturer, I have seen looks
of confusion or disappointment in my hosts' faces at both national
and international Aboriginal events. Breaking stereotypes, however
inadvertently, can be an entertaining experience. A number of Native
writers have in fact developed satirical works around this experience
(Johnston 1978; Warrior 1992; Taylor 1992; Kane 1992). But non-Native
disappointment can have more serious implications. Not only might
we lose our audiences, but perhaps even opportunities in various government or university positions or even in Native organizations. It
is not an uncommon experience for contemporary Native peoples to
be judged as especially inferior to the Noble Savage ideal (Doxtator
1992, 13), an ideal which has been internalized by the colonizer and
colonized alike.

Not unlike the plain old savage, the Noble Savage has engendered
tension between fantasy and reality. But noble or not, one is as dead and
unreal as the other. Yet, it is obvious that each new generation needs an
"authentic Indian"; hence, the survivability of the Noble Savage. Even
plastic shamans and imposters such as Grey Owl continue to fascinate
both Native and White audiences. The crux of the matter may lie in the

Urban Cowboys' (and now the Urban Indians') needs for an authentic Indian, although for different reasons. If the Wild West Cowboy needed the Ignoble Savage, the Urban Cowboy needs the Noble Savage to authenticate his (or her) place on the American landscape. The Cowboy's need, as has been suggested by many writers and scholars, comes out of a complex of guilt, rationalization, and a search for an authentic White North American culture. And however misguided they are by the image industry, many descendants of the colonial enterprise do also have a genuine interest in Aboriginal peoples and cultures. Fed by a concern for the quality of life in our society, such peoples believe that the indigenous valuation for balance between humans and the environment would benefit an over-industrialized planet. Hopefully, this concern includes the will for justice and goes beyond the proverbial use of the Indian as prop for the conscience of a morally lethargic corporate world.

For the Urban Indian, the need for the authentic Indian is indicative of the identity crisis Aboriginal peoples now face. Such a crisis is to be expected, since Native identity has been constricted to romanticized nature/religion and consigned forever to the past. How can contemporary generations make sense of their world or feel secure in their choices? Centuries of mixing up ideas of an authentic Indian culture with the primitive past, and now feeling the political pressure to remain culturally "different," that is, unlike the Whites, can only result in bewilderment and guilt for Native youth. While other groups, including the English and the French, treat themselves as the norm and any cultural change as normal, Natives face charges of assimilation or imitation. Given the contradictory and culture-stultifying messages conveyed in society, it is not surprising that the Urban Indian might hang on to the identity of the Noble Savage to authenticate his/her place in contemporary culture.

Of course, I am not suggesting Native people, rural or urban, are bereft of culture, traditions, or authenticity. But obviously, "authenticity," both as a stereotype and an imposition, is unacceptable. Aboriginal peoples are normal human beings who must have the right to address misrepresentations, have some control over the images being produced, and the right to live, define, and determine their everyday lives. And to reiterate a point I began to make in an earlier work (LaRocque 1975), Aboriginal cultures are not cultures of the past, they are as inherently dynamic as anyone else's cultures. It is true, of course, that Cowboyism has arrested Aboriginal cultural development, but it is just as true that it has not entirely erased it from the North American landscape. It is as important to make a distinction between politics, culture, and

134 The Emma LaRocque Reader

stereotypes as it is to acknowledge the possibilities of cultural elasticity, adaptability, and political agency.

But the Wild West machine does persist and constantly puts us in a reactive situation. How might we respond beyond the obviously self-destructive modes of confrontation or co-option? Is there ever any way to have the Cowboys and Indians come to terms with each other without violence or gross commercialization? What would it mean? Can we redefine Cowboys and Indians? Can we take seriously the facts of change in both divides? Surely, we have all changed since the invention of the ol' dusters. Can we follow up on these changes with some name changes? Is there any reason to continue with signposts such as Ft. Whoop-Up, Indian Head or Squaw Valley? For that matter, is there any reason to revive Wild West themes? Recently, in July 2000, I was quite astonished to see a billboard calling for Indian actors to act in a re-staging of the Buffalo Bill's Wild West Show in Paris! I am not sure what got my attention more, the Parisian audacity or the fact the ad was posted in an Alberta reserve community hall.

Cowboys and Indians might have more in common than previously believed! After five hundred years, I suppose this should not be so surprising! Notwithstanding the political differences (or the post-colonial caution re: "common humanity"), the irony is that today, Cowboys and Indians can look and behave a lot alike. There are, of course, cultural differences, but they have been exaggerated by political rifts; further, the differences do not preclude shared humanity or even similar lifestyles. And what is more, in *Legends of our Times: Native Cowboy Life*, Baillargeon and Tepper (1998) present Native peoples of the plains and plateau as the first cowboys of North America. They are not referring to the Wild West type, but to a ranching lifestyle which does involve a realistically based love for land, horses and riding, and the outdoors. City slickers perhaps envy this tough but rewarding way of life.

But of course, and alas, there is that other Cowboy, the Wild West Cowboy With Guns…. And there is that other Indian, the White Man's creation, that Savage Indian. These are the Cowboy and Indians we have to confront. And since the Noble Savage is an integral part of the Cowboy/Indian complex, we must resist internalizing this too. Native intellectuals face a daunting task. The burden of confrontation is well expressed by McMaster and Martin, editors of *Indigena*: "To be an Aboriginal person, to identify with an indigenous heritage in these late colonial times, requires a life of reflection, critique, persistence and struggle" (McMaster and Martin 1992, 11). But on whom does the onus fall in confronting Cowboys and Indians? Are confrontation or co-option the only possible responses? Do Native artists and intellectuals always have to be looking in from the outside? What do we do when Native actors play the Indians? What do we do when we just want to have fun too – are we the only ones to bear the so-serious burden of the real Cowboy/Indian history? Can we have fun without telling lies? Can we have fun without falsifying, stereotyping or in any way perpetuating the colonial origins of the Cowboy/Indian complex?

Maybe a little, the fun is trickling in. I always thought *McLintock* was a hilarious movie! There is the French-made cartoon *Lucky Luke and Daisy Town*. And there is Graham Greene in *Maverick*. And we're even starting to sing a song about John Wayne's teeth (*Smoke Signals*) – maybe just a little we are tumbling the weeds, we are sifting the sands …

To me what is most important is to come to grips with both colonial history and contemporary life. As responsible members of contemporary society our task is to safeguard the human rights and human resources of all peoples, certainly for Aboriginal peoples as specifically situated by themselves. As scholars our task today is to ensure we tell the truth about the original Cowboy/Indian encounter so that we will not repeat ourselves. As artists our task is to imagine, to inspire, to create, to cross and challenge the borders without having to over-romanticize ourselves. But the moral challenge is this: how might Canadians most constructively expand the meaning of the West in these late colonial times? Might Canadians do so in the spirit of Métis visionary Louis Riel, whose dream it was that the West, in parts, become the haven for the oppressed of the world? But of course, it must first become the homeland for the well-being and identity of First Nation and Métis peoples. This may be the only way to bring meaning and sense into a Plains Cree-Métis child's jangling experience of Cowboys and Indians.

2006

Sweeping

I read the books
I saw the looks
I stooped to the downward
                          sweep

of Canada's eye
               lids

cast in lead
cast in red
          neck

But inside my head
I burst with dreams
In my belly
I roared
In my throat
I chanted
In the wombs of my mind
I made love
with words and earth.

In the beginning was the word
and the new   story
was the earth
and the new   earth
was image   nation.

With sweetgrass I

      up
swept
          wards
the down
with sage I
swallowed
              lids
the leaded eye

2006

Sources of Inspiration: The Birth of "For the Love of Words": Aboriginal Writers of Canada[1]

As early as the late 1970s, when I first began teaching the Canadian Native Literature course in what was then the quite new Department of Native Studies at the University of Manitoba, I started thinking of a conference that would celebrate Aboriginal peoples' "love of words." Even then and even in works of non-fiction it was difficult to miss the earlier First Nation and Métis writers' inventive use of the English language. However, I noticed with some concern that what little critical attention was given Aboriginal literatures – including poetry, short stories, or other creative writing – was primarily focussed on personal tragedy, social issues, or anthropology.

Over the last thirty years there has been exciting growth in both Aboriginal writing and the critical study of it. But again, critical

---

1 This was originally written as an afterword to a conference. Renate Eigenbrod and Jennifer Andrews (2006) explain the origins of the event: "Held in the fall of 2004 in Winnipeg, with the generous support of the University of Manitoba, the Social Sciences and Humanities Research Council, and The Canada Council for the Arts, "'For the Love of Words': Aboriginal Writers of Canada" was a landmark conference. Inspired by Emma LaRocque's vision, "For the Love of Words" brought together Native and non-Native scholars and Aboriginal writers/community activists for an intensive three-day gathering that combined creative readings, plenary speeches, and academic sessions examining the significance of language in the context of Native Canadian writing. It was organized by Emma LaRocque in collaboration with Renate Eigenbrod, her colleague in the Department of Native Studies (with much appreciated help from Warren Cariou, Department of English, and Native Studies graduate student Karen Froman). The sharp focus and congenial atmosphere of the conference led to a great deal of stimulating discussion and lively debate within sessions and readings – and just as intensively over morning coffee, lunch, or dinner – about the benefits and limitations of traditional approaches to Native literature and other possible frameworks for expanding and reassessing the goals of Native Studies, particularly through a closer examination of Aboriginal literary aesthetics."

treatment has largely ignored the stylized quality in Native writing, focussing instead on culture and postcolonial politics. Given our colonial history, this is perhaps inevitable. Nonetheless, as I point out in my opening address (LaRocque 2006), even in resistance there is much beauty, grace, and complexity in Aboriginal literatures. A love of words kneaded skilfully is intrinsic to Aboriginal cultures, and it is important that this is not only appreciated but given the attention it deserves in contemporary critical contexts.

I grew up in Cree with Wehsakehcha, that chameleon teaser of the human condition. Wehsakehcha stories were not merely "told" or anthropologically recounted. Nor were they intended to be explicitly or necessarily functional or didactic. That would be too mundane. At least for my mother and grandmother, who dramatized Wehsakehcha into my heart. There was animation, movement, song, and play with words. There was a sense of pure joy in the performative wording of metaphors, similes, and other tropes. Telling "stories" was a highly crafted art for the enjoyment of words – and it was the beginning of my long-held dream for this historic conference.

The objectives of the conference, "'For the Love of Words': Aboriginal Writers of Canada," was to bring together scholars and writers to explore the qualitative richness and fluidity of oral traditions and contemporary productions. It was an inspiring experience, and the participants brought such depth, illumination, and artistic and intellectual energy to the conference that we all felt a special issue based on the conference theme should be published. I know that what is "lived" in a gathering is quite different from what is written on paper. Still, I could not help but notice that in many of the papers given, the presenters avoided dealing with the artistic merits of the texts they were examining, and instead emphasized sociopolitical realities as well as cultural information, all of which is of course integral to Aboriginal experience. While all this generated stimulating discussions and lively debates around the implications of resistance aesthetics, I did find myself thinking that perhaps we could have another conference where we could further explore ways in which we can analyze and theorize imagination, beauty, and play of words, which is the stuff of Aboriginal reflection, satire, novels, novellas, plays, and poetry. And the stuff of Wehsakehcha. The challenge now is for all of us to find and/or to translate such a "love of words" in/to English.

2007

Métis and Feminist: Ethical Reflections on Feminism, Human Rights and Decolonization

To speak or write on matters of human rights for Aboriginal peoples, especially for Aboriginal women, is to be confronted with extraordinary challenges, in part because there are so many issues to address. I have struggled with what issues to foreground with respect to Aboriginal women and feminism, reviewing a menu of socio-political items such as poverty, racism/sexism, violence and the culturalization of violence, the criminal justice system, self-government, exclusions of Aboriginal women in constitutional processes and so forth. Yet, one feels compelled to offer a more positive portrait of the ways in which Aboriginal women live: as victims of colonization and patriarchy, yet as activists and agents in their lives; as oppressed, yet as fighters and survivors; and as among the most stereotyped, dehumanized and objectified of women, yet as the strong, gracious and determined women that they are. I also wondered whether I should just concentrate on Métis Nation women as their histories and contemporary concerns are frequently submerged, if not erased, under the umbrella terms and treatment of Aboriginal women, which almost always means dealing exclusively with status Indian issues.

Perhaps a way to bring together some of these wide-ranging concerns is to offer reflections on my engagement with feminism as a scholar and educator, a writer and social critic, a human rights advocate and most pertinently, as a Métis woman who grew up with all the contradictions and burdens of a community wracked with the colonial situation, and in a society inured to this situation.

I am aware that many, perhaps even the majority of, status Indian and Métis women do not identify with or readily use the label "feminist." Joyce Green has observed that:

> "Feminist identification and feminist analysis [are] weak within Aboriginal communities and organizations, and [are] not widespread among individual

women. Aboriginal women have been urged to identify as Aboriginal, in the context of the domination and exploitation by the newcomer community, to the exclusion of identification as women with women across cultures, and with the experience of exploitation and domination by men within Aboriginal communities" (1993, 111).

Reasons for this are complex and include political, historical, cultural and socio-economic factors as well as some misunderstanding about feminism. For some Aboriginal women, such misunderstanding reflects their disadvantaged socio-economic position and marginalization, which, among other things, deprives them of attaining adequate education. But there are also Native women intellectuals who charge white feminism with having little or no understanding of colonial history, Aboriginal peoples or race oppression (Stevenson 1993; Monture-Angus 1995; Ouellette 2002).

Given that feminism is neither well-understood nor readily received by many Aboriginal women, it is useful to offer some basic assumptions, definitions and understandings about feminism. Josephine Donovan writes that "historical and anthropological studies reveal" four "determinant structures under which women, unlike men, have nearly universally existed" (1990, 172). I find her concise overview of these structures helpful:

> First and foremost, women have experienced political oppression.... Second, nearly everywhere and in nearly every period, women have been assigned to the domestic sphere.... Third, women's historical economic function has been production for use, not production for exchange.... Fourth, women experience significant physical events that are different from men's. (1990, 172–3)

Is this also true for Aboriginal women? Without going into all the possible nuances and exceptions to the rule, and taking somewhat of a different direction from Donovan, I have no hesitation in accepting that such determinant structures are most definitely present in the lives of the majority of Aboriginal women. While there are some notable exceptions in history, such as some semi matriarchal-oriented societies among Indigenous peoples, and while we can pinpoint colonization as the major factor in our present conditions, it remains true that we currently live under structures that proscribe or marginalize our lives. Aboriginal women experience political oppression in a number of ways. Our alienation from constitutional processes and from positions of leadership in white and Native male-dominated institutions are evidence of this. Aboriginal women have not enjoyed automatic inclusion or leadership roles in the public sphere of either Canadian society or in the upper echelons of national Aboriginal political organizations. Nor have they enjoyed equal treatment in Canadian legislation or in Aboriginal governance. They continue to face discrimination in a wide spectrum of social and economic settings. Even in areas of religion or spirituality, Aboriginal women's roles are circumscribed by church doctrines or by some renderings of Aboriginal traditions. Women are politically oppressed when their roles and standing in the political and cultural life of their societies are restricted when compared to men.

While much has been made of "balance" between genders in Aboriginal traditions, there is overwhelming evidence that, by and large, Aboriginal women's roles have been confined to the domestic sphere. As in the area of domestic roles, Donovan explains that women have "been consigned to the domestic sphere and to domestic duties – including child-rearing or mothering – throughout recorded history" (1990, 172). We also need to ask what is maybe meant by balance. Does the rhetoric of "balance" necessarily or automatically mean gender equality? It could merely mean that male and female roles are to be interdependent or complementary but from within gender-specified stations. The problem is in the definition of the roles. For instance, I have heard a male elder baldly declare that "man is the law, and woman is to serve the man and to nurture the family." Here, the elder is equating balance not with gender equality but with maintaining the status quo, that men maintain their over-arching dominance in the family, the stuff of patriarchy. "Balance" then becomes a new buzzword for keeping women to domestic and nurturing roles. I am sure not all people who promote balance between genders mean to say that women's roles should be restricted to home life. However, it does remain that for many, idealization of nurturing/motherhood has been reified and has gained political currency within nationalist and cultural difference discourses. I come back to this later.

Concerning women's economic function, I would be careful – as is Donovan – not to apply western-based economic ideas onto pre-industrial societies, and in our case, original Indigenous societies. Concepts such as "production for use" versus "production for exchange" may not be applicable to land-based, non-capitalist cultures. Living off the land does tend to encourage greater flexibility in gender/labour roles. However, we can see that Aboriginal women's gender roles, including economic roles, became more restricted with the arrival of European missionaries, "explorers" and fur traders. Separation between home (domestic) life and work (productive) life (the public/private dichotomy identified by feminist analysis) certainly increased. The fur traders, for example, encouraged male labour and travel, which of course meant that women were left to attend to child-rearing and other family

142 The Emma LaRocque Reader

and home demands for much longer periods than was customary. Missionaries twisted such gender role and economic changes into moral mandates. Within a few years of Confederation in 1867, the Canadian government legislated Indian status/non-status identity, rights and gender roles along patriarchal lines.

Donovan invokes "significant physical events that are different from men's," citing menstruation, childbirth and breastfeeding as examples, and uses these differences as a springboard towards formulating a particularly female epistemology and ethic (1990, 173). Donovan does not name sexuality or sexual violence here. However, Aboriginal women need to consider violence as a significant physical event (or series of events) as Aboriginal females of all ages continue to suffer from child abuse, wife battering, sexual assault and murder in epidemic proportions. As Patricia Monture-Angus explains: "It is likely Aboriginal women experience violence in their lives with greater frequency than any other collective of women in Canadian society"; further, that "violence is not a mere incident in the lives of Aboriginal women" (1995, 170).

Deploying Donovan's approach, then, we can see that Aboriginal women's experiences and socio-political positions in both Native and white communities fall within these structural determinants. Thus, we cannot remove Aboriginal women's concerns from other women's concerns for we too live under over-arching male-dominated conditions both as Canadian citizens and Aboriginal people. And although we must be sensitive to racial, cultural or economic differences, we can address Aboriginal women's multiple layers of oppressions from a feminist perspective.

Feminism

What then is "Feminism"? I understand feminism as a struggle to end sexism and gender-based inequality in society. "Feminism ... is comprised of the well-founded belief that girls and women are legally, politically and socially disadvantaged on the grounds of their sex; the ethical stance that this oppression is morally wrong; and the pragmatic commitment to ending injustice to all female human beings" (Overall 1998, 15).

bell hooks has a more comprehensive definition:

> Feminism is the struggle to end sexist oppression. Its aim is not to benefit any specific group of women, any particular race or class of women. It does not privilege women over men. It has the power to transform in a meaningful way all our lives. Most importantly, feminism is neither a lifestyle nor a ready-made identity or role one can step in to. (1994, 24)

Feminism, then, does not belong to any particular group, and those who understand and practise this social idea of ending gender inequality and injustice are feminist. In this sense, men and women of all backgrounds can be feminists, and feminists should be among our best allies, and many are. Aboriginal writers, artists, scholars and community activists resisting our dehumanization and our dispossession are doing work very similar to feminist principles and objectives. Feminist and Aboriginal resistance entails both deconstruction and reconstruction. Aboriginal, non-Aboriginal, male and female feminists will especially examine theories, portrayals, political positions or social treatments of Aboriginal women. Feminism provides us with theoretical tools with which we can analyze historical realities such as patriarchy. Feminism is not so much complaining about one particular man, event or even piece of legislation (i.e., the *Indian Act*); rather, feminism is an analysis of how cultural, political and social systems work to privilege men and disadvantage women. Feminism has an ethical component in that feminist analysis interrogates, confronts and seeks to transform those realities that compromise women's well-being and human rights.

Being Métis

Given the seemingly innocuous and even grand principles and objectives for human rights embedded in feminism, I have often been surprised, at times even startled, at the negative reactions to this concept. Because the labels "feminist" or "feminism" carry such a negative or unclear meaning for many women, perhaps it is best not to fixate on terminology or on oppositional politics but rather to begin by trying to find what is important to us as Aboriginal women. Here I outline what is important to me with the inference that what is important to me may or ought also be important to other women.

I do not come from any racially or economically equal, much less privileged, background.[1] The Métis in my community have been written up from an urban-centric bias as "bush people" living in "isolated" or "remote Indian" communities along a railroad line in northeastern Alberta (Garvin 1992). Although we spoke Plains Cree (with Michif) and lived off the land, legally we were/are not status Indians and so never lived on reserves. We were/are Métis but never lived in the

---

1 As part of my resistance scholarship theory, I have refused to stand aloof from some of my research and published works, and accordingly locate some family or community contexts. For more biographical information see chapter "Tides, Towns and Trains."

144 The Emma LaRocque Reader

Alberta Métis Settlements, or "Colonies" as they were once called. We knew ourselves as Apeetowgusanuk (or "half-sons" in Cree) who were descended from both the Red River Métis and locally originated Métis[2] communities with deep kinship connections to both status and non-status Indian peoples. And although Métis do originate from the early fur trade era of First Nations and European peoples, both my maternal and paternal family histories are grounded in Métis Nation lineage with no remembrance of or relational ties with non-Aboriginal people. My parents, aunts and uncles all spoke of "scrip"[3] and how Apeetowgusanuk lost and were continuing to lose beloved domains of lands either through scrip or simply through urban, industrial and farming encroachments. Legally, we did not own any land but in those years we could still definitely live on, from and with the land, for morally, it was our land.[4] My grandparents occupied, used and loved this land long before Confederation, and my father was born before Alberta became a province.

My parents' generation made a living from the many resources of the land, including hunting and trapping, as well as from wage labour, wherever such could be found. And although most Apeetowgusanuk were hard-working, proudly independent, or Ootayemsuak peoples, they/we were suffering from unimaginable poverty and racism, complete with layers and waves of both legal and social dispossession.

Among the multiple sites of dispossession, public schooling contributed significantly to my generation's sense of cultural dislocation and intellectual alienation. Not only did schooling aim to extract us from our mother language and our motherland with its particular western ethos, it failed to teach us basic classroom reading and writing skills, thereby failing to prepare us for the new brave world of industrialization/

---

2 Some capitalize "Métis" to indicate those who originate from the Red River in order to make distinctions from other métis who do not have Red River lineage. See Peterson and Brown (1985).

3 Between 1870 and 1900, the federal government issued a series of tickets with monetary or land value (scrip) to "Halfbreed Heads of Families" as a form of recognizing Métis rights to land. However, in large part, the Métis were divested of the scrips by speculators, fraud, government legislation and cultural processes alien to them (see RCAP 1996).

4 I am grateful to my younger brother, who has remained on our original land area but like my father before him, can only lease the land as we have never had resources to purchase this land. But if there was any justice for Métis people the governments should simply transfer ownership to those Métis families who have loved and tended specific lands – and continue to do so – long before Confederation.

Métis and Feminist

urbanization, even as this world was fast overtaking us, especially after World War II. Undergirding this pedagogy was the colonialist version of history and the "National Dream," all equated with "progress." Not surprisingly, the vast majority of Métis students left school as fast as they could do so legally. In 1971, the average grade level for Métis people in Alberta was four. This and more have left many people of my generation and their children in a socio-cultural vacuum. This is the direct and continuing legacy of colonization, and it is the sociological after-effects of this colonial earthquake that has dislocated and disoriented many of our youth.

Two things have always followed me from my early years: on one hand, our richly woven cultural life based on our blended land and railroad line ways, textured with our Métized (my coin) Cree oral literature, language and worldview; and on the other hand, our extreme poverty and alienation from the financial and material privileges of mainstream Canada. I do not speak of poverty in any abstract sense. Depending on seasons (trapping or non-trapping), wage-labour employment or non-employment, we could also go without much food for months, for years. My parents typically struggled to outfit us with adequate or socially acceptable clothing, lunches and other school supplies during school terms. Poverty in my family and community translated into social warfare on our bodies. As virtually penniless people of the land who spoke only Cree and often lived miles away from town, we had minimal access to doctors or hospitals throughout the 1900s, but most relevant for my generation, in the 1940s–70s. Consequently, many people died, often from tuberculosis or other diseases. Many of my relatives were sent away to sanitoriums due to TB, among them, my older sister and brother. Some came back in coffins. We were lucky: my older brother and sister survived and came home. Some children were never returned from hospitals, and those who were orphaned (but were taken care of within extended kinship systems) were often confiscated by state welfare agencies. The now infamous "sixties scoop," social welfare systems taking children away from Native families, was also practised on northern Métis communities. Those who survived were left with bewilderment and broken hearts along with a wide array of medical or social problems. Some individuals and some families increasingly displayed fragmentation, depression, alcohol abuse, anger and violence.

Yet, remarkably, numerous Métis individuals and families kept body and soul together, and I hasten to add, many men including my father did not take to violence under any circumstances. In my home there was no physical violence (except for the rare disciplinary willow lashings from my mother); as a rule, I grew up safe and secure inside our home.

146   The Emma LaRocque Reader

But my mother (1918–1981) did not grow up so safe. Somewhere, during the Depression, my maternal grandfather had been dispossessed of his scrip, his store, his land and dairy farm, uprooting his large family. Apparently, he took to drinking and family violence. Overnight my mother's young life had become one of abject poverty, and she and her sisters suffered the most immediate consequences. As part of making ends meet, my grandfather pushed his many daughters out of the home as soon as they became "of age." In a patriarchal world, they were left to find men who could take care of them.

I cannot say whether my grandfather's treatment of his daughters was typical of Métis attitudes of those times but I can say that patriarchy did not end with my grandfather. The Métis community of my generation was by no means free from patriarchal notions and practises. Take the name we had for ourselves: Apeetowgusanuk, or "half-son." Why not "half-daughters"? In my own family, all the men got two given names, and all the women had one name. This practise goes back to my grandparents and great grandparents. There was also the typical double standard about male and female sexual behaviour. To put it in the vernacular, men could "run around," women could not. If women exercised sexual freedom they could expect censorship. In the Roman Catholic Church, boys could assist priests in the service, girls could not. In our home, however, my mother, who integrated Cree Métis traditions with Roman Catholic rituals, assumed spiritual leadership. She also led the way in many of our family decisions and activities. Although my own parents allowed the girls as much freedom of expression as the boys, I do recall one incident that indicated they had been much influenced by male-favoured thinking. When I was quite young I was told by my mother not to walk over my father's and brothers' trapping/hunting supplies and preparations. I immediately asked why not? She explained that it would bring bad luck to their trapping/hunting. I do not remember her answer, if any, to my next "why?" but I called on natural justice – if my brothers could walk over them, so could I. I was left to my youthful logic but the message was disturbing: girls are contaminated, girls bring bad luck and girls can't do all the things boys can, simply because they are girls. I am aware that today people attach spiritual power to menstrual taboos, but I was premenstrual, indicating that this taboo reflected wider and deeper gender biases and could be generalized at will.

To me all this problematizes human customs that are biology-linked. World-wide, women and girls suffer horrific mutilations, so-called "honour killings" within families, as well as extreme confinements, which the international post-colonial community has largely tolerated

Métis and Feminist 147

in deference to nationalisms, cross-culturalism or tradition. Given our scientific knowledge today,[5] it seems to me we should ask whether any biology-based restrictions, even if spiritualized, are benign. Of course, I am raising normative questions, unlike my parents who tended to let things be for they were raised in an ethic of non-interference.[6] I am of a different generation – I marvel and am often concerned at the power tradition has over human beings. Yet, my mom was by no means sanguine about traditions that impacted her more directly.

Even though my mom was a remarkably resourceful woman who took exceptional care of us, she was by no means a happy homemaker. She most definitely did not romanticize motherhood; if anything, she resented the fact that responsibility fell on her to do the major portion of child-rearing and other home-related duties. This is all the more interesting because my amiable father, unlike many other fathers, assisted with many of the household chores, such as cooking, making our lunches for school and so forth, whenever he was home. Conversely, my mother enjoyed working outside alongside my dad. My mom was as free to trap and do many other so-called masculine-assigned tasks as my father was free to work in the home. Yet the key difference for my mom lay in the fact my father had a choice concerning childcare and kitchen work whereas my mother did not. And she really had no other choice. Although highly gifted and creative, my mom, along with the vast majority of other Métis women of her generation (and even my older sisters' generation), never had any opportunity to go to school or to develop her many gifts, much less to have a career or even get a job. So my mom lived with the frustration of remaining financially dependent on my father – something she viewed as an affront to her dignity.

Poverty also sets up social conditions that facilitate violence against women. In my mother's generation, white males, including police and priests, attacked Native women because they knew the women were in no position to bring them to justice. Similarly, home-grown predators in

---

5 It is theorized that most biology-linked customs that tend to injure or constrict females in "traditional" societies were created in pre-scientific eras when people did not understand bodily functions and so tended to mystify them. It is interesting, however, that so many such customs were invented to circumscribe women more than men.

6 There is much beauty to this ethic as it facilitates tolerance for difference, among other things. But ethically it does have its limitations for many social evils such as slavery, which existed because it was tolerated by society. Similarly, sexism flourishes because it is tolerated. What should we tolerate and to what extent?

148 The Emma LaRocque Reader

our communities targeted the most defenceless because they too knew they could get away with it. Generally, many women in our area were bullied, battered or assaulted. Aboriginal women's relocations to urban centres is in part a result of such poverty and violence.

Previously, I have addressed the topic of violence against women within Native communities (see chapter "Violence in Aboriginal Communities," LaRocque 1997). I have tried to place this troubling issue in the context of colonialism, yet at the same time, have emphasized that for many reasons, male violence cannot be fully explained by social or political conditions. In other words, neither colonization nor poverty explains everything about why or how Native men and boys (and societies) may assume sexist attitudes or mysogynistic behaviours. This point has to be emphasized because male violence continues to be much tolerated, explained or virtually absolved by many women of colour, including Aboriginal women, usually in defence of cultural difference, community loyalties or nationalist agendas, or out of reaction to white feminist critiques. I am concerned too that sexual violence, in particular, is often treated as only one of many colonial-generated problems that we face. But as numerous studies show, this is no ordinary problem. Sexual violence devastates human dignity and freedom and rips apart the lives of victims, their families, kinships and other crucial community seams, and when it is internal such violence is even more severe and life-lasting (Shkilnyk 1977). As far back as humans have existed this crime against humanity has existed and remains global in scope and runs across all cultures and classes, obviously requiring much greater analysis and confrontation than it has received.

Clearly, poverty is a social evil that steals from poor people a quality of life each Canadian citizen should have the right to expect. Poverty severely compromises the physical, cultural and psychological well-being of children, women and men, but it is the case that the most defenceless, usually women, children, the disabled and the elderly, often bear the greatest burdens. These are issues that centrally concern women who most certainly have a great stake in working towards a society in which every citizen has access to fundamental resources for a safe and decent quality of life. Indeed, this should be a fundamental human right in our world. At the very least, this must mean ending poverty and violence.

Criticism and Feminism

On a philosophical level, freedom to choose is fundamental to our humanity. It is theorized (Freire 1970; Puxley 1977) that what makes us human is our capacity to make choices, which in turn, gives us moral agency. This is why colonization or any other form of coercion is a form of dehumanization. The human need and the human right to be able to have and to make choices, then, is an act of humanization. The freedom, the means or the capacity to make choices is really what self-determination is all about. Although the international community recognizes self-determination as a basic human right, all too often the concept of self-determination is applied only to cultural, ethnic or political forms and movements. But self-determination cannot be limited to constitutions, cultures or collectivities; it must be extended to individuals. Self-determination must mean that all individuals – whether they are under a sovereign Indigenous nation or not – have a basic right to a certain quality of life, free from the violence of colonialism, racism/sexism and poverty, as well as from the violence of other humans, even if these other humans are one's people, or even one's relations, or are themselves suffering from colonial conditions. For multiple reasons, Aboriginal women have the greatest stake in self-determination, both as part of a people struggling to decolonize and as individuals struggling to enjoy basic human rights.

Self-determination must also mean intellectual freedom. I turn to this issue from the context of my work in Native studies for four decades now. Many of us in Native studies have made a living deconstructing the Euro-Canadian master narrative with its canons and ideologies; but we must also have the right to exercise our analytical skills and training in the service of advancing Aboriginal scholarship and humanity. We must maintain our freedoms to practise our scholarship. I emphasize intellectual and academic freedom because as feminist scholars or professors, we face political problems in pedagogical settings. I used to teach what I thought was a fairly benign seminar on Native women. I noticed that students responded well to history or information on the social conditions confronting Aboriginal women. However, when I presented them with literature or thinking that was remotely "feminist," I was greeted with silence. Interestingly, my student numbers from this course started dwindling; I do not know whether or not this was the result of an organized effort, but I certainly received the message that any critical reflection on the place of Aboriginal women in Aboriginal communities was not open for discussion. I was, on one hand, chided by a Native male student for "airing our dirty laundry in public," and on the other, I was labelled and psychologized by white students, especially those who were unhappy about their marks. These are two tactics used to discredit Aboriginal and feminist analyses.

I am painfully aware that social and political realities place Native academics in unusual circumstances. In the first place, we are still a very small community, making it difficult to treat each other's works critically. I feel this pressure with this chapter! Moreover, there seems to be an unstated expectation that women not criticize women, or that Native scholars not criticize Native scholars. This is unfortunate because it detracts from the important theoretical work that needs to be done, and it hampers intellectual vibrancy. Aboriginal scholars walk a tightrope between keeping a wary eye on western-defined canons and negotiating cultural and/or community interests. Of course, cultural issues are urgently important to contemporary Native peoples. Issues of cultural, social or political urgency can, however, present conflicting interests for scholars as critical thinkers and as decolonizing educators.

For example, stereotypes about traditional knowledge and how this is expected to function in gender roles, usually with inferences that Native women be all-embracing mothers and healers, poses particular problems to those who disagree or practise roles outside of these expectations. Many popular creeds portray Aboriginal women as centrally maternal, nurturing and feminine. Typically authenticated by biology, culture or tradition, such characterizations are widely articulated by academics, writers and policy-makers as well as many community platforms. I am partial to a female epistemology and appreciate what is nurturing and feminine but I find certain idealizations of this role quite problematic.

For purposes of discussion I will take up some representations from Kim Anderson's *A Recognition of Being: Reconstructing Native Womanhood* (2000). This is an important and substantial book, one of a handful of books that focusses on Aboriginal women's experiences and issues. It is compassionate, thoughtful and well written, and the author made an effort to respectfully include a wide variety of views, including mine. This book has gained wide readership and is a useful springboard for debate on Aboriginal feminist theory.

Anderson's objective is to facilitate as many Native women's voices as possible. However, although Anderson allows for different voices, no debate is generated, for she foregrounds those views of motherhood as central to Aboriginal women's epistemology. She writes: "Motherhood was an affirmation of a woman's power and defined her central role in traditional Aboriginal societies" (2000, 83). To be sure, Anderson takes great pains to extend the "Aboriginal ideology of motherhood" (2000, 171) to those women without children and employs the concept of "aunties" in a very positive way. She also points to special women who have done great international work of healing, women with no

Métis and Feminist 151

biological children but "their role is the same as that of any mother: to teach, nurture and heal all people" (2000, 171). This is indeed a sterling vocation and ethic, echoing some feminist directions which have argued for a maternal-based "moral vision" (Donovan 1990, 173). Nonetheless, such maternalization is totalizing and exclusionary. Many women today choose not to be mothers, and they neither have desire nor appreciate being forced into what is essentially a heterosexist framework, even if a feminine one. Ultimately, motherhood does imply biology, and, as deployed in Anderson, defines "womanhood."

Even more disconcerting is the notion that a skirt is a way of accessing connectedness to the earth (2000, 167). Anderson explains that the skirt is "another symbol related to woman's ability to produce and nurture life" (2000, 166). This is then extrapolated into a rather startling view of what constitutes womanhood, or femininity. Anderson quotes a young woman who remarks: "The skirt itself represents the hoop of life. So, as a woman, you need to walk like a woman, you need to sit like a woman, you need to conduct yourself like a woman, and part of that is being recognized, not only on this earth, but also in the spirit world, as a woman" (2000, 168).

Such an assertion reflects a statement of faith, and while we must respect people's faiths, what do we do when faith turns to dogma that requires submission or contradicts other rights? I do not wear skirts, and I most certainly do not feel any less connected to the earth. Indeed, I take umbrage to any suggestion that my spirituality is wanting simply because of clothing or ceremony! But my take here is much more than personal: as a scholar and as a feminist, I question such a remark. In the first instance, this view is strikingly similar to patriarchal Christian and other fundamentalist constructions of "woman," and one wonders to what extent the influence of residential schools and other patriarchal agencies and attitudes, both old and new, is at work here.

It is simply not true that there was any universalized Aboriginal understanding about "womanhood," especially one that made much of masculinity or femininity in the western sense. In fact, archival records reveal that European men reacted to the fact that, in some Aboriginal nations, there was little difference between men and women in roles, appearance, clothing or even physical strength.[7] Furthermore, there were widely divergent traditions around gender roles.

---

7 In a scathing critique of Alexander Mackenzie's journals, Parker Duchemin notes that MacKenzie interpreted Sekani women's height and "lusty make" (that Mackenzie imagined) as "inverting normal distinctions of gender" (Duchemin 1990, 60–1).

152   The Emma LaRocque Reader

Equally problematic is the naturalizing of human gestures to bio-logical determinism, which has every potential to discriminate against those who do not fit certain expectations. Gender stereotypes such as walking "like a woman" or "like a man" carry heterosexist preferences and prejudices that perpetuate the oppression of gay people, among others. And I might add, as one who grew up in the bush with no mod-ern amenities, we did not think in terms of gender-proscribed ways of walking when we picked berries, chopped wood, carried water or walked for miles to towns or to our traplines, and so forth. There is much scholarly evidence to suggest that gender, and with it notions of femininity, or masculinity, are constructed (Roscoe 1998). It remains debatable whether one walks, talks or gestures "like a woman" or "like a man" naturally, or is taught to do so. The other and perhaps more important point is that traditionally, Indigenous nations demonstrated much tolerance for difference and individuality (LaRocque 1997). Even in cultures that practised fairly rigid sex roles there were allowances, even honour, for those who assumed cross-gender roles, although it appears there was more honour given to women who took on male roles than men who took on female ones (Hungry Wolf 1980, 60–4, 67). This implies a cultural bias in favour of male-defined roles.

With respect to assigning gender quality to certain clothing, a study of Native women's roles in the fur trade shows that European men, reflecting their westernized notions about femininity, modesty and chastity (sexual mores), pressured their Native wives and their half-breed daughters to conduct themselves with "lady-like" manners and to adopt the wearing of western clothing such as skirts and other "femi-nine," usually English, accoutrements (Van Kirk 1980). Further, many Aboriginal cultures did not produce skirts or dresses as we know them today, and both men and women wore either robes, pants or pant-like leggings. It was European husbands and fathers assuming authority over their Native families who pressured Native peoples to associate clothing with gender roles or even with spirituality. We see here that colonization is almost completely about over-arching male dominance, which clearly had a domino effect on Aboriginal cultures and practises.

While intending to affirm Aboriginal women and cultures, both much beleaguered in white North American archival records, histories and popular culture, many writers readily criticize Euro-Canadian colonial forces (not a bad thing in and of itself), but they tend to both gloss over Aboriginal practises that discriminate(d) against women, and they generalize and romanticize traditions. There is an over-riding assump-tion that Aboriginal traditions were universally historically non-sexist and therefore, are universally liberating today. Besides the fact that not all traditions were non-sexist, we must be careful that, in an effort to celebrate ourselves, we not go to the other extreme of biological essentialism of our roles as women by confining them to the domestic and maternal spheres, or romanticizing our traditions by closing our eyes to certain practises and attitudes that privilege men over women.

There is no doubt that many pre-Columbian cultures developed political systems and spiritual practises in which women held significant power and influence. Nor was this power relegated to the domestic sphere. And there is no question that colonial forces have seriously disrupted Aboriginal thought and institutions. There is no question that we need to rebuild and restore ourselves and our cultures. However, this cannot mean that we refrain from confronting patriarchal and sexist attitudes or oppressive behaviours. The fact remains that there is an awful lot of gender inequality within Native families, communities, organizations and governments. In the final analysis, it does not much matter what the ultimate cause of sexism or misogyny may be. What matters is that, on a fairly universal level, it permeates the lives of women throughout the world today, and it certainly permeates our lives, and that is what feminism attends to.

Women cannot saddle ourselves with the staggering responsibility of teaching or nurturing the whole world; nor should we assume sole responsibility for "healing" or "nurturing" Aboriginal men. To assume such roles is tantamount to accepting patriarchal definitions about the nature and role of women, and it results in assuming responsibility for our oppression and our inequality. And to do this is to deny our historical and sociological experience as women. This is not in any way to dismiss men's experiences or to suggest we should be aloof or callous towards those men who also suffer from racism and colonialism (and in some instances, even from female violence). I know too well how hard my beloved Bapa worked to take care of us because he had no other opportunities than to be a labourer; I know too well how much my two brothers continue to struggle to make ends meet even today because school failed them. However, men and women experience colonialism differently. This is not about "blaming our men" but of assessing women's situation in an historical and social context. The point is, colonialism and patriarchy are systemic problems, and we cannot address colonialism and patriarchy adequately by assuming personal or collective female responsibility for how the world hurts or how men may behave.

I believe that some of the maternalist claims about roles and positions are taken without adequate historical or anthropological research, and without awareness about their implications. But they are also taken in an effort to outline our difference from western definitions. "Difference" serves rhetorically as part of an anti-colonial arsenal in the process of culture re-building. However, in decolonization movements traditions about women are often framed as largely domestic and supportive in nature. The disturbing pattern in nationalist movements is that while women are celebrated abstractly as carriers of culture and guardians of tradition, their fundamental human rights are often denied (Young 2003). "Historically ... women do not reap equal benefits from decolonization for reasons of gender inequality [because] the decolonised nation is hardly interested in female liberation [as men become] chief beneficiaries of political and economic power gained through the nationalist struggle" (McLeod 2000, 115). My hope is that First Nations and Métis peoples can avoid these pitfalls. But it is worrisome that a discernible pattern is already there: Native women are "honoured" as "keepers" of tradition, defined as nurturing/healing, while Native men control political power. What concerns me even more is that in the interest of being markers of difference, many non-western women are apparently willing to accept certain proscriptions, even fundamental inequalities. Why is it women are always the ones to do this? In Canada, much of the rhetoric of Indigenous nationalism is filtered through the language of "cultural difference" requiring "culturally appropriate" responses and models.

The question is, to what extent is difference discourse serving us as women? How different are we, and from whom, exactly, are we to be different? Who is defining the difference? Feminism invites us to think seriously about difference, but to also remain focussed on women's human rights.

This is not to say that we are exactly the same as white Canadians or that we want to be. Of course we are different! But our difference today, as it was in pre-Columbian times, is much more dynamic, diverse, complex and nuanced than what the popularized and stereotyped "cultural differences" discourse suggests. That these "differences" are often neatly typologized into a handful of traits[8] may be convenient for many, and they are certainly more political than cultural, but I believe they serve to entrench the colonizer's model (to borrow J.M. Blaut's [1993] phrase) of "the Indian," rendering women marginalized and vulnerable to unequal treatment.

The irony is that, generally, there is a tendency to lump Native scholars and/or writers, perhaps especially Native women, under certain universalized and prescribed notions of experience or of expression. For all the talk on difference we continue to be stereotyped as some

---

8 See my analysis of this (LaRocque 1997).

mother-earthy mass of battered bodies. Both Aboriginal and non-Aboriginal writers tend to do this. While many of us may have much in common, the generalized treatment to our selves or to our work is an act of erasure, to each of us.

Further, it is unacceptable that many feminist writers, perhaps especially white and African American writers, seem unaware of our existence, both as politically situated women and/or as intellectuals and scholars. There is in mainstream Canadian and American feminist writings a decided lack of inclusion of our experience, analysis or perspectives. A while ago, I perused about fifteen textbooks on feminist theory, most of them published in the 1990s. With the exception of about three authors,[9] not one of them wrote a single word on Aboriginal people (American or Canadian), including women; much less referred to any of our deconstructions, Indigenous-based anti-colonial theories; to the contemporizing of Aboriginal epistemologies in our classrooms; or to our matrifocal societies and traditions, even though most of them had several chapters on "women of colour." However, there are some more recent works, especially by women of colour, that have treated Aboriginal women seriously and respectfully.[10]

Clearly, there remain problems with white-constructed feminism, and just as clearly, Aboriginal women must deal with multiple sites of being othered. But, to use an old aphorism, let's not throw out the baby with the bath water! As we address white feminist exclusions we must be careful that we not sabotage our human rights or our critical capacities. I do not think it is fruitful for us to weaken our resources or our analysis by fixing upon what is now a very common argument, namely, that feminism is irrelevant because white women have conceptualized it (and presumably know nothing about racism or colonial history), or because race/racism is more urgent and fundamental to Native women than sex/sexism. Racism/sexism is a package experience and it is virtually impossible to untangle one from the other (LaRocque 1990). But the integrity of my sexuality and my body will not be sacrificed for race, for religion, for "difference," for "culture" or for "nation."

---

9 The authors (in my collection at the time) that included some treatment of Aboriginal women are Emberly (1993), Hunter (1996), and Stalker and Prentice (1998). While Emberly and Hunter take a respectful and considered approach, Stalker and Prentice include one puzzling chapter on "Native Students and Quebec Colleges," which is written by a non-Aboriginal woman.

10 I am thinking especially of Sherene Razack's works, *Looking White People in the Eye* (1998) and *Race, Space and the Law* (2002). See also Bannerji (1993).

156 The Emma LaRocque Reader

Much work is needed to decolonize the feminist/academic community concerning the treatment and reading of Aboriginal women's material and intellectual locations. That we are diverse, complex and divided is all the more reason for greater efforts to be made by all intellectuals. New theoretical directions are urgently needed to help think through the issues confronting Aboriginal women today.

Nonetheless, despite these problems, and despite the substantive socio-economic disparities between Native and non-Native women (Frideres 2003), and even despite the colonial chasms that do exist, I do believe that feminism is viable as a basis for analysis and as an ideal for equitable gender relations. This feminism though cannot be read as solely belonging to white women; Aboriginal women have fought for their rights long before and long after European arrival or influence even if they have not used white feminist language. Further, being feminist cannot and does not mean abandoning our commitments to the Aboriginal community.

The relationship between Native and white women cannot be unidirectional. The Canadian or international women's movements cannot define all the terms nor expect Native women to assume dominant cultures as their own, even if we share common interests around gender. Native women's cultures challenge state and cultural systems. White women must do some consciousness-raising about the quality of life and the nature of political and intellectual colonialism in our country.

Aboriginal values and worldviews offer genuine alternatives to our over-industrialized, over-bureaucratized, corporate-controlled society. Many Aboriginal beliefs and practises, *the real* traditionally based practises – and those reinvented – also offer models and concepts on gender equality that can enhance woman-centred notions of equality and valuation. Naturally, we need to transform those traditions that obstruct gender equality; we need to confront thinking and institutions that violate our rights and we need to ensure that our contemporary First Nations and Métis liberation efforts move away from that either-or pattern of sacrificing women's equality in the interests of the ever amorphous "collective." We must be both decolonizers and feminists.

Finally, I am painfully aware that I have raised questions and issues that are politically charged and may cause discomfort. I am highly conscious of the fact that there are ideological divisions and methodological disagreements among us as we seek to find common ground in the theorizing of our lives, both as women and as diverse Aboriginal peoples. I am equally aware that we are oppressed peoples and that we are making valiant efforts to restore ourselves to rebuild our stolen and fragmented cultures and traditions. I appreciate that it is difficult for us to bear any further criticism. Yet, history teaches us that it is in moments of nationalisms that we are most vulnerable not only to essentialisms/fundamentalisms (Green 2003), but to the disempowerment of women. It is in moments of nationalisms that we must exercise our critical capacities towards the enhancement of our human freedoms.

Freedom from imperial, systemic and personal dominations must remain the basis of our emancipatory efforts. This must mean that, paramount among our principles, is an abhorrence of violations against other human beings. Specifically, in this discussion, no injustice against any persons, whether constitutional, cultural or physical/sexual, should ever be tolerated in the name of advancing any collective or political interests, even when idealized as some kind of a decolonizing reconstructive process. We must understand that it is not in the interest of any collective or culture to dismiss or abuse individual rights, particularly matters as crucial as citizenship, identity or personal safety and integrity. It is not deliverance if some people's rights within any decolonizing or liberation movements are sacrificed.

In the final analysis, what matters to me is that, as we rebuild, we have an opportunity to create contemporary cultures based on human rights that extend to all members of our communities. Such rights will respect cultures and traditions but, at the same time we must be vigilant that cultures and traditions uphold the human rights of all peoples, certainly children and women.

2009

Reflections on Cultural Continuity through Aboriginal Women's Writings

This chapter presents a selective survey of contemporary Indian and Métis women's writing and shows how these writers have translated the Aboriginal achievements, world views, and colonial challenges into meaningful and compelling art. This is not a literary or critical study of Aboriginal literatures; rather, it is a peek at cultural agency and accomplishments through literature. I will draw largely on auto-biographical and creative works produced by Aboriginal women from different cultures and locations. Inevitably, I can only be selective: it is simply impossible to include all writers, or to discuss them in equal proportions, because it would take volumes to produce a thorough treatment of all literature by Native women. This, of course, points to the mass and the importance of Aboriginal literature, including that written by women.

I also want to deal with some troublesome issues concerning identity and terminology. As a writer and scholar of Métis Nation heritage, being invited to write a chapter focussing on the cultural contributions of First Nations women necessitates that I begin with a brief evaluative review of terms such as "Aboriginal," "Indian," "Métis," and "First Nations." These are all highly problematic terms, not only because they are, of course, colonial in origin, but also because they result in prejudicial treatment of many Aboriginal people, and so create, quite spuriously, political divisions. For example, who writes or speaks on behalf of, or about, Aboriginal and/or First Nations women? The relationship between identity and privilege is a discourse that yet needs to be opened up, but currently, it is virtually swollen shut with politics; here I can only offer some observations about the history and use of these terms.

Let's begin with the word "Métis," about which there is considerable misunderstanding or plain lack of knowledge. Some think being Métis is very much like being French. Or that simply having some Indian in one's background, however generationally or culturally remote, constitutes the full meaning of being Métis. Others assume being Métis is the same as being half-white, half-Native. Still others think being Métis is the same as "non-Status." More recently, sociodemographic phenomena described as "hybridization" and "border crossing" – mostly by non-Aboriginal academics – further blurs the uniqueness of Métis Nation peoples. The usage, adoption, and even appropriation of the designation "métis" has become so broad and generalized that most Canadians are not familiar with the historical and ethnographic fact that vast numbers of Métis peoples, especially from western Canada, though a unique ethnocultural group, are also Aboriginal, whose connection to Aboriginal is genetic, familial, linguistic, epistemological, and ecological.[1] For example, the Prairies, perhaps especially the more central northern parts, are filled with Cree-Métis peoples who, of course, originate from both Europeans and Indians during the fur-trade era, but over time formed their own ethnicity (i.e., Métis marrying Métis) with a culture blended, yet distinct, from both groups.[2] Although these peoples were excluded from the *Indian Act* and treaties, they were and remain primarily connected to *Nehiyawewak* (Cree-speaking people), who themselves speak or grew up with *Nehiyawewin* (Cree language). Most were raised with parents, kin, and communities whose cultural lifestyles were intimately connected with the land and with other Aboriginal people. All these things are important to repeat because all the confusion, not to mention politics, surrounding the term "métis" can obscure the Aboriginal rights of those Métis Nation peoples whose cultures are centrally indigenous and whose lives contribute to the cultural continuity of all Aboriginal peoples.

As is well known, the term "Indian" is an imposed historical and legal designation first associated with Columbus's erroneous geography, and, in Canada, with the *Indian Act*, an Act quintessentially colonial in nature. The *Indian Act* and the treaties have defined a legally

---

1 My necessarily brief treatment here of the history, politics and identity of the Métis Nation peoples, particularly my argument that they, as Native-mated peoples, should be accorded the same rights and resources as other Aboriginal peoples, is based on my article (see chapter "Native Identity and the Métis: Otehpayimsuak Peoples").

2 In an effort to show ethnic differences among the Métis/métis, some scholars have used small-m "métis" as opposed to the capitalized "Métis." Métis with a capital M generally refers to those peoples who became a distinct ethnic group by marrying within the group, that is, Métis marrying Métis. These peoples developed a distinct culture, especially around the Red River area. For an excellent exploration on the many origins of the Métis/métis, see (Peterson and Brown 1985).

distinct identity and have, at least, offered a certain measure of rights and resources for those designated as Status and/or Treaty Indians. Less well known is that the Métis Nation peoples, though connected to Indian peoples, as noted above, were excluded from the *Indian Act*. This exclusion has had numerous socio-political and economic consequences for the Métis in terms of identity, land, and resource rights.[3] And although the Métis were included as Aboriginal in the 1982 Canadian Constitution, they still struggle to have this put into practise.

Since the repatriation of the Constitution and the drive for self-government, Status Indian people have adopted the term "First Nations," a term now mostly understood as meaning exclusively those people who have historically had a "status" and "treaty" relationship with the Canadian government under the *Indian Act*. "First Nations" is in many ways an appropriate political self-designation for Aboriginal people. Unfortunately, "First Nations" has come to be used exclusively by and for Status and Treaty peoples, and with it the association of the term with Aboriginal rights. This, along with the unnecessary and often politicized confusion about the term "métis," has made it even more convenient for the Canadian governments to use the term "First Nations" in a way that especially excludes the Métis Nation, and perhaps those who are "non-Status Indian," of enfranchisement legacy. This has generally led to serious abrogation of rights for those Aboriginal people who are not "Status Indians" as per the *Indian Act*. By persisting in the association of Aboriginal rights almost exclusively with the phrase "First Nations," the Canadian government, whose constitutional mandate is to recognize equally the rights of all Aboriginal people, is in fact exercising inequality.

We should all be troubled by this, not only from the perspective of human rights and, in particular, Aboriginal rights, but also and certainly from a cultural perspective. In relation to this, and in every respect significant to indigenous culture building, western Métis Nation women, for example, are among Aboriginal women who should be included when considering cultural continuity and contemporary "contributions" to Aboriginal communities.

---

3 See the Royal Commission on Aboriginal Peoples (RCAP 1996), volume 4, chapter 5, on the regional differences of Métis (or métis) identity, especially as these differences have been used to stall recognition of Aboriginal rights for the various Métis communities across Canada. The Royal Commission on Aboriginal Peoples provided many legal avenues by which the Canadian governments could and should recognize Métis peoples' rights.

Reflections on Cultural Continuity

I begin here because I must locate myself in writing this paper. I am Métis and decidedly Aboriginal. The Cree-speaking, hunting/trapping and railroad-working community I come from is of the Métis Nation (Red River and far northwest) cultural group. In Cree we referred to ourselves as *Apeetowgusanuk*, or "half-sons"; other Cree peoples often referred to us also as *Otehpayimsuak*, "the people who own themselves" (see chapter "Native Identity and the Métis: Otehpayimsuak Peoples."). In other words, Aboriginality is not exclusive to those people who have been defined by the *Indian Act* as "Indian" and who today generally refer to themselves as "First Nations."

Since culture is so much more than legal status, it is imperative that we include all Aboriginal people when considering something as vital as cultural continuity, especially on behalf of all those Aboriginal women who have kept their cultures alive despite all odds and despite colonial machinations of marginalization. This is in honour of my *Nokum*, my *Ama*, and *Nemis* (grand-mother, mother, and older sister) as well as my aunts – all who have left this earth but all who have left me and this world with a rich Cree-Métis heritage and culture. Because they kept their *Nehiyowewin* (Plains Cree) and their *atowkehwin* (myths and legends) and their skills, among other things, they kept their cultures alive; because of that, I am alive. We are alive. By "alive" I mean literally and culturally.

When studying Aboriginal writing, it becomes quickly apparent that our sense of cultural knowledge, depth, and experience would be incomplete were we to exclude Métis Nation writers and scholars. Writers such as Jeannette Armstrong, Maria Campbell, Beatrice Culleton, Marilyn Dumont, Louise Halfe, Rita Joe, Lenore Keeshig-Tobias, Margo Kane, Lee Maracle, Eden Robinson, and Ruby Slipperjack, among others, are keepers of their cultures in contemporary modes. Not only have they confronted colonial history and misrepresentation, which I would argue is a "positive" response to colonial realities, they have drawn deeply from the well of their cultural memories, myths, and mother languages. And, as artists, Aboriginal writers form bridges in areas Western thinkers traditionally thought unbridgeable: many, perhaps especially poets, move easily from the oral to the written; all move from the ancient to the post-colonial and from historic trauma to contemporary vibrancy. Some form bridges from personal invasions to personal triumph. Native women have moved far beyond "survival"; they have moved with remarkable grace and accomplishments right onto the international stage. These writers not only retrieve our histories and experiences, a process that is both necessary and painful, but they also collect and thread together our scattered parts and so nurture our spirits and rebuild our cultures.

The Civ/Sav Dichotomy

Generally, Western-biased historians have done a great disservice to knowledge and to Aboriginal peoples in their classically colonial renderings of Aboriginal peoples as stone-age primitives, with no significant cultural accomplishments or civilization. The ideological but systematized paradigm of civilization versus the savage, what I have come to call the "civ/sav dichotomy," is still deeply entrenched in our educational and media institutions. But, in fact, indigenous cultures of the Americas have produced significant material and non-material aspects of culture. The most obvious examples of great material production come from central America, particularly from the Aztecs, Incas, and Mayans, who developed city states, built massive pyramids, along with other marvellous stone, adobe, and wooden structures, and developed mathematically precise calendars requiring knowledge of astronomy. Throughout the Americas, indigenous peoples developed a wealth of horticultural and agricultural skills (such as terracing and irrigation), foods, products, pharmaceutical and medicinal knowledge, and a fascinating array of techniques, tools, and textiles. Native peoples also invented unique dwellings, efficient means of transportation, precise tools, and numerous other land-based technologies suited to their cultural needs. For example, they practised perhaps the most effective resource-management systems anywhere in the world. The more northern peoples controlled the forest in such a way that both forest and humans thrived.

On non-material levels, indigenous peoples have invented thousands of wondrous and cultivated languages and literatures, and a great variety of political, economic, and religious systems. Such systems merit special attention because they were based on values that often continue to be relevant in today's society. Here, I want to caution that we avoid romanticizing or stereotyping by keeping in mind that cultural values are ideals we aspire to, not ones we always demonstrate. Human beings do not always live up to the best ideals within their communities. Nonetheless, it is important that we maintain values that enrich life. In Aboriginal societies, these values include the integration of the ecological system, which demands environmental sensibilities and ethics, and, with it, organization and standards for human dignity, egalitarianism, consensual decision making, and balance between humans and the earth, as well as between men and women. Some Native cultures were organized around matriarchal or semi-matriarchal systems, reflecting advanced understanding of the role of women in human and cultural development.

Native societies also developed exacting protocols for justice, ceremony, and art, with emphasis on the dignity and freedom of the human spirit. The notion of "human dignity," though, means different things to different peoples; in my culture, human dignity includes the valuation of personhood and individuality in the context of community and kinship responsibilities. And in these times of aggressive fundamentalism on one hand, and, yet, gross tolerance of mysogynistic behaviour on the other, we cannot emphasize enough the greatness and beauty of such values. These are often expressed in Native spirituality, a spirituality rooted deep into the soil and in the feminine, and which nourished the land, individual freedom for both genders, vision, and tolerance of difference. The achievements in the arts include sculptures, pottery, sand painting, rock painting, hieroglyphics, weaving, crafts, oral literatures, poetry, oratory, drama, music, and other fine creations of the heart and intellect.

This "quick list" overview is but a glimpse into the original accomplishments of our ancestors, the original peoples of the Americas.[4] This overview does not include the ingenious cultural adaptations after the arrivals of Columbus, the conquistadores, the Jesuits, the Daniel Boones, the cowboys, the fur traders, and Confederation. Such a quick view list is not complete without making the additional point that not only has the world borrowed (or appropriated) much from Aboriginal wealth, resources, and cultures but that modern North and South America is built on indigenous roots. As anthropologist Jack Weatherford has put it so precisely: "These ancient and often ignored roots still nourish our modern society, political life, economy, art, agriculture, language and distinctly American modes of thought" (Weatherford 1991, 18).

And what can we say of our achievements in cultural tenacity, spiritual integrity, and human endurance in the face of sustained cultural and legislated assaults? Europeans and their more modern descendants have indeed borrowed – or divested – much from indigenous peoples. In the last few decades, considerable scholarly attention has been given to colonization and its effects on Aboriginal peoples. Although this reading of history has been kind, it has recently evoked some interesting responses by some Native groups or individuals. Some feel that to explain everything about Aboriginal peoples in terms of colonization has a totalizing effect. They argue that they are more than the sum of

---

4 For a fascinating perspective on the cultural contributions of indigenous peoples of the Americas, see Weatherford (1988) and Weatherford (1991). For a sensitive anthropological overview of Aboriginal cultures in Canada, see Morrison and Wilson (2004).

164 The Emma LaRocque Reader

colonization and that colonization does not define or even determine their existence in total. Such emphasis clearly calls for reflection on not only what has been lost, but also what has been kept, borrowed, adapted, or changed. For all the losses, Native peoples have shown remarkable elasticity, tenacity, and agency. This can be seen in the Aboriginal responses and transactions, from those with early Europeans right through to our contemporary times. We can trace women's cultural tenacity from the fur-trade era, even through the residential school era,[5] and on to the mid-1900s and now modern times.

When the European fur traders began to trade and form relationships with Aboriginal peoples, they were not dealing with peoples without culture. Women, in particular, were keepers of their cultures. Even though they were faced with new burdens and opportunities generated by the fur trade, Aboriginal women still acted as keepers of their families, languages, oral literatures, land-based technologies and skills, foods, clothing, art, music, and much more. They also served as cultural brokers between various Native peoples and cultures throughout the fur-trade era. Their roles, of course, were complicated and traumatized by the imperial mercantilist situation. The legacy of this historic trauma remains evident today, but, nevertheless, many of the skills and ways of life from the fur-trade era survived for many years, and were practised by my mother's generation among northern Alberta Native (many of whom are Métis) women. Because of that, such skills are still alive and well, especially in northern communities.

Contemporary Aboriginal Women's Writings

In the tradition of our grandmothers and mothers, Aboriginal women have continued to work for the preservation of our families, communities, and cultures, and, in so doing, are keeping our peoples and cultures alive and current. Writing is one such expression of both creativity and continuity. Since the late 1960s, Aboriginal women have been creating a significant body of writing, which serves in many respects as a vehicle of cultural teaching and reinvention as well as cultural and political resistance to colonialism with its Western-defined impositions, requirements, and biases. But writing is also about the love of words, which at once expresses indigenous roots, social agency, and individual creativity.

---

5 See for example, Fiske's (1996) study of Carrier women resistance responses to residential schooling.

Reflections on Cultural Continuity

A chronological, albeit incomplete and selective survey of this writing will serve to introduce a sense of the depth and scope of Native women's contributions to both Aboriginal and the larger Canadian cultures. Though the focus is on contemporary writing, any discussion on Aboriginal women writers must begin with Mohawk/Métis poet Pauline Johnson. Born in 1862 to an English mother and a Mohawk father on the Six Nations Indian Reserve, Johnson was to become the first Aboriginal poet, and the first Canadian woman, to be published. For all her firsts, and for her stature as a popular Canadian poet, Johnson was never free from the colonizer's language and imagery, as evidenced in some of her poetry in *Flint and Feather* (1972 [1917]) as well as in the persona of Indian princess she assumed during her recitations. Put in the difficult position of having to meet the demands set by the prejudices of a racially conscious Victorian-based Canadian society, she nonetheless vigorously championed Indian and Métis rights and humanity. Interestingly, my generation grew up reading her famous and delightful poem "The Song My Paddle Sings," but never read her resistance poems such as "The Cattle Thief" or "A Cry from an Indian Wife."

In Pauline Johnson's lifetime, the Canadian government shored up its urban and industrial encroachment on eastern Native peoples' lands, quashed western Métis Nation resistance, dispossessed Métis and Indian lands and resources through scrip and treaties, and then legislated the *Indian Act*, which gave the government control over "Status" Indian peoples while creating enfranchised "non-Status" Indians and bumping the Métis Nation peoples from their Aboriginal rights. In Johnson's lifetime, reserves, scrip, residential schools, Batoche, and "road allowance" were established. Canadian society enforced segregation, gender discrimination, and containment through local and social avenues. "Indians" became wards under the *Indian Act*, numerous Status Indian women lost their rights, and the Métis lost their Red River as well as their far northwestern lands under Confederation.

Once sidelined from mainstream Canada, Indian and Métis peoples were politically silenced for about a century. It was not until the late 1960s that the next (and now unstoppable) wave of Native writing was born. The next popular and socially revolutionary publication by an Aboriginal woman was produced by Métis author Maria Campbell. Her autobiography *Halfbreed* (1973) exploded Canada's naive notions of itself as a fair and caring country by situating her life of loss and abuse against the historical oppression of Métis Nation peoples. Her community and her family, rich in humour and Métis culture, was subjected to harsh poverty and racial discrimination in their town and public schools. Also published in the same year was Jane Willis's (1973) autobiography

Geneish: an Indian Girlhood. Perhaps shadowed by the overwhelming reception of *Halfbreed*, this work remains less well known, but the story it tells is no less important. Jane Willis tells of her years in residential school in northern Quebec as a time of mental, intellectual, and corporal abuse. Routinely denounced as "savages" and stripped of all things Indian, Willis and fellow students were repeatedly subjected to hard labour and racist humiliations. Willis's book foreshadowed the stories to come about the Native experience in residential schools.

Racist humiliations were everywhere in these times. Salish/Métis writer Lee Maracle produced an autobiographical, edited account of largely urban-based life in *Bobbi Lee: Indian Rebel – Struggles of a Native Canadian Woman* (1975). This story showed that racism, sexism, and even cruel treatment of Native peoples was not confined to public or residential schools. Hot, harsh, poverty-ridden streets of Canada's cities exacted punishment on urban Native peoples, particularly in the era from the 1940s to the 1970s.

Not surprisingly, then, Native women were involved in a host of socio-economic issues, including legislated and social discrimination, poverty, violence, health, (in)justice, education, identity, and cultural renewal in the late 1960s on to the 1970s. Much of their writing from this period comes from Native newspapers, editorials, or essays in collections. The Native women, many of them educators, who wrote at this time include Victoria Callihoo, Ethel Brant Monture, Edith Josie, Verna Kirkness, Marlene Castellano, Gloria Bird, and Beverly Hungry Wolf, among others. Mi'kmaq poet Rita Joe, perhaps the most well-known Native woman poet of that era, wrote simply but movingly about the struggles and losses of her community and family, but also about the beauty of her people and culture.

The 1980s opened with a powerful, raw novel by Métis writer Beatrice Culleton. *In Search of April Raintree* (1983), a story of two adopted Métis sisters, is an unflinching exposé of the callous abuses of the 1960s' scoop of Indian and Métis children by the child and welfare system. It is equally an account of devastating violence and racism against Native women in urban centres. Several years later, [Culleton] wrote *Spirit of the White Bison* (1985), an allegory of the wrenching consequences of separating child from parent. Though written softly, so softly it reduces one to tears, it is nevertheless a thunderous criticism of man's inhumanity to the great buffalo of the plains.

In the same year, Okanagan educator, activist, and writer Jeannette Armstrong published *Slash* (1985), a much-read historical novel set in the 1970s era of political resistance by Native peoples in both Canada and the United States. Jeannette chronicled the colonization of

Reflections on Cultural Continuity

Native peoples in North America through her main character, Slash, a young Okanagan man who drifts from one political rally to another, but eventually finds his way back to home, to his traditions and to his homeland.

Ojibwa writer and educator from Sioux Lookout, Ruby Slipperjack, gently addresses community and family disintegration in *Honour the Sun* (1987). The story is told in the form of a diary written by Owl, who begins her diary as a carefree, funny, precocious, ten-year-old Ojibwa girl, but concludes it as a saddened teenager who must leave home as her life and the lives of her beloved family are disrupted by changes outside their control. The following year, Lee Maracle's *I Am Woman* (1988), although not a novel, became popular reading in Canadian literary and academic circles. Maracle's book roars against poverty, male violence, and Native organizational lethargy, but situates these problems in the context of colonialism and Canadian negligence.

During the 1990s, streams of Native-authored works were written in almost every genre. Often, Native authors cross genres, such as Shirley Sterling's *My Name Is Seepeetza* (1992). This has been classified as a children's book, but is also studied as adult-level fiction in literature courses. It is a semi-autobiographical novel about a Native girl's experience in a residential school. Lee Maracle (*Sundogs* 1992; *Ravensong* 1993) and Ruby Slipperjack (*Silent Words* 1992) published more novels, but the 1990s especially saw a growing list of anthologies with Native women's biographical and political essays, as well as creative writing, including short stories, plays, reinterpretation of legends, and, of course, poetry. Such anthologies include *All My Relations* (edited by Thomas King 1990); *Seventh Generation* (edited by Heather Hodgson 1989); *Native Writers and Canadian Literature* (edited by W.H. New 1990); *Our Bit of Truth* (edited by Agnes Grant 1990); *Voices: Being Native in Canada* (edited by Linda Jaine and Drew Hayden Taylor 1992); and *An Anthology of Canadian Native Literature in English* (edited by Daniel David Moses and Terry Goldie 1992). Two anthologies during that period featured exclusively writing by Native women: *Writing the Circle* (edited by Jeanne Perreault and Sylvia Vance 1990) and *The Colour of Resistance: A Contemporary Collection of Writing by Aboriginal Women* (edited by Connie Fife 1993). Also published in the 1990s was *Native Literature in Canada: From the Oral Tradition to the Present* (edited by Penny Petrone 1990), the first critical study and survey of Native literature authored by a non-Native academic. And the first collection of critical essays on Native writing by Native academics, many women, and edited by Jeannette Armstrong, was also published as *Looking at the Words of My People: First Nations Analysis of Literature* (1993).

168   The Emma LaRocque Reader

Of course, Native women writers have not stopped writing. The year 2000 opened with the publication of more novels: *Whispering in Shadows* by Jeannette Armstrong, *Monkey Beach* by Haisla sensation Eden Robinson, and *Weesquachak and the Lost Ones* by Ruby Slipperjack. These three novels have as their main character an Aboriginal female. Penny, in *Whispering in Shadows*, is a young, restless artist who breaks out of the apple orchards of the Okanagan, as well as a stifling relationship, in pursuit of her dreams to go to art school for a university education. She becomes an environmentalist who yearns to bring healing to the suffering indigenous humanity she encounters in her international travels. Penny is named after her grandmother, from whom she learns to see the extrasensory contours and colours of the land. Paced and quiet, yet seething with the spirituality of indigenous indignation, Armstrong lets the land do the speaking. Her book is a critique of globalization with its relentless and insatiable capitalist tentacles, drive, and greed.

In *Monkey Beach*, Lisa Marie, named after Elvis Presley's daughter, is a Haisla teenager haunted by ancestral and familial ghosts and half-hidden personal devastations. Set in both contemporary Kitimat and the Haisla ancestral beaches along Canada's Pacific coast, *Monkey Beach* features seaside and urban *b'gwuses*, monsters camouflaged as sometimes human and sometimes not.

Ruby Slipperjack's protagonist in *Weesquachak* is a young Ojibwa woman, Janine, who, after having gone to the city, comes back to her northern community. She gets involved with a trapper and both find themselves shadowed by something or someone. This "something" or "someone" provides a sense of menace and eeriness to this novel. In the bush Janine feels watched, even stalked, at times. Is it an ex-boyfriend? Is it just a clever raven? Surely, it is the Trickster. But what purpose does the Trickster serve in contemporary times?

Poetry is also a strong and active avenue of creative expression for Aboriginal women. Since the 1960s, thousands of published poems have been written by Aboriginal women. In the 1960s and 1970s, much of this poetry was found in Native newspapers and magazines, as well as in the earlier anthologies. Jeannette Armstrong remembers finding "small poems scattered like gems here and there in the pages of mimeographed Native flyers and bulletins which appeared at every Native political gathering" (Armstrong in Armstrong and Grauer 2001, xviii). Over time, Native poetry eventually appeared in some of Canada's leading literary journals and academic anthologies, such as *Ariel, Prairie Fire, Descant, Border Crossings*, and others. The growing list of books of poetry by Native women is an indication of the significance of poetry in our cultures.

Mi'kmaq poet Rita Joe (*Poems of Rita Joe* 1978; *The Song of Eskasoni*; *More Poems of Rita Joe* 1988) was among the first published poets. Other Native women who have published books of poetry include Jeannette Armstrong (*Breath Tracks* 1991); Beth Cuthand (*Voices in the Waterfall* 1989); Marie Annharte Baker (*Being on the Moon* 1990; *Exercises in Lip Pointing* 2003; *Coyote Columbus Café* 1994); Joan Crate (*Pale as Real Ladies: Poems for Pauline Johnson* 1991; *Foreign Homes* 2002); Joanne Arnott (*Wiles of Girlhood* 1991; *Steepy Mountain* 2004); Kateri Akiwenzie-Damm (*My Heart is a Stray Bullet* 1993; and as editor, *Without Reservation: Indigenous Erotica* 2003); Marilyn Dumont (*A Really Good Brown Girl* 1996; *Green Girl Dreams Mountains* 2001); Louise Halfe (*Bear Bones and Feathers* 1994; *Blue Marrow* 2004 rev); Lee Maracle (*Bent Box* 2000); and Sharron Proulx-Turner (*What the Auntys Say* 2002).

Collaborative works that carry essays, poetry, or art by Aboriginal women include *My Home As I Remember*, edited by Lee Maracle and Sandra Laronde (2000); *Into the Moon*, edited by Lenore Keeshig-Tobias (1996); *Sweetgrass Grows All Around Her*, edited by Beth Brant and Sandra Laronde (1994); *Kelusultiek: Original Women's Voices Atlantic Canada*, edited by R. Ursmiant (1994); and *Indigena*, edited by Gerald McMaster and Lee-Ann Martin (1992).

There is more. In addition to poetry and novels, autobiographies and biographies, Native women also produce short stories, plays, children's books, ethnographic material, social and political commentaries, and contemporary retellings of legends. Aboriginal women academics are literally, in the words of Joyce Green, "transforming the academy" with their research and by the intellectual challenges they pose to old Western frameworks and biases.[6] Those who have produced semi-biographical and semi-autobiographical works mixing analysis with voice and narrative include Janice Acoose (*Iskwewak* 1995), Beth Brant (*Mohawk Trail* 1985), and Patricia Monture-Angus (*Thunder in My Soul* 1995). Gail Guthrie Valaskakis integrates personal Native narrative and socio-political experience with a critical and theoretical cultural studies approach in *Indian Country: Essays on Contemporary Native Culture* (2005).

To say that Native women's literary contributions are substantial is, obviously, to understate the volume and significance of what these women have produced. Indeed, their writing has evoked much intellectual excitement among literary critics and scholars from around the world. And, in time, as more Aboriginal people take to contemporary

---

6 Unattributed in the text but see, for instance, Green (2000, 2007, 2017) –Elaine Coburn, editor's note.

170 The Emma LaRocque Reader

art and literature, Native writing will assume its high place within the Aboriginal community. Much has actually been written about Native women writers, particularly about Maria Campbell, Lee Maracle, Beatrice Culleton, and Jeannette Armstrong. Critics have generally focussed on their life stories, with an emphasis on the Native colonial experience. That is, much has been written about women's oppression and disempowerment. In effect, the emphasis has been on cultural discontinuity. For the most part, non-Native critics, particularly feminist-conscious men and women, have tried to be respectful and sensitive. This is especially noticeable since the 1990s. However, such critics have generally tended to look more for ancient cultural secrets or patterns[7] amid what I call "ethno-graphic tidbits" than for those crucial spaces of contemporaneity and agency that actually fill the pages of Native writing, as, of course, they fill the lives of Aboriginal people.

Cultural Continuity through Writing

Although I do often remark on cultural "tidbits" with some tongue-in-cheek, the question does arise: how do readers find cultural continuity in Aboriginal women's writings? One can ask such a question only if one views this writing as alien to Aboriginal peoples; and one can think this only if one believes in what J.M. Blaut (1993) calls "the colonizer's model of the world," which is the model that claims Europe is inherently progressive, in contrast to non-Europe, which is backward. Blaut challenges this presumed progressiveness, which he dubs the "European Miracle" that has been diffused throughout the globe through colonialism, enabling non-European peoples to finally evolve towards progress and modernization. In other words, the model claims that the colonized owe their lives to the colonizer; the non-European world owes its cultural life to Europe.

With respect to indigenous peoples of the Americas, the colonizer's model of the world has largely been translated and deduced into that "civ/sav" dichotomy mentioned earlier. That is, history of Native/white relations in the Americas has been presented as a moral "encounter" between civilization and savagism in which "savages" or "Indians" inevitably give way to civilized Euro-white North Americans.[8] In plain words, white North American history and school texts, as well

---

7 See, for instance, Rasporich (1996).
8 Classic studies on civilization/savagism include Pearce (1967) and Jennings (1976). See also Dickason (1984).

Reflections on Cultural Continuity

as the media, have traditionally portrayed Aboriginal peoples as aimlessly wandering (read "nomadic"), uncultivated ("wild"), violent ("bloodthirsty") savages clearly inferior to Euro-white Americans or Canadians.[9] The legacy of such twisty and self-serving history and anthropology has classically cast Native peoples as unable to adapt to cultural change. Or, if they do adapt, they are, at best, borrowing, at worst, mimicking the colonizers' gifts flowing from the diffusion of the "European Miracle." Writing has been treated as one such gift. However, in historical and anthropological fact, Aboriginal peoples were not stone-age savages waiting for the European alphabet on the seashore. Aboriginal cultures were not in some frozen state of primitivity, unable to change or to adapt. Aboriginal peoples were and are uncongealed and dynamic. Writing is, in fact, an example of Native cultural fluidity.

That Aboriginal people are writing is in itself an act of cultural continuity. Any form of expression that is instrumental to our renewal is cultural continuity. Writing is really about "telling," and "telling" originates in orality. Whatever it is that we are telling, whether it is *atowkehwin* (myths and legends) or *achimoowin* (factual or non-fictional type of "stories") or *ehmamtowaytameh* (thinking, reflecting, analysing), and however we do it, orally or in writing, as long as we are doing it, we are expressing a live and dynamic culture. Some indigenous peoples had their own writing systems and all had effective communication systems centuries prior to European incursion. It is not surprising that Native peoples did not greet the technique of writing as being alien to them. In Canada, for example, two Métis persons from northern Manitoba co-developed with a missionary the syllabic system that quickly spread throughout northern communities. It is not uncommon to find that there has been Native collaboration, input, or direction to creative works or socio-political systems that have been appropriated as originating solely from White authorship (Weatherford 1991). Writing is as much our culture as clay tablets used to be for Europeans.

Since this essay reflects on cultural continuity, let us look at how Aboriginal women writers are dealing with these issues of cultural discontinuity and continuity. It is, of course, relatively easy to find examples of discontinuity, given our colonial stories, but how does a reader find cultural continuity? What does cultural continuity look like,

---

9 For a more thorough treatment of historical writing which assumes this "civ/sav" dichotomy, see Emma LaRocque, "Native Writers Resisting Colonizing Practices in Canadian Historiography and Literature" (PhD dissertation, University of Manitoba, 1999), in particular, chapter 2.

172 The Emma LaRocque Reader

especially when, for example, the majority of my generation left home and built our lives around very different economic, material, and cultural environments? Most of us who left home, myself included, no longer know or no longer replicate the ways of our parents, much less the ways of our grandmothers. Nonetheless, there is evidence of cultural continuity being demonstrated by those of us who are in quite different locations from our original homes.

Cultural continuity is much more than about material or even linguistic replications that sociologists and anthropologists have traditionally identified as sustained "cultural markers" and by which they have judged cultural change among Aboriginal peoples. Indeed, and consistent with the civ/sav (or progress/primitive) view, both society and academia, including some Aboriginal people, have traditionally assumed any cultural change by Aboriginal peoples must ipso facto be viewed as assimilation. But Aboriginal peoples have long demonstrated that change, even under enforced circumstances, does not result in cultural amnesia. Culture shock or even catastrophic trauma are not the same as cultural amnesia. Obviously, cultural change for Aboriginal peoples has been complicated by colonization but it is equally true and still must be emphasized that cultural change is not alien to Aboriginal cultures. We must certainly shed the view that all things highly cultivated or "developed" and "modern" come from Europeans. We must also shed the notion that cultural change is foreign to indigenous cultures, whether in pre-contact times or now. We must rethink our own responses to all the twists and turns of colonial assumptions and stereotypes about us. We must assume our birthright to be whoever we are in today's world. For example, there is in this country an expectation that we be culturally different. The dialectics of cultural difference go squarely back to early colonial times in which it served and continues to serve colonizers to keep "natives" in their place, and one way to do that is to create a stereotype of difference. It is imperative we challenge the assumptions that attend these expectations. Further, notice that "difference" is almost always associated with traditionalism (which is itself stereo-typed). This is consistent with the civ/sav view that Westerners, being inherently progressive, make history, but "natives," being statically primitive, can only maintain tradition.[10]

---

10 Doxtator (1992), provides a perceptive analysis of how "Indians" are stereotyped as traditional in contrast to whites as makers of history. See my treatment of notions of progress in context of stereotypes in LaRocque (1975). See also Francis (1992), 57–60.

Reflections on Cultural Continuity

Clearly, the Native community faces many tough and interesting issues. The point here is that by taking our rightful place in our contemporary world, we are breathing cultural continuity. The act of writing is an act of agency, and agency is cultural continuity in its articulation of our histories, our invasions, and our cultural values. Aboriginal writers' cultural contributions to the Aboriginal (and wider) communities are profound. Among numerous other contributions, writers provide historical information and analysis of the Native colonial experience. Writers offer an inside perspective of ethnographic data. Interestingly, writers do say much about "difference," but in ways surprising and even unexpected. Writers certainly challenge both standard academic notions about cultural difference and change as well as political and societal demands that we stay different, that is, stereotyped.

Expressing the Materiality of
Aboriginal Culture through Writing

Not much is said about how Native writers express their cultures through their detailed descriptions of the materiality of their cultural backgrounds, particularly about their homes and the economic bases to their daily living. Undoubtedly, I am reflecting on my own generation, but I begin by pointing this out in a number of works written by Aboriginal women.

I turn again to Maria Campbell. For any Métis youth who wonders about his or her cultural heritage, that is, who asks the question of how Métis Nation people expressed their culture, say from the 1800s to the 1970s, reading Campbell would provide considerable cultural information. Campbell is of Cree/Scottish Métis Nation ancestry. Her parents raised her and her siblings with Métis material culture, as well as Métis values. It is of some interest that Maria Campbell begins her facts of biography with this: "I should tell you about our home now before I go any further" (1973, 16). She then gives minute details about their "two-roomed large hewed log house," telling us about their homemade tables and chairs, beds and hay-filled canvas mattresses, the hammock that babies swung from, the huge black wood stove in the kitchen, the medicines and herbs that hung on the walls, the wide planks of floors scoured evenly white with lye soap, and so forth. She reminisces, "The kitchen and living room were combined into one of the most beautiful rooms I have ever known" (1973, 17). Maria's parents were typically hard-working, resourceful Métis folks who lived well off the land but who also used as many modern conveniences as they were able to procure. In addition to store-bought goods, her parents relied on foods

174 The Emma LaRocque Reader

of the land, which meant they engaged in hunting/trapping, fishing, berry picking, and some gardening. They would have acquired and developed techniques and tools consistent with having to kill or harvest the resources. Skills such as hunting, trapping, snaring, shooting, fishing, boating, and building satellite camps and cabins were vital. Related skills in the butchering, dressing, and preserving of the foods were equally vital. Animals also offered shelter, clothing, accessories, and tools, as well as techniques of art. In this kind of setting, there was little demarcation between home and work.

As a rule, living from the land necessitates mutual respect between men and women, even though there were/are some gender divisions of labour. For example, men did big game hunting and trapping, so they left their homes during particular seasons. But this did not translate into the devaluation of women who stayed home to tend to their children and families. Nor were men and women confined to rigid gender-defined roles. Men could do housework and, indeed, were expected to assist, and women could go out hunting, and those who did were expected to carry their share of work out on the land. This theme is also evident in Maria's *Stories of the Road Allowance People* (Campbell 1995).

An internationally respected environmentalist, intellectual, and activist, Okanagan author Jeannette Armstrong also turns to home and land as key themes in her first novel, *Slash* (1985). Set in the heydays of the early 1970s American Indian Movement and confrontations with the FBI in the United States, *Slash* is an historical novel that recounts the historical and continuing impact of colonization as seen through the life of Slash, a young Okanagan man. The novel is rich with political commentary, but, for me, the most moving parts in the novel centre on Slash's relationship with his home and his land. His home is set on a ranch among the sage-brush hills of the Okanagan. His parents (and kin) are hard-working ranchers who tend to their homes and their children. Slash grows up with the Okanagan language and myths as well as strong family values and work ethic. Of course, the story is complicated by the legacy of colonization, and, all too soon, Slash finds himself adrift. For quite some time, he is lost between the safety and coherence of family traditions and the disruption of town and school, and then the post-colonial chaos of political rallies. Many times throughout the novel, the smells of home cooking and the texture of the Okanagan hills lead Slash back to his home. Finally, Slash grounds himself literally by coming home to stay. By this, he is reclaiming his homeland, his culture.

Land or the landscape (or sea and seascape, as in the case of Eden Robinson's *Monkey Beach* 2000) features significantly in women's writing. This is not surprising as land is the backbone to original cultures of the Americas. In *Honour the Sun* (1987), Ojibwa novelist Ruby Slipperjack treats us to her character Owl's landscape. Owl, a carefree ten-year-old girl, enjoys her childhood by playing outside for much of the novel. Owl's summer playground is nestled in the heart of the Canadian Shield, home to bears and blueberries. Home also to the Ojibwa of northern Ontario, Owl's landscape is contoured with spruce trees, birch, poplars, craggy hills, rocks, sloping meadows, and lakes. And rail-road tracks. Owl's large family consists of her mother and numerous brothers and sisters. Owl's widowed mother, a strong, enduring matriarch of the family, keeps her many children fed and organized. Owl's "Mom" knows the ways of the land and lake. She routinely fills their canoe with her children and paddles them to a small island, where the family camps and relaxes. Many skills of the land are required for such an event. Making and cooking bannock, picking berries, fishing, filleting and frying fish, collecting and chopping firewood, usually birch, provide an oasis from the chaos of community. She feeds her kids with fish and berries, macaroni, potatoes, and bannock. Slipperjack's exquisite details of this land-based culture are lovely. One can almost hear the fire crackling and smell with Owl the "birchbark and wood smoke drift into the tent."

Of course, having to make a living by using resources from the land (or waters), whether those resources are animals, fowl, fish, or gardening, or wood or plants, roots and berries, takes hard work and intimate knowledge of one's resources and ecological environment. Nor is the environment always gentle or non-violent, for being carnivores living off the land means killing animals for food. Living on the land can be difficult and harsh. We should be careful not to insult the hard work involved by romanticizing it inappropriately. Naturally, it has its beautiful, even "Hiawathian," aspects and moments, but this is a culture that entails much work, patience, knowledge, and expertise. It is not just camping: it is a whole way of life.

By providing us with such exquisite detail, these writers offer numerous teachings as well as anthropological and ecological data about our various cultures. There is much to learn from our writers. The data about Aboriginal use of both modern and natural resources, land or waters, tell us much about the intelligence, the planning, the organization, and, generally, the ingenuity and science of these cultures.

The academic community rather quickly cast such Aboriginal-derived knowledge as "traditional ecological knowledge" (now TK), different from Western science. Numerous studies – or, rather, typological charts – came out comparing presumed differences and similarities between Aboriginal (read traditional) and Western (read scientific)

176 The Emma LaRocque Reader

knowledge. While this discussion is ever changing, there remain stereotypes about indigenous knowledge.[11] However, even a quick overview of indigenous cultural developments immediately points to an Aboriginal-based science to not only the building of materially evident cultures, but to the collection and arrangement of data about the land and the animals, seasons, climate, geography, astronomy, and the environment. In other words, there is a science to knowing the nooks and crannies of land-based life, but much of this has gone unnoticed – or if noted, stereotyped – by both Aboriginal and non-Aboriginal readers and critics, especially by those who have grown up in cities and have no way to relate to rural or bush life. Such inability to fully appreciate this lifestyle is compounded by the Western bias for urbanization and industrialization.

But there is also much said, both explicitly and implicitly, about urbanization in Aboriginal writing. This is to be expected, not only because urbanization and industrialization has had an impact on Aboriginal cultures, but also because the Aboriginal population is increasingly urban. Since the 1950s, the numbers of Aboriginal people have been steadily growing in Canadian cities, and the 2006 census indicates that 53 percent of Aboriginal people reside in urban centres located outside reserve communities. And those who still live in rural areas, whether on reserves or in other settlements, have long been integrating urban and industrial aspects of Canadian life. Indigenous cultures built towns and cities long before Europeans arrived in the Americas. Also, particularly in northern Canada, as long as Native peoples have been engaged in the fur trade, they have been integrating metropolitan aspects of world culture. Perhaps globalization began with the fur trade. It is not surprising, then, that writers treat crackerjack popcorn, bubblegum, clocks, radios, railroads, boats, books, ranching, farming, flying, cars and trucks, or Elvis Presley, as being as commonplace as *Wisakehcha* or Seneca roots.

Writers treat urbanization as being both impositional and natural. What are considered impositional are governmental policies, interference, forced relocation, forced education, and other legal manoeuvres that threaten both the cultural and resource base of Aboriginal peoples. Material cultural change, on the other hand, is treated as part of the cultural landscape natural to Native peoples. Many policy analysts as well as academics have missed this Aboriginal approach to cultural change. To repeat a point made earlier, contemporary Aboriginal thinkers

---

11 I pursue some of these issues in "From the Land to the Classroom: Broadening Epistemology" (see chapter).

treating cultural change (when it is voluntary) as natural to Aboriginal peoples is consistent with all the archeological and anthropological evidence that indicates that our ancestors in the Americas were, under normal, that is, politically balanced, circumstances, dynamic peoples who engaged not only in material international trade but in the exchange of ideas, customs, and beliefs. Indigenous trade goes far back into indigenous history, much farther back than trade with Europeans. Again, it was the European colonizers who treated indigenous peoples as primitives afraid of change. It was colonizers who developed into an art form the various but well-known stereotypes of Aboriginal peoples as "traditional" peoples without history, that is, peoples stuck in ceremonial repetition (albeit "colourful") but peoples who cannot change without disintegrating or peoples who do not assume agency for their life. And, to the extent Native peoples have internalized these stereotypes, it has paralysed our peoples, perhaps especially our youth, from assuming our/their birthright as contemporary Canadians.

Yet, writers have long demonstrated the vibrancy of Aboriginal individuals and communities. Writers do not treat Native peoples as an amorphous collective. Rather, like all storytellers throughout the ages, writers present Native characters, whether fictional or non-fictional, as unique individuals who have names and personalities and the full range of humanity, that is, persons who are capable of the good and the bad. Some are very funny. Some are downright evil. Some are heroic. Most are ordinary, imperfect folks who laugh, cry, and work very hard to keep their families fed, well clothed, and safe. Colonial processes, such as land theft, forced relocation, residential schools, encroaching urbanization and industrialization, violence, and racial and cultural discrimination have certainly caused catastrophic trauma, as social conditions continue to indicate, but Native peoples have demonstrated personal and cultural strength, perseverance, and enormous creativity. They have continued to live their lives in inventive ways even throughout those moments in Canadian history when "out of sight, out of mind" was much in practise by most non-Native Canadians.

Aboriginal writing is, of course, infused with Aboriginal languages, ideals, values, norms, faiths, and belief systems. Many writers draw on myths and legends not only to keep the legends alive, but also often to make resistance statements about colonization. Lee Maracle (1993) opens her haunting novel, *Ravensong*, with the sound of Raven weeping. The novel tells the story about a deadly flu epidemic in the 1950s that claimed numerous lives of an urban Native family. Raven is a central mythological figure to cultures along the Pacific northwest coast, and it is Raven who sounds the cry from the

178 The Emma LaRocque Reader

bowels of the earth and sea in an effort to wake up the seemingly unconscious Native and white communities. Raven and Cedar work to get "white town" to notice the devastations and to guide Native women towards recovery.

Ojibwa writer Lenore Keeshig-Tobias (1992) uses the metaphor of Trickster to make multi-layered critical comments about the white man in her wonderfully sharp poem, "Trickster Beyond 1992: Our Relationship." But she also turns the critical knife towards Trickster, charging him with having disappeared at a crucial time in history. Ultimately, she is critical about herself and the newcomer: "He is like me, a Trickster, a liar ... a new kind of man is coming, a White Man."

Aboriginal languages are honoured in a great variety of ways in these writings. Eden Robinson (2000) opens her novel with six crows that speak to her in Haisla, "La'es, they say, la'es, la'es." Characters are given Aboriginal names or nick-names. Scholars use Native words to explain Native world views and philosophies. Or to correct misrepresentation. But perhaps no one writer has foregrounded a Native language like Cree poet Louise Halfe. The first time I came across Louise's poetry (1993) was when I was reading the manuscript for *Writing the Circle*. My heart sang when I read ["Pakak" about] "Pahkakhos" – the flying skeleton of Cree legend, a legend my mother often cited to us. Of course, my mother had her own version, quite different from Louise's, but just to see it in print made me smile right out loud. From a cornucopia of Cree thought and grit of experience, the writer's love of words, Cree words, spill out, roar out onto the pages in all her publications. And into our own bones. [Halfe]'s poetry teases us to the edges of human encounters with bears, bones, rocks, ghosts, spirits, tricksters. She takes us even to the marrow of shadows and light that humans are – she lifts the rocks and makes us look at what is under there. For Louise Halfe, as it is for all great writers and thinkers, "healing" is no sweet, meditational journey; it is raw, terrible, and gutsy: "Flying Skeleton/I used to wonder/Where you kept yourself ... You lifted your boney hands/To greet me and I/ Ran without a tongue" (1994, 8).

As colonized peoples, we all ran without our tongues in many phases or parts of our lives. In a previous era, Rita Joe (2001 [1988], 17) wrote, "I lost my talk." But writing has served as the vehicle to recovering our tongues. By articulating our histories, our traumas, or our cultures, writing becomes the process, the result, and the expression of decolonization. Intellectual resistance in the form of writing opens possibilities for liberation. Louise Halfe, like most writers, has more than found her tongue. She has reinvented both Cree and English. Her "leddars" to the "Poop" are simply resistance par excellence. In her second collection of poetry, *Blue Marrow*, Halfe (2004 [1998]) takes us to places of terror and laughter. We hear voices of those who had the courage to test the edges of human senses. These courageous souls are our ancestors.

Writers serve our cultures by being reflective, often analytical. This work is known as criticism. But writers also mirror to us who we are. They deal with greatness as well as our smallnesses. They comment on our contemporary predicaments. For example, Lee Maracle (2002) lays open the cycle of abuse and neglect in Native families in her novel, *Daughters Are Forever*. Margo Kane's (1990) play, *Moonlodge*, confronts issues of identity wrapped up in stereotypes to which some Native characters succumb.

Writers serve our cultures by assuming the role of cultural critics. It is often assumed that criticism is only negative and that Aboriginal writers should just focus on what is positive. Or that we should just criticize white society and not Aboriginal actions, beliefs, proposals, communities, organizations, or leadership. In tandem with this, there is much anti-intellectualism in our society, both in the Native and larger communities. I believe such attitudes reflect a misunderstanding as to the nature of criticism and the social purpose of knowledge. When practised with social awareness, responsibility, and compassion, the critic's job is as positive as, say, a musician's job.

The need to be positive is understandable, given the magnitude of misrepresentation to which we have been subjected. It is a corrective response to the stereotyping of Native peoples as social problems. Further, there is no question that humans gravitate towards creativity and constructiveness. However, we do need to pay attention to R.D. Laing's meaning of "selective inattention,"[12] or false consciousness. We, as peoples in Canada, are not yet fully liberated or decolonized. We have not even begun to explore the seductive use of words often framed within positivism. For example, we now have "historic trauma" instead of colonization. We now pursue "healing" instead of decolonization. The two are not to be confused. The language of "healing" assumes woundedness and invites therapy; the language of decolonization assumes power politics and should invite exploration of political liberation (not to be confused with violence). The language of "healing" assumes personal responsibility; the language of decolonization assumes a confrontation with colonial forces and the rearrangement of the status quo. We must remain vigilant against being "psychologized" just as we must remain

---

12 Sullivan (1955) is responsible for the concept of "selective inattention." Laing (1967) wrote about "mystification," among other concerns – Elaine Coburn, editor's note.

180 The Emma LaRocque Reader

alert to being exclusively politicized (and culturalized, for that matter). We need to be clear that agency does not mean the abandonment of decolonization work. Of course, neither does it mean the shucking of our responsibilities as human beings. Accordingly, we should pay greater attention to our self-constructed mythical portraits of ourselves as well as to the vocation of being a critic. All this can be accomplished without neglecting to emphasize the much-needed corrective view of Native peoples, and certainly Native women, as peoples of persistence, adaptability, and regeneration.

Concluding Thoughts

Women writers demonstrate great love and valuation of their people and many specifically honour their grandmothers, grandfathers, mothers, fathers, siblings, and other kin. I notice that many poems are dedicated to specific individuals. In several of my own poems, I recall the names of my *Ama*, *Bapa*, as well as the names of my sisters, aunts, and uncles, all people who have suffered enormously under the weight of colonial forces but people who also loved life and laughter. These were people who drummed along with my guitar, people who tickled and teased us and made us laugh. People who told us stories into the night. But they also sang haunting songs about loneliness, wanting to come home, about lost loves and times. They also wept for their fathers, mothers, and siblings. And many had to weep for their children lost to sickness. These were people who gave us language and culture. People who have left this earth, many in untimely, even jarring, fashion. And with their leaving, our families, our communities got so much smaller, numerically and, in some ways, culturally. Yet, despite these losses, rebirthing always takes place, whether with new generations or by creative processes. On these same lands or on new lands. Footpaths through ferns and spruce or sidewalk in the city – these are all our lands now. We all have the honour and the challenge of living our cultures for all generations, those of our ancestors and those for tomorrow.

Perhaps culture is ultimately about what people do together. It has been suggested that as long as Aboriginal people continue to do things together, there will be Aboriginal cultures alive. It is important, therefore, that we facilitate get-togethers – think tanks, conferences, potlatches, achievement celebrations, remembrances, sun dances, sweats, smudges, potluck dinners. And that we do this in our communities as well as on national levels.

As we all know, all sorts of conferences do go on all around us. Often, these conferences focus on socio-political and economic issues. All very important. But I notice there are not many conferences on Aboriginal writing or writers (or on other Aboriginal artists). It was with this in mind that I envisaged a conference on Native writers and writing, and, finally in 2004, with the assistance of a good friend and colleague, we organized a conference "For the Love of Words" (see chapter "Sources of Inspiration: The Birth of 'For the Love of Words': Aboriginal Writers of Canada"). It was truly a wonderful experience to read and listen to amazing, cultivated, indigenous-rooted, inspiring words of prose, poetry, plays, biography, and criticism, largely created by Aboriginal writers and scholars. Many writers expressed great appreciation for this rare opportunity to share creativity, one's inner being, and love of words with each other. This conference highlighted the great work of recovery and renaissance, not to mention the artistic and intellectual work that writers perform in our communities, in our country, and in our world. In this sense, doing things together, then, is decolonization. It is reconstructive. It confirmed to me the crying need for Native and white communities to celebrate artists, certainly writers.

Native women's writings have reached deep into the Canadian and Aboriginal intellectual culture. In very significant ways, Native women's writings have had a profound impact on both Native and non-Native communities. Aboriginal university students, for example, gain a greater understanding of cultural expression, critique, and political resistance; non-Native readers may gain a new appreciation of Aboriginal cultural and political locations in Canada with new commitments to supporting Aboriginal rights, lands, and resources. Today, Native women are not only cited by intellectuals on the international stage, they are among the sought-after intellectuals on the international stage.

When all the political wranglings have passed, what will stay will be the great thoughts, the great words. I find in Jeannette Armstrong's (2000, 19) poetry of the soul a great call for human liberation:

Wake up. All the shadows are gone. There is daylight even in the swamps. The bluejays are laughing…. Laughing at the humans who don't know the sun is up and it's a new day…. You are all turning yellow from too much sleep.

2010

Insider Notes: Reframing
the Narratives

The prairie is full of bones.
The bones stand and sing
and I feel the weight of them
as they guide my fingers on this page

– Louise Halfe, Blue Marrow

In the summer of 1974, I worked for the Native Curriculum Resource Project, part of the Province of Alberta's Department of Education. My job was to research alternatives to Alberta's provincial curriculum with respect to its treatment of Native peoples. I was struck immediately by the endless layers of stereotypes in both elementary and secondary textbooks, particularly in history and social studies. I easily connected what I was discovering – and in an important sense, re-discovering – with what I had known as a Métis student in public schools. I was connecting my knowledge with my experience, or, as I have written earlier, my footnotes with my voice.[1] This research enabled me to write *Defeathering the Indian* (LaRocque 1975), which addresses the problem of stereotypes in schools and in society. *Defeathering the Indian* is, on one level, a curriculum handbook for teachers. On another, perhaps more important level, it is a resistance book without the political language to mark it as such. What I was protesting – that is, resisting – was the portrayal of Native peoples as befeathered savages. I pointed out the prevalence of the stereotypes in school textbooks, classroom politics, and in society, particularly as promoted by the media and marketplace.

---

1 For a beginning discussion of Native "voice" in response to the notion of Native "voicelessness" in literature (and society) see chapter "Preface: Here Are Our Voices – Who Will Hear?"

Insider Notes: Reframing the Narratives

I explained how dehumanizing it is to be seen and treated as savages, as less than human creatures bereft of valuable culture, coherent language, and multidimensional personalities. I turned to facts of biography and cultural information, and used humour, among other things, to highlight our (Native) humanity and challenge the Canadian historical record and its gamut of culturally produced stereotypes. I turned the tables to point out, however meekly, who the "real savages" (meaning the American cavalry) were. In the end, I optimistically (naively, some would say) appealed to our common humanity, to common sense and common decency. I tried to be subtle rather than explosive, but I think such a concern was more a mark of my colonization than of my liberation. And, certainly, I was unaware of sexist language. I was young and in the early stages of decolonization. In many ways I was not particularly aware of Western-defined politics. I was just beginning to shore up my Plains Cree-Métis–based youthful knowledge with another kind of knowledge, the outside world of many voices and the protocols of Western scholarship.

I was also entering a particular kind of discourse. I was quite unaware, at the time, that I was well within an established and ever developing Native resistance tradition, in facts, process, tone, and approach. Indeed, the unity of experience, presentation, and argumentation across the centuries of this tradition is dramatic. Whether in the form of social and historical commentaries, autobiographies, short stories, legends, poetry, or plays, whether it is in the 1790s or 1990s, whether it is lands, reserves, homesteads, homes, parents, children, or women personally invaded, or whether it is languages, ceremonies, epistemologies, or faiths suppressed, there is a striking unity of occurrence. Native writers record historical and personal incursions, social upheavals, a range of emotions, and unique individual and cultural backgrounds, and struggle for hope and determination. The earlier style of recording these many realities is often a mixture of rhetoric, extraordinary insight, moral outrage, and dignified poignancy. Literary devices are both inventive and prosaic. The argumentation combines historical and current Aboriginal traditions, including resistance and postcolonial strategies. The writing is more complex than first meets the eye.

Is Native Writing Resistance Literature?

Native activists and intellectuals have long been *resisting* Canada's political and intellectual treatment of Native peoples. However, situating Native writing as resistance literature requires some discussion because, for a number of historical and cultural reasons, Native writing

184 The Emma LaRocque Reader

does present its own unique problems, approaches, and features. In *Resistance Literature*, Barbara Harlow (1987) traces the development of the theory of resistance literature to organized resistance militant movements for national liberation and independence "on the part of the colonized peoples in those areas of the world over which Western Europe and North America have sought socio-economic control and cultural dominion". These movements have produced "a significant corpus of literary writing, both narrative and poetic, as well as a broad spectrum of theoretical analysis of the political, ideological, and cultural parameters of this struggle" (Harlow 1987, xvi). The writers, ideologues, and theoreticians of these movements "have articulated a role for literature and poets within the struggle alongside the gun, the pamphlet and the diplomatic delegation" (Harlow 1987, xvii).

Given these parameters, Native writing does not strictly follow "resistance literature within the early Third World"[2] terms. In the first instance, Native peoples of Canada did not have written languages[3]; therefore, they did not leave their own written records of their resistance activities against the early European intruders. Indeed, it is not until the late 1700s and early 1800s that a few individual Natives were able to write in English, having learned the skills of Western literacy from missionaries. Reflecting the complexity of the Native people's relationship with the missionaries and the Canadian school system, be it public or residential, Native writing as a form of any significant collective expression was not possible until about the 1970s, if not the 1980s.[4] This is not to imply that English literacy is a necessary foundation to resistance, for clearly Native people resisted the European oppressions long before they took up the English alphabet. Indeed, resisting colonial languages has been an integral part of the resistance.

Native writers have a complicated relationship with the English language, a relationship that reflects more than 500 years of cultural, linguistic, and political appropriations, exchanges, and confrontations. As Albert Memmi (1957, 106–9) points out, literacy is a linguistic, political, and psychological challenge for colonized peoples of oral traditions

---

2 Harlow also traces the problematic term "Third World", noting that it "sees to possess more rhetorical power than precision" (1987, 4).

3 Writing in English is not the only kind of literacy. Kulchyski (2005) makes compelling observations that particular inscriptions, on the Pangnirtung landscape, "marks perhaps on one level a written response, the construction of a different sort of text" (189). See also Mildon (2008).

4 For an adequate summary of Native people's experiences of the Canadian school system, see Frideres (1998, 148–68). Frideres presents figures indicating that about 60 per cent of Native students do not complete high school.

who move on to the technique of writing – that is, adopting, and surely tweaking – the colonizer's language.

Many Native writers have certainly commented on the difficulties of adopting the colonizer's language(s). This awareness is perhaps why many Native writers and speakers have felt compelled to acknowledge our oral traditions. Apparently self-conscious of the fact Native North Americans presumably did not have written languages, Native writers have extolled their spoken languages as well as their methods of recollection. But, more than self-consciousness or concession, we are assigning equal value to oral traditions which, of course, include an array of communication signs and systems that may form a "sort of text." One of the earliest Native writers, George Copway (1818–1869), begins his cultural defence in 1847 by what at first appears to be concession: "I have not the happiness of being able to refer to written records in narrating the history of my forefathers." But he also immediately stakes out the value of oral tradition by calling on his memory: "but I can reveal to the world what has long been laid up in my memory" (Copway 1992 [1847], 19[5]). Similarly, a century later, Chief Dan George wrote, "My people's memory/Reaches into the/Beginning of all things" (1974, 85). The final report of the Royal Commission on Aboriginal Peoples, issued in 1996, also highlights an anonymous statement by one of the Native presenters: "I have no written speech. Everything that I have said I had been carrying in my heart, because I have seen it. I have experienced it."

In 1969 northwest coast folklorist, artist, and actor George Clutesi (1905–1988) introduced his collection of Tse-Shat traditions, traditions he translated into English, by declaring that he avoids documentation: "This narrative is not meant to be documentary. In fact, it is meant to evade documents. It is meant for the reader to feel and to say I was there and indeed I saw."[6]

---

5 The writings of Copway are printed originally in this form:

Copway, George. *The life, history and travels of Kah-ge-ga-bowh (George Copway): a young Indian chief of the Ojebwa nation, a convert to the Christian faith and a missionary to his people for twelve years; with a sketch of the present state of the Ojebwa nation in regard to Christianity and their future prospects: also, an appeal with all the names of the chiefs now living, who have been christianized, and the missionaries now laboring among them.* 6th ed. Philadelphia: J. Harmstead, 1847.

More recently, they were printed in other editions, including Copway, George. *The Traditional History and Characteristic Sketches of the Ojibway Nation.* New York: AMS Press, 1972. – Elaine Coburn, editor's note.

6 Clutesi (1969) emphasizes this point by setting the whole statement in an unnumbered page at the beginning of his book.

186   The Emma LaRocque Reader

It is often taken for granted that literacy is an enormous improvement in human evolution. Those of us who come from oral traditions have quite different perspectives on literacy (and evolution). In fact, literacy becomes the enemy when printed words are used for "extinguishment" purposes, as nineteenth-century Ojibway activist Catherine Soneegoh Sutton (1823–1865) put it so poignantly.[7] Not only is English (or French) the vehicle for the extinguishment of Aboriginal rights, it is also the expressive means of dehumanization. Mohawk lawyer, educator, activist, and writer Patricia Monture-Angus explains that "it is probably fortunate for Aboriginal people today that so many of our histories are oral histories. Information that was kept in people's heads was not available to Europeans, could not be changed and moulded into pictures of 'savagery' and 'paganism'" (Monture-Angus 1995, 11). For these reasons, and as George Clutesi knew so well, in certain contexts documentation must be assiduously avoided. My parents, who were of Clutesi's generation, but, unlike Clutesi, never attended school, knew this too. This is why my father refused to let me go to school until he had no choice. This is why my grand-mother and my mother told us stories deep into the winter nights. Clearly, it is not by accident that I grew up so close to my language, a language that remains closest to my soul, and just as clearly I have my parents to thank for their insightful resistance, a resistance I did not fully appreciate until I began to understand that language is the epistemological basis of culture.

As Ojibway writer and ethnographer Basil Johnston argues, it is through our languages we carry our world views, which are, in turn, expressed in our epistemologies (Johnston 1990, 10–15). This means, then, that our approaches to the notion and application of knowledge may be quite different from those that inform Western conventions. Anthropologist Robin Ridington (1990) has posited that oral-based, hunting Aboriginal societies approach knowledge rather than materials as technology and "they code information about their world differently from those of us whose discourse is conditioned by written documents" (277). These "differences," as Ridington (1995) appreciates, are much more involved than the oversimplified comparative charts that have become current in discussions on Aboriginal cultural differences or "traditions." Among non-Native scholars, Ridington has among the most perceptive understandings of how northern hunting societies conceive of and apply knowledge, and that this knowledge

---

7 Sutton quoted from a letter written to the editor of *The Leader* in 1876; as quoted in Petrone (1990, 65–8).

Insider Notes: Reframing the Narratives

is intimately linked to language, land, and skills. Land-based Aboriginal cultures are nuanced and intricate, and this should raise questions about how we translate them into our urban lives, literatures, and criticisms.[8] In any event, the indigenous *eh-tay-ta-moowin* (in Cree it approximates "hypothesizing") and *eh-too-ta-moo-win* ("praxis") have implications for those of us engaged in scholarly activities. Cree writer and educator Janice Acoose finds "writing in the colonizer's language simultaneously painful and liberating" (1995, 12). Painful because English provides her "the only recourse ... to convey the reality of the Indigenous peoples." Painful because our words have been infantilized, stolen, silenced, or erased. Yet, "writing in the colonizer's language" is also facilitative (I am not sure I can agree that it is liberating), for as Acoose puts it, "doing research and writing encourages re-creation, renaming and empowerment of both Indigenous peoples and non-indigenous peoples" (1995, 12).

There is no question but that literacy and the art and politics of documentation present us with cultural problems when, for example, literacy steals the nuances of oral expressions, and with political problems when words are used to vilify or to dispossess. But literacy in and of itself is a great human achievement; obviously, literacy is a two-edged sword dependent on whether humans use it for oppressive or emancipatory purposes. In certain contexts I can certainly appreciate George Clutesi's strategy of avoiding documentation, but those of us today engaged in scholarship and writing cannot and must not avoid documentation. For now we are here. And document we must, for much of the "war" is in the words. And document we do.

Further, we are in the twenty-first century, and English (or French) is as much our birthright as our Aboriginal languages. English is in many respects our new "native" language, not only because English may become the only language known to future Native generations (I shudder at the thought) but also because it has become the common language through which we now communicate. English is now serving to unite us, and, in many ironic respects, serving to decolonize us. In this sense, perhaps we can say literacy is liberating. Our usage of English is, of course, not necessarily that of the colonizer. Since we have a painful and political relationship with this language, we attend to the task of "reinventing the enemy's language" as Native American poet

---

8 I explore a complex of pedagogical and epistemological issues concerning the translation of land-based cultures into our classrooms in "From the Land to the Classroom: Broadening Epistemology" (see chapter).

188 The Emma LaRocque Reader

Joy Harjo has so aptly put it.[9] To re-invent the enemies' language is a re-creative process, and for Cree poets, a Cree-ative process, and, as such, English is now as much our vehicle of creative expression as it is our vehicle of resistance.

Assessing Native resistance writing is also complicated by the fact Natives are still expressing the presentness of their colonization. It is apparent that Native peoples are not uniformly conscious of or resistant to their colonized condition, one expression of which is the internalization of the colonizer's standards and stereotypes. One consequence of this internalization is the Natives' sense of shame concerning their Indianness, a theme many Native writers treat. This sense of shame is another indication of having taken on the images, standards, or expectations of the colonizer, which Métis historian and social critic Howard Adams (1975) referred to as the "White Ideal" in *Prison of Grass*. Powerful media through which White North Americans' conceptions of beauty, status, acceptability, privilege, or reality become established have had damaging effects on both White and Native self-images. Whereas for Whites the White Ideal has, as a rule, provided them with an exaggerated self-assurance, Native peoples, much like other oppressed or "minority" groups,[10] have struggled with self-acceptance in the face of formidable racial and cultural rejection. And such racism continues to harass contemporary generations even if it appears to some that there is an Aboriginal "industry" of privilege! There are no socio-economic privileges for Aboriginal peoples, but more, they are still being hounded and haunted by White North America's image machine, which has persistently portrayed them in extremes as either the grotesque ignoble or noble savage. Internalization is just one of our struggles against misrepresentation, which in our literatures are reflected in both overt and subtle ways. The study of Native writing must take into consideration this not so inconsiderable problem evident in our works and across generations ...[]

In any case, resistance literature is no longer limited to specific historical liberation movements in Africa, Central and South America, or the Far and Middle East; it has broadened to include what is now generally referred to as postcolonial literatures. Ashcroft, Griffiths, and Tiffin (1989) use the term "post-colonial" to "cover all the culture affected

---

9 This phrase is original to Harjo and is the title of an anthology co-edited with Gloria Bird (Harjo and Bird 1997).

10 Some of the classic Afro-American statements on this include Baldwin (1949), X (1965), and Haley (1977).

by the imperial process from the moment of colonization to the present day" in which there is concern "with the world as it exists during and after the period of European imperial domination and the effects of this on contemporary literatures." And they suggest that "it is most appropriate as the term for the new cross-cultural criticism which has emerged in recent years and for the discourse through which this is constituted" (Ashcroft, Griffiths, and Tiffin 1989, 2).

Native peoples certainly fall within (and outside) the inclusive terms as set out here, although Native Canadians hardly enjoy "postcoloniality" since their colonial experience is imbricated with the past and present. Neither is the Native experience of colonialism universally understood nor has Native writing as resistance been consistently recognized at home or abroad. Nevertheless, we have been protesting being othered or dominated by re-settler colonies. We have certainly been articulating the experience and, to rephrase Ashcroft, Griffiths, and Tiffin (1989, 2), *talking back* "to the imperial centre."

Articulating the experience and "talking back" constitutes, according to Peter Hitchcock (1993), a "dialogics of the oppressed," and while dialogics does not end the oppression, it does "constitute a significant logic of resistance and an array of contestatory practises" (4). Native peoples of Canada have been engaging in contestatory practises right from the initial contact with Europeans to the present. But more to the point, Native writers and critics are not going to depend on external definitions as to whether they have written resistance literature. It is to Native writing and theorizing that critics must turn to be able to assess the cause and nature of the resisting Native in Canada.

To be sure, resistance may not always be immediately apparent to the unstudied; for examples we can turn to a range of works by authors that include Chief Dan George, Ruby Slipperjack, Tomson Highway, Tom King, Richard Wagamese, Richard Van Camp, or Eden Robinson, among others. With respect to producing literature along with armed resistance, no one Native nation or peoples has produced literature from an "organized resistance movement" within a "specific historical context," as defined by Harlow (1987, 11). This is undoubtedly due to the vast cultural, linguistic, and geographical differences among the indigenous peoples of Canada. Perhaps Louis Riel, who today would be understood as a liberation resistance fighter, came closest to producing literature within an organized resistance movement, but he had no colleagues in this pursuit. Certainly, many Native works cannot be considered works of resistance in the tradition of liberationist Third World thinkers and writers or the explosive American Black writers of the 1960s, such as Eldridge Cleaver or Malcolm X, but, as I have argued, a simple assertion of one's (Native) humanity is a form of resistance, given the magnitude of dehumanization over a span of 500 years. In this overarching history of colonization, Native peoples have developed a collective sense of relationship to the land and to each other, and to the common cause of decolonization. In this sense, every politically aware Native teacher, scholar, writer, artist, filmmaker, poet, or activist is ultimately a producer of resistance material. In fact, precisely because Native writers have not written "alongside the gun" (Harlow 1987, xvii), their writing is all the more the form of articulate resistance in Canada.

Native Writers Resisting Colonial Practises

Not only is this writing articulate, it is in fact quite extensive, as Penny Petrone (1990) documents in *Native Literature in Canada: From Oral Tradition*.[11] Petrone produced the first comprehensive study of Native literatures and showed how much and how long Natives have been writing. Although she acknowledges the social protest element to this literature, her reading is more an ethnography than a study in intellectual agency. But Native writing is much more the story of strategic contestation than it is of ethnographic testaments, and when cultural information is provided it is usually a device of contestation.

Now, of course, an increasing assortment of scholars are paying increasing attention to Aboriginal perspectives. But I am not sure to what extent these scholars appreciate the oppressive nature of colonial canons and their pernicious workings in our respective intellectual lives. The problem has centrally to do with the "civ/sav" ideology,[12] which dichotomizes Native-White relations in terms of civilization inevitably winning over savagery, as most Western writers have assumed throughout the centuries. This ideology circles the wagon, so to speak, on any Native action and reaction as something infantile or less than human. Historical and literary treatment of so-called "Indian Wars" is a case in point: Aboriginal Nations fighting to save their persons, communities, cultures, and lands was propagandized as simply irrational violence of bloodthirsty savages.

---

11 German scholar Hartmut Lutz has also produced a number of works detailing various writings by Native peoples. See also chapter "Preface: Here Are Our Voices – Who Will Hear?" and Hulan (1999).

12 My discussion of the civ/sav dichotomy was first published in "The Métis in English Canadian Literature" (see chapter).

But once the Native-White encounter is understood as colonially framed, and once Native peoples are accorded humanity, we can find their many contestations in a variety of genres going back to the earliest encounters. So read, the subtext to the very records that sought to denigrate Native humanity is a power struggle between newcomer and indigenous discourses. For example, as recorded in the *Jesuit Relations*, Father Brébeuf remarks on Huron challenge to the Jesuit tenets of creation and "our other mysteries." Apparently miffed that the "headstrong" Huron approached this discussion with cultural relativism, Brebeuf points out to them "by means of a little globe ... that there is only one world," to which the Huron "remain without reply" (Mealing 1965, 44). This is a fairly classic instance of early Europeans resorting to technical trickery to strengthen their claim to superiority, especially when they were confronted with Native cultural and intellectual scepticism or resistance. Parker Duchemin (1990) in "'A Parcel of Whelps,' Alexander Mackenzie among the Indians," explains that, as a way of establishing White authority over Native peoples, "a charade of white omniscience and omnipotence ... was played and replayed" by European explorers (53–4). It had to be replayed because Native peoples were not so easily impressed. The point is Native peoples were not glazed-eyed savages sitting on their haunches by the seashore waiting for European gods and baubles. In the understated words of Olive Dickason (1992) in *Canada's First Nations*, "most authorities agree that it is highly unlikely that 'civilization' was brought over whole to a welcoming population waiting to be enlightened" (60). A decolonized critical review of archival records shows Native peoples resisted ideological impositions, economic exploitation, cultural insults, and personal abuse.[13]

Similarly, a critical review of contemporary Native writing shows that Natives have been resisting colonizing practises as long as they have been writing. The depth and scope of Natives engaging in contestatory literature is such that we can refer to it as a tradition in the sense of canon. We can trace this tradition from – as Petrone (1990) puts it – the "first literary coterie of Indians in Canada" (35) of the mid-1800s. Of course the most dramatic growth of Native writing has taken place since 1969 when Harold Cardinal signalled the arrival of contemporary resistance writing with his *Unjust Society*. If any era birthed Native resistance literature proper, it is the 1970s, for, on the heels of Cardinal

---

13 Native resistance is amply recorded in fur-trade journals: see (Ray and Freeman 1977; Saum 1965).

came, first, a steady stream of socio-political commentaries, then poetry, and autobiographies. Also published in this era were a miscellany of collections that presented a cross-section of biographies, essays of social and literary criticism, interviews, government reports or proposals, newspaper articles and editorials, short stories, plays, and poetry.

This was followed in the 1980s, finally, by novels. Beatrice Culleton's *In Search of April Raintree* (1983), Jeannette Armstrong's *Slash* (1985), Ruby Slipperjack's *Honour the Sun* (1987), and Lee Maracle's *I am Woman* (1988) – which is not a novel – became popular reading and made it into mainstream classrooms studying Canadian Native peoples. These works have gained considerable attention, especially as resistance works. Since then, streams of novels have been published, most of them after 1990; among the most well known include Thomas King (*Medicine River; Green Grass, Running Water*), Ruby Slipperjack (*Silent Words*), Lee Maracle (*Sundogs; Raven*), Richard Wagamese (*Keeper 'n Me; A Quality of Light*), Richard Van Camp (*The Lesser Blessed*), Tomson Highway (*Kiss of the Fur Queen*), Jeannette Armstrong (*Whispering in Shadows*), and Eden Robinson (*Monkey Beach*).

Poetry has continued to pour in from a host of writers, much of which is to be found in current anthologies on Native literature as well as in literary journals and periodicals. A number of poets have also published books of poetry (e.g., Rita Joe, Duke Redbird, Louise Halfe, Marilyn Dumont, Beth Cuthand, Annharte Baker, Duncan Mercredi, Gregory Scofield). Short stories and plays are also to be found in both old and new anthologies. Entertaining short-story writers include Richard Van Camp, the humorist and prolific writer/playwright Drew Hayden Taylor, and veteran writer and ethnologist Basil Johnston. And, of course, plays by Tomson Highway (*The Rez Sisters, Dry Lips Oughta Move to Kapuskasing*) have received international recognition. Other notable playwrights include Margo Kane, Floyd Favel, Daniel David Moses, Ian Ross, Armand Ruffo, and Monique Mojica.

There are resistance themes common to all these works, irrespective of genre, gender, era, or even chronology. They engage fairly overt postcolonial and decolonization themes that include the re-establishing of Native cultures and the challenging of historical and cultural records. The texts also expose destructive government policies and social injustices. Many novelists, short-story writers, poets, and biographers recount cultural fragmentation in the form of community and personal crises. Others analyse colonial records, and some focus on the struggle for revitalization and self-determination. Finally, I take note that Native literary criticism is forming into a new formidable intellectual genre since the arrival of *Looking at the Words of Our People: First Nations*

Analysis of Literature (1993), edited by Jeannette Armstrong. A first of its kind, this Native Canadian–published collection of critical essays situates Native North American writing in American and Canadian intellectual life. Although many of the essays focus on American material, essays by Janice Acoose, Kateri Damm, and Gerry William treat Canadian writers such as Maria Campbell, Howard Adams, Beatrice Culleton, and Thomas King. Since then a number of other publications of critical essays authored largely by Native writers and academics have appeared, and they include: *(Ad)dressing Our Words* (2001), ed. by Armand Garnet Ruffo; *Creating Community: A Roundtable on Canadian Aboriginal Literature* (2002), ed. by Renate Eigenbrod and Jo-Ann Episkenew; *Aboriginal Oral Traditions* (2008), ed. by Renée Hulan and Renate Eigenbord. In addition to Native-authored literary criticism published in journals, anthologies, and some books, Native peoples have been producing other kinds of critical works as well; for example, there are numerous theses and a considerable number of dissertations produced by Native graduate students. There are also legends, children's stories, ethnographies, arts and crafts manuals, and so forth. I have previously considered these as "soft sell literature," but they are, in fact, forms of resistance as they too represent contemporary efforts to re-establish the validity of Aboriginal aesthetics and formats.

Voice as Resistance Scholarship

Many of us who are writers are also scholars. As a writer and a long-standing professor in Native Studies, I have per force been dealing with issues that confront resistance writers who work inside the academic community and mandates.[14] For me, there has always been an insider/outsider tension, although much of my three decades in the university I have experienced as an outsider. To this day, in fact, the only time I feel more or less like an insider is when I am mentoring grad students or meeting with my colleagues. Arun Mukherjee's (1994) *Oppositional Aesthetics* describes experiences strikingly similar to my own, particularly the struggle to assume intellectual agency in the face of Western scholarship's continuing practise of universalizing Western experience and knowledge. Take the notion and politics of theory, especially in the study of literature. In the context of discussing rankings and promotions

---

14 Parts of this discussion have been presented in LaRocque (see chapters "Preface: Hear Are Our Voices – Who Will Hear?" and "The Colonization of a Native Woman Scholar").

194 The Emma LaRocque Reader

in universities, Mukherjee points to the pressure to "write in sanctioned ways," and to get "published in the right places," which, she explains, is not simply a matter of "disagreements with other scholars in a dialogical mode" (1994, xiii).

To write and research in sanctioned ways often involve the invocation of theory. Barbara Christian (1995) questions what she calls "the race for theory" in an article of the same title. Christian notes that "there has been a takeover in the literary world by Western philosophers" such that "they have re-invented the meaning of theory" (457). She believes that this has served to silence and to intimidate "peoples of colour" whether they are creative writers or academics. She argues that this represents a new version of Western hegemony: "I see the language it creates as one which mystifies rather than clarifies our condition, making it possible for a few people who know that particular language to control the critical scene." She adds that this took place "interestingly enough, just when the literature of peoples of colour ... began to move to 'the centre'" (Christian 1995, 459). And like Mukherjee, Christian (1995) argues this is political. "It is difficult to ignore this takeover," she explains, "since theory has become a commodity which helps determine whether we are hired or promoted in academic institutions – worse whether we are heard at all" (459). Christian further argues that "people of colour have always theorized – but in forms quite different from the western form of abstract logic" (1995, 457).

Cree Métis people engaged in abstract logic, but not necessarily or totally in the same way or about the same things as Western peoples. That this is so must make a difference in our theories and research. I have been investigating how and where these places of difference emerge for someone like me who carries an indigenous ethos and epistemological basis and also works within Western scholarship, yet calls for decolonization (for everyone and on many levels). Needless to say, I have been confronted with extraordinary pedagogical and canonical challenges, contradictions, anomalies, and, at times, insults. In my earlier years at the university, practising positionality of resistance in scholarship was sacrilege, and not fashionable as it now appears to have become.

How well I remember a particular letter of reference in my application for doctoral studies in history. A professor I trusted and held in some regard (who was also a colleague, as I had been publishing and teaching long before I was able to take up doctoral studies) characterized my work as suffering from "too much introspection and the facts of her own biography." He patronized me as a "remarkably talented" but "undisciplined scholar," and ended with a gratuitous slap by asking the department to "assist [me] in taking this step towards realizing [my]

Insider Notes: Reframing the Narratives   195

full potential as a scholar." This was in 1990, when it was not uncommon for mainstream academics to undermine the work of Native scholars with charges of parochialism, "advocacy history,"[15] or even reverse racism. This was done with the confidence of objectivity, a confidence only colonialist scholars have enjoyed.

To say the least, such accusations are glaringly ironic, given the racism evident in White texts on Native peoples and cultures, a racism unabashedly inflammatory, patronizing, and subjective. And yes, there is advocacy history – it is stitched into the very core of the re-settler canon. Plainly, there is overwhelming evidence that the Western argument for "objectivity" is a self-serving tool of those accustomed to managing history.

The discourse of "bias" – or its apparent opposite, "objectivity" – is of particular interest to Aboriginal scholars. The essence of the dominant Western narrative is its claim to "objectivity." As Russell Ferguson (1990) writes, objectivity is simply assumed by utilizing techniques of supposed absence: "In our society discourse tries never to speak its own name. Its authority is based on absence. The absence is not just that of the various groups classified as 'other,' although members of these groups are routinely denied power. It is also the lack of any overt acknowledgement of the specificity of the dominant culture, which is simply assumed to be the all-encompassing norm. This is the basis of its power" (11).

This technique of absence, or what may be called the subterraneous Western voice, as practised especially by earlier anthropologists and historians but still echoed by many mainstream intellectuals, is a tool in the politics of power. While Native voice in scholarship has been swiftly stigmatized, White North American voice over Native history and cultures has been normalized. Techniques of absence are nowhere more present than in the classically colonial, archival, and academic descriptions and data about Natives' tools, physical features, beliefs (which are often degraded to "rituals"), or even geography. There is, as Parker Duchemin (1990) explains, an "appearance of impartiality" to these descriptions, and it is this appearance that has been mistaken for objectivity. Such appearances are in fact imperial and not at all objective or impartial…. To the point here, such airs of detachment are in direct contrast to my Plains Cree-Métis

---

15 Historian Doug Sprague essentially charges Métis historian and critic Howard Adams with "advocacy history," although he also implicates "academic historians" of the same – as if Métis cannot be academic historians! See Sprague (1988), 13 note 19.

196 The Emma LaRocque Reader

socialization, which encourages integration between the "self" and the "word" (63).

Cree clearly differentiates *achimoowin* ("fact") from *atowkehwin* ("fiction"). It allows the speaker to speak in his or her own voice without assuming that voice is mired in what Kathleen Rockhill (1987) calls "chaos of subjectivity" (12). One's own voice is never totally of one's self, in isolation from community. At the same time, one's self is not a communal replica of the collective. The Cree knew themselves as *Nehiyawehwak*, the Exact Speaking People.[16] As a *Nehiyohsquoh* (exact-speaking woman), I choose to use my exact-speaking voice whether I am writing history or whether I am writing poetry. Or teaching in a university classroom. Of course, voice is not primarily about oneself or even of "one's people" (a favourite colonial expression) – it is more a recognition of the relationship between power and knowledge, which then reveals positionality. From this theoretical base I have pursued my academic career.

I am in good company, for many scholars and writers from non-Western traditions (and feminists from a variety of traditions) are refusing to remain alienated from their "selves."[17] Likewise, by refusing to remain distant from my words and works, I am not only attempting to remain true to my heritage, I am also seeking cultural agency. Peter Hitchcock's (1989) exploration of dialogics in which "both subject and object are decentered" is helpful here:

> Rather than assume subaltern subjectivity as forever the concern of what has been derisively called 'victim studies' a dialogic approach emphasizes the cultural agency of the oppressed and also shows what political implications this might have for literary analysis in general and cultural studies in particular ... the underlying concern is to develop a critique of the epistemological bases of the academy that marginalize or ghettoize those cultures that would call its authority into question. (Hitchcock 1989, xi)

But I do not approach scholarship only from a cultural location, especially one that is often reductively and categorically classified as

---

16 In some dialects, it can also refer to "people of four directions."

17 Jeanne Perreault (1995) writes that feminist writers and theorists "of all races, sexualities and classes" (1) have been "grappling with modes of expression that evade the familiar narrative of life events" (3), and out of this "a new kind of subjectivity is evolving" (4). In the process of writing "self-in-the-making," concepts such as subjectivity, agency, and self are being reframed. See also, Brown and Strega (2005).

"different," which I take to be the colonizer's strategy. Rather, as one who comes from a dispossessed people, I engage with my research. A key part of this necessarily and unavoidably means disturbing the re-settler canon.

Palestinian writer and critic Ghassan Kanafani (in Harlow 1987) challenged Western scholarship by arguing that research of the subjugated was finally legitimized only by the researcher's engagement in the language and resistance of the subjugated. Kanafani asserted that "no research of this kind can be complete unless the researcher is located within the resistance movement itself inside the occupied land, taking his testimony from the place in which it is born ... the lips of the people." Kanafani, as Harlow (1987) explains, "not only disclaims any pretence to 'academic objectivity' or 'scientific dispassion,' he rejects too the very relevance in a study of resistance literature of such critical stances or poses" (3).

Kanafani's stand is not entirely unprecedented, even in Western practises. The questions and debates concerning the study of history that came out of Michelet's (1967) passionate and engaging *History of the French Revolution* (1833–1867) comes to mind. In his introduction to Michelet's translated work, Gordon Wright argues that "Michelet could never be the impartial judge, weighing evidence and letting it guide his decision. He was an historian *engagé*, the impassioned evangelizer of a new gospel" (Wright in Michelet 1967, xv). Michelet would have taken to Kanafani. Or perhaps Said.

Edward W. Said wrote extensively on the relationship of power to knowledge. In *Orientalism* (1978), he points out that while the West's requirement for knowledge to be non-political, that is, "scholarly, academic, impartial, above partisan or small-minded doctrinal belief," it is an "ambition in theory." In practise it is "much more problematic" because no one "has ever devised a method for detaching the scholar from the circumstances of life, from the fact of his involvement (conscious or unconscious) with a class, a set of beliefs, a social position, or from the mere activity of being a member of society" (Said 1978, 9). He challenges too the "general liberal consensus that 'true' knowledge is fundamentally non-political (and conversely that overtly political knowledge is not 'true' knowledge)." In fact, he cautions, "No one is helped in understanding this today when the adjective 'political' is used as a label to discredit any work for daring to violate the protocol of pretended surrapolitical objectivity" (Said 1978, 10).

Said's observations are certainly applicable to the Canadian academic community and its treatment of Aboriginal history, text, and scholarship. The political nature of the colonizer's language(s), his/her

The Emma LaRocque Reader

ownership of "history" (or who qualifies as "historian"), "objectivity," and other hegemonic practises have inspired what should most appropriately be understood as Native resistance scholarship and discourse. Much like other non-Western scholars before us, we are grappling with the relationship between knowledge and power, between misrepresentation and resistance.

Resistance is in me and in the literature I document and analyse. However, at multiple levels, I am constantly negotiating practises and canons of the colonizer and yet remaining one of the voices of the colonized. Obviously, I value and enjoy university scholarship and at the same time I respect my Plains Cree-Métis knowledge and ways of approaching knowledge. For example, I try to maintain orality both in my style of teaching and, in certain contexts, also in my academic writing.[18] I find it useful to make a distinction between scholarship as a disciplined way of approaching knowledge that requires training in certain academic skills and language, and scholarship (purportedly) that advances a particular ideology. The question is whether we can separate skill or craft from ideology.

In order for me to exercise liberation, I must create an intellectual practise that claims my own humanity and style, one that builds scholarship based on this humanity. I consider my use of "voice" good scholarship, not a contradiction, as some might argue. My use of voice is a textual resistance technique in that it concerns discourse and presentation, not simply or necessarily personal or familial matters. Voice is much more than about introspection or even about "sounding differences," to borrow the phrase from Janice Williamson (1993). It is, in large part, corrective scholarship. Native scholars and writers are demonstrating that voice can be, must be, used within academic studies, not only as an expression of cultural agency, but as a form of resisting misrepresentation in Canadian scholarship and popular culture.

The implication for me as a practising academic is that when I use my voice (say, through references to first-person commentaries, or to community, family, experiences, perceptions, anecdotes, or facts of biography for instructional purposes), I am assuming a contrapuntal space concerning Western conventions; I am not in any way abandoning the canon of scholarly circumspection. In fact, as a scholar, I am exposing

---

18 For an insightful commentary on the Aboriginal writers' use of orality in their written works, see Eigenbrod (1995). The question, though, is this: does the use of orality in writing reflect an in-between-ness, or is it more a reflection of an ongoing-ness, that is, recreating and reinventing a language and literature from Aboriginal poetics?

bias – in this case Western bias. I am, as Barbara Harlow (1997) writes, "imposing a review" of what is understood as "literature, literary studies and the historical record" (4).

Does it need saying that my exposition of bias is not restricted to White partisanship? Native intellectuals are not immune to their own forms of bias, but they are no more predisposed to it than are Western intellectuals. What's more, as part of claiming my own distinctiveness and exercising my ideals of scholarship, I will not serve merely as a conduit of other voices, Native or otherwise. I am observing that as various Native communities are flexing their political or cultural muscles, Native scholars may find themselves in difficult positions. We are no different from any other human community in that we hold dearly some beliefs and assumptions, which if challenged, even with all the best data and argumentation, may evoke responses that could affect our research. Studies of violence, traditions, women, spirituality, or even images of "Indians" are fraught with potential politics. The Native community is as vulnerable as the White community in its internalization and perpetuation of stereotypes, an issue I return to in my discussion of romanticism ...[]

Even though stereotypes exist, we are a diverse peoples criss-crossing geographies, languages, culture areas, faiths, legally divided identities, politics, and so forth. We do not have a uniform Native identity even if we have a common experience under colonization. Of course, in important ways, we have many things in common, which come from our colonial experience as well as shared indigeneity. But we are also truly different from each other, not only as individuals or cultures, but also in our personal socio-economic circumstances and perspectives. It is as important to name our differences as it is to articulate the common experience of invasions in our lives. We have all experienced colonial intrusion, but we have not all experienced it at the same time or in the same way or to the same degree. I, for one, cannot entertain racist, sexist, or ideological injunctions that I must be a carbon copy of other colonized persons and colleagues. For that matter, nor do I unquestioningly accept postcolonial buzz labels such as "essentialist," "subaltern," "hybridity" or "mimicry," which can be similarly universalizing. At some point, agency has to mean something actual, like having the right and the freedom to name one's identity without someone theorizing it and us to yet newer forms of erasure and generalization.

It is imperative that we treat with respect other people's works upon which we build our dialogics and, for many of us, our academic degrees; it is also important to maintain our right to disagree. Writers owe much to each other, and I acknowledge my debt to all these writers (and scholars) I use, but I must also retain my right to debate and to question. My goal is not to settle for politically correct or kitschy notions. My objective is to offer valuable criticism. Edward Said (1983) in *The World, The Text, and the Critic* writes that "criticism must think of itself as life-enhancing and constitutively opposed to every form of tyranny, domination and abuse; its social goals are noncoercive knowledge produced in the interests of human freedom" (29). The important thing is that we all have the right to speak, the right to be represented fairly, as well as the obligation to represent fairly, and the right to express ourselves true to our lives, experiences, and research. As Abenaki resistance filmmaker, poet, and singer Alanis Obomsawin explains,

> The basic purpose is for our people to have a voice. To be heard is the important thing, no matter what it is that we are talking about ... and that we have a lot to offer society. But we also have to look at the bad stuff, and what has happened to us, and why.... We cannot do this without going through the past ... because we are carrying a pain that is 400 years old. We don't carry just our everyday pain. We're carrying the pain of our fathers, our mothers, our grandfathers, our grandmothers ... it's part of this land. (Alieoof and Levine 1987)

I too carry "the 400 year pain," a "pain" that is part of this land; I too carry the pain of my mother, my father, my sister, my brothers, my nieces and nephews, my grandfathers and mothers, my aunts and uncles. And I carry my own pain. Here I offer vignettes of life experiences relevant to the profound sense of alienation I have experienced in the world of education, an experience that has propelled me to pursue scholarship – particularly, the story of dehumanization – so passionately. I must emphasize that, to me, it is not enough to simply tell the story, it is equally important that we name, locate, and situate the "story."

Neegan (First) Narrative

"Get 'em, Daniel Boone, get 'em." My eyes were wide open, my hands clutching the sides of my desk. I waited breathlessly as America's mythic frontiersman Daniel Boone, with a cast-iron frying pan in hand, stood readying to spring upon a hideously painted Indian stealthily crawling into his boathouse. Then "boinng" – and our grade four (mostly Métis) classroom burst into gleeful applause – the gallant frontiersman had "got 'em."

Of course, it was not my first and certainly not my last exposure to such imagery. My relatives and I were well acquainted with the scene of the tomahawk-swinging savage who took shrieking delight in rushing upon wagon trains and defenceless White women and children.

Niso (Second) Narrative

When my brothers and I were in elementary school, we were required to draw Columbus's ship. I drew a large, detailed picture of a multi-storeyed clipper, its tall white sails fluttering against a cerulean blue sky, the sky touching the deep blue sea. It must have been then that I had to memorize the famous ditty: "in 1492/Columbus sailed the ocean/deep and blue."

I was a northern Canadian Cree Métis child with a political and cultural heritage in contradiction to the Columbus narrative. At the time I, of course, had no knowledge of the ramifications behind Columbus's ship, but I was left with the distinct impression that he was some godlike White hero who had done the universe an inestimable, not to mention irreversible, favour by "discovering" the "New World."

Neesto (Third) Narrative

In Goshen College, Indiana, the showing of the 1969 BBC film series *Civilisation*, written and narrated by Kenneth Clark, was a campuswide mandatory event. Clark begins by arguing that Greco-Roman cultural accomplishments defined civilization against the powerful but impermanent achievements of African masks or wandering Viking ships. What has stayed with me about this series is how Clark compared a surviving "pitifully crude" stone baptistery to a wigwam by saying: "But at least this miserable construction is built to last. It isn't just a wigwam."

I could not speak.

Nehwi (Fourth) Narrative

In the summer of 1976, prior to enrolling in Canadian history at the University of Manitoba, I had an occasion to visit the Martyr's Shrine in Midland, Ontario. From the outside the Martyr's Shrine looked like any eastern Roman Catholic cathedral – stone-built, large, and reminiscent

202 The Emma LaRocque Reader

of edifices shown in Kenneth Clark's *Civilisation* television series. On the inside, it looked like a large version of the Catholic churches my parents and teachers had made my siblings and me attend – dark, echoing, and full of flickering candles. I really had no idea what the Martyr's Shrine represented until my eyes adjusted to the darkness – there, at the very front of the pews, were looming life-sized wax museum figures. I slowly realized what they were: kneeling priests angelically looking up, hands folded, praying for mercy as open-mouthed, hideously painted, evil-eyed savages tower over them, about to bury hatchets in their skulls!

Postcards and pamphlets were handed out – still photography to lock in the master view, perhaps to keep it safe from exposure. Inside myself, I resolved to know the truth behind such soul-numbing presentations. I walked out of that structure with fire in my head. Consciousness was seeping in. Liberation resistance scholarship was in the making.

Rediscovering the Narrative

Of course, Columbus or the Jesuits were but the beginning of an endless string of White heroes who filled the pages of my comics and my school textbooks. The Explorers, the Conquistadores, the Missionaries, the Fur Traders, the Pilgrims and Puritans, the Daniel Boones, the American Cavalry and the Cowboys, the Fathers of Canadian Confederation – they were all presented as "great" and their greatness was and still is directly related to the degree to which they othered, killed, dehumanized, or de-Indianized Indians.

Hollywood put in motion the glorification of the White man. While Whites could experience a vicarious greatness watching Cowboys beat the Indians (no matter how ferocious and "cunning"), Native audiences crouched in their seats, grateful for the theatre's darkness. Similarly, in so many of Canada's signal places, Native peoples have had to cringe within themselves, having to cope with the re-settler's heroic point of view. I have noted that at every important juncture and place in my life, or in that of my family or community, our worlds have been either deleted, belittled, or decontextualized by an assortment of White North America's propaganda machines.

As can be surmised from my narratives, my student life was filled with considerable distress.[19] Before I was in any position to critically

---

19 Some of these experiences of racism in the educational system are included in my autobiographical essay "Tides, Towns and Trains" (see chapter).

examine the history and sociology of racism, I experienced a sense of shame and alienation from teachers, textbooks, comics, and movies that portrayed Indians as savages. Later, as I pursued "higher" education, I soon discovered that many university professors and most textbooks presented Native peoples in as distorted and insulting ways as the elementary texts had done. The racist theme of Western civilization/ Indian savagery was ever-present. Some professors were less subtle than others.

I have been a professor for three decades, and I continue to battle this epic myth. Indeed, I continue to be astonished by some White academics' obsessions in the defence of "civilization." For instance, Tom Flanagan (2000) flagrantly waves his star-spangled civ/sav banner in his book *First Nations, Second Thoughts*.[20] In a chapter called "Whatever Happened to Civilization," he bemoans the contemporary enlightened direction of assuming cultural equality for Aboriginal peoples. Further, not only does he actually believe the civ/sav construct is objective, he argues his thesis is not racist. Of course, throughout he draws on the American expansionist doctrine of Manifest Destiny.

As Joyce Green points out, "Flanagan's book is arguably not in fact about second thoughts, but about first thoughts: the justifications that have always legitimated colonialism on Turtle Island" (2002, 2). The notion of "civilization" and its antithesis "savagery" are invariably defined and measured by Euro-White North American standards. It should be needless to point out that such an un-scientific belief is racist because it sets up Whites as superior and non-Whites as inferior. Yet such racialized evolutionism has not entirely disappeared from the Western intellectual tradition. In disciplines of anthropology, history, political science, psychology, sociology, religion, and even in earlier Marxist thought, theories on human development were and still are largely premised on patriarchal, Eurocentric and evolutionary ideas about so-called primitive peoples.

I have not been impressed. I have experienced Canada's archives, libraries, cathedrals, martyrs' shrines, museums, movies, forts, and university hallways – all places that reflect Eurocentrism – as places of exile.

---

20 Doctrinaire theses such as Flanagan's jolt us to practise anti-racist pedagogy. For an excellent race analysis see Schick (2002). See also Carol Schick and Verna St. Denis, 2005.

The Emma LaRocque Reader

Reframing the Narrative

My liberation has come from rediscovering the Columbus narrative for what it is: a self-serving White cultural myth, which has been effectively transmitted from generation to generation and institutionalized by White North America's powerful educational and cultural systems. The other aspect of my liberation has come from the "knowing" that Native peoples were not as they were imagined.

I have always known that there was absolutely no connection between the othering of "the Indian" and the consummate humanity of my parents, brothers and sister, my *nokom* (grandmother), my aunts and uncles, my nieces and nephews. It is this unsung humanity, as much as the vilification of Native peoples, that has compelled me to this place of engaged research and discourse. It is important that we understand colonial subterfuge behind the fantastic hero-ification of the White man. It is imperative that our understanding is taken from the words of those who have suffered from this proselytizing, the Native peoples of Canada. In *There Is My People Sleeping*, Sarain Stump (1970) speaks movingly to the significance of understanding:

> I was mixing stars and sand
> In front of him
> But he couldn't understand
> I was keeping the lightning of
> The thunder in my purse
> Just in front of him
> But he couldn't understand
> And I had been killed a thousand times
> Right at his feet
> But he hadn't understood

Before "he" can "understand," we must situate Native response in the context of colonization; in particular, room must necessarily be given to the exposition of what Parker Duchemin (1990, 63) calls "textual strategies of domination" in Euro-Canadian writing.

2013

For the Love of Place – Not Just Any Place: Selected Métis Writings

This essay has an express purpose of exuding orality, with the objective of raising awareness about Métis love of land, or of landedness. As such, I am approaching the discussion more from a literary and creative approach. I am of course aware that any mention of the Métis can bring up any number of issues from pretty much any number of disciplines. I will not try to address these multi-faceted issues which can involve historical, constitutional, social and ethnographic questions. My discussion here is obviously quite exploratory, and I have taken some poetic liberties with style and organization.

While the displacement and dispossession of the Red River Métis is more or less a well-known historical fact within academia (and to a lesser extent, in the wider community), ironically rarely is the theme of place associated with the Métis. By place I mean more than geographical location or mapping, though all that is included; by "place" I mean more like attachment, rootedness, groundedness, materiality. Familiality. Home. Homelands. A particular and unique land area in this country where we carry out body and home-stitching everydayness. A place where we live. And go to work from. Or in. A place where we come to know the ways and voices of family and neighbours. A place where we become familiar with pots and pans, woodpiles and water pails. Or computers and iPods. A garden we tend. Blueberry meadows we work or rest in, meadows surrounded in sunlight streaming through poplars and birch. A place where we dream. Yes there was the Red River and that was and is a place. To be sure a very significant place. But Red River has been so over-politicized that we can barely recognize it for the love of place – not just any place as a real place where real people practised their everyday ways of life and livelihoods. What did Riel eat?

Let me put this matter of place in another way. People in western Canada, and especially Manitoba, know about the Red River Métis. Or should. Everyone knows that Riel defended Métis interests and died for the Métis cause. And everyone knows the prairie Métis (or a handful of them) took a sort of last stand at Batoche, put up a good fight but lost.[1]

And everyone knows the other Canadian story – the sanitized school story – the pioneer version of how the coureurs de bois, or the voyageurs in early fur-trade times, sang and joshed their way up and down the St. Lawrence, portaging their way into the interior. Strapping, jovial "halfbreed" men who seemed to be forever paddling.

Another theme of halfbreed wanderings is to be found in Norma Bailey's Daughters of the Country series produced by the National Film Board. In the third film, titled *Places Not Our Own*, there is a scene where a Métis family is travelling by horse and wagon. It is sometime in the Depression. It is somewhere in the Prairies. Here the Métis are the prairie gypsies – apparently homeless and with no specific place to go.[2] And where did Morag's Métis lover in Margaret Laurence's (1974) *The Diviners* live? Where does he come from? Where does he go? Like an apparition, he fades in and out of Morag's life (Laurence 1974, 184). Whether the Métis are presented as portaging minstrels, prairie gypsies or inconstant lovers, popular culture has romanticized and perpetuated the myth of Métis as roaming transients with little or no sense of rootedness to homes and lands, to homelands.[3]

Yet everyone knows the Métis fiddler. Or the Métis fighter. And the Métis martyr. But who knows the people? Who knows where they played their fiddles? Who really knows why they fought, or why they sacrificed their lives? Who knows who the Métis are and what they love and hold dear? Who knows where they have lived – or where they live now? Who knows how they felt or how they feel now about being displaced, then replaced? And today – where are their places? How do they live in those places? What do they feel about these places? Or that one place?

---

1 I am referring to the Northwest Métis Resistance at the Battle of Batoche in 1885 where some 250 Métis men fought some 900 Canadian Militia troops. The Métis took a last stand to protect their lands against imperial forces. See Hildebrandt (2007). See also Barron and Waldram (1986).

2 *Places Not Our Own*, directed by Derek Mazur (National Film Board, 1986), available online at www.nfb.ca/film/places_not_our_own, accessed 6 October 2011.

3 I am not suggesting that we confine any Indigenous group, including the Red River Métis, to the sort of rootedness that freezes them to the past which would keep them "in their place" so that colonizers can gaze or segregate them. For an interesting discussion on the uses and abuses of notions of "roots" see Eigenbrod (2005), especially the chapter on "The Rhetoric of Mobility."

Of course, I am not going to answer these questions or issues. I raise them poetically rather than ethnographically. Here I only have time to offer vignettes of thoughts from several Métis writers and to highlight those facets and issues which often get neglected in film, literature, and other popular productions, but even in critical discussions. Generally, critical attention to Métis writers focus on socio-economic and identity issues.[4] Here I take three well-known Métis – Maria Campbell, Marilyn Dumont, and Greg Scofield – who clearly express their profound attachments to home and landedness. I turn first to Maria Campbell, who in *Halfbreed* (1973) offers considerable cultural information tracing Métis life from the Métis Resistance era of the late 1800s to her own era of the 1950s–70s from which she wrote the memoir. Maria Campbell is of Cree/Scottish Métis Nation ancestry from Saskatchewan. Her parents raised her and her siblings with Métis material culture as well as Métis values. It is not incidental that [Campbell] (1973) begins her facts of biography with this: "I should tell you about our home now before I go any further." She then proceeds to describe their "two-roomed large hewed log house," detailing their homemade tables and chairs, beds and hay-filled canvas mattresses, the hammock that babies swung from, the huge black wood stove in the kitchen, the medicines and herbs that hung on the walls, the wide planks of floors scoured evenly white with lye soap, and so forth. I am sure it was with tears of love that she reminisced: "The kitchen and living room were combined into one of the most beautiful rooms I have ever known" (Campbell 1973, 17). Clearly, these tangible everyday objects remain a cultural palate of warm memory and strong attachment from which Maria Campbell has written and lived.

In a very short non-fiction piece called "The Gift," Alberta Métis writer Marilyn Dumont (1990) writes about watching her father revisit and linger over a beloved spot of land he had long ago lost. This land, located in northeastern Alberta, had been given to him as a wedding gift by his father – but he and his wife (Marilyn's parents) were unable to keep it due to the Depression in the 1930s. Many years later Marilyn and her aging father climb up a hill to see – and to say a final goodbye – to this place. Before leaving this ancestral high ground, Marilyn watches with pain as her father "tucked some blades of grass and twigs into his wallet." She describes her own reaction: "My thoughts raced. I wanted to take something too. Something to say I'd been here. My

---

4 For example, see Kateri Damm (1993, 93–114). For a more post-colonial reading see Hoy (2001).

eyes searched in the grass. A light flickered. I picked up a brown piece of glass. The heavy broken bottom of a jug. I didn't know what I'd do with it. It didn't matter; I gripped it against me" (Dumont 1990, 46). His fact-based story is another very moving testament to Métis attachment to place, in this case a parcel of land. Not just any land. But a very site-specific, family-significant, and much-loved place. It is excruciatingly difficult to lose places we love. As Marilyn Dumont puts it: "Who knows what it's like to leave, to give up a piece of land? If you do, it might haunt you forever, follow you til you come back" (Dumont 1990, 44).

Many Métis – not all, but altogether too many – have been forced in some way or other to leave their special places. In this sense, there is some truth to the image of the Métis as prairie gypsies, but this should be seen as a consequence of displacement – not as a cultural or individual trait to be romanticized. The sad fact is that many Métis cannot come back to their places of origin due to urban and industrial encroachments, or outright dispossession by either federal or provincial laws and actions. But even this reality does not erase the Métis love of home, kin, or community. Some have had to adopt symbolic places that hold great significance. One such place is Batoche. In his autobiography *Thunder Through My Veins* (1999), Métis poet Gregory Scofield titles one chapter "Pekewe, Pekewe" ("Come Home, Come Home" in Cree). He had come home to Saskatchewan, to the prairies, to what he calls his roots. After a very long and troubled and confused youth, [Scofield] had finally discovered Batoche – on one hand a historic place of sacrifice, loss, and pain, but for him, a new place of peace and belonging. A place, a people, a culture that he could identify as his very own (Scofield 1999). These prairie writers, each work reflecting a different period of time, nonetheless experienced some form of uprootedness in their personal and community lives – yet each is deeply rooted to particular histories, places, geographies, and families. To be sure, there are many differences between these writers (age, gender, experience, and genre among them), yet one constant stands out – a strong identification with placeness. Landedness for the Métis remains an unbroken bond.

My father used to say we are nothing without land. Rarely did my gentle father make such categorical pronouncements. He was born at the turn of the twentieth century in northeastern Alberta, his roots coming directly through the Red River Métis of the 1870s–90s. Bapa was a hard-working man forced by colonial history to raise his family in a road allowance section of land he never got to own. "We are nothing without land." It took me some time to realize the full profundity of his

Selected Métis Writings 209

statement. He was not just talking about legal ownership of property – although land and resource rights, of course, remain an unfinished business for the Métis, certainly for the Red River Métis. My father (and mother), who never had the means to own property, had a philosophy and praxis about land that was far greater than capitalist notions of land as real estate commodity. Métis writers reflect and express what Métis peoples know and feel – that they are deeply, ancestrally, Indigenously, and fundamentally rooted to their lands and families. To my Métis parents land represented identity, culture, self-sufficiency, and independence. Landedness also meant family, home life, kin, and community. Landedness is purposeful; it gives meaning to language and life.

For all our efforts to explain our identity and our epistemic world views in relation to land and place, stereotypes and ignorance about the Métis persist. I come back to the beginning. I have just spoken to the well-known and perhaps worn-out old stereotypes. Earlier in my research I had been struck by the portrayals of Métis as alienated loners who insert into Native or white lives without context or belonging. Like Billy Jack in the movie *Billy Jack*.[5] Sometimes they were romanticized. Like Morag's lover in *The Diviners* (Laurence 1974). Often they were demonized. Historians and novelists alike presented Métis as volatile males splintered between the chasms of civilization and savagery.[6] These should be old stereotypes, yet have these rather classic images changed? I am not so sure. I have noticed that some place and replace Native American writers and academics make no distinction between individuals who are half-white/half-Indian, and those Métis Nation peoples of western Canada who formed a distinct ethnic culture and community.[7] The more recent post-colonial emphasis on hybridity or border-crossing, useful concepts in some contexts, can serve to further obscure Métis national identity and culture and, in turn, Métis land and resource entitlements.[8] But even in Canada we still have films,

---

5 A 1971 film about a "half-breed" American Navajo who is also a Vietnam War veteran, launching a four-film series. Elaine Coburn – editor's note.

6 See chapter "The Métis in English Canadian Literature."

7 Native American writer and academic Elizabeth Cook-Lynn in (1996) takes a very troubling view of "Métis" as halfbreed individuals who threaten Native "tribal" identity. There is no mention or appreciation of the Red River Métis as Indigenous with Indigenous identity. See also Harrison's (1985) treatment of the Métis as people in between in her book.

8 For further explorations of these issues, see chapter "Native Identity and the Métis: *Otehpayimsuak* Peoples" and see chapter "Reflections on Cultural Continuity Through Aboriginal Women's Writings"; LaRocque (2010).

The Emma LaRocque Reader

poems, stories and books, titles and academic treatments that tend to focus on Métis homelessness, identity crises, marginalization, or an in-betweenness. Of course, there is some sad truth to these images. The Red River Métis did lose their beloved lands in the Red River, and about 83 percent of this population were forced to relocate and many could not find a new place or new homelands.[9] If they did, they would face other dragons such as the "scrip" that the federal government gave as poor compensation for Métis claims, the Gatling gun at Batoche, provincial confiscations of traplines through Natural Resource laws, or the oil sands in northeastern Alberta. To name but a few. And notwithstanding the somewhat recent Powley Supreme Court Decision (2003)[10] that recognized specific Métis harvesting rights, neither the provincial nor federal governments are anywhere near fulfilling the Canadian constitution – that is, of actualizing Métis land and resource rights as Aboriginal peoples. But despite all these historic pressures, Métis managed to stay together and even to develop strong communities in central and northern parts of the prairie provinces, many along road allowances. The Métis Nation story is a remarkable feat of survival and cultural tenacity. For despite all the succession of losses and obstacles, there are thousands of Métis Nation families and individuals across western Canada who live lives quite similar to those of "ordinary Canadians." That is, they have homes – maybe even "home-lands" – and culturally cohesive and functioning family lives with meaningful occupations. Without in any way seeking to minimize those Métis who have suffered much personal and cultural dislocation, some of us Métis have had to say "Hey – not all of us were stolen or fostered, not all of us suffered identity crises (even despite huge obstacles) and not all of us had to look for homes and places." Historians and literary critics now need to refocus and enlarge their portrayals and treatment of Métis peoples, issues, and themes. I say this to draw attention to our rootedness, to our integrated identity as Métis Nation peoples. To our love of our lands.

Love of land does not depend on property ownership (though that certainly should be a right that Métis have). My family still owns no lands. But long before the province of Alberta was established, long before Confederation was arranged, my paternal and maternal Plains and Woodlands Cree/Métis ancestors filled these lands by use and love

---

9 See Sawchuk et al. (1981). See also RCAP (1996) Volume 4, Chapter 5 on "Métis Perspectives" "Métis Perspectives," 198–386. See also Sprague (1988), Chapter 3.

10 *R. v. Powley*, [2003] 2 S.C.R. 207, 2003 SCC 43. Also see the recent *Manitoba Métis Federation v. Canada* decision at http://scc.lexum.org/decisia-scc-csc/scc-csc/scc-csc/en/item/12888/index.do.

Selected Métis Writings

of the land. Like other Red River Métis Nation peoples of their generation, my parents knew every nook and cranny of lands stretching hundreds of miles within their areas. My brothers – along with others of our generation and their children – still know, occupy and use these lands. Métis scholars, and writers and poets such as Maria Campbell, Marilyn Dumont and Greg Scofield carry the nooks and crannies in their hearts. As do I. I end with Marilyn Dumont's (1996, 46) poem "not just a platform for my dance":

This land is not
just a place to set my house my car my fence

This land is not
just a plot to bury my dead my seed

This land is
my tongue my eyes my mouth

This headstrong grass and relenting willow
these flat-footed fields and applauding leaves
these frank winds and electric sky

are my prayer
they are my medicine
and they become my song

this land is not just a platform for my dance

2015

"Resist No Longer": Reflections on Resistance Writing and Teaching

The words "resist no longer" from the 1986 musical *Phantom of the Opera* run through my mind as I contemplate the changes of focus in research and writing in the discipline and field of study that I have been engaged in for more than three decades. The purpose of this essay is to provide a reflective overview of what I have come to call "resistance scholarship," an intellectual positionality I have practised in my research, teaching and writing style. And since most of my academic years have been spent in Native Studies I, of course, draw on this discipline as one model for resistance and for invention. My objective is not to detail the programme of our department but to discuss what Peter Kulchyski, scholar, colleague and veteran of Native Studies, calls "the ethical impulse" (2000, 20). This ethical impulse directs the research and teaching we do, and is embedded both in resistance and invention or what I have elsewhere referred to as both deconstruction and reconstruction (LaRocque 2010).

Situating Myself: Personal and Political Contexts

But first, consistent with my decolonizing approach, I begin by briefly situating (and linking) my personal and political location that forms the context to my thinking and pedagogy. I am Metis[1] and grew up in

---

1 Metis are one of three Indigenous groups recognized as *Aboriginal* in the Canadian Constitution. Metis' dual (First Nation-European) ancestry emerged out of the First Nation, French and English fur trade during the seventeenth century. However, these first "halfbreed" peoples evolved into a distinct Indigenous ethnic culture, and by the early 1800s, the majority of Metis located in the Red River area, and there developed a sense of nationhood. While there are a number of different Metis communities across Canada, the Red River Metis, now known as Metis Nation, the majority of whom live in western Canada, remain the most prominent. For more on the development of Metis identity, see Peterson and Brown (1985) and see chapter "Native Identity and the Metis."

Reflections on Resistance Writing and Teaching 213

a land-based, Cree-speaking Metis culture in northeastern Alberta at a time when our socio-economic conditions as a family and as a community were very bleak. Indeed, throughout the Depression era and into the 1960s, and really, since the days of Red River (1869–70) and Northwest (1884–5) resistances against colonial incursions, the Metis were suffering extensively from land loss and displacement, poverty and deadly diseases such as tuberculosis. In the aftermath of these resistances,[2] the Metis in Alberta (and throughout western Canada) had become so marginalized that neither residential nor public schools were available to most.[3] Metis were often stranded between federal and provincial jurisdictions as neither governments wanted to recognize or acknowledge Metis as Indigenous peoples with land and resource rights.[4] And even though many Metis communities or families such as ours lived near or had access to urban centres, it was not until the 1950s that some small and socially segregated – and characteristically underfunded – public schools for Metis children became available.[5] While not going to residential schools served to protect us from cultural and familial severance and the darker horrors of residential schools, we were not protected from psychological, cultural or corporeal abuse in public schools. Much like residential schools, public schools embraced colonial pedagogy and most teachers engaged in racist practises and punitive treatment of Metis and other Aboriginal children. The vast majority of those of my

---

2 For a detailed study of the two resistances, see Doug Sprague (1988); see also Sawchuk and Sawchuk et al. (1981).

3 Although some Metis – or those arbitrarily identified as Metis by colonial agents such as priests, police or treaty commissioners – did attend residential schools, most Metis could not as legally they were excluded from the *Indian Act*. Residential schools were established for "registered Indians" as defined by the *Indian Act*, a federal statute. On Metis and residential schools, see Chartrand, Logan, and Daniels (2006).

4 For a useful survey of the different Aboriginal groups in relation to legal distinctions and exclusions in Canada, see James Frideres and Rene Gadacz (2001). For a good discussion on the complexities of Metis constitutional, Aboriginal and/or land rights, see the Royal Commission on Aboriginal Peoples (Vol. 4, Chapter 5, 1996).

5 The exception to this may be found in the Metis Settlements which were set aside through Alberta's Metis Population Betterment Act in 1938. Public schools were probably available by the late 1940s to children whose parents lived in such settlements. However, the province's definition of "metis" was somewhat loose, and the Settlements were restricted to those "metis" seen as particularly "destitute." For a number of reasons, the majority of Metis in northeastern Alberta did not go into the Metis Settlements. My family and community (with Red River roots) were among those. For more on the Settlements, see Pocklington (1991); and Sawchuk and Sawchuk et al. (1981), especially chapter six.

214   The Emma LaRocque Reader

generation quit school early, and usually at around grades four to five, because public schools were so dehumanizing and alienating.

School was not available for my parent's generation (pre-1950s) in our area. Ironically – and thankfully – my parent's lack of formal schooling meant they were able to keep their children, speak their language and practise their land-based culture (which was combined with seasonal wage labour). It was my parents who, despite all odds, not only provided us with love, food and shelter, but also the beauty and the vitality of their Cree-Metis/Michif cultural literacy, and by so doing, instilled and inspired in me a spirit of determination, independence and a love of knowledge. However, my love of learning was many times badly shaken as my school experiences – which were often pierced with bullying, classicism, racism and colonial denigration of Native histories – became fairly intolerable with each passing grade. But I was lucky for in grade seven I could go to a new (public) school where I had the great fortune of having the kindest and most perceptive teacher for grades seven to nine. This teacher helped me regain my confidence in learning, and he helped me go on to high school, and from there I finally made it to university. I finished my BA and my first MA in the United States, then came back to Canada to do graduate work in history at the University of Manitoba. While there, and again more by luck than my station in life, I was hired to teach a summer course for a newly established department of Native Studies (in the Faculty of Arts) – I have been with the department ever since, rising eventually to the rank of professor.

Developing the Native Studies Canon

Specifically, I have been teaching in the department of Native Studies almost from the very beginning of its inception (1975), and while I am not technically one of the founders of it, in the formal or institutional sense, I developed or re-designed the majority of the core undergraduate courses taught in the early years (at the time the department offered a BA programme). This entailed developing historical, theoretical and conceptual frameworks relevant to Aboriginal (First Nation, Metis and Inuit) histories, cultures and contemporary experience. Of course, this is quite different from the task usually faced by novice professors who adapt their courses from pre-existing canons. In the 1970s, the Native Studies canon did not exist but had to be invented, which required an enormous amount of intellectual and practical energies. We were an under-resourced and very small department. There were no role models and it meant going against the grain in many instances; throughout the 1970s, 1980s and even into the 1990s, Native Studies was largely dismissed as a "cross-cultural" remedial programme and not taken seriously as a scholarly unit. However, we were developing indigenously-based critical scholarship and creating courses which not only respected and foregrounded Aboriginal cultures and peoples, but also questioned colonial history and knowledge. At the same time we were aware that we had to make these courses meaningful to Aboriginal students and non-alienating for white Canadian students. These courses (and many more since that colleagues and I have continued to develop as we now offer a doctoral programme) have become critically central to our field, and in effect, have become part of a "Native Studies canon."

But what is a canon? In the context of academic disciplines, Joyce Green, Metis scholar in political science, describes a canon as "that core of material which is viewed as foundational to the discipline ... and is considered essential reading for students, and is considered to be the base on which newer knowledge is based" (2001, 39). Green is quick to point out that the canon was "constructed primarily by western European intellectuals, was imbued with and propagated the dominant philosophies, ideologies and analytical forms of the dominators" (39). In other words, the "canon" privileged European knowledge while it justified the colonial project. In contrast, the very basis of Native Studies depends upon Indigenous knowledges and experiences which considerably expand upon and in many crucial ways contradict or confront traditional western notions of what constitutes "knowledge" or "literature," and so radically transforms the idea of the "canon." In short, and among many other ways, we can know outside of textbooks, we can create oral-based literatures, and we can "read" in multiple, not singular (Western) ways. As decolonizing professors we were engaged in an interpretative undertaking, bringing our worldviews, our colonial experience, our modes of understanding and research and of course, our personal styles into the curriculum and into our university classrooms. Some of us also brought our languages and our "lands," the epistemological bases to our cultures, into the classrooms; however, in my case, I was not doing any ordinary "cultural" or "cross-cultural" teaching, rather, I was "combining cultural ethos with critical 'resistance' analysis" (see chapter "From the Land to the Classroom: Broadening Epistemology"), that is, I was deconstructing colonial records and building Indigenous presence.[6] As Peter Kulchyski explains, "Native Studies can

---

6 I have written about some of these earlier challenges of teaching in a number of previous works; see especially chapters "Preface – or – Here Are Our Voices, Who Will Hear?"; "The Colonization of a Native Woman Scholar"; "From the Land to the Classroom: Broadening Epistemology"; LaRocque (2002).

be seen as an interpretive practise, a mode and an ethics of reading that depends upon an exploded concept of text" (2000, 23). We "exploded" the concept of text in a wide variety of ways, and in so doing, we also challenged what it means to know and that what we "know" is culturally and politically informed.

Knowledge and Resistance Scholarship

It is particularly important in Native Studies that students appreciate the environment in which scholarship develops. Most of us have been led to believe that scholarship is objective, impartial and apolitical (Said 1979, 9–10). But in fact, knowledge is culturally and politically produced, perhaps especially in the so-called Social Sciences. More specifically, we now understand that much of archival "knowledge" about Indigenous peoples was saturated with ideological content, to say nothing about distortion and just plain racism. Ethnohistorian Francis Jennings bluntly points out what Aboriginal scholars know so well – that the historical labelling and anthropological classifications of "the Indian" as Savage juxtaposed against the European as Civilized "reflect words and concepts which have evolved from centuries of conquest and have been created for the purposes of conquest rather than the purposes of knowledge" (1976, 12).

J.M. Blaut in *The Colonizer's Model of the World* argues that scholarly beliefs are "shaped by culture" (1993, 10), and "the ethnography of beliefs" or "belief licencing" (30–43; 59), and that Eurocentric scholars have shaped knowledge from a single theory (the "European Miracle"), in fact, a "super theory" from which other smaller theories have evolved that were and continue to be instrumental for colonialism. In brief, the "European Miracle" is the powerfully legitimating colonizer's belief that:

> European civilization – 'The West' – has had some unique historical advantage, some special quality of race or culture or environment or mind or spirit, which gives this human community a permanent superiority over all other communities, at all times in history and down to the present.... Europeans are seen as the 'makers of history.' Europe eternally advances, progresses, modernizes. The rest of the world advances more sluggishly, or stagnates: it is 'traditional society.' (Blaut 1993, 1)

This belief is at the same time "Eurocentric diffusionism," a related theory "about the way cultural processes tend to move over the surface of the world as a whole. They tend to flow out of the European sector and toward the non-European sector" (1). Colonialism then "must mean for the Africans, Asians and Americans, not spoilation and cultural destruction but, rather, the receipt by diffusion of European civilization: modernization" (2). Colonialism is re-fashioned as progress and enlightenment. Further, "the development of a body of Eurocentric beliefs, justifying and assisting Europe's colonial activities has been and still is, of very great importance. Eurocentrism is quite simply the colonizer's model of the world" (10). What is more, all other European ideas and philosophies have been advanced as universal truths, not as ideas bound to and limited by specifically European cultures and places. Such Eurocentric approaches and theories, embedded in Western scholarship, have been promoted as empirical and scientific, and until recently, have enjoyed uncontested dominance.

The dominant western narrative is knowledge which has been selected, assembled and arranged in such a way as to facilitate and advance the heroification of the European in the Americas (and everywhere else), much to the expense of Indigenous peoples, including Canada's Aboriginal peoples (Duchemin 1990; LaRocque 2010). Clearly, and as so many scholars have long documented, there are ways to see the European/Indigenous encounter as other than the super theory of "civilization" conquering "savagery." Exploring these "other ways to see" is one of the critical tasks of Native Studies.

Native Studies then challenges dominant and hegemonic knowledge and theories. In Canada, the history, the diversity and the complexity of Aboriginal cultures has, until quite recently, been ignored or simply infantilized. The colonial project has been glossed over. And in terms of representation, Native peoples have been universally stereotyped and savagely dehumanized. On a more material level, there is virtually no end to the list of all the ways Indigenous peoples have lost entire populations, cultures, communities, lands and resources.

The Ethical Imperative of Native Studies

In such a context, there is no way we can avoid taking ethical positions; as decolonizing scholars, and not just from Native Studies, we must interrogate false history which is, on one hand, the glorification of Euro-resettlement of Canada, and on the other, the denigration of Aboriginal cultures. We must also respond to the ongoing injustices and other urgent needs as well as the resilience of Aboriginal communities. Therefore, central to Native Studies is the manifold task of challenging the resettler text and repositioning the place of Aboriginal peoples in

218   The Emma LaRocque Reader

Canadian (and international) history and society. For example, we hold that the construction of Canada was a political act, and equally, that the construction of Canadian historical and literary knowledge with respect to Aboriginal peoples was, and largely remains, a political act. In part, and as Joyce Green (2001) argues, "Native Studies exists because of relations of oppression. It exists because of historical colonial relationship, in which the oppressor constructed knowledge as first, its own cultural and intellectual production; and second, as that which legitimated the colonial enterprise" (40).

And precisely because of such constructions both in political life and in the production of knowledge, and in many ways as a corrective response, Native Studies places Aboriginal peoples at the centre of our inquiry and investigation from which we challenge hegemonic canons and/or reassert Indigenous life, or totally create anew, theories and methodologies. It is in this sense that Native Studies appears as a form of "resistance scholarship." Of course, as scholars we include a variety of meanings and interpretations; as scholars, we must constantly modify our data base, our understanding, our research methods and theories. In contrast to the European Miracle tunnel vision or "tunnel history" which views non-European peoples as "rockbound" by supposedly "timeless, changeless tradition" (Blaut 1993, 5),[7] I have always understood our intellectual and scholarly lives as dynamic, dialogical and creative – much like how Native cultures have always approached life.

Green has also pointed out that Native Studies exists because other disciplines in universities have failed to treat adequately or fairly, either Indigenous knowledge or the Native experience (2001, 42). Given this, a large part of our Native Studies efforts has necessarily involved the legitimation of Aboriginal cultures, knowledges and experience. However, more recently, focus has shifted from the more explanatory position of "legitimation" to the more pro-active stance of cultural affirmation. Today's younger Aboriginal scholars are not so heavily burdened as my generation was to correct misinformation and to deconstruct racist portrayals and language; today's generation can and is moving on to more "positive" and (self)-affirmative work.

---

7 Today I do not think European scholarship views all non-European peoples in this way; after all, some of the most brilliant post-colonial scholars are non-European. But the notion lingers on that indigenous peoples are still "traditional" in the sense Blaut (1993) means by that, that is "Europe eternally advances, progresses…. The rest of the world advances more sluggishly, or stagnates: it is 'traditional society'" (1).

Reflections on Resistance Writing and Teaching 219

But the differences in approach are actually slight because as I have just noted resistance work that perhaps characterizes previous generations has always been affirmative work. Doing a critique of archival or Hollywood stereotypes is asserting and affirming the integrity of Aboriginal cultures and the humanity of Aboriginal peoples. And really, in the context of this discourse, any validation of Aboriginal cultures is, in the final analysis, also a form of challenge to the mainstream canon. In any case, all this has been exciting for not only are we rebuilding our cultures by establishing new intellectual traditions for future generations but also because we are pushing the margins of western academia as well as redefining it.

Not only do we seek to dismantle colonial paradigms and stereotypes, we create new genres and languages. For instance, take the concept of "settler." Within what I have called the "civ/sav dichotomy" (see chapter "The Métis in English Canadian Literature"; LaRocque 2010), Europeans used the concept of "settlers/settlement" as a mark of civilization (assumed to be European) in direct opposition to the "nomadic" "Indians," nomadism being a sign of savagism.[8] So in archival literature "Indians" are often described as "roaming" or "ranging rather than inhabiting" – an early colonialist mantra that rationalized and soon legalized dispossession of Native lands, resources and communities. The stereotype of the underpopulated, wandering and warring savage Indian on "empty lands" became the Cowboy/Indian genre in the comic book and movie industry. In courts, where the colonizers are at once party and judge, Native people have had to prove their "occupancy and use" of ancestral lands in order to win back portions of their stolen lands! The concept "Settlement/settler" became a moral argument eagerly advanced by European justifiers of colonization. Settlement along with agriculture became associated with "progress" and cultural evolution, with the nifty notion that farmers had prior land rights over hunters because they used and "settled" the land; hunters, or "savages," merely roamed over it (Pearce 1965, 70–1). This is one of many examples of how Aboriginal histories and cultures were/are falsified or grossly distorted.

In fact, there were a great variety of cultures, with many Indigenous groups engaging in forms of agriculture (Jennings 1976; Weatherford

---

8 And not romanticized as it now appears to be, even in some post-colonial thinking. For an absorbing discussion on the conceptual and political problematics of rootedness, migrancy and nomadism, see the chapter on "The Rhetoric of Mobility" in *Travelling Knowledges* by Renate Eigenbrod (2005, 21–38).

220 The Emma LaRocque Reader

1988, 1991; Wright 1993). But more importantly, those who were not farmers (in the European sense) such as the coastal, Plains and northern peoples used and occupied and variously cultivated and harvested their resources, lands and waters. They had their own forms of territorial usage and settlements (Dickason 1992; Morrison and Wilson 1995). As we now know pre-Columbian Indigenous peoples of the Americas were very heavily populated (Blaut 1993, 184; Jennings 1976, 30)[9] with extensive settlements and other modes and lifeways of rootedness to certain domains of lands. Those Native peoples such as the Plains and some Northern peoples who did migrate did so for resource management reasons and within bounded areas of lands; they were not aimlessly wandering[10] (which is Webster's original meaning for the word "nomadic"). Mobilization and rootedness within the context of land use by Indigenous peoples are not mutually exclusive – as European colonists very well knew given they were often dependent on Native geographical expertise and/or produce.[11] The ultimate irony is that Europeans were just as mobile as anyone else, yet for obvious political interests, they claimed ownership of the concept of civilization/settlement. There is no objective moral basis for the idea that those who built permanent settlements or practised certain styles of farming had/have prior rights to those who have other relational uses, methods and attachments to lands. Frankly, I am not enamoured with the concepts and words "settler," or "settlement" given their colonial utility; but to make an obvious statement: Indigenous peoples were the original settlers of the Americas, whether they lived in city states or commuted between satellite camp sites. For this reason I cannot call Europeans "settlers" – to do so is to imply as well as to entrench the idea that Aboriginal peoples were not! In actuality, colonizers dispossessed and displaced Native (including Metis) settlers and settlements (as well as other relational attachments to lands), and re-settled the lands. In the words of Jennings, "The so-called settlement of America was a *re*settlement"

---

9 For a fuller discussion on Indigenous populations prior to Columbus' arrival, see Blaut (1993), especially chapter four; and Jennings (1976), chapter two.

10 Of course, at different periods and in different ways, post-Columbian Indigenous peoples were literally vanishing by the millions (Blaut 1993; Jennings 1976), and of those who survived, many were left homeless, and in various ways, forced to wander, particularly Native Americans. The Hollywood version of either "nomadic" or "Vanishing Indians" straggling behind one lone horse with travois is in fact a political picture – and one that tells a very different story than what Hollywood meant to portray. For more on the Vanishing Indian, see Berkhofer (1978); see also Francis (1992): chapters two and three.

11 See, for example, Jennings (1976, 80).

Reflections on Resistance Writing and Teaching 221

(30, his emphasis). This is why I refer to Euro-White North Americans as resettlers.

There are many other colonial words and descriptions of Native life in areas of organization, governance, leadership, gender, spirituality and so forth, that serve to downgrade the cultures and dehumanize Native peoples (LaRocque 2010, 50).[12] Indeed, as Ronald Wright puts it, "An entire vocabulary is tainted with prejudice and condescension" (1993, xi). Such colonial texts invite "explosion," yet our challenge to such tendentious, sexist and racist use of words has been slow and uneven. One response has been to "reclaim" words (i.e. "squaw") that were meant to debase Native women and men. Another response is to use Native words and concepts, which in many contexts is a much needed cultural and political sign, and in literature, is a thing of beauty. However, it is French and English words (within which we work in North America) as well as some ideological and/or discipline-bound phraseologies (i.e. tribal, traditional, hunters and gatherers, subsistence, chief, warrior) and concepts that, at the very least, require rethinking. Much work remains to be done in these areas of stereotyping, belittlement and disempowerment through language manipulation. We are now in [the] process of reworking and establishing new vocabularies, languages and canons in our fields. Of course, such struggles at the level of language and institutionalized canons are connected with material and legal struggles, given that the "subjectifying nature" (Coulthard 2007, 455) of colonial languages serves to undermine our humanity as well as our inherent rights to lands and governance, which are of course based on our settlement/s and continued occupation, use and relationship of lands since time immemorial.

Reworking and Establishing New Canons

In Native Studies "reworking and establishing new canons" is actually a very fluid process, one that requires respectful disagreements with colleagues for we are not uniform in this work and development. Because Native Studies is meta-disciplinary in nature, our faculties represent a wide variety of disciplines, research directions, methodologies and

---

12 In *When the Other Is Me* (LaRocque 2010), I analyse in chapters two and three, "lexical strategies of belittlement that especially serve to degrade and infantilize Native peoples" (38); the instrumental role of the "war of words" (72) in colonial writing, and its impact on Native peoples is quite immense. See also Adams (1975) and Duchemin (1990).

222 The Emma LaRocque Reader

even ideologies. Our own department reflects such diversity. Some of our faculty emphasize community research, some tend to "traditional knowledge," others focus on law and legislation or other urgent issues such as racism, poverty, violence against women, urbanization, while still others do archival, historical or literary work. But all of us concern ourselves with and as Peter Kulchyski put it, "the righting of" and "the writing of" (2000, 3) the names and places erased, lands and resources stolen, or beliefs, stories and visual arts distorted by both resettler colonial renderings and colonial governments.

Naturally, we each work in the areas we specialize in. While I have focussed on the deconstruction of colonial misrepresentation in Canadian historiography, literature and popular culture, particularly the civ/sav paradigm, I have also advanced an Indigenous-based critical voice and theory (1990). For example, I have demonstrated that it is possible to appreciate Aboriginal "voice," rooted in Indigenous and colonial experience, without compromising either that voice or scholarly protocols. This kind of critical positionality is an outgrowth of my "resistance" research in Native/White relations, an area of discourse and study which cannot be dealt with effectively only by standard western models or by a unidisciplinary approach. Others may refer to such approaches as "engaged research." It depends somewhat on our respective disciplines but, again, all of us in Native (or Indigenous) Studies do not accept without challenge the massive falsification of our histories, or all the insults to our cultures and intelligence extant in colonial records and literatures, and in the media and marketplace, for that matter.

It is the legacy of colonization that makes us resistance scholars. But this work is not unscholarly, parochial or blindly subjective; nor is it merely defensive (or offensive). It is not insular, simplistic or necessarily culturalist or nationalist in basis. Native Studies is an ambitious project. Our knowledge of the fields involved is wide ranging, spanning five centuries of archival material, historical, anthropological and/or literary scholarship. We pursue our investigations and our arguments through the discourse of colonizer fur traders, explorers, missionaries, jurists, historians, anthropologists, playwrights, poets and novelists, from the sixteenth to the twenty-first centuries, and through the counter-discourse of Aboriginal intellectuals including artists, writers and the growing numbers of Aboriginal scholars who have perforce challenged old imperialist schools of thought which continue even today to stereotype, ignore or discredit us. Needless to say, we are complex and diverse in our research, approaches and argumentations. Resistance scholarship entails and requires ethical and critical study, engaged research, and intellectual freedom.

Playing Defence, Playing Offence

However, not everyone agrees or is comfortable with the word "resistance," and some may find the phrase "resistance scholarship" an oxymoron. This may partly indicate the shift from having to play defence to being able to play offence. In the literary world for instance, some Aboriginal novelists or poets and literary critics have turned to "writing home" (McLeod 2001), rather than "writing back" at the proverbial "Empire" (Ashcroft, Griffith and Tiffens 1989); other scholars (both Aboriginal and non-Aboriginal including some grad students) in various fields have turned their attention to the retrieval and foregrounding of cultural knowledge, both traditional and contemporary, with a focus on languages, literatures, land ways, epistemologies and philosophies, kinship and political systems, ideas of treaties, use of resources, or material art and so forth. In these contexts, if the meaning of the word "resistance" is taken literally (i.e. "striving against"), then perhaps the notion of resistance research may be limiting. But it is also the case that many students and some scholars associate the word "resistance" as only oppositional and negative, whereas cultural matters or cultural portraiture is seen as inherently constructive, hence, positive. Some find that the word "resistance" is too "post-colonial" and as such, unbalanced and singular in its scope, and neglects centuries of indigenous knowledge prior to colonial incursions. Aboriginal novelist and scholar Thomas King in "Godzilla vs. Post-Colonial" finds the term "post-colonial" problematic for a number of reasons:

> And worst of all, the idea of post-colonial writing effectively cuts us off from *our* traditions, traditions that were in place before colonialism ever became a question, traditions which have come down to us through our cultures in spite of colonization, and it supposes that contemporary Native writing is largely a construct of oppression. (1997, 242–3)

Indigenous knowledge has indeed existed eons prior to European invasions, and Thomas King, of course, makes a very important observation. To what extent colonization has impacted on Indigenous knowledge, and whether or not this is even any longer important to consider, especially within post-colonial theory (or theories) remain issues of debate and perhaps some contention. More recently, Anishnabe (Ojibway) scholar and colleague Niigonwedom James Sinclair has argued that:

> critical lenses of protest and resistance in Aboriginal literatures have now become so commonplace they are beginning to mirror the one-dimensional

treatment Indigenous peoples receive in mainstream media.... The issue is not that Indigenous peoples resist, for they must and do, but that these acts are fetishized, romanticized, and commodified into comfortable and consumable narratives. (2010, 26)

Sinclair goes on to advocate for an interpretive lens of "continuance" as a "methodology that considers Indigenous literatures not only as narratives of resistance but engages the other countless activities Native authors undertake as active and responsible members of communities and creation" (28). Such engagements and "lens" "opens up Indigenous literatures (and arguably Indigenous cultures) as expansive and adaptive, growing and innovative, instead of only staving off a colonial tidal wave" (28).

There has also been a thought that resistance work (associated with post-colonial criticism) necessarily re-centres the colonizer. J. Edward Chamberlin, for example, has stated that post-colonial theories "reinforce the dominance it seeks to replace" (as quoted in Sinclair 2010, 26). Judith Leggat in a very thoughtful essay, "Native Writing, Academic Theory, Post-colonialism across the Cultural Divide," states that in an instance of unequal power relations between Aboriginal writer and White academic, "the act of literary analysis can reinscribe colonialism" (in Moss 2003, 120). In some ways and in certain contexts all these cautionary arguments about the uses or abuses of post-colonial theories (under which resistance theory is often subsumed) have merit of course. It may be true that for every theory and frame of interpretation Aboriginal artists, scholars and other intellectuals invent, there will be those who will not comprehend or who will oversimplify and form new stereotypes. And it may be true that in some cases our work will be used to "reinscribe" or re-centre colonialism. Given the magnitude of western arrogance and ignorance about Indigenous peoples and cultures, we should perhaps expect these sorts of obtuse and defensive manoeuvres. But surely, such obstructive devices cannot block our work; nor should they in any way limit our scholarship and our right to theorize ourselves (or anyone else), our cultures and our experience, or to employ (always reflexively and critically, of course) or create whatever theories best assist in our work of deconstructing and reconstructing. Or simply because we love scholarship. It seems to me that there is a "European miracle" diffusionist assumption to all these obstructions, and the implications are unsettling. Is it that every time we Indigenous scholars and artists employ so-called western tools or concepts, we are no longer who we are? Or that we re-colonize or enslave ourselves just by using certain terms, languages or schools of thought? That we have none of our own thoughts? Obviously, this is a dead-end road to go on. This is to buy into the European diffusionist notion that everything originates or comes from Europe. That nothing belongs to us! That all we can ever do is borrow "the master's tools"! Intellectually speaking, there is no master here – unless we give it that power. "Borrowing" is a two-way street – if Indigenous peoples "borrowed" European tools, Europeans did so as well, more than amply at that (Axtell 2001; Jennings 1976; Weatherford 1988; Wright 1993). But there is another perhaps more important point here – we not only have dynamic cultural heritages, we also have a birthright to this contemporary world. And these two aspects, cultural heritage and contemporaneity is a matter of imbrication, not a matter of absolute ontological or fathomless chasm. We all have blended heritages, Europeans no less so, but it has obviously been to the advantage of colonizers to emphasize our differences, those real and those imagined or constructed.

I am not minimizing the challenges that confront us; the "master narrative" is powerful because it exercises what Said calls "flexible positional superiority" (1979, 7). That is, Eurocentric perspectives do have tendencies to absorb counter-knowledges and re-frame them within their own perspectives and for their own purposes. Or to shift terms of arguments or definitions both as "techniques of mastery" (Duchemin 55), and as a means of maintaining their super theory of civilization/ savagery (LaRocque 2010, 47–55). And it is still largely the case that the "globalization of knowledge and Western culture constantly reaffirms the West's view of itself as the centre of legitimate knowledge, the arbiter of what counts as knowledge and the source of "civilized knowledge" (Smith 1999, 63). However, we cannot keep giving power away by acquiescing to the popular but mistaken notion that all things belong to Europeans!! Or that "everything that belongs to the colonizer is not appropriate for the colonized," which Memmi deduces is "a confused and misleading conviction" (1967, 138). As far as I am concerned, Shakespeare, for instance, is as much my heritage as a human being, as is *Wehsakehcha*, the central Cree comic-psychologist shape-shifting character in the numerous stories my mother entertained her children with. To believe otherwise or to in any way limit ourselves in our use of theory or terminology is to fall into the colonizer's model of the world, which is exactly where neo-imperialist thinkers would contain us. Moreover, we have our own tools. We have our languages, our literatures, our concepts, our theories, our ways of knowing and of discovering and arranging knowledge. And our knowledge cannot be defined by or confined to some old colonial stereotypes of "Native culture" or "traditional (now 'Indigenous') knowledge." Our knowledges are trans-colonial, expansive, unsedimented and both ancient and contemporary. In many ways Indigenous scholars can speak many languages; we too can exercise flexible positionality!

It is very true that Indigenous peoples' histories, languages, literatures, religions, worldviews, political systems, technologies, architectures, sciences and the arts did not begin with European arrivals! And amazingly much has survived. To be sure, survival has not been universal or even in texture, but what has not survived in whole we have and continue to re-invent. As I have long argued, pre-Columbian Indigenous peoples were dynamic and adaptive, and have continued to be despite all the invasions and with it, massive depopulation and dispossession. Of course, we are not who we were, but neither is Europe: it is not as though the world that Shakespeare lived in hundreds of years ago, inhabited by monsters, witches and countless other religious beliefs and secular speculations that had no basis in observational truths (Dickason 1984), is the world of contemporary Europeans. Both Indigenous and Western cultures, hence scholars, are confronted with the historical realities of continuance and discontinuance.

But it is European-based scholarship that has traditionally treated Indigenous cultures as stagnant, primitive clay pots into which progressive varnished European cultures infuse their "European miracle" through colonial diffusion. Such a view constantly measures Indigenous change and difference solely from western cultural tenets which are assumed to be "the hub of the human wheel out of which emanate all things progressive in culture and intellect" (LaRocque 2010, 163). This sort of neo-colonial thinking places, yet again, Indigenous peoples in an absolutely no-win situation. In fact, it translates to intellectual genocide because it demands that Indigenous peoples remain "traditional," that is, fixed and frozen in time; and when they change, they are charged with "assimilation" (even when assimilation is forced) – one way or another we are consigned to irrelevance, a modern version for the Vanishing Indian! (Francis 1992; LaRocque 2010). Meanwhile, the western world, which has more than liberally taken from the Indigenous (both materially and conceptually), acts as if it has neither been acculturated, indigenized, hybridized nor colonized by its own colonial globe trotting.

Resistance Scholarship as Critical Inquiry

Some may also assume that the very nature of "resistance" cannot be used in the same breath as "scholarship." Those who believe this are those who carry on old colonial ideas of scholarship as pure and uncontaminated by "the mud of politics" (Said 1979, 13). But as Said has argued, now echoed by numerous other decolonizing scholars since, scholars are products of their societies and as such are never free of their culturally-formed perspectives and political locations. This is not to say that this renders scholarship useless or a joke. Arguably, no one was more passionate about scholarship than Edward Said. He practised and advocated intellectual rigour, critical awareness and self-reflexivity in the pursuit of knowledge. What he understood is the intimate connection between "knowledge" and power. It is this connection that we seek to expose through our scholarship

I for one believe strongly in critical scholarship, otherwise I would not be in this vocation. There are protocols of research and study in the best of scholarly activity and dialogue that I believe has the capacity to enhance humanity. On a more personal note, my own resistance research approach has never been confined to western knowledge, presuppositions or methodologies or to western definitions or theories. But, and again, I do not believe scholarship or science or technologies or any other cultural acquirements belong solely to the west. Innovation and learning have never been alien to Indigenous cultures; scholarship is as much my birthright as anything else, period.

I am in this work not only because I love knowledge and obviously, all the complexities and nuances and questions of knowledge production, but also because I am ethically committed to the vocation of humanization, that is, both to the ending of injustice and oppression, whether social or intellectual, and at the same time, to the reconstruction of Indigenous humanity. And ultimately, all humanity. I do not know how we can study colonization and all its manifestations through mass media stereotypes, or the ongoing destruction and invasion of Indigenous lands, or the daily indecencies of sexism and racism without addressing the ethical, social and political ramifications of such study. To study any kind of human violation is *ipso facto* to be challenged in our ethics, and to be called into resistance! In this Native Studies is decidedly and unavoidably political.

However, there is also much that we can and must celebrate. Decades – centuries really – of Indigenous resistance has produced many positive political, socio-economic and cultural changes. In Canada, a number of our original languages are still in use; our philosophies, worldviews and narratives are increasingly studied and understood, spiritual beliefs and protocols are being practised; we are re-inventing many aspects of our arts including song, storytelling, sculpture and many other forms of material and visual art; our written literatures are flourishing; our scholars are increasing as is our largely excellent

228   The Emma LaRocque Reader

scholarship; some socio-economic conditions have certainly improved, relatively speaking,[13] and our populations are rising; we are winning some significant battles over land and resource rights in courts, even as we face ongoing incursions in the form of industrial encroachments, legitimized by governments and "the national interest." Our presence in the culture and politics of Canada can no longer be dismissed or ignored. We are always resurfacing. And what may be called "resurgence" today is actually a continuation of Indigenous resistance and resilience. Take the 1970s. How well I remember as a university student reading Harold Cardinal's book *The Unjust Society* (1969). It had a revolutionary effect on me. As did the many protests held by various Native (both First Nation and Metis) communities in northern Alberta. In that era I witnessed and was part of the political awakening of Aboriginal peoples across Canada. If there is resurgence today it is because of previous generations who refused to give up, who believed in the value of who they were/are, and who took their aspirations to the streets and to the courts, and to the cameras for all Canadians to see. Some of us took to schools and scholarship.

We Cannot Be Owned

Today, as always, the topic of Native peoples is politically charged. This renders scholars in Native Studies vulnerable to multiple criticisms or attacks, not only from westernist intellectuals, or societal conflicts which wind their way into our classrooms, but also from cultural and political interests that come from the Native communities.

Although we wish to be supportive to the work of reconstruction that Aboriginal nations are undertaking, we must be careful; we cannot become mouthpieces for any particular political or ethnic group, nor propagandists for any movement. We cannot be owned or dictated by any organization or constituencies, be they communities or universities.

---

13 This is not to suggest all is glowing in the socio-economic area – Aboriginal peoples in Canada do still lag behind other Canadians in areas of education, employment, housing, health, and so forth. Further, Aboriginal peoples suffer the highest rates of youth suicide and homicide, as well as the highest rates of incarceration. Poverty, racism and sexism are still a daily reality for Aboriginal peoples. But compared to the 1950s–70s eras, the era I grew up in, the socio-economic picture was in certain respects much more grim than it is now. See Frideres and Gadacz (2001) chapters 3–6. See also Statistics Canada, 2006 Census.

Said reminds us:

> Loyalty to the group's fight for survival cannot draw in the intellectual so far as to narcotize the critical sense, or reduce its imperatives, which are always to go beyond survival to questions of political liberation, to critiques of the leadership, to presenting alternatives that are too often marginalized or pushed aside as irrelevant to the main battle at hand. (1996, 41)

Many of us in Native Studies, or other resistance-based studies, have made a living deconstructing Western hegemonic canons and ideologies; but we must also have the right to exercise our analytical skills and training in the service of advancing Aboriginal humanity, and sometimes, this means we must offer some critical reflections. There are no flawless cultures in the world, even those that have been oppressed. Naturally, our analyses or criticisms may not be welcomed or understood. Indeed, given the educational and socio-economic gap between Aboriginal scholars and the wider community, our critiques may be experienced as hurtful. The university culture of criticism is a very particular, if not esoteric, culture which many non-university people, Native and non-Native alike, may misunderstand as simply "too negative." Put another way, there is tension between our critical, analytical commitments and the need to support Native struggles for social justice. Nonetheless, we must maintain our freedoms to practise our scholarship, our mandates to review information, and to evaluate it, and if necessary, to debate and to disagree.

As may be appreciated, intellectual freedom ranks as one of my most cherished treasures, and indeed, practising this freedom is one reason I have been a life-long scholar. But this is not only because of my profession, but because I believe our freedom to research and to reflect is requisite to advancing our humanity. However, I hasten to add, such freedoms are not without context or social responsibilities. As a decolonizing Indigenously situated feminist scholar, I believe in the social purpose of knowledge, and further, that my knowledge gained from intellectual freedom is informed by my cultural and social responsibilities.

The effects of colonization on both white and Native scholars and scholarship in Canada is just beginning to be appreciated; and indeed, in the area of scholarship, much has improved since the 1970s! There are now in North America works (too numerous to reference) from almost all disciplines which reflect appreciation of our cultural heritages as well as sound understanding of our colonial experiences. But as long as

230 The Emma LaRocque Reader

all the racist and dehumanizing archival, historical and literary portrayals continue to circulate in our library and publication systems, as they do, we are put in a situation of having to continually address this material, especially as each new generation of students enter our classrooms. In addition, it is clear that we do still face misunderstanding and some resistance in the way our knowledge base and cultural information as well as our decolonized methodologies are received. For all these reasons and more we are not in a position to "resist no longer."

However, although we have a significant role to play in resisting oppression, in theorizing its origins and demonstrating its social consequences as well as assisting in reconstruction, we cannot be distracted from our vocation as critical thinkers. Our research must be rigorous but it cannot be aloof. Our research must be thorough, thoughtful, thought-provoking, and our scholarship must exude the highest of standards, but also be "transgressive" and humanized with a compassionate voice. As an intellectual and a scholar, I often call for that "critical and relatively independent spirit of analysis and judgement," which Edward Said argues "ought to be the intellectual's contribution" (1996, 86). This is the primary contribution that we can all can make; this is the spirit in which I carry out my scholarly studies within a Native Studies mandate and programme that is as open, vibrant and international in scope as any critical human inquiry. For me this is the meaning of "resistance" scholarship.

2015

Contemporary Métis Literature:
Resistance, Roots, Innovation

Dear John: I'm still here and halfbreed,
after all these years

– Dumont (1996, 52)

I was born
into the world
speaking Mechif
a language
whose base is Cree
with a whole bunch
of French thrown in
for good measure
Kipaha la porte! I say   *Mechif for "close the door"*

– Bouvier 37

The history of the Métis people is marked by a complexity that reflects the duality of their origins and the many forms of resistance that have characterized their ongoing relations with the Canadian nation-state.[1] The Métis are a distinct ethnic Indigenous people who are recognized as Aboriginal in the Canadian constitution, and whose history, ancestry, and cultural expression emerged out of the First Nations, French, and English fur trade during the seventeenth century. The first "Métis" were children of relations between First Nations women and European men. From these early relations grew "halfbreed" families, who by a process of endogamy (marrying within their own group), became

---

1 Because not all the Métis are necessarily francophone in origin, I write the word without the accent on the "e." [This Reader adopts the more common Métis spelling. Elaine Coburn – editor's note]

Métis peoples. By the early 1800s large populations of Métis merged and located in the Red River Valley. By 1869 there were about 10,000 Métis in the Red River Settlement (Weinstein 2007, 5).

Early Métis cultural development largely revolved around the fur trade, as their familial knowledge of Native cultures, languages, and lands were indispensable to the Hudson's Bay and North West companies. The Métis played central and distinguished roles as guides, voyageurs, provisioners, traders, interpreters, and cultural brokers. They were known and respected for their hard work and independence, and in Red River for their growing sense of nationalism as they fought to protect their bison-hunting territories as well as their right to trade freely with competing fur trade companies. Their unique blending of cultures was reflected in the iconography of the Métis flag, an infinity symbol whose double loops indicate the strength of Métis duality, which was first used by Métis resistance fighters in the Battle of Seven Oaks in 1816.

Métis determination to protect their lands and distinct culture took on a more dramatic form in the mid-1800s when they were excluded from land negotiations between the newly formed country of Canada and the Hudson's Bay Company. The Métis, who formed the vast majority of the Red River Settlement, established a provisional government in 1869 under the leadership of Louis Riel to represent their interests when land surveyors arrived in the Red River area (now Winnipeg and the vicinity) to facilitate the transfer of western lands to Canada. Relations broke down as the Métis stood their ground; the "Red River Rebellion" of that same year led to the Manitoba Act and that province's entry into Confederation. Although the Métis wrested legal recognition for their lands through the *Manitoba Act* of 1870, they suffered widespread dispossession; by the early 1880s, two-thirds of the Métis had moved out of the province (Weinstein 2007, 13). The majority moved west and northwest.

The unresolved issues of land loss and displacement in Red River followed the Métis to the Northwest, giving rise to the second Métis resistance, known in Canadian history as "the 1885 Northwest Rebellion." This resistance in northern Saskatchewan – again led by Louis Riel (who had been retrieved from exile in the United States) – culminated in the unsuccessful Battle of Batoche with the Canadian militia, leaving the Métis with loss of lives, lands, and leadership. Riel and his men, along with Native supporters, were arrested, and Riel was executed in November 1885. Military strategist Gabriel Dumont escaped into exile in the United States.

After 1885 the Métis made more mass migrations further west and north, once again in search of lands and legal recognition for ownership of these lands. What is of note is that despite the massive losses, repeated dispersals, and political isolation, and the harsh socio-economic conditions that followed, the Métis continued to adapt, finding ways to re-establish communities and to maintain a strong sense of their Métis identity. Today there are about 400,000 Métis who live in both rural and urban communities across Canada. Métis communities with their distinct culture and traditions continue to exist; 90% live in Manitoba, Saskatchewan, and Alberta (Métis National Council 2013). However, the issue of Métis identity has grown complicated, in part due to government policies. These complications have impacted the Métis in many crucial ways with respect to Aboriginal land rights, but also in the defining and reading of Métis literature.

Métis literature reaches as far back as the European and Indigenous peoples' inscriptions, and it will reach as far forward as the next "new peoples" generate text. This is not to romanticize "Métissage"; it is to point out that Métis peoples have inherited a wealth of literatures – literatures spoken, sung, performed, painted, carved, engraved, pictographed, penned, and stereo/typed (pun intended). And now cybered. It is not surprising, then, that from the very beginnings of Métis ethnopolitical consciousness, the Métis were multilingual, and within the bison-hunting context on the Red River plains, invented a language (Michif) that combined mostly Cree with French, though in some regions it also mixed some English and Saulteux (Bakker 2001, 177–9). In all these languages, the Métis "re-cree-ated" or invented anew stories and traditions steeped in European and Indigenous oralities and alphabets. They were also involved, along with their Cree and Anishinaabe (Ojibway) kin, in the development of the Cree syllabary, "a mixed system containing both syllabic and alphabetic characters" that was collaboratively created by the Wesleyan missionary James Evans in the 1840s (Nichols 1984, 4). Not only did the northern Native peoples such as the Cree, Métis, Anishinaabe, and perhaps Dene assist in the invention of this system, but once available, they "spread it across Rupert's Land" (1).

It is interesting to speculate that, were it not for political interventions in Red River and Saskatchewan, the Métis may very well have developed literatures written in the syllabic system as well as a standardized Michif writing system.[2] But the prairie Métis did not have

---

2 Métis Elder Rita Flamand of Manitoba has developed and teaches a standardized Michif writing system. See Rita Flamand at http://speakingmytruth.ca/downloads /AHFvol2/08_flamand. Accessed 11 July 2013.

234 The Emma LaRocque Reader

much opportunity to develop written literatures, for in the words of Pamela Sing, "Different histories of displacement have resulted in different linguistic and cultural practises" among the Métis (2006, 100). Michif as a language could not develop under the diasporic conditions in the aftermath of the Red River (1869) and Northwest (1885) Métis Resistances[3]; however, it certainly did not disappear. As Sing points out, Michif can be found in writings by Riel, Dumont, and others, and is now inserted into some contemporary Métis writings as a marker of cultural belonging, distinction, and resistance (Sing 2006, 102–3). But whether or not Michif is used, Métis peoples continue to be among the great storytellers and writers of Canada. This writing, however, is not without genealogical and sociocultural politics.

Definitional Problems

Métis literature has been subject to a series of misrepresentations and misnomers emerging from the legacy of colonial history. The problem for most scholars and theorists – and for many writers who identify or have been identified as Métis – centres on identity. It is virtually impossible to treat Métis literature without dealing with the intricacies of identity. One of the most significant obstacles is the issue of terminology. It has become common practise to universalize the Métis as "Métis" (to replace the word *halfbreed*, which some find offensive but is actually a term used by most Métis people right into the 1970s), a term that encompasses all individuals of any mixed White-Native (or "mixed blood") ancestry.[4] What this difficult matter of terminology reveals is that Métis identity or identities is/are not uniform. Just as there were "many roads to Red River" (Peterson and Brown 1985, 37–72), so there are many different ways through which individuals or communities have come to identify as "Métis."

Indeed, the shifting terrain of identity politics and legislative changes have dogged the Métis, no less so for the post-1990 writing community, as many well-known Aboriginal writers[5] relocated from Métis (or

---

3 For a detailed study of the two resistances, see Sprague (1988).
4 This chapter focusses entirely on Métis issues in Canada. The term "mixed-blood" is used mostly in the United States, where mixed ancestry is approached quite differently by Native American communities, writers, and theorists. See, for example, Owen (1998). See also Braz (2005).
5 Such writers include Duke Redbird and Lee Maracle (who were prominent in the 1970s wave of "Métis" writers), Drew Hayden Taylor, Ian Ross, Duncan Mercredi, Margo Kane, Kateri Akiwenzie-Damm, and Jordan Wheeler. These writers have made significant contributions to the Métis writing community.

Contemporary Métis Literature 235

mixed ancestry) to First Nation memberships (see Frideres).[6] However, some have continued to associate as Métis by hyphenating their identities, for example, the veteran Cree/Métis poet Duncan Mercredi (*Spirit of the Wolf* 1991), or the recently published Métis/Mennonite poet Katherena Vermette (*End Love Songs* 2012), or the very innovative Métis/Dene dramatist Marie Clements (*DraMétis* 2001). Marilyn Dumont and I also hyphenate as Cree/Métis, even though our identities are decidedly Métis Nation, a distinction that I will take up later.

On the other hand, not all peoples who have assumed Métis identities are necessarily Métis. To put it rather baldly, what distinguishes a first-generation mixed-blood from being a Métis is ethnicity. Métis identity is not just biologic; Métis peoples developed families, communities, and culture (or *cultures*, because there are a number of different Métis cultures – the Red River ones became the Métis Nation and remain the most prominent). But there are other communities that sprang up all over North America that had no direct relationship to or with the Red River Métis. Among the many com-plicating factors concerning Métis/Métis identity,[7] it is the common and generalized use of the term *Métis* that is perhaps the most controversial – and the most confusing. The confusion lies in conflating the term *Métis*, a racial category, with *The Métis*, a sociopolitical and ethnic category. In an effort to explain and keep this distinction, the Métis National Council, an umbrella organization for the Métis Nation peoples, presented the following to the United Nations in 1984: "Written with a small '*m*', *Métis* is a racial term for anyone of mixed Indian and European ancestry. Written with a capital '*M*', *Métis* is a sociocultural or political term for those of mixed ancestry who evolved into a distinct indigenous people during a certain historical period in a certain region of Canada" (Métis Nation Council in Peterson and Brown 1985, 6). The "certain region of Canada" includes the historic fur-trade areas from Ontario westward and into the Territories.

In the landmark study *The New Peoples: Being and Becoming Métis in North America* (1985), Jacqueline Peterson and Jennifer S.H. Brown trace

---

6 This was in large part due to Bill C-31 (1985), which reinstated *non-status Indians* to *status* under the *Indian Act* (1876). For a broad survey of the different Aboriginal groups in rela-tion to legal distinctions and exclusions, see Frideres. The recent ruling that the Metis now qualify as "Indian" under the Constitution Act (1867) bears on Metis Aboriginal rights, not on Metis Nation identity per se.

7 Such factors include confusing legal distinctions, a wide variety of individual and community backgrounds, and outsider definitions. For more details, see chapter "Native Identity and the Metis: Otehpayimsuak Peoples." See also (Dickason 1992, 359–65).

the development of Métis peoples whose identity moved from their beginnings in the fur trade as "half-Native and half-White" to that of a "new people," that is, to an unhyphenated ethnicity, or "ethno-genesis," which they explain is about "how new peoples, new ethnicities and new nationalities come into being" (8). By the late 1600s, such new peoples were developing their own communities throughout North America but were especially concentrated in the Great Lakes/Ohio Valley areas. By the early 1800s a distinct Métis population converged in the Red River Valley region. According to Peterson and Brown, these "new peoples" were:

> not merely biracial, multilingual and bicultural, but the proud owners of a new language; of a syncretic cosmology and religious repertoire: of distinctive modes of dress, cuisine, architecture, vehicles of transport, music and dance; and after 1815 of a quasi-military political organization, a flag, a bardic tradition, a rich folklore and a national history. (Peterson and Brown 1985, 4)

These are the peoples that the wandering artist Paul Kane took such an interest in, and about whom he opined that this "race, in keeping themselves distinct from both Indians and whites, form a tribe of themselves; and although they have adopted some of the customs and manners of the French voyageurs, are much more attached to the wild and savage manners of the Red Man" (Kane in *Minnesota History* 1959, 310). Kane was, of course, viewing the people through "imperial eyes," particularly from the perspective of European travel writing (Pratt 1992), but he also indicates the strong Indigenous foundation of Red River Métis identity. As already noted, this Indigenous-based, ethnically cohesive, and increasingly nationalist population, concentrated in the Red River Valley area, was seriously dislocated by political developments in the 1870s (and again in the late nineteenth and early twentieth centuries in the Northwest), which ushered in an expanded Confederation, a Confederation that resolutely refused to acknowledge their unique peoplehood or to respect their culture and lands as separate from Indians or Whites (Weinstein 2007, 11).

In the ungenerous and polarizing words of Prime Minister John A. Macdonald in the House of Commons debate in 1885 regarding land settlements: "If they are Indians, they go with the tribe ... if they are Halfbreeds, they are whites" (Macdonald in Jannetta 2001, 33). This attitude and policy had a devastating impact on the Métis. While prairie Indians secured reserves and other rights through treaties, and White re-settlers received homesteads and other assistance, the Métis were

Contemporary Métis Literature 237

subjected to a chaotic *scrip* programme, both in Red River and again in the North West, which left them largely without ownership of lands, either as individuals or as a collective (Sprague 1980; Sprague 1988; see also Sawchuk et al. 1981).[8] As a result, the Métis found themselves squatters on lands not yet claimed by White immigrants, or on "road allowance" strips of land in unoccupied Crown lands, literally living on the edge of roads and valiantly making a living both from harvesting the land and wage-based seasonal labour. For about a century the Métis were indeed Canada's "forgotten people" (Sealey and Lussier 1975).

The Métis, particularly in Saskatchewan and Alberta, continued to organize and press for their well-being and land settlements through the Depression era, but it is only since the early 1970s, and as part of the larger Native political movements throughout Canada, that the Métis could indicate the severe extent of their dispossession and eventually begin to gain recognition as *Métis* with Aboriginal rights (Weinstein 2007). As happened in decolonizing movements throughout the world, intellectuals, artists, and writers became the voice and vehicle for articulating peoples' histories, experiences, and aspirations. In Canada, contemporary Métis Nation resistance discourse relies on its own resistance history; this discourse is located in "an arena of struggle" (Harlow 1987, 2) for justice, recovery, and historiographic and constitutional redress.[9] Necessarily contestatory in its beginnings, Métis writing involves a recollection of scattered parts, both personal and communal, and while in its initial stages it talks back and *at* the proverbial imperial centre, it quickly repositions by decentring the "empire" (Ashcroft, Griffiths, and Tiffin 1995), "coming home" (McLeod 2001), and foregrounding "healing" (Episkenew 2009), cultural rebuilding, and self-determination. The body of literature that forms a Métis literary aesthetic is marked by mixing, transgression, and a reinvention of genres, languages, tropes, and techniques. It is characterized by a style of deconstructing and reconstructing, often mixing documentation with "voice" informed by cultural ethos (see chapter "Preface: Here Are Our Voices – Who Will Hear?" xviii; LaRocque 2010, 18, 164). Threaded through all of this is a "love of words," a point I will return to at the end.

---

8 The *scrip* system (certificates redeemable as cash or land given to individuals) was complicated and in part grew from the 1870 *Manitoba Act* which had guaranteed lands for the Metis. See the recent *Manitoba Metis Federation (2013) v. Canada* decision.

9 For an excellent discussion on the complexities of Métis constitutional, Aboriginal, and/or land rights, see the Royal Commission on Aboriginal Peoples (Vol. 4, Chap. 5, 1996).

238 The Emma LaRocque Reader

Métis Nation Literature

The first wave of Métis writers who published between the early and mid-1970s articulated the multilayered facets of this discursive resistance, as have subsequent (post-1990) writers. Given the historical significance and literary importance assigned to the first wave, and given that these writers have consistently produced a body of work that is clearly identified as Métis literature, I will begin by foregrounding the major texts by Maria Campbell, Howard Adams, and Beatrice Culleton (now Mosionier). I will also discuss the post-1990 work of Marilyn Dumont and Gregory Scofield, who are widely recognized as two of the major contemporary Métis poets. These writers all have strong (though not uniform) connections to the historic Red River Métis.

Maria Campbell is best known for her (1973) autobiography *Halfbreed*. The book contains her devastating revelations about "what it is like to be a Halfbreed woman in our country, about the joys and sorrows, the oppressing poverty, the frustrations and dreams" (*Halfbreed* 1973, 2). For Campbell, the personal is historical. Campbell, raised in a Saskatchewan Métis hamlet, tells of both warm and funny family and community events, but also of the long history of marginalization and tragic despair that she traces back to the Northwest Resistance at Batoche. Indeed, Campbell herself is a descendant of Gabriel Dumont. Like Harold Cardinal's *The Unjust Society* (1969), which revealed the inequities and hypocrisies that girded Canadian liberal-state philosophy with respect to Status and Treaty Indian (now First Nations) peoples in the country, *Halfbreed* shattered the benevolent White Canadian self-image, a critique of Canada that was to be repeated by most Métis and other Aboriginal writers that followed these early exposés of dispossession, neglect, extreme poverty, brutal racism, and sexism. Campbell barely survived to tell her story. With directness and uncompromising politics, *Halfbreed* relates her struggles with poverty, racism, domestic violence, drug addiction, and prostitution.

The publication of *Halfbreed* (1973) changed the course of Aboriginal writing, and ultimately non-Aboriginal literary criticism in Canada, for it not only inspired younger generations of Indigenous authors to re-inscribe the Canadian narrative, but also provoked White Canadian readership to see Aboriginal peoples in a new light. Campbell's book proved that the extreme conditions of the Métis had not happened by any fault of their own; in other words, this was not a choice or a sign of a defect on their part, but rather part of societal prejudice that had long historical roots. Because it is sometimes difficult to see these historical roots from the context of the present, Campbell begins her book with the history of Louis Riel and the Red River Resistance – to show that her people's problems did not begin with her generation, but with the refusal of the Canadian government to acknowledge the Métis people's claim to recognition and land. In this way, *Halfbreed* was a source of affirmation and political awakening, since it affirmed Métis experience while at the same time uttering a challenge to dominant interpretations of Canadian history.

Since then, Campbell has worked as a teacher and cultural activist. She has written television and radio plays and has published many other works, including children's stories, a play based on her life entitled "Jessica" (published in *The Book of Jessica* 1987), and the popular collection of Métis short stories, *Stories of the Road Allowance People* (1995). Reprinted in 2010 with fresh, bold illustrations by Sherry Farrell-Racette, *Stories of the Road Allowance People* is a rich collection of prose poems that give voice to the great storytelling traditions of the Michif Métis. Using humour, irony, and a combination of "village English" and Michif, Campbell in a new way tells stories of racism and colonization, but most of all, stories that are filled with colourful Métis personalities, ghosts, and legendary shape-shifters (both human and not), along with gentle chiding of mischief-making within the community.

On the heels of *Halfbreed*, Howard Adams's docu-biography, *Prison of Grass*, was published in 1975. Adams was an academic, an author, and a social activist who believed that the Aboriginal struggle was best understood as an international struggle "against world capitalism" (Lutz, Hamilton, and Heimbecker 2005, 228). Although *Prison of Grass* was labelled (or dismissed) as "protest writing" (Petrone 1990, 383–8), and certainly was not considered a literary work, it is an important autobiographical and historical text that rings with orality in style. It tells a similar story to *Halfbreed*. Adams, too, was raised in a caring Métis home scarred by abject poverty and racial segregation in rural Saskatchewan. Unapologetic and raw, *Prison of Grass* (1975) rips the hide off the grand Euro-Canadian myth of White "civilization" naturally overpowering Indian "savagery," and unmasks Canadian society's racist treatment of Native peoples. Interspersing documentation with his personal account, Adams reveals the heartbreaking legacy of colonial racism: the racial shame and disintegrating effects of internalizing the "White Ideal" (1975, 16).

The theme of racial shame is also central in Beatrice Culleton Mosionier's first novel, *In Search of April Raintree* (1983). While Mosionier has published several children's stories, including a moving allegory of the white bison, plus another novel (*In the Shadow of Evil* 2000), and, recently, a memoir (*Come Walk with Me* 2009), her revised *April Raintree*, often described as fictionalized autobiography, continues to receive both popular and scholarly readings. *In Search of April Raintree* (1983) is a graphically violent story of two Métis sisters, April and Cheryl, whose tragic lives are largely determined by the different colour of their skins. Separated through foster care but reunited as young adults, the sisters often argue (through letters) about their relation to their mixed-race identity. Cheryl identifies with "Indians"; April feels ashamed of being Native. After a series of traumatic and disturbing experiences, Cheryl commits suicide. Sadly, it is only after Cheryl's death that April comes to a greater understanding of her feelings and explains that, although "[s]hame doesn't dissolve overnight" (Mosionier 1983, 168), she will embrace her Métis heritage.

Interestingly, in *April Raintree*, both Cheryl and April blur "Métis" with "Indian" in their search. There are no Red River or any other Métis community cultural markers in the novel. To be sure, there are many references to the term *Métis*, and Cheryl does adopt a "Métis" identity (which she gets from her foster mother Mrs. MacAdams), but it is often cast in historical terms and often elided into "Indianness." For example, in one letter to April, Cheryl enthuses about her school speeches and papers on "the history of the Métis" (which she associates with buffalo hunts) and in the next paragraph remarks that she may need a pair of glasses but would not want to wear them because "It's unIndian" (Mosionier 1983, 77). Deeply impacted by school and societal stereotypes about "halfbreeds," it is onerous for Cheryl and April to embrace their Métis heritage. Cheryl, in reference to Louis Riel, exclaims, "He's a Métis like us.... It means we're part Indian and part white. I wish we were whole Indians" (Mosionier 1983, 44–5). Coming to accept the distinctive nature of Métis culture and heritage, what I describe as a form of "returning home" later in this chapter, is a consistent theme in Métis (or Métis) writing of the twentieth century.

This arduous process of self-acceptance and "returning home" is clearly evident in the writing of poets Gregory Scofield and Marilyn Dumont, two of the most well-known post-1990 wave of Métis writers. Like their literary elders, Scofield and Dumont foreground themes of racial shame and defiance. In his first published collection of poetry, *The Gathering: Stories for the Medicine Wheel* (1993), Scofield writes "survival poetry," of keeping his "head down" and ducking "the put downs/Shoved it all down" (44). In his autobiography *Thunder Through My Veins* (1999), Scofield tells of his multilayered identity struggles, fuelled by racism and poverty and, in large measure, homophobia and homelessness. Like Culleton, Scofield was not raised in a stable,

Métis-affirming home, which initially led him to turn to "Indian" instead of Métis cultural markers in an effort to clarify his identity. When he first learned that his family was "halfbreed," he "was disappointed that [they] weren't pure Indians" (Scofield 1999, 107), and for some time he refused to accept this and assumed his great-great-grandmother's (Kohkum Otter's) Cree identity. He begins his process of "returning home" when he first visits a Métis cultural centre in Batoche and learns about Métis history and culture. He weeps "openly" when he first meets "the heroes" he "was ashamed of in school" at a Batoche museum and watches a re-enactment of the 1885 "Northwest Rebellion" (1993, 48). He adopts Batoche as his homeland: "The importance that I had once placed on being Cree – a true and pure Indian – seemed to disappear with the sinking sun…. Never again would I search for a place of belonging. This place, Batoche, would always be 'home.' My home" (1999, 166–7). By adopting Batoche as his homeland, by honouring his mother and adopted aunt in *I Knew Two Métis Women* (1999a), and by relearning Cree, Scofield reconstructs and regains his Métis family and community origins. In *Singing Home the Bones* (2005), Scofield collects and embraces the many pieces that finally make up his identity. Through "conversations" with the dead and the living, he reconnects with his Cree-Métis ancestors and simultaneously discovers that his father was Jewish; by linking all these bones with his own, he celebrates his Métis heritage. This collection of poetry, like many of his other poems, is not merely ethnographic or historic; rather, *Singing Home the Bones* (2005) reveals the full splendour of his own humanness. Like life, bones are brittle, even if connective. Known for his performative presentations that blend haunting Cree chants with contemporary lyrical readings, Scofield metaphorically brings home the diasporic Métis bones, including his own, and, most recently, Riel's in *Louis: The Heretic Poems* (Scofield 2011).

Like Scofield, Marilyn Dumont deals with Métis dispossession, racism, and "half-breed" identity in her three books of poetry: *A Really Good Brown Girl* (1996), *green girl dreams Mountains* (2001), and *that tongued belonging* (2007). In her first book she confronts Canadian icons such as John A. Macdonald, as well as "squaw" stereotypes and other gross misrepresentations of Aboriginal peoples. Her poems mix genres and languages and are marked by political edginess, yet never lose sight of human needs and emotions about love, loss, family, friends, and the beauty of the land. In *A Really Good Brown Girl* (1996), Dumont recounts a childhood humiliation that is on one level about racialization. On another level, it offers us an opportunity to review

242 The Emma LaRocque Reader

what standards are employed when assessing Métis identity and literature. Dumont (1996) recalls:

> My skin always gave me away.... a little white girl stared at the colour of my arms and exclaimed, "Are you ever brown!". I wanted to pull my short sleeves down ... but she persisted, "Are you Indian?" ...
>
> How could I respond? If I said yes, she'd reject me: worse, she might tell the other kids my secret and then they'd laugh and shun me. If I said no, I'd be lying ...
>
> I said "No," and walked away. (14–15)

In one sense, Dumont was not lying; she is not "Indian," she is Métis, or "halfbreed," as she sometimes puts it. Of course, as a child she could not explain this. She could only respond to the power of the White colonial gaze, which in numerous ways distorted her identity.[10] That she is not Indian is brought home to her later in life when in a con-versation with "this treaty guy," she finds herself saying, "I'm Métis like it's an apology and he says, 'mmh,' like he forgives me ... he's got 'this look,' that says he's leather and I'm naughahyde" (1996, 58).

The issue of identity varies considerably among other post-1990 Métis writers such as Joanne Arnott, Sharron Proulx-Turner, Rita Bouvier, and Warren Cariou. Joanne Arnott, who identifies as Métis/mixed blood, is the author of seven books, including poetry, nonfiction, and children's literature. *Wiles of Girlhood* (Arnott 1991), a collection of poetry, is her first publication. Her material deals with social issues such as abuse, poverty, women, and mixed-race identity. Sharron Proulx-Turner, who comes from a mélange of Native and European ancestry from the Ottawa Valley but is now a member of the Métis Nation of Alberta, has published a memoir (under a pseudonym) and three other books. The theme of rebirthing and revisioning, which draws from and points to a new order of Indigenous, woman-centred spirituality and hybridity, runs through her mixed-genre writing. In her episodic storytelling poem *what the auntys say* (Proulx-Turner 2002), she sees stories as giving "one long birth of one old Métisse lady," and explains "Métisse means Métis woman-girl/two half-bloods not half and half like cream" (13). Rita Bouvier is a Saskatchewan Métis teacher, community worker, and author of three books of poetry, *Blueberry Clouds* (1999), *Papiyahtak*

---

10 Almost all Métis writers across eras and genres deal with the destructive power of White looking. For yet another example, see Cariou (2000) "The Racialized Subject in James Tyman's *Inside Out*." It is not clear that Tyman is Métis – he was labelled as "metis Indian" by social workers.

Contemporary Métis Literature

(2004), and *Better That Way* (2008). Expressive and politically conscious, Bouvier's poetry clearly reflects her Métis cultural grounding in her use of Michif Cree and her moving memories of her grandfather, who gently showed her the ways of the land.

Warren Cariou, well known to mainstream Canadian literary culture, represents yet another facet to the complexities of identification. Cariou is a scholar, novelist (*The Exalted Company of Roadside Martyrs* 1999), filmmaker, and an emerging poet. Born in northern Saskatchewan to a German mother and a father whose Métis ancestry was a "family secret," indicating "the historical stigma attached" to Native ancestry, Cariou grew up as "a white kid" who identified himself as "French, German and Norwegian" (2002, 76). It was not until he was in his twenties that he slowly learned about his Red River Métis roots. In his wonderfully written autobiography, *Lake of the Prairies* (2002), Cariou takes a tentative position regarding his identity: "I feel closely connected ... particularly to the Métis, but it doesn't seem quite right to claim that I am one" (2002, 224). However, he now identifies as "of mixed Métis and European Heritage" (*Manitowapow*) and is active in the Native academic and writing community.

Many of these first-and second-wave Métis writers have received or have been short-listed for an array of literary awards. This is not only an indication of the quality of their work, but also of the fact that the wider Canadian literary community has paid increasing attention to Aboriginal writers. Indeed, critical reception of First Nations and Métis writing has changed dramatically, particularly since the 1990s. While much Indigenous writing from the 1970s to the late 80s was met with initial incomprehension, defensiveness, and labelling – confirming what the writers were articulating, namely, that there was a huge divide between Native and White peoples – subsequent reception has become more open and judicious.

The early years of the 1990s stand out as a dramatic turning point in Aboriginal writing and in criticism, as indicated by the appearance of a number of anthologies at that time, including *All My Relations* (King 1990), *Writing the Circle* (Perreault and Vance 1990), *Native Writers and Canadian Literature* (New 1990), and *An Anthology of Canadian Native Literature in English* (Moses and Goldie 1992). However, none of the "Native literature" anthologies published between the late 1980s and the 2000s has a "Métis literature" category, though all of them include or analyze authors of Métis or "mixed" ancestry. Although both mainstream Canadian literary critics (Fee 1990; Godard 1990; Grant 1990; Hoy 2001) and Indigenous critics (Acoose 1995; Akiwenzie-Damm 1993; Fagan et al. 2009; Ruffo 2003) have, since the 1980s, given overwhelming attention to Campbell's (1973) *Halfbreed* and Mosionier's (1983) *April Raintree*, the time is overdue for a more focussed study of Métis literature.

244   The Emma LaRocque Reader

Métis Aesthetics

The only substantial book-length study of Métis writing is Armando Jannetta's *Ethnopoetics of the Minority Voice: An Introduction to the Politics of Dialogism and Difference in Métis Literature* (2001). Employing concepts of dialogism, hybridity, and border-crossing, Jannetta links three Métis men's nineteenth-century (largely 1840s–1930s) landscapes of vanishing open spaces and "nomadic" lifestyles to Campbell's and Mosionier's autobiographical narratives, arguing that "the experience of open spaces and the subversive historical tradition of 'border-jumping' reemerge and have been recovered by male and female Métis writers in order to decolonize literary discourse and to counter colonial mentality" (161). Jannetta profiles what might be taken as a Métis aesthetics in his rather large leaps of linking these five different, if not disparate, auto/biographies:

> all the texts of the Métis writers discussed share a perception of a holistic universe in which humour and tragic vision are balanced, as well as a dialogic orientation and nomadic quality. The peripatetic element of contemporary Métis literature is characterised by a constant process of becoming, rootlessness, displacement and restlessness, a reality of multiple belonging, of being caught between cultures and loyalties, wandering a mindscape and landscape that is neither white nor Indian. Finally, however, it reclaims a vision beyond the lost savage, reasserting a Native consciousness and legitimising Native epistemologies in a third space located in communal relations outside the white-Indian dichotomy. (162)

This portrayal of a supposed Métis genre is actually quite a classic stereotype of the wandering halfbreed caught between White and Indian worlds. Although Jannetta advances the notion of a "third space," he never demonstrates what exactly that might be. In fact, the only option he presents for the Métis writers is that they jump back into the borders of Native (rather than Métis) consciousness and epistemology, which, in effect, is not outside the White-Indian dichotomy. Further, I am troubled by his unfortunate wording about "the lost savage," which recalls the *civ/sav* lens of the colonizer's gaze (see chapter "The Metis in English Canadian Literature").

Jannetta (2001) does insist that "Métis life histories ... in a space of contestation, participate in the creation of 'new genres'" (160), and he extrapolates from my argument in my 1990 essay (see chapter "Preface: Here Are Our Voices – Who Will Hear?"), but he somewhat misreads my point, which was not about border-jumping but rather that Native

Contemporary Métis Literature

(in the inclusive sense of the times) contestation had developed new genres which, among other things, combined "footnotes" with "facts of biography" (see chapter "Preface: Here Are Our Voices – Who Will Hear?"). Indigenous writers and literary critics Kateri Akiwenzie-Damm and Armand Ruffo have also noted this pattern in Métis writing. In her essay on Maria Campbell and Beatrice Culleton, Akiwenzie-Damm (then named Damm) describes their style as "dispelling and telling" (1993, 93); Ruffo notes that there is a Métis literary tradition in "the documentary/autobiographical mode of writing [which] continues a tradition of speaking out to address the colonizer ... which can be traced back to the likes of Louis Riel" (2003, 86). In fact, quite contrary to Jannetta's thesis, most contemporary Métis writers and scholars seek to deconstruct the West's stereotype of the itinerant hybrid and to re-inscribe or, more properly, re-root the Métis with home(land), community, culture, and agency. As Nehiyaw (Cree)-Métis literary scholar Janice Acoose states, "Campbell's text challenges existing stereotypes and images ... by providing vivid spiritual, social, political and economic context to her Halfbreed ... way of life" (1995, 90). Métis aesthetics, then, is a re-humanization art – a discourse that counters dehumanizing romanticizations of the tragic lost "Hybrid" and at the same time offers "cultural signifiers such as language, song, dance, and social protocol" (Ruffo 2003, 80), which should guide how we understand the cultural category of "Métis" (see chapter "Reflections on Cultural Continuity through Aboriginal Women's Writings"). Métis do in fact cross or integrate many borders, but this does not mean that they are rootless or can only bounce from White to "Indian" – they are more than the sum of the two.

But knowing how to read Métis culture remains a difficult issue for many critics. Part of the problem is that the struggles that Métis writers have shared have been taken to mean that the Métis lack a coherent core culture, despite the fact that most of these writers also offer much cultural information. The other problem is that most critics cannot make any distinction between First Nations cultures and the Métis. There are some significant distinctions, but these are issues that require much greater treatment than I can give them here. Suffice it to say, colonial imaginings and the "White-Indian dichotomy" continue to plague the study of Métis peoples and literatures. Some critics reach for a concept of "whole Indians" as the standard by which they measure Métis aesthetics. Julie A. Davies (1996), an American teacher, characterizes *April Raintree* as "neither entirely Native nor entirely white ... a work that is also not firmly grounded.... There are no recurring Native themes such as connection to the land, spirituality, communal cooperative living,

246   The Emma LaRocque Reader

or the wisdom of elders". This list is problematic for the Métis (and other Aboriginal people, for that matter) for a number of reasons. First, it is quite simply too categorical. But what is at issue for the Métis is that even if this list typified "Nativeness" (which in its generalized, typologized, and ruralized way it does not), it is not Métis. While Métis have profound Indigenous roots to their identity, such a list does not encompass Métis culture(s). But how do we read Métis writing in light of Métis standards of culture and aesthetics, rather than Indian or White standards?

The critical literature seems not to know what to do at this juncture – what are the standards, what are the cultural markers from which one could appraise Métis identity and aesthetics discourse? As a rule, and with the exception of Jannetta, non-Native critics shy away from asking this question and, perhaps understandably, side-step the issue with acknowledgements that it is "extremely difficult" (Andrews 2013, 11) or "highly charged" (Lutz 2009, 190). And while Native critics in Canada have long been calling for criticism that respects cultural diversity and specificity,[11] there is little attempt to outline what this may actually mean when it comes to a Métis aesthetics discourse. It seems straightforward enough to outline Métis difference from Whites, and indeed most theorists (and even some writers) use "White" instead of "Indian" standards to measure "difference" in the Métis. But what about the differences between Métis and First Nations cultures? Here there is a noticeable tendency to subsume Métis under pan-Aboriginal cultural criteria. At the same time, as I noted earlier, there is some insistence on blurring the racial category "Métis" with the ethno-political Métis Nation.[12] If Métis Nation culture is distinct, coherent, and present, which it is, then the literary community must properly identify and respect this ethno-cultural coherence. It is here that the universalized use of "Métis" is a problem. And it is here that "hybridity" as the fulcrum from which the generalized Métis are theorized serves to obscure rather than clarify Métis identity (and literature). Perhaps the clarion call for "Indigeneity" (and "indigenization") serves to drown out Métis distinctiveness,

---

11 Most Aboriginal writers and critics have long been citing their specific cultural locations. This practice is now being reworked in terms of "Indigenous literary nationalism" advanced by some Native American literary theorists. For Canadian considerations, see Fagan et al. (2009). See also Weaver, Womack, and Warrior (2006).

12 Note, for example, the way the media and critics have conferred a "Metis" identity on Joseph Boyden, even though Boyden does not come from any Metis community. See www.quillandquire.com/authors/profile.cfm?article-i.d.=6573. Accessed 5 May 2013.

although this is complicated by the fact that Métis Nation peoples are also Indigenous, and many First Nations peoples are of mixed ancestry or are closely related to the Métis. The simultaneous appeals to Indigeneity and hybridity seem to be a difficult combination or concept to grasp for some critics (and politicians), but for the Métis Nation peoples there is no necessary conflict. The myriad and convoluted theories and contentious debates surrounding hybridity are beyond the scope of this chapter[13]; however, there is no discussion of the Métis/Métis without some consideration of hybridity. The worst use of "hybridity" is to be found in colonial writings and popular culture, which have characterized "halfbreeds" as suffering from unresolvable conflict innate to their presumed polarized "civilized/savage" natures (see chapter "The Metis in English Canadian Literature"). The old academic version of this is the frontier view of the Métis caught between "the chase" and "civilization" (87). The new version may be the "neither Native nor White" formulation still evident in some creative and theoretical works.

A more nuanced reading of hybridity emphasizes "both and more" (Lutz 2009, 197), a plurality or blending rather than a straddling of cultures, a syncretic thing. This liminal or "third space" is outside the White-Indian polarization and offers room for 5goes beyond mere "dialogics" or "border-jumping," and does not impose the "colonizer's model of the world" (Blaut 1993, 10), which assumes that everything belongs to Europeans and that hybridity is a one-way street. Obviously, weaving the master narrative into hybridity theories premised on the belief that the (post)colonial world begins and ends with Europe is the problem, not hybridity or halfbreedness itself.

Further, while there is some basis for thinking of the Métis as located in hybrid space, and while this has been difficult for a certain generation of Métis writers, such portrayals should not be generalized because they serve to distort and obscure specific unfragmented cultures (or homes), particularly for the Métis Nation, who are arguably no longer a "hybrid race" (see Lundgren 1995, 63) but a "new people,"[14] and not necessarily suffering from an "in-between" location; or if they do,

---

13 Niigonwedom James Sinclair (2010) in "Tending to Ourselves" reviews some of the arguments between Native American literary theorists and some postcolonial renderings of "hybridity." See also Daniel Heath Justice's (2010) essay in this same collection.

14 For those of us who come from many generations of Metis ancestry – not uncommon in numerous Metis communities in western Canada – how long are we to be "a hybrid race"? See chapter "Native Identity and the Metis: Otehpayimsuak Peoples", especially note 5.

248   The Emma LaRocque Reader

their suffering is caused by external social and political disruptions, prejudices, and misperceptions, rather than their Métis identity. Care should be taken that a Métis aesthetics is not developed solely from "the icon of the confused and alienated Halfbreed," as Jo-Ann Episkenew puts it (2002, 57). There is a powerful "returning home" motif that runs throughout Métis writing, obviously suggesting that there is an unbroken and cohesive home to return to. As complex as the discussion of Métis identity is, Métis Nation peoples have a very strong sense of identity as a distinct culture. While this culture is not congealed, neither is it culturally unmarked.

When we employ a reading strategy that does not privilege theory over people, what is striking is the extreme racism (and sexism) and marginalization that Métis writers across the eras have experienced and confronted – not only because they were/are Native but specifically because they were/are "halfbreed." This racism is what has con-founded their lives and their identities. The racism, hostility, and antipathy expressed and exercised against peoples of mixed ancestry reaches very far back into human history and is certainly conjoined to colonialism (Young 1995; Stoler 2002). My discussion of the Métis Nation as constituting "new peoples" is an ethnographic and historical fact, but the thorny politics of identity – especially challenging for Métis Nation peoples, as their particular identity faces erasure by conflation of terms – necessitates delineations and name changes. Needless to say, those peoples with "mixed ancestry" but not of Métis Nation backgrounds also have their own cultures; what is needed are new designations to clarify the differences. Terms and notions such as "whole" or "pure" cultures (and their reverse, "contaminated"), "mixed" or "full blood," and certain derogatory usages of "halfbreed" – all terms that come from eras of unscientific folk biology and racist ethnography – are problematic.

Most Metis/Métis align themselves with the iconic Red River and with Indigeneity, whether they come to this identity after a process of genealogical self-discovery or whether they grew up Métis with clear Métis heritage and culture. Earlier I noted that Marilyn Dumont and I hyphenate our identities. I believe Dumont does this to accentuate her alliance with the Cree language as she fills "that tongued belonging" (the title of Dumont's 2007 collection of poetry) with a Cree-sense. I do it to show a simultaneity, not a straddling, of heritages. Most important, I identify as Cree/Métis because my "soul language" is Plains Cree/ Michif, and because I was raised in a family and community whose lives and cultures were of the land (see chapter "For the Love of Place – Not Just Any Place: Selected Métis Writing"), who approached the world –

Contemporary Métis Literature

and still do – with a *Nehiyawew Apeetowgusanak* ("Cree-speaking half-sons") epistemology, which is at once multi-holistic and dynamic. As I have argued in my book *When the Other Is Me* (LaRocque 2010), I resist being read as an ethnographic "other" hybrid.

Indigeneity and halfbreedness run deep in Aboriginal literary expression. Memorializing *nohkomak* (the grandmothers) in her haunting honour song *Blue Marrow* (1998), the brilliant Cree poet Louise Halfe gives vision to the Native women in the fur trade who "Ribboned the Sky" (1998, 89).[15] The ribbons are the halfbreed children who carried their *Nehiyawewin* (Cree), their *atowkehwin* (mythologies/worldviews), and their *aski pimatsewin* (life from the land) to become the Métis Nation. And like their Indigenous and European forebears, the Métis Nation is resilient and enjoys a very rich "storied" and literary inheritance. In my case, not only did I grow up with Cree Michif orality, but also with a mother who corresponded with her sisters in Cree Michif syllabics right into the 1970s. And while my own English literacy did not officially begin until the age of nine when I started (public) school,[16] I was "pre-schooled" through comic books (now elevated to "graphic novels") since infancy. And most of all, my mother, like my grandmother, could mesmerize us with her vast cultured storehouse of lexical magic in her animated telling of *atowkehwin* (myths and legends) or *achimoowin* (non-fiction). It is through my Métis heritage and culture, reaching back many generations, that I learned to appreciate literature, in all its presentations: oral, visual, performative, musical, syllabic, and alphabetic.[17]

While I have noted the "resistance" voice and aesthetics of the writers foregrounded here, it is important not only to place this in the national context from which it grew, but equally, to appreciate the poetics of this literature. Métis writers have inventively gathered roots, relations,

---

15 Ribbons are important symbolic art pieces in Métis culture. Louise Halfe's grandparents were halfbreed, probably from among some Métis who had "taken treaty" in the heyday of de-territorialization.

16 As a rule, Métis in Alberta did not go to residential schools, but public schools were not available until the mid-1950s. English was not spoken in many communities until well into the 1970s; my parents managed with "store" English. On Métis and residential schools, see Chartrand, Logan, and Daniels (2006).

17 For a good overview of Métis culture and heritage in land use, language, music, clothing, traditional and contemporary art, as well as historiographic essays on contemporary Métis writing and scholarship, see the voluminous collection edited by Barkwell, Dorion, and Prefontaine (2001). For Métis recipes, see *Metis Cook Book and Guide to Healthy Living* (Ottawa: Métis Centre/National Aboriginal Health Organization, 2008).

stones, bones, beads, and songs as their work has developed in range, depth, and style. Many reviewers have noted the innovative qualities of this art; indeed, most of these writers have themselves expressed a desire to be read as poets, as creative writers, not merely as ethnographic exhibits or political signs. Much remains to be explored about Métis writing and criticism. The future will bring a new generation who will continue to push the edges of identity and genre. My chapter has not addressed the many other forms of Métis literature: drama, short stories, diaries, journals, songs, commentaries, children's literature, war memoirs, Riel's religious and resistance diaries, petitions, the bardic Pierre Falcon's songs, to say nothing of the wealth of archival material. And this list does not include what may be available in French, in Michif, or in syllabics.

Literature is perhaps finally about words. Love of words. Attention to imagination and creativity might be the task for the next generation of both writers and critics. Of course, this does not mean we can ignore our cultural groundings or political locations, but the very nature of literature demands innovation and exploration into what makes us human. Any study of Métis literature must include not only the meaning of nationalism, resistance, or agency in Métis history and ethnocultural development, but also an interest in Indigenous-based but decidedly Métis poetics. We write for many reasons, but ultimately we write because, like Marilyn Dumont (2010), we are "fascinated with language" or languages, as befits Métis inheritance.

2016

Colonialism Lived

I don't remember when I first heard the words "colonization" or "racism," or when exactly I first began to make a conceptual connection between those words and my experience. But I sure remember my first experience of them. I was eight or nine years old, perhaps younger. I was in a café in a small town in northeastern Alberta, a town we frequented as a family as it was a major meeting place for commercial and community exchanges for Métis and other Native people. I was sitting on one of those 1950s revolving red vinyl stools with metallic edges, sipping pink cream soda and looking at a comic book, waiting for my parents. I heard an odd noise, and saw a quarter rolling right past my little nose. Then I heard awful words drip from some awful place: "Hey, little squaw, wanna go for a ride?"

I looked up and saw this fat, red-faced white man, sneering at me. I quickly mumbled no and put my nose back in my comic book. Mercifully, he left – perhaps because it was broad daylight in a café full of people. But no one had paid attention. I think back now and shudder with horror at what could have happened to me. At the time I didn't know the word "squaw" and I had no idea what the fat man meant. I just knew instinctively he was disgusting and dangerous.

It was not to be my only encounter with racism (and sexism, but that is another essay). Sadly, it has been a lifelong challenge. I'll begin with just some of my elementary school experiences. The first school I went to at the age of nine was a typical one-room schoolhouse complete with a pot-belly stove and large chalk blackboards. This school housed one (white) teacher and about twenty mostly Métis children, ranging from Grades 1 to 8. My parents were not keen on me going to school but I had staged a sit-down strike at home and howled until my parents relented. I had fallen in love with the idea of school because my older brother had taught me how to read those little Red, Blue and

252   The Emma LaRocque Reader

Yellow books. And my mother had instilled a love of learning from her vast storehouse of Cree/Métis knowledge. So I walked into that one-room schoolhouse with confidence and anticipation. In just a few years I was to dread going to any school. Like most children in the country, I learned about Dick, Jane, and Sally, with Puff and Spot, and Shakespeare and settlers, but nothing good about Big Bear, or Riel, and nothing at all about George Copway or Pauline Johnson, two of the first accomplished Aboriginal writers in Canada, or anything about Peheh-soo or Wesahkehcha (mythical Cree characters). Instead, I read stories about "great explorers" and "heroic settlers" in combat against horrid and inhumane "savages." This cowboy/Indian message was conveyed everywhere – in schools, in stores, in movie houses, and in the comic books most of us grew up reading. We would have seen them on television too if our homes had had electricity.

Indeed, I don't remember learning about Cree people, much less about the Métis. Nor were we allowed to speak Cree/Michif even though most of the school population was Plains Cree Métis. We were strapped if we spoke Cree/Michif or were two minutes late to school – even though we had to walk three kilometres to get to school. Old fan belts from vehicles were used for the strappings. We could also be slapped at whim. I saw many children slapped or strapped or roughed up. I myself was strapped for being two minutes late. The same teacher also slapped me once – in front of my mother no less! What was my crime? It was clinic day when all the children were getting vaccinated and for some reason parents were also invited. We were all to stay outside until our names were called. Being my first year at school, I must have misunderstood because I opened the door, thinking my mom had stayed inside. Just as I opened the door, the teacher, who was right there, backhanded me across the face. I was stung – more so because my mom witnessed him hitting me. Clearly hurt and furious, she swore at the teacher in Cree but he had already shut the door on us. Beyond that she was powerless to do anything. Neither she nor my father could read, write, or speak English. We knew nothing about school boards or complaints processes; that world was entirely foreign and inaccessible to my parents and community. There were no police who would have ever listened.

This was us in the early 1960s, on our lands, where we owned no property and had no access to any established centre of power. I had to endure that teacher for several years, and even though he passed me speedily from grade to grade, and made much of my ability to read and spell (often making fun of my older brother as he placed stars after my name, setting me up for bullying in the playground), I never felt safe or happy around him. I was relieved when we were finally bused to another school.

That was a larger and more modern school. There were more white children but the Métis were still the majority. I was in Grade 4. What I remember most about this school was that we had to exchange Christmas gifts. Names were chosen at random and I remember having to buy a gift for a white boy I knew nothing about, which made me nervous. Then came the dreaded day of the exchange, and when the boy opened his gift from me, it became apparent that whatever I had gotten was incomplete. Actually, I think my father had bought the toy – he did not read and would not have known batteries were not included. He would have bought according to the picture on the box. I also did not understand or see the fine print of instructions. The boy did not make a fuss; it was the teacher who had a tantrum and publicly shamed me. What was so strange about this teacher's behaviour was that she should have known better. She and her family lived just a few miles from my aunt and uncle's place and my uncle did odd jobs for them, like clearing the land that they had mysteriously come to own, land that morally belonged to Native people. It was not as if she was unaware of our socio-economic conditions. Surely she must have known that many Métis parents, though they worked hard on traplines or at waged jobs, could hardly afford toys for their own children, much less Christmas gifts for school! Besides, in those years the Métis celebrated New Year's, not Christmas. Why she made us exchange gifts in a school full of low-income children remains a puzzle to me! What did she think she was teaching us – white Christian generosity?

The following year we were once more moved to a different school, right in the middle of winter term – and again, without any consultation whatsoever with our parents. This time we (me, my younger brother, and a handful of cousins) were bused to a much larger town school whose population was mostly white. It was the same town where that fat man had tossed a quarter at me. Overnight we became a crouching minority. The all-white teachers knew nothing about us or even that we were coming. They were very strict and often disdainful towards Native children, and I remember three teachers who were especially unkind and easily violent towards us. Our Grade 6 teacher in particular seemed to have a great dislike of non-white children. One day he called the names of all the non-white children and had a private chat in the hallway with them. Most of us were Native (Métis, Status Indian, and non-Status, and most of us with Cree and/or Métis cultural backgrounds) but several were Lebanese or Chinese. One by one he went asking each of us how many times a week we bathed! On another occasion he punished a boy from a nearby Cree reserve with one of those classic three-foot rulers. He made the boy bend over a desk and he hit him with this ruler over and over as hard as he could. To this day I can still hear the echo of that ruler as it smacked the boy's buttocks. The rest of us sat frozen and terrified. I have no idea what that boy had done – I just know it broke his spirit that day. And maybe some of our spirits as well.

This school also had Catechism for kids of Roman Catholic faith. It was assumed all Native children were Roman Catholic so we were all forced to attend. I don't remember if the classes were for thirty or sixty minutes, but I do remember every minute was hell. We were made to memorize Latin prayers and to sit perfectly still. The teacher was known for her meanness and her demand of absolute obedience. If we so much as moved our faces one degree from the front, we could expect a hard slap in the face. I learned this on my first or second day of class when I turned to see if my younger brother was there. As I turned my head back, my twelve-year-old face collided with a plump but solid backhand.

Everything about this school felt like a very bad dream. Playgrounds were no easier than classrooms as the white children also taunted me. I was often hurt and humiliated but never told my parents. In fact, until now I have hardly told anyone, and I have rarely written about these particular experiences. In an unexpected way, I was saved from that horrid school by having to be hospitalized in Edmonton. And shortly after my return from the hospital, I was able to leave this school and attend a new one in a new place where I had the great fortune of having my first kind white (Mennonite) teacher. Under his caring guidance through Grades 7 to 9, I regained my love for learning. I also regained my confidence and was able to keep going, making it to high school, then to university.

These were not the residential schools that Canadians are just starting to learn about. These were public schools. In my area Métis children went only to public schools. My parents' generation of Métis never went to residential schools. As a rule most had no schooling at all. Ironically, the fact that Métis had no opportunity until the 1950s to go to any school was probably what saved my generation as far as retaining our cultures and languages. However, it did not save us or protect us from teachers who physically abused us and shamed us for who we were. It did not save us from feeling frightened or inferior. I am not aware of any sexual abuse in these public schools, and we were able to go home at the end of the day, but in every other way, they were just as bad as residential schools.

Colonialism Lived

Recently someone suggested I should write my memoir (a sure indication of aging), and I thought if I told all the stories of all the times I or members of my family, or members of my community, have faced racism (or sexism, or classism, or every other ism), no one would believe me. Especially white Canadian people. The reality is that I can no longer count all the times I have either experienced or observed racism against Aboriginal peoples. Yet at the same time I remember almost every dehumanizing instance of racism directed at me or at my family. Racism is not abstract; it is an experience. Each encounter, each stare seething with stereotypic assumptions, each distrust, each discrimination, each punitive measure taken, each ignorant and insulting tweet posted – they sit like lava in the core of one's being. Experiencing racism to this magnitude is like being branded with a searing iron. It is impossible to forget. And essential to put in perspective.

So how does one survive such an environment of hate (for it is racial hate), disdain, and hostility? A cursory look at statistics on Aboriginal peoples tells us many do not survive such environments. Suicides and homicides, as well as other forms of unnatural death, are extremely high compared to national rates. And for those who survive, such experiences can lead to a variety of difficult directions. At some point in my young life I chose to survive, and for me, survival has meant a lifelong vocation of researching and educating on Native/white relations and their social and political ramifications.

Somewhere in high school I began to fight back intellectually whenever I heard racist remarks, whether made by friends, teachers, taxi drivers, storekeepers, police, priests and Protestant preachers, nuns, nurses, or train conductors (my dad worked on the railroad so our family was often in trains). But it was during my first two years in university that I began to make a connection between racism and historical events in North America. In sociology classes I learned about racism, although it was mostly about slavery and racism in the United States. In my education foundation classes I had an extraordinary professor who encouraged me to read parts of an essay I had written about my community's alienation from school. Well, what a firestorm my class presentation generated. It so happened the father of one of my classmates was the superintendent of the school I was writing about. The classmate jumped up and in a quivering angry voice defended his dad (whom I did not know), the school, the teachers, the town, and basically called me a liar. This was not to be the only time I would encounter such defensive reactions, and it would certainly not be the only time my integrity would be insulted. However, my classmate's reaction only confirmed the chasm of experience between my (Native) world and his (white) world.

This was probably the beginning of my life's work trying to educate Canadians about the ugly nature of racism. Around the same time I read Harold Cardinal's book *The Unjust Society* (1969), a book I could relate to on so many levels. Even though I did not come from a Status or Treaty Indian (now First Nation) or reserve or residential school background, I could of course relate to the racism and colonialism that Cardinal detailed. The attempts to assimilate Status people were very similar to the attempts to deny Métis identity. And in complete contradiction to so-called assimilation policies, the Canadian governments and society were just as determined to segregate the Métis as they were to keep Status people in geographical and social isolation – to keep us in our places. The prejudices, the discrimination, the hostilities, and the diseases that confronted Status peoples were exactly what we were confronted with. And even though we were not legally – and in some respects culturally "Indians," my generation (and later some of my nieces and nephews) were subjected to much cruelty as well as denigration of our Métis cultures and histories. Every attempt was made to whip us into white English Canadians, yet we were kept marginalized.

If Truth and Reconciliation commissions mea[n] anything to white Canadians, there should be commissions on public schools about their falsification of history and ignorance and disdain of Aboriginal cultures, as well as their mistreatment of Native children. Public schools are just as guilty and should be just as liable as residential schools for their abuse of these children and attempted destruction of Indigenous cultures. And there should be commissions on Métis people whose cultures, achievements, massive losses of lands and resources, and suffering have been too long ignored.

It is easy for the majority of Canadians to dismiss Aboriginal accounts of racism. After all, it is part of the profound denial that racism even exists in a "nice" country like Canada. And while some white people have been open to learning the true history of Canada, many continue to believe in white superiority and blame Native peoples for their problems. And even when mainstream media feature racism, they often do so superficially. It was discouraging to read the article on Winnipeg's racism in the February 2015 issue of Maclean's magazine, for example. First, it appears that racism is getting worse. Equally troubling, though, it appears as if journalists have not quite gotten the hand-in-glove connection between colonization, white privilege, and racism. It is easy to report on specific incidences of racism, and, of course, these should always be reported. However, it is just as, if not more, crucial to understand how racism is so deeply embedded in Canadian institutions, laws, and practises. How racism is shored up with mythologies of civilization, hard work, fairness and innocence. But the history of Canada is largely the history of the colonization of Native peoples. It is a history of dispossession, rationalization, and control. This means, among other things, that racism against Aboriginal peoples has been so normalized that many non-Native peoples feel entitled to spew hateful slurs, or even to engage in physical (or sexual) assaults against Aboriginal men, women, or children. Racism is so normalized that those who expose it or challenge it are often dismissed, labelled, or psychologized. All these are classic colonizer techniques designed to deny, discredit, and censor.

Many non-Native people also believe that only "rednecks" are overtly racist. But they do not seem to realize the reason these rednecks can spew racial hate is because they live in a colonialist society that has benefited from racism and tolerates this kind of behaviour. In a sense, there is no such thing as individual racism; individuals become racist because they grow up in a racist society. But obviously some hide it better than others, and some are just more plain cruel than others.

If reconciliation is to mean anything, Canadians need to look at the ways that Canada has nurtured racism against Native peoples. This means looking at all the major institutions that make this country run. For example, how does a judge in Winnipeg get away with refusing to look at racism as a major factor in the death of Brian Sinclair, a Native man, in one of Winnipeg's most central hospital ERs? This is a perfect example of systemic racism where at least four or five very powerful systems (Winnipeg Regional Health, the hospital, the unions, lawyers and courts) protected seventeen medical and security staff members from facing legal or medical charges. As far as I know, in the end no one was held accountable for Mr. Sinclair's death because everyone was protected within what one hospital lawyer called "a perfect storm" of events. I have studied this case and I have no hesitation in saying that racism killed Mr. Sinclair. As it has countless numbers of other Native peoples, whether these deaths were caused by sexual predators, police shootings, homicides, suicides, or diseases that come with poverty and inadequate accessibility to first-rate education or medical attention. Racism is lethal and no country with any conscience should ever tolerate it, much less live off its spoils.

I believe Canadians want to be kind. I personally have many beautiful and socially aware friends who are white Canadian and I know they are caring. But kindness, however important, is not enough. And telling stories, though important, is not enough, because when it comes to Aboriginal peoples, many Canadians are more likely to judge than to help. They need to understand why this is so, because this is in stark contrast to how most Canadians respond to international crises. Clearly, some fundamental change in thinking and knowledge about Native/white relations is required. Notions of Europeans bearing fruits of civilization to savages need to be dismantled from our textbooks, popular culture, boardrooms, and courts, and there needs to be an acknowledgement that Indigenous cultures were coherent, cohesive, and purposeful. There needs to be an understanding of how First Nation and Métis and Inuit peoples have lost and continue to lose their lands and resources, and the devastating impact this has had on them. There needs to be an understanding of how racism is instrumental to colonialism. And there needs to be an understanding of how Canadian society has benefited from all this.

There is no peace without justice. And there is no reconciliation without justice and restitution. And there is no justice without righting historical and current wrongs. Canada has a long way to go before we can say with assurance that our country is a just country.

2017

Powerlines

powerlines
in northerncanadasouthafrica
are not just
telephone poles
by railroad tracks
thick green glass
transformers
that call for target practice
with railroad rocks
when we were kids
walking home from school

powerlines
in northerncanadasouthafrica
are not just
hydro poles
along gravelled highways
now all paved
cutting through the great forests
felling poplars, pine, spruce and birch
making foxes run, owls screech
squirrels scold
bear and deer hide
bluejays, robins and chickadees
growing silent
even crows sit sullen

powerlines
in northerncanadasouthafrica

are not just
gas lines
burrowing under the earth
ground hogging
bulldozing blueberry meadows
flattening green slopes and hills
pushing off my Nokom's house
pushing her to the town ditch

powerlines
are not just shiny black cables
making lines across the sky
now hiding everywhere under the earth
and even seas
powerlines
were in my comic books
in the pages of my schools
in the Hollywood history teachers told
making heroes of themselves
powerlines
are on my face
my kidneys, my lungs
my eyes
maybe my mind
powerlines run all over
already they run over the heroes too

2022

Wehsakehcha, Comics, Shakespeare and the Dictionary

How does a Cree/Michif-speaking Métis with an orally-based land culture begin the road to becoming a professor; a profession that, in large measure, is all about amassing books and filling one's life with the written and urban culture of colonial education? A more concrete way of putting this, and in terms of experience, is to say that my early childhood years were filled with the comical and yet complex *Wehsakehcha* (the Cree legendary figure also known as "trickster") and my school years were full of white-invented savages, settlers and "Shakespeare" (among the numerous fictional and non-fictional readings public schools offered). For me those years were both easy transition and difficult dissonance.

I started this transition from orality to English literacy a long time ago; perhaps it began at age 4 or 5, the moment in which I opened Cowboys and Indians comic books such as Billy the Kid, Davey Crocket, The Lone Ranger and Tonto, and so forth. Or when I first saw pictures of Dick and Jane, Sally, Spot and Puff in my older brother's Red, Yellow and Blue readers.

These sources did two things to me: one, I wanted desperately to learn how to read; and two, I became unconsciously more alienated from my childhood upbringing. I wanted to learn how to read for a very practical reason – I wanted to know what the little alphabets inside the cloud over each character's head were saying. In part, comic books spurred my thirst for literacy, and for a long time I thought literacy was the best thing ever invented. I thought so without realizing for many years that learning to read carried a cultural price. Without my knowing these readings were the beginnings of my Otherness. My intellectual exile in my own homeland. The dissonance between *Wehsakehcha* and *Cowboys and Indians*. In short, *Wehsakehcha* brought me laughter and wonder; *Cowboys and Indians* comics (and movies) caused me discomfort, confusion and racial shame. *Wehsakehcha* is ultimately about being human; Cowboys were all about dehumanizing and killing "Indians." But all this is a big story that requires more space than I can give it here, and one that is relayed in a number of my writings (LaRocque 2010, for instance).

The other "big story" about my journey from orality to literacy is actually more complex than just moving from a culture of words to a culture of writing. And that is difficult enough. What is not well known is that Métis Nation people can claim a rich literary heritage from both First Nation and Euro-Canadian peoples. They have inherited, as I have said elsewhere, "a wealth of literatures – literatures spoken, sung, performed, painted, carved, engraved, pictographed, penned and stereo/typed (pun intended). And now cybered" (see chapter "Contemporary Métis Literature: Resistance, Roots, Innovation").

In addition to this heritage, the Métis of Rupert's Land, along with other Native people, were involved in the development of the Cree syllabary in the 1840s. Syllabic literacy spread among Native peoples throughout the plains and the north. Right up to the 1970s my mother and her sisters were literate women who wrote to each other in the syllabic system. My mother used to read the Roman Catholic Bible and other religious material in syllabics. In effect, I grew up in literacy. And in orality. Perhaps this is why learning the English alphabet and phonetic system came so easy for me. And actually, I learned how to read before I entered grade one, and once in school, I loved reading and spelling the most.

I still love words. Whether Cree, Michif, English or the little of French I learned in high school. And this love began by listening to my mother and sometimes grandmother tell us Cree legends and myths in Cree. Or my mother reading to us from her syllabic Bible and pamphlets, or letters from her sisters. Both my grandmother and mother were fantastic storytellers; they did not just tell stories, they virtually performed them in their animated ways of speaking. Their ways of telling stories transported us to worlds and characters that were magical and transcendent.

I loved pictures too. Some comic books were also magical and transcendent, not only because of their storylines but because of the visual art that inspired imagination. Like a giant yellow moon against a navy blue starry sky, moon reflected off a perfectly still river which carried a man in a birchbark canoe. Like in *The Book of Hiawatha*. Or the giant yellow moon that lit the way in the dark for *The Singing Donkey* and his menagerie of fellow-abandoned friends in search of a home.

There is considerable universality to stories whether told or written. In Coyote and the Roadrunner, for example, Coyote's attempts to trick

Roadrunner which always backfired on him reminded me of *Wehsake-hcha*'s antics. Like Coyote, *Wehsakehcha* was often wiley, scheming and over-confident, if not a downright braggart! Yet his schemes to outwit others often failed and we could laugh with him, knowing intuitively that we all have tricksterisms in us. And so it is with Coyote. Stories can be a bridge between cultures – in an unexpected way, *Wehsakehcha* and comics provided that bridge for me. I have retained my orality and at the same time my youthful encounters with comics turned into my love of books.

Today I have more books than I know what to do with! Books on nearly everything and of course, loads related to my work and area of specialization. Do I have any special attachment to any particular books? I would have to say dictionaries. I have a lot of dictionaries and thesauruses. English, after all, is my second language and I have had to look up a lot of words – a necessity I enjoyed early in high school. Indeed, as a graduate student I often carried a dictionary right into my university classes. In the field that I teach, Native Studies, some students, Native and non-Native alike, have difficulties writing essays. Part of that has to do with lack of timely research but it also has to do with lack of facility with the English language. Students often seem surprised when I tell them that English is my second language and that it is the humble (and oft neglected) dictionary that has enabled me to deepen my knowledge of English. And these days one does not even have to go to a library for a dictionary – they just have to go to their smart phones! Still, learning a second language is really a lifelong challenge.

I never kept my comic books but I have never forgotten them – both the few beautiful ones, and the all too numerous racist ones. Neither have I forgotten *Wehsakehcha*. Yes, I have more books than I have shelf space. In fact, my mother, a fastidious and organized woman, would be horrified at how untidy my book stacks are – but I know she would be most happy that I still speak Cree and laugh with *Wehsakehcha* quite often.

Afterword

When I first started writing, there were few contemporary Indigenous writers in Canada. This was in 1971. My first ever published essay was on Alberta public schools as I and numerous other Indigenous kids, both Métis and Status Indian, or First Nation as they are now known, experienced it. I had written the essay for an assignment in a university class. My very kind professor sent it to a Native weekly newspaper, *The Native People*, which published it. At the time, I knew nothing about this newspaper or the organization, the Alberta Native Communications Society, which produced it. A few months later, in the summer of 1971, the organization hired me as a reporter for the paper. I was not trained in journalism, but I took to it because I enjoyed writing. And because I was born "living colonialism" (see chapter "Colonialism Lived"), a fiery sense of justice had long lived in my being. Reporting on various (and usually very political) Native events was one way I could begin to express that commitment to justice.

In Alberta in the early 1970s both Status Indians (as they were then known) and the Métis referred to themselves as "Native people," which we all were since most Métis then grew up in Cree and with land-based cultures. But there are some significant differences between First Nation and Métis peoples. Besides lineage and identity, there are historical, cultural, and legislative differences. Despite the Métis displacements and subsequent diaspora after the Red River Resistances of the late 1800s, the majority of Red River Métis remained a cohesive functioning and living culture with many generations of Métis in our genealogies; in western Canada most Métis have Red River roots with knowledge as to our historic homelands.[1] Today, largely due to John A. McDonald's

---

1 Over the years I have written a number of articles on the Métis. Recently, we have had non-Métis people claiming they have some "Indian" in their background, no matter

266 Afterword

antipathy to Métis peoples, and Manitoba's failure to honour its moral and legal obligations under the Manitoba Act of 1870, many Métis are landless. Or live on lands they do not legally own but morally belongs to them. Métis do not have treaties or live in reserves. And the majority of Métis went to public schools. Throughout the early to mid-twentieth century, many Métis lived under dire socio-economic conditions.

As I have written in a number of essays, I did not grow up in a White middle-class home or community; as a Cree-speaking Red River Métis (rural) community in northeastern Alberta, we were wracked with devastating poverty, marginalization, and precarious health. Add to this the pervasive racism we experienced from the nearby town we frequented: from peers, police, priests, storekeepers, restaurants, hospitals, clinics, public schools, and so forth, the racism was both systemic and up close and personal.

All throughout my schooling I learned in various degrees all about "Settlers" and "Savages." On the playgrounds and town cafes and sidewalks my ears rang with classist, racist, and sexist name-callings. As Métis resistance scholar and writer Howard Adams put it in *Prison of Grass*, "Even in solitary silence, I felt the word 'savage' deep in my soul" (1975, 16). For me, not only did I have to contend with the word savage or "dirty Indian" but also the label "squaw." These experiences became the driving force to my research on White North America's constructions of "The Indian." I soon learned that the core of this construction centred on Euro-White North American weaponized ideology (Jennings 1976) I have come to call "the civ/sav dichotomy" (see chapter "The Metis in English Canadian Literature") from which Indigenous peoples, on a cultural and intellectual scale, were degraded as savages in direct contrast to Euro-White peoples who were glorified as civilages (my word). And from this have come numerous images and stereotypes resulting in racial and cultural shaming of Indigenous peoples. In policy and in concept the civ/sav arsenal was, in effect, a "colonizer's model of the world" (Blaut 1993) which served to

---

how remote, and pose as Métis in order to be able to claim fishing and hunting rights or other resources. Others with mixed-race backgrounds but with no Métis culture or lineage have also claimed the word "Métis" for their identity. My article on Métis identity (2001) establishes who the Métis are not, and who they are. And why there is so much confusion. It is very important to the Métis that Canadians understand who exactly the Red River Métis are. Not only are hunting or fishing rights (such as they are) at stake, but we struggle to be recognized as the distinct ethnic, Indigenously based culture that we are.

Afterword 267

dispossess and dehumanize peoples of the Americas. This has had a huge destructive impact on Indigenous peoples but also, and inversely, on non-Indigenous peoples.

The gross misrepresentation in schools and society, combined with our poverty and marginalization, had a profound effect on my community and on me. It took some time for me to understand that our socio-economic situation was due to historical factors, namely, colonialization. To live colonialism is to witness and to experience assorted inequities and injustices. As my youthful political consciousness grew, so did my hunger for justice and my resolve to educate.

A keen sense of social justice (or injustice) is a passion I carried into academia, and into academic writing. In 1975, when I became, rather unexpectedly, an author of *Defeathering the Indian* (see chapter "A Personal Essay on Poverty"), which was meant to be a curriculum guide for public school teachers in Alberta, I had just completed my first three years of university and did not consider myself an academic, nor did I ever imagine that I would become one, much less a professor with a life-long love of scholarship. And poetry.

In the summer of 1976 I started teaching, also unexpectedly, in Native Studies, a department at the University of Manitoba that had just been officially established the year prior by the Board of Governors. I had not known such a department existed, but for me it was the beginning of a lifetime career, as it turned out.[2] But teaching "Native Studies" was not just a career, it was a vocation. In the department I was assigned to teach an introductory course covering a wide survey of First Nation and Métis historical and social issues, and Native literatures. I was not trained specifically in these areas, and in my early years, my academic writing was directed by the need to carry out research to be able to teach such a wide variety of topics with some confidence. Later I also developed some courses specific to my interest and doctoral work. For my dissertation I concentrated on Euro-White North American colonial (and patriarchal) misrepresentation of Indigenous peoples, focusing on Canadian historiography and literature. Some of this research provides a foundation to my book *When*

---

2 Several years ago, in an interview, I was asked what my career goals were when I was a youngster. I explained to the interviewer that there was no such thing as "career goals" where I grew up. People were too busy trying to survive. My parents worked very hard to shelter, clothe, and feed us; of course, they wanted what was best for us, but "career goals" as a concept or option were culturally and sociologically nonexistent for us. My life in the university has not been a career goal but, as I explain, a vocation.

the Other Is Me (2010), which in addition features Native writers' resistance, or "contrapuntal" (Said 1994, 66–7) counter-discourse to racist, stereotypic, and dehumanizing portrayals found in Canadian colonial records and historical and literary material.

This Reader is not a complete list of my publications, but the selection reflects my intellectual interests and pursuits, which were and are informed by my sociopolitical standing in Canadian society. Academic readers will note that many of the works take an inter- and multidisciplinary approach. Native Studies as an intellectual discipline is, by its very nature, latticed with many disciplines as we deal with archival material, history, ethnography, literatures, law, governance, social issues, gender studies, community/participatory research, and more. Such an approach also reflects what has become a fairly universal understanding that most Indigenous cultures exude a world view in which all life is interconnected and relational. A tree is never just a tree, for instance, and a fallen tree is never definitively "dead." Similarly, knowledge is imbricated from the ancient to the contemporary and cannot be strictly divided into categorical bits and pieces.

The articles selected for this Reader deal with colonial history and misrepresentation; feminist analysis, particularly on violence against women; racism; Métis identity; contemporary First Nation and Métis writing; and what I have called resistance scholarship, extending Barbara Harlow's work on *Resistance Literature* (1987). The Reader also includes some of my published poetry.

I have now been writing for about fifty years and I have taught for more than forty-five years, and my foremost objective has been the humanization of Indigenous peoples. It is imperative that White and other non-Indigenous peoples learn the truth about the colonization process and also about the cultural achievements and humanity of Indigenous peoples. I believe only then will society really change, and only then can reconciliation truly happen. Equally, it is just as crucial that Indigenous peoples learn the same truth so that they can be justly proud of their histories, heritages, and cultures. They then can take their rightful place in society as equal and valuable human beings, as they should be. These were my hopes and objectives when I began to write, as well as when I began to teach. I wanted my research and pedagogy to be transformative. I am happy to say that I have seen many positive changes over the years – many more and increasing numbers of both White and Indigenous peoples are gaining a much greater knowledge and appreciation of Indigeneity. It will take both groups to transform a colonial relationship – however, the onus is on colonial actors to change

Afterword

269

their perspectives and economic priorities, as well as their social and political privileges.

Much has changed over the last fifty years, and certainly much has changed since the 1950s and 1960s, the era in which I grew up. Our populations have grown. Our life expectancies have lengthened. Our socio-economic profile has improved. Our education levels have substantially improved. There have been significant land claim and self-determination gains. On the creative front, our literary output (in English) has virtually exploded since the 1990s. This dramatic growth both in Indigenous writing and the critical study of it has practically revolutionized our pedagogies for those of us who teach Indigenous literatures. We have great novelists, poets, playwrights, sci-fi fictionalists, political/social commentators, biographers, essayists, and many other creative producers in music, acting, film, and various other mediums, such as digitalization. We have great artists, and many artworks are featured in art galleries, museums, and assorted ivory hallways across Canada. We are increasingly represented in diverse careers and educational attainments.

On the political front First Nations have not looked back since their political awakening in the early 1970s, an awakening spurred on by the federal government's White Paper proposal of 1969. Around the same time the Métis were also awakening, as indicated by Métis writers such as Maria Campbell in *Halfbreed* (1973) and Howard Adams in *Prison of Grass* (1989, first edition 1975). History began to be revisited and retold through Native poetry, novels, autobiographies, and other forms of writing. Native Studies and, with it, Native scholars began to appear. The rebirth, as Harold Cardinal named it in his second book, *The Rebirth of Canada's Indians* (1977; following Cardinal's *The Unjust Society*, published in 1969), included the renewing and/or reinventing of spiritual and artistic traditions, beliefs, ceremonies, protocols, languages, storytelling, songs and dancing, drumming, fiddling, foods, and many other cultural activities. Pow Wows and the Elder movement became popular. As did political protests.

While we have much to celebrate, and while both political and cultural resurgence has continued, sadly, we still have much to protect, protest, and resist. Industrial and urban encroachments onto First Nation and Métis lands and resources continue. For both First Nation and Métis, pollution and lack of clean water and decent housing remain significant concerns for many communities. Self-government is not yet comprehensively realized. Nor is quality education or basic medical care easily accessible, be it in more remote areas or in towns and cities. There is yet much poverty, homelessness, violence, and other socio-economic problems plaguing too many First Nation and Métis families and communities. Too many Indigenous individuals have been killed, either by police or by other White men. A disproportionate number of Indigenous men and women are incarcerated. And who or what can heal the broken dreams and lives of those abused in residential schools?

I never went to residential school, but I consider myself a public school survivor. Not much has been said about how abusive public schools were to my generation. Many Status and non-Status First Nation students and the majority of Métis students attended public schools. My siblings and I experienced public schools as repressive, punitive, assimilationist, and classist (see chapter "Colonialism Lived"). Teachers used corporal means to punish us – often without cause. We were not allowed to speak Cree, and we were forced to attend religious classes that were taught by a cruel woman teacher who readily slapped us even if we only turned away for a moment. Whatever minimal history was taught about "Indians" was generally pejorative and racist. And there was a lot of bullying and violence in the school playgrounds. Of course, there were some fundamental differences between residential and public schools. At the end of the day we were able to go home and, while there was physical, psychological, cultural, and authoritarian violence, there were no sexual assaults – as far as I know.

Overall and over the centuries there has been tremendous violence against Indigenous people. What is perhaps the most troubling is the continuing violence against First Nation, Métis, and Inuit women and girls. And undoubtedly, some men and boys. The violence has been extensive and deadly. There have been a number of reports and inquiries from organizations such as Amnesty International (2004, 2009), the Native Women's Association of Canada (2009, 2010), Missing Women Commission of Inquiry (2012), and even the RCMP (2014, 2015). In 2016 the federal government finally issued a National Inquiry into Missing and Murdered Indigenous Women and Girls and released a two-volume report in 2020. As significant and important as these reports and the inquiry are, the response addressing the violence has been slow. It seems to me not much has changed as Indigenous women and girls continue to suffer "domestic" abuse, kidnappings, sex trafficking, sexual assaults, and murder. Indigenous women, often young women, continue to be missing. And way too many continue to be assaulted from within or outside their homes and communities. Such disregard of female humanity is, in part, what moved me to feminism and to research and publication of essays on misogyny and violence against women. This violence is also profoundly racist.

Afterword

Those of us who are writers and scholars, among others, have been arduously informing Canadians about racism (embedded in colonialism) and its destructive effects. For a very long time now. As far back as the 1800s Native men and women, as soon as they could speak and write in English, wrote vociferously against colonial usurpation of lands, with it, racist stereotypes. Yet racism still runs strong in Canadian (and American) society, much of it produced at the outset of European arrivals and continued through numerous and assorted colonial fiction and non-fiction. Not surprisingly, White supremacy is deeply embedded in society. Racism is not only about stereotyping (which is bad enough); it insinuates itself in societal structures such that it becomes normalized and is expressed in what sociologists refer to as "everyday racism." Has the racism lessened over the centuries? It is difficult to tell.

Because I believe in the social purpose of knowledge, I have concentrated on researching and publishing these troubling historical and contemporary social issues. When I started as a Lecturer in Native Studies, I was a graduate student in history and did not sufficiently understand the power and pervasiveness of the university expectations or protocols which were largely western, patriarchal, and overwhelmingly White middle class. Ironically, I was the one often accused of being "biased" reflecting the colonial notion that western scholarship was objective. Apparently, teaching about colonization, even though it is solidly documented, was not considered "objective" by both White students and administration, especially when taught by an Indigenous instructor. At the time I did not know how to defend or explain my positionality. I was an idealist, and I thought the university was for learning and open to all peoples and to new ideas that were not western-centric. It was only later that I began to articulate the politics of "objectivity" and explained that in Cree one does not distance one's words from one's context yet at the same time knows the difference between subjectivity and objectivity (see chapter "Preface: Hear Are Our Voices – Who Will Hear"). Today much of what and how I was teaching is now understood as Indigenous Methodology and widely practised by many Indigenous academics. More widely, particularly in feminist, post-colonial, and resistance studies, positionality is now part of understanding the ethnocultural (Blaut 1993) and political partisanship of scholarship and research (Said 1978).

A word on poetry. In the Indigenous literary community, we have way more poets than novelists or dramatists. There are probably as many reasons for this as there are poets. But I do think we have gravitated towards poetry partly because poetry facilitates transition from orality to writing, especially for my generation. I take to poetry for many reasons, perhaps the biggest reason is my love of words. Obviously, poetry is a different form of writing in format and style from academic and other prose. Each genre meets different parts of me. Poetry allows a creative expression of the nitty-gritty aspects of life, but also of beauty that surrounds us. I write poetry also for the challenge of creativity and just for the love of words.

But I do also love knowledge and the discipline of scholarship; I very much enjoy critical analysis and (discernible) theory. As an inherent part of my decolonization and counter-discourse or resistance to the colonial discourse of the dominant western narrative I use my "voice" in my academic writing, and I try to use language that many readers can understand. Using voice is considerably more complex than storytelling or facts of biography. Nor is it for its own sake. When I refer to the person it is to voice my positionality and to make larger arguments in contrapuntal response to the dominant "settler" (or more properly, resettler) narrative (LaRocque 2010, 7–8, 31–3). It is instructional in purpose – one might say it is for "the pedagogy of the oppressor" (to twist Freire's 2020 [1970] formulation).

Knowledge is not something we own. Scholarship is built on centuries of other researchers' knowledges and cultures. All of us borrow ideas or data from countless sources, beginning with our parents and cultures. It is difficult to say which writers and scholars have had the biggest impact on me. My knowledge base extends from Wehsakehcha stories in Cree to store-bought comic books to outstanding novelists and poets to brilliant thinkers and scholars.

My dream for Native Studies (now Indigenous Studies) has always been to develop it as an intellectual discipline, with concentrated focus on scholarship that nurtures research, critical thinking, and analysis (LaRocque 2015). I have long been concerned that universities (administration, faculty, students, both mainstream and Indigenous) have tended to relegate Native Studies to "cultural portraiture" and more recently to "community." Both of these concepts are often oversimplified and even stereotypical; moreover, "community" is highly politicized. Culture and community are important, of course, and we certainly include aspects of these two elements in our teaching, research, and service. However, Indigenous Studies is and ought to be so much broader in scope and research. My hope is that we not lose sight of the centrality of scholarship where one can concentrate on intellectual/theoretical knowledge and critical reflection in an environment of academic freedom and institutional support. This does not mean we abandon the social purpose of knowledge – far from it. We use our knowledge – gained from good scholarship – for the betterment of humanity. As I stated in my article

Afterword 273

on "resistance teaching" (see chapter "Resist No Longer: Reflections on Resistance Writing and Teaching"):

> although we have a significant role to play in resisting oppression, in theorizing its origins and demonstrating its social consequences as well as assisting in reconstruction, we cannot be distracted from our vocation as critical thinkers …
>
> As an intellectual and a scholar, I often call for that "critical and relatively independent spirit of analysis and judgement," which Edward Said argues "ought to be the intellectual's contribution." (1996, 86)

This is the contribution I have worked to make. This is the legacy I hope to leave. But I am not leaving just yet! There are so many more things to learn, so much more deconstruction and reconstruction to do, so many more theories to enjoy, conversations to engage in. And poems to write.

Emma LaRocque
Winnipeg, 2021

References

Aboriginal Women's Council of Saskatchewan. "Child Sexual Abuse: Words from Concerned Women." *Canadian Woman Studies/Les Cahiers de la femme* 10, no. 1–2 (1989/90ty;èop): 90–1.

Acoose, Janice. "Halfbreed: A Revisiting of Maria Campbell's Text from an Indigenous Perspective." In *Looking at the Words of Our People: First Nations Analysis of Literature*, edited by Jeannette Armstrong, 137–50. Penticton: Theytus, 1993.

– "Post Halfbreed: Indigenous Writers as Authors of Their Own Realities." In *Looking at the Words of Our People: First Nations Analysis of Literature*, edited by Jeannette Armstrong, 27–42. Penticton, BC: Theytus, 1993.

– *Iskewawek: Kah 'Ki Yaw Ni Wahkomakanak*. Toronto: Women's Press, 1995.

Adams, Howard. *Prison of Grass: Canada from a Native Point of View*, 2nd revised ed. Saskatoon: Fifth House Publishers, 1989 (1st ed. 1975).

– *A Tortured People: The Politics of Colonization*. Penticton: Theytus Books, 1995.

Akiwenzie-Damm, Kateri. "Dispelling and Telling: Speaking Native Realities in Maria Campbell's *Halfbreed* and Beatrice Culleton's *In Search of April Raintree*." In *Armstrong*, 93–114. 1993.

– *My Heart Is a Stray Bullet*. Cape Croker: Kegedonce Press, 1993.

– *Without Reservation: Indigenous Erotica*. Wiarton, ON: Kegedonce Press, 2003.

Alioff, Maurie, and Susan Schouten Levine. "Interview: The Long Walk of Alanis Obomsawin." Cinema Canada (June 1987): 10–15.

Allan, Luke. *Blue Pete: Rebel*. London: Herbert Jenkins, 1940.

Allard-Tremblay, Yann, and Elaine Coburn. "The Flying Heads of Settler Colonialism: Or the Ideological Erasures of Indigenous Peoples in Political Theorizing." *Political Studies* 71, no. 2 (2023): 359–78. https://doi.org/10.1177/00323217211018127

Amnesty International. "Stolen Sisters: A Human Rights Response to Discrimination and Violence against Indigenous Women in Canada." Accessed 2004. www.amnesty.ca/sites/amnesty/files/amr200032004enstolensisters.pdf

276 References

– "No More Stolen Sisters: The Need for a Comprehensive Response to Discrimination and Violence against Indigenous Women in Canada." Accessed 2009. www.amnesty.ca/sites/amnesty/files /amr200122009en.pdf

Andersen, Chris. *Métis: Race, Recognition, and the Struggle for Indigenous Peoplehood*. Vancouver: University of British Columbia Press, 2014.

Anderson, Kim. *A Recognition of Being: Reconstructing Native Womanhood*. Toronto: Second Story Press, 2000.

Andrews, Jennifer. "Irony, Métis Style: Reading the Poetry of Marilyn Dumont and Gregory Scofield." *Canadian Poetry*, 2013. Accessed May 16, 2013. http://canadianpoetry.org/volumes/vol50/andrews.html.

Andrews, Jennifer, Renate Eigenbrod, and Emma LaRocque, eds. *"For the Love of Words": Aboriginal Writers of Canada*. Spec. issue of *Studies in Canadian Literature*, Vol. 31, no. 1, 2006.

Angelou, Maya. *I Know Why the Caged Bird Sings*. New York: Bantam Books, 1970.

Armstrong, Jeannette. *Slash*. Penticton: Theytus Books, 1985.

– *Breath Tracks*. Toronto: Williams-Wallace Publishers, 1991.

– "The Disempowerment of First North American Native Peoples and Empowerment through Their Writing." In *An Anthology of Canadian Native Literature in English*, edited by Daniel David Moses and Terry Goldie. Toronto: Oxford University Press, 1992.

– *Looking at the Words of My People: First Nations Analysis of Literature*. Peneticton: Theytus Books, 1993.

– *Whispering in the Shadows*. Penticton: Theytus Books, 2001.

Armstrong, Jeannette, and Lally Grauer, eds. *Native Poetry in Canada: A Contemporary Anthology*. Peterborough: Broadview Press, 2001.

Arnott, Joanne. *Wiles of Girlhood*. Vancouver: Press Gang, 1991.

– *Steepy Mountain Love Poetry*. Cape Croker: Kegedonce Press, 2004.

Ashcroft, Bill, Gareth Griffiths, and Helen Tiffin. *The Empire Writes Back: Theory and Practice in Post-Colonial Literatures*. London: Routledge, 1989.

– eds. *Post-Colonial Studies Reader*. London and New York: Routledge, 1995.

Axtell, James. *Natives and Newcomers: The Cultural Origins of North America*. New York and Oxford: Oxford University Press, 2001.

Bailey, Alfred Goldsworthy. *The Conflict of European and Eastern Algonkian Cultures, 1505–1700*, 2nd ed. Toronto: University of Toronto Press, 1969.

Baillargeon, Morgan, and Leslie Tepper. *Legends of Our Times: Native Cowboy Life*. Vancouver: UBC Press, 1998.

Baker, Marie Annharte. *Being on the Moon*. Winlaw, BC: Polestar Press, 1990.

– *Coyote Columbus Café*. Winnipeg: Moonprint, 1994.

– *Exercises in Lip Pointing*. Vancouver: New Sky Books, 2003.

References

Bakker, Peter. "The Michif Language of the Metis." In *Metis Legacy: A Metis Historiography and Annotated Bibliography*, edited by Lawrence J. Barkwell, Leah Dorion, and Darren R. Prefontaine, 177–9. Winnipeg: Pemmican, 2001.

Baldwin, James. *Notes of a Native Son.* Boston: Beacon Press, 1949.

Bannerji, Himani, ed. *Returning the Gaze: Essays on Racism, Feminism and Politics.* Toronto: Sister Vision Press, 1993.

Barron, Laurie F., and James B. Waldram, eds. *1885 and After: Native Society in Transition.* Regina: Canadian Plains Research Center, 1986.

Barton, Willow. "Where Have the Warriors Gone." In *Writing the Circle: Native Women of Western Canada*, edited by Jeanne Perrault and Sylvia Vance, 8–18. Edmonton: NeWest, 1993.

Battiste, Marie. "You Can't Be the Doctor If You're the Disease: Eurocentrism and Indigenous Renaissance." In *CAUT Distinguished Academic Lecture* 26, 2013. www.caut.ca/sites/default/files/marie_battiste_caut_lecture _final_2013_2.pdf.

Bell, Diane. "Considering Gender – Are Human Rights for Women Too?" Paper presented at the International Conference on Human Rights in Cross Cultural Perspectives. College of Law, University of Saskatchewan, 1989.

Berger, Thomas R. *Northern Frontier, Northern Homeland: The Report of the Mackenzie Valley Pipeline Inquiry, Volume 1.* Ottawa: Minister of Supply and Services, 1997.

Berkes, Fikret. *Traditional Ecological Knowledge in Perspective: Traditional Ecological Knowledge: Concepts and Cases.* Edited by J. Inglis. Ottawa: Canadian Museum of Nature, 1993.

Berkes, Fikret, and Thomas Henley. "Co-Management and Traditional Knowledge: Threat or Opportunity?" *Policy Options* 18, no. 2 (1997): 29–31.

Berkhofer, Robert F. *The White Man's Indian: Images of the American Indian from Columbus to the Present.* New York: Alfred Knopf, 1978.

Blaut, J.M. *The Colonizer's Model of the World: Geographical Diffusionism and Eurocentric History.* New York and London: Guilford Press, 1993.

Bouvier, Rita. *Blueberry Clouds.* Saskatoon: Thistledown, 1999.

– *Papiyahtak.* Saskatoon: Thistledown, 2004.

– *Better That Way.* Saskatoon: Gabriel Dumont Institute, 2008.

Brant, Beth. *Mohawk Trails.* Ithaca: Firebrand Books, 1985.

Brant, Beth, and Sandra Laronde, eds. *Sweetgrass Grows All Around Her.* Toronto: Native Women in the Arts, 1996.

Braz, Albert. "North of America." *Comparative American Studies* 3, no. 1 (2005): 79–88. https://doi.org/10.1177/1477570005050951

Brody, Hugh. "Indians on Skid Row: The Role of Alcohol and Community in the Adaptive Process of Indian Urban Migrants." Northern Science Research Group, Dept. of Indian Affairs and Northern Development, 1971.

Brown, Chester. *Louis Riel.* Drawn & Quarterly, 2021.

278   References

Brown, Dee. *Bury My Heart at Wounded Knee*. New York: Holt, Rinehart & Winston, 1970.

Brown, Jennifer SH, and Robert Alain Brightman. *The Orders of the Dreamed: George Nelson on Cree and Northern Ojibwa Religion and Myth, 1823*, Vol. 3. Minnesota Historical Society Press, 1988. https://doi.org/10.1515/9780887553059

Brown, Leslie, and Susan Strega, eds. *Research as Resistance: Critical, Indigenous, and Anti-Oppressive Approaches*. Toronto: Canadian Scholars' Press, 2005.

Brown, Michael F. "Cultural Relativism 2.0." *Current Anthropology* 49, no. 3 (2008): 363–83. https://doi.org/10.1086/529261

Campbell, Maria. *Halfbreed*. Toronto: McClelland and Stewart, 1973.

– *Stories of the Road Allowance People*. Penticton: Theytus Books, 1995.

Campbell, Maria, and Linda Griffiths. *The Book of Jessica: A Theatrical Transformation*. Toronto: Coach House, 1989.

Cardinal, Douglas. *Of the Spirit: Writings – Douglas Cardinal*. Edited by George Melnyk. Edmonton: Newest Press, 1977.

Cardinal, Harold. *The Unjust Society*. Edmonton: Hurtig Publishers, 1969.

– *The Rebirth of Canada's Indians*. Edmonton: Hurtig Publishers, 1977.

Careless, James Maurice Stockford. "Frontierism, Metropolitanism, and Canadian History." *Canadian Historical Review* 35, no. 1 (1954): 1–21. https://doi.org/10.3138/chr-035-01-01

Cariou, Warren. *The Exalted Company of Roadside Martyrs: Two Novellas*. Regina: Coteau, 1999.

– "Hybrid Imaginings." *Review of Gregory Scofield's I Knew Two Métis Women and Thunder Through My Veins*, David Day's *The Visions and Revelations of St. Louis the Martyr*, and Robert Hunter's *Red Blood. Canadian Literature* 167 (2000): 141–4. Print.

– "The Racialized Subject in James Tyman's Inside Out." *Canadian Literature* 167 (2000): 68–84. Print.

– *Lake of the Prairies: Stories of Belonging*. Scarborough: Doubleday, 2002.

Carpenter, W. *Guidelines for Responsible Research in Northern Canada: Discussion Paper, ACUNS Conference*, Ft. Smith, NWT, October 2, 1993.

Chartrand, Lionel, T.E. Logan, and J.D. Daniels. *Metis History and Experience and Residential Schools in Canada*. Ottawa: Aboriginal Healing Foundation, 2006.

Chartrand, Paul L.A.H. "Aboriginal Rights: The Dispossession of the Métis." *Osgoode Hall Law Journal* 29, no. 3 (Fall 1991): 457–82. https://doi.org/10.60082/2817-5069.1743

Chisaakay, Molly. "Shadows." In *Writing the Circle: Native Women of Western Canada*, edited by Jeanne Perrault and Sylvia Vance, 31. Edmonton: NeWest, 1993.

Christian, Barbara. "*The Race for Theory*." In *Post-Colonial Studies Reader*, edited by Bill Ashcroft, Gareth Griffiths and Helen Tiffin. London and New York: Routledge, 1995.

References

Chrystos. *Not Vanishing*. Vancouver: Press Gang, 1988.

Clements, Marie, Greg Daniels, and Margo Kane. *DraMétis: Three Métis Plays*. Toronto: University of Toronto Press, 2001.

Clutesi, George. *Potlatch*. Sidney: Grays, 1969.

Coburn, Elaine. "'Theorizing Our Place': Indigenous Women's Scholarship from 1985–2020 and the Emerging Dialogue with Anti-Racist Feminisms." *Studies in Social Justice* 14, no. 2 (2020): 429–53. https://doi.org/10.26522/ssj.v14i2.2295

— " I was Born Asking": An Interview with Emma LaRocque. *Canadian Journal of Native Studies* 37 no. 2 (2017): 159–178.

Colorado, Pam. "Bridging Native and Western Science." *Convergence* 21, no. 2/3 (1988): 49–67.

Connor, Ralph. *The Foreigner: A Tale of Saskatchewan*. Toronto: Westminster, 1909.

Cook-Lynn, Elizabeth. *Why I Can't Read Wallace Stegner and Other Essays*. Madison: University of Wisconsin Press, 1996.

Copway, George. *An Anthology of Canadian Native Literature in English*. Edited by Daniel David Moses and Terry Goldie. Toronto: Oxford University Press, 1991.

Coulthard, Glen S. "Subjects of Empire: Indigenous Peoples and the 'Politics of Recognition' in Canada." Contemporary Political Theory 6 (2007): 437–60.

Crate, Joan. *Pale as Real Ladies: Poems for Pauline Johnson*. London: Brick Books, 1991.

– *Foreign Homes*. London: Brick Books, 2002.

Crawford, John C. "What is Michif?: Language in the Métis Tradition." In The New Peoples: Being and Becoming Métis, edited by Jacqueline Peterson and Jennifer S.H. Brown, 231–41. Winnipeg: University of Manitoba Press, 1985.

Creighton, Donald Grant. *The Story of Canada*. Houghton, Mifflin, 1959.

Culhane Speck, Dara. *An Error in Judgement: The Politics of Medical Care in an Indian/White Community*. Vancouver: Talonbooks, 1987.

Culleton, Mosionier Beatrice. *In Search of April Raintree*. Winnipeg: Pemmican, 1983.

– *Spirit of the White Bison*. Winnipeg: Pemmican Publications, 1985.

Cuthand, Beth. *Voices in the Waterfall*. Penticton: Theytus Books, 1989.

Dailey, R. "The Role of Alcohol among North American Indian Tribes as Reported in the Jesuit Relations." *Anthropologica* 10, no. 1 (1968): 45–59. https://doi.org/10.2307/25604758

Damm, Kateri. "Dispelling and Telling: Speaking Native Realities in Maria Campbell's *Halfbreed* and Beatrice Culleton's *In Search of April Raintree*." In *Looking at the Words of Our People*, edited by Jeannette Armstrong, 93–114. Penticton: Theytus Books, 1993.

Davies, Julie A. "Beatrice Culleton (1949–)." In *Writers of Multicultural Fiction for Young Adults: A Bio-Critical Sourcebook*. Westport: Greenwood, 1996.

Day, David, and Marilyn Bowering, eds. *Many Voices: An Anthology of Contemporary Canadian Indian Poetry*. Vancouver: J.J. Douglas, 1977.

Deloria, Vine. *God Is Red*. New York: Dunlop, 1973.

References

DePasquale, Paul, Renate Eigenbrod, and Emma LaRocque, eds. *Across Cultures/Across Borders: Canadian Aboriginal and Native American Literatures.* Peterborough: Broadview, 2010.

Dickason, Olive. *The Myth of the Savage and the Beginnings of French Colonialism in the Americas.* Edmonton: University of Alberta Press, 1984.

– *Canada's First Nations: A History of Founding Peoples from Earliest Times.* Toronto: McClelland and Stewart, 1992.

Donovan, Josephine. *Feminist Theory: The Intellectual Traditions of American Feminism.* New York: Continuum Publishing, 1990.

Dosman, Edgar. *Indians: The Urban Dilemma.* Toronto: McLelland and Stewart Lts, 1972.

Doxtator, Deborah. *Fluffs and Feathers.* Brantford: Woodland Cultural Center, 1992.

Duchemin, Parker. "'A Parcel of Whelps': Alexander Mackenzie among the Indians." In *Native Writers and Canadian Writing,* edited by WH New, 49–74. Vancouver: University of British Columbia Press, 1990.

Dumont, Marilyn. "The Gift." In *Writing the Circle: Native Women of Western Canada – An Anthology,* edited by Jeanne Perreault and Sylvia Vance, 44–6. Edmonton: NeWest Press, 1990.

– *A Really Good Brown Girl.* London: Brick Books, 1996.

– *Green Girl Dreams Mountains.* Lantville: Ooolichan Books, 2001.

– *That Tongued Belonging.* Cape Croker Reserve: Kegedonce, 2007.

– "BCP Honours Indigenous Sovereignty Week 2010: Interview with Cree/ Metis Poet Marilyn Dumont." *Black Coffee Poet,* November 2010. Accessed February 10, 2014. http://blackcoffeepot.com/2010/11/23bcp -honours-ind.

Dunn, Marty. *Red on White: The Biography of Duke Redbird.* Toronto: New Press, 1971.

Eigenbrod, Renate. "The Oral in the Written: A Literature between Two Cultures." *Canadian Journal of Native Studies* 15, no. 1 (1995): 89–102.

– *Travelling Knowledges: Positioning the Im/Migrant Reader of Aboriginal Literatures in Canada.* Winnipeg: University of Manitoba Press, 2005.

Eigenbrod, Renate, and Jennifer Andrews. "Introduction: From Conference to Special Issue: Selected Articles on 'the Love of Words'". *Studies in Canadian Literature* 31, no. 1 (2006). https://journals.lib.unb.ca/index.php/SCL/article /view/10191

Eigenbrod, Renate, and Jo-Ann Episkenew, eds. *Creating Community: A Roundtable on Canadian Aboriginal Literature.* Brandon University: Bearpaw Publishing, 2002.

Emberley, Julia. *Thresholds of Difference: Feminist Critique, Native Women's Writings, Postcolonial Theory.* Toronto: University of Toronto Press, 1993.

Emery, Alan R. and Associates. *Guidelines for Environmental Assessments and Traditional Knowledge.* A Report from the Centre for Traditional Knowledge. Hull, QC: Can. Int. Dev. Agency and Environment Canada, 1997.

References

Episkenew, Jo-Ann. "Socially Responsible Criticism: Aboriginal Literature, Ideology, and the Literary Canon." In Eigenbrod and Episkenew, 2002, 51–68.

– *Taking Back Our Spirits: Indigenous Literature, Public Policy, and Healing.* Winnipeg: University of Manitoba Press, 2009.

Estes, Nick. *Our History Is the Future: Standing Rock versus the Dakota Access Pipeline, and the Long Tradition of Indigenous Resistance.* Verso Books, 2019.

Ewers, John C. *People and Pelts.* Winnipeg: Pequis Publications, n.d.

Fagan, Kristina, Stephanie Danyluk, Bryce Donaldson, Amelia Horsburgh, Robyn Moore, and Martin Winquist. "Reading the Reception of Maria Campbell's Halfbreed." *Canadian Journal of Native Studies* 29, no. 1–2 (2009): 257–81

Fagan, Kristina, Daniel Heath Justice, Keavy Martin, Sam McKegney, Deanna Reder, and Niigonwedom Sinclair. "Canadian Indian Literary Nationalism?" *Canadian Journal of Native Studies* 29, no. 1–2 (2009): 19–44. https://doi.org/10.51644/9781554584178-004

Fee, Margery. "Upsetting Fake Ideas: Jeannette Armstrong's 'Slash' and Beatrice Culleton's 'April Raintree.'" In *Native Writers and Canadian Writing*, edited by W.H. New, 168–82. Vancouver: University of British Columbia Press, 1990.

Feit, Harvey. "Hunting and the Quest for Power: The James Bay Cree and White-Men in the 20th Century." In *Native Peoples: The Canadian Experience*, edited by R. Morrison and C. Wilson. Toronto: McClelland & Stewart, 1986.

Ferguson, Russell. "Introduction: Invisible Center." In *Out There: Marginalisation and Contemporary Cultures.* New York: The New Museum of Contemporary Art, 1990.

Fife, Connie. *The Colour of Resistance: A Contemporary Collection of Writing by Aboriginal Women.* Toronto: Sister Vision Press, 1993.

Fisher, Anthony Dwight. "A Colonial Education System: Historical Changes and Schooling in Fort Chipewyan". *Canadian Journal of Anthropology* 2, no. 1 (1981): 37–44.

Fiske, Jo-Ann. "Gender and the Paradox of Residential Education in Carrier Society." In *Women of the First Nations: Power, Wisdom, and Strength*, edited by Christine Miller and Patricia Chuchryk. Winnipeg: University of Manitoba Press, 1996.

Flaherty, Martha. *Freedom of Expression or Freedom of Exploitation.* Speech to the Association of Canadian Universities for Northern Studies 4th National Students' Conference on Northern Studies, November 27, Ottawa, 1994.

Flanagan, Thomas. *Riel and the Rebellion 1885 Reconsidered.* Saskatoon: Western Producer Prairie Books, 1983.

Flanagan, Tom. *First Nations, Second Thoughts.* Montreal: McGill-Queen's University Press, 2000.

282 References

Forer, Mort. *The Humback*. Toronto: McClelland and Stewart, 1969.

Francis, Daniel. *The Imaginary Indian*. Vancouver: Arsenal Pulp Press, 1992.

Freire, Paolo. *Pedagogy of the Oppressed: 50th Anniversary Edition*. New York: Bloomsbury Academic, 2018 (1st ed. 1970).

Frideres, James S. *Canada's Indians – Contemporary Conflicts*. Scarborough: Prentice Hall of Canada, 1974.

– *Aboriginal Peoples in Canada: Contemporary Conflicts*. Scarborough: Prentice Hall Allyn and Bacon Canada, 1998 (1st ed. 1984)

– *Aboriginal Peoples in Canada: Contemporary Conflicts*. Scarborough: Prentice Hall Allyn and Bacon, 2003.

Frideres, James S., and R. Gadacz. *Aboriginal Peoples in Canada: Contemporary Conflicts*. Toronto: Prentice Hall, 2001.

Fry, Alan. *How a People Die: A Novel*. Doubleday, 1970.

Gadgil, Madhav, Fikret Berkes, and Carl Folke. "Indigenous Knowledge for Biodiversity Conservation." *Ambio* 22, no. 2–3 (1993): 151–6. https://doi .org/10.1007/s13280-020-01478-7 Medline:33566330

Garvin, Terry. *Bush Land People*. Calgary: Arctic Institute of North America of the University of Calgary, 1992.

Gates, Henry Louis, Jr. *Black Literature and Literary Theory*. New York: Methuen, 1984.

Gaudry, Adam. "Communing with the Dead: The "New Métis," Métis Identity Appropriation, and the Displacement of Living Métis Culture." *American Indian Quarterly* 42, no. 2 (2018): 162–90. https://doi.org/10.1353 /aiq.2018.a693376

George, Chief Dan. "My Very Good Dear Friends." In *The Only Good Indian*, edited by Waubageshig. Don Mills: New Press, 1970.

– *My Heart Soars*. Saanichton, BC: Hancock House, 1974.

Gladue, Norma. "Broken Promises." In *Writing the Circle: Native Women of Western Canada*, edited by Jeanne Perrault and Sylvia Vance, 62–74. Edmonton: NeWest, 1993.

Godard, Barbara. "The Politics of Representation: Some Native Canadian Women Writers." *New* (1990): 183–228.

Government of Manitoba. "The Aboriginal Justice Inquiry." 1991. www.ajic .mb.ca/reports/final_ch01.html

— *Aboriginal Justice Implementation Commission Final Report*. 2001. Winnipeg. http://www.ajic.mb.ca/reports/final_toc.html

Grant, Agnes, ed. *Our Bit of Truth: An Anthology of Canadian Native Literature*. Winnipeg, Manitoba: Pemmican Publications, 1990.

– "Contemporary Native Women's Voices in Literature." *New* 124–32.

Green, Joyce. "Constitutionalizing the Patriarchy: Aboriginal Women and Aboriginal Government." *Constitutional Forum* 4, no. 4 (1993): 110–20. https:// doi.org/10.21991/C9908S

References

- "Democracy, Gender and Aboriginal Rights," unpublished manuscript, November, 1993.
- "Transforming at the Margins of the Academy." In *Pushing the Margins: Native and Northern Research*, edited by Jill Oakes, Rick Riewe, Maryilyn Bennett and B. Chisholm. Winnipeg: Native Studies Press, 2000.
- "Canon Fodder: Examining the Future of Native Studies." In *Pushing the Margins: Native and Northern Studies*, edited by Jill Oakes, R. Riewe, M. Bennet, and B. Chisholm. Winnipeg: Native Studies Press, 2001.
- "Theoretical, Methodological and Empirical Issues in the Study of Indigenous Politics," *Canadian Political Science Association*, 2002.
- *A Cultural and Ethnic Fundamentalism: The Mixed Potential for Identity, Liberation, and Oppression*. The Scholar Series. University of Regina: Saskatchewan Institute of Public Policy, 2003. (This also appears as a chapter in Carol Schick, JoAnn Jaffe, and Alisa Watkinson, eds. *Contesting Fundamentalisms*. Halifax: Fernwood Publishing, 2004).
- ed. *Making Space for Indigenous Feminisms*. Halifax: Fernwood Press, 2007.
- ed. *Making Space for Indigenous Feminisms* (2nd ed.). Halifax: Fernwood Press, 2017.

Green, Rayna. "The Pocahontas Perplex: The Image of Indian Women in American Culture." *Massachusetts Review* 16, no. 4 (1975): 698–714. https://doi.org/10.1515/9783110978926.150

Griffiths, Linda, and Maria Campbell. *The Book of Jessica: A Theatrical Transformation*. Coach House Press, 1989.

Haley, Alex. *Roots*. New York: Bantam Books, 1977.

Halfe, Louise Bernice. "Pakak." In *Writing the Circle: Native Women of Western Canada*, edited by Jeanne Perrault and Sylvia Vance, 79–80. Edmonton: NeWest, 1993.

- *Bear Bones and Feathers*. Regina: Coteau Books, 1994.
- *Blue Marrow*. Regina: Coteau Books, 2004 (First published 1998 by McClelland and Stewart).

Harjo, Joy. "I Give You Back." In *She Had Some Horses*. New York: Thunder's Mouth Press Inc, 1983.

Harjo, Joy, and Gloria Bird, eds. *Reinventing the Enemy's Language: Contemporary Native Women's Writings of North America*. New York: W.W. Norton, 1997.

Harlow, Barbara. *Resistance Literature*. New York: Methuen, 1987.

Harrison, Julia D. *Métis: People Between Two Worlds*. Vancouver: Douglas & McIntyre, 1985.

Heath Justice, Daniel. "A Relevant Resonance: Considering the Study of Indigenous National Literatures." In DePasquale et al., 2010, 61–76.

Hermann, Elisabeth. "'Academic Squaws': Some Aspects of Culture Contact in the Literature and Criticism of Paula Gunn Allen and Wendy Rose."

In *Minority Literatures in North America*, edited by Wolfgang Karrer and Hartmut Lutz. Frankfurt/M.: Peter Lang, 1990.

Higgens, Barbara. "God's Man on Earth or First Communion." In *Writing the Circle: Native Women of Western Canada*, edited by Jeanne Perrault and Sylvia Vance, 87–108. Edmonton: NeWest, 1993.

Highway, Tomson. *The Rez Sisters*. Saskatoon: Fifth House Books, 1987.

– *Dry Lips Oughta Move to Kapuskasing*. Saskatoon: Fifth House Books, 1989.

Hildebrandt, Walter. "The Battle of Batoche." In *The Western Métis: Profile of a People*, edited by Patrick C. Douad. Regina: Canadian Plains Research Center, 2007.

Hilger, Michael. *The American Indian in Film*. Metuchen, NJ and London: The Scarecrow Press, 1986.

Hitchcock, Peter. *Dialogics of the Oppressed*. Minneapolis: University of Minnesota Press, 1989.

Hoare, Tony, Chris Levy, and Michael Robinson. "Participatory Action Research in Native Communities: Cultural Opportunities and Legal Implications." *The Canadian Journal of Native Studies* 13, no. 1 (1993): 43–68.

Hodgson, Hodgson, ed. *Seventh Generation: Contemporary Native Writing*. Penticton, BC: Theytus Books, 1999.

Hokowhitu, Brendan, Aileen Moreton-Robinson, Linda Tuhiwai-Smith, Chris Andersen, and S. Larkin, eds. *Routledge Handbook of Critical Indigenous Studies*. London: Routledge, 2020.

Honour, Hugh. *The New Golden Land*. New York: Pantheon Books, 1975.

hooks, bell. *Feminist Theory: From Margin to Center*. Boston: South End Press, 1984.

Hoy, Helen. *How Should I Read These? Native Women Writers in Canada*. Toronto: University of Toronto Press, 2001.

Hubert, Cam. *Dreamspeaker*. HarperCollins Publishers, 1981.

Hulan, Renée, ed. *Native North America: Critical and Cultural Perspectives*. Toronto: ECW Press, 1999.

Hulan, Renée, and Renate Eigenbrod, eds. *Aboriginal Oral Traditions*. Halifax and Winnipeg: Fernwood Publishing, 2008.

Hungry Wolf, Beverly. *The Ways of My Grandmothers*. New York: William Morrow and Company, 1980.

Hunter, Lynette. *Outsider Notes: Feminist Approaches to Nation/State Ideology, Writers/Reads and Publishing*. Vancouver: Talon Books, 1996.

Inuit Tapirisat of Canada. *Negotiating Research Relationships in the North: A Background Paper for a Workshop on Guidelines for Responsible Research*. Yellowknife, NWT, 1993.

Jaenen, Cornelius J. *Friend and Foe: Aspects of French-American Cultural Contact in the 16th and 17th Century*. New York: Columbia University Press, 1976.

Jaine, Linda, and Drew Hayden Taylor, eds. *Voices: Being Native in Canada*. Saskatoon: University of Saskatchewan, Extension Division, 1992.

References 285

Jannetta, Armando E. "Metis Autobiography: The Emergence of a Genre amid Alienation, Resistance and Healing in the Context of Maria Campbell's *Halfbreed* (1973)." *International Journal of Canadian Studies* 12 (1995): 168–81.

– *Ethnopoetics of the Minority Voice: An Introduction to the Politics of Dialogism and Difference in Metis Literature.* Augsburg, Germany: WiBner-Verlag, 2001.

Jeannette Armstrong, ed. *Looking at the Words of Our People: First Nations Analysis of Literature.* Penticton: Theytus Books, 1993.

Jennings, Francis. *Invasion of America: Indians, Colonialism, and the Cant of Conquest.* Chapel Hill: University of North Carolina Press, 1975.

Joe, Rita. *Poems of Rita Joe.* Charlottetown: Ragweed Press, 1978.

– *The Song of Eskasoni: More Poems of Rita Joe.* Charlottetown: Ragweed Press, 1988.

– "I Lost My Talk." In *Native Poetry in Canada: A Contemporary Anthology*, edited by Jeannette C. Armstrong and Lally Grauer. Peterborough: Broadview Press, 2001 (1988).

Johnson, E. Pauline. *Flint and Feather: The Complete Poems of E. Pauline Johnson.* Mass Market Paperbacks, 1972 (1917).

Johnson, Martha. Dené Traditional Knowledge. Excerpt from *Lore, Capturing Traditional Environmental Knowledge.* Ottawa: Dené Cultural Institute / International Development Research Centre, 1992.

Johnston, Basil. *Moose Meat and Wild Rice.* Toronto: McClelland and Stewart, 1978.

– "One Generation from Extinction." In *Native Writers and Canadian Writing: Canadian Literature Special Issue*, edited by W.H. New. Vancouver: University of British Columbia Press, 1990.

Johnston, Patrick. *Native Children and the Child Welfare System.* Toronto: James Lorimer and Co. Publishers, in association with Canadian Council on Social Development, 1983.

Kane, Margo. "Moonlodge." In *An Anthology of Canadian Native Literature in English*, edited by D.D. Moses and T. Goldie, 279–91. Toronto: Oxford University Press, 1992.

Karrer, Wolfgang, and Hartmut Lutz. *Minority Literatures in North America: Contemporary Perspectives.* Toronto: Peter Lang, 1990.

Keeshig-Tobias, Lenore. "Trickster Beyond 1992: Our Relationship." In *Indigena: ContemporaryNative Perspectives*, edited by Gerald McMaster and Lee-Ann Martin, 101–1. Vancouver: Douglas and McIntyre, 1992.

– ed. *Into the Moon.* Toronto: Sisters Vision, 1996.

Kennedy, Jacqueline. "Ft. Qu'Appelle Industrial School." M.A. thesis. Carleton University, 1970.

Kenny, George. *Indians Don't Cry.* Toronto: Chimo Publishing, 1977.

King, Thomas, ed. *All My Relations: An Anthology of Contemporary Canadian Native Fiction.* Toronto: McClelland and Stewart, 1990.

286 References

- "Godzilla vs Post-Colonial." In *New Contexts of Canadian Criticism*, edited by Ajay Heble, D. Palmateer Pennee and J.R. Struthers. Peterborough: Broadview Press, 1997.

Kino-nda-niimi Collective, eds. *The Winter We Danced: Voices from the Past, the Future, and the Idle No More Movement*. Winnipeg: ARP Books, 2014.

Kinsella, W.P. *Dance Me Outside*. Oberon Press, 1977.

Knudtson, Peter, and David Suzuki. *Wisdom of the Elders*. Toronto: Stoddart, 1992.

Kovach, Maggie, Jeannine Carriere, Harpell Montgomery, M.J. Barrett, and Carmen Gilles. *Indigenous Presence: Experiencing and Envisioning Indigenous Knowledges within Selected Postsecondary Sites of Education and Social Work*. University of Saskatchewan, Indigenous Studies Report. Saskatoon, SK, 2015.

Kroetsch, Robert. *Gone Indian*. Nanaimo: Theytus, 1973.

Krotz, Larry. *Urban Indians: The Strangers in Canada's Cities*. Edmonton: Hurtig Publishers, 1980.

Kulchyski, Peter. "What Is Native Studies?" In *Expressions in Canadian Native Studies*, edited by Ron F. Laliberte, P. Settee, J.B. Waldram, R. Innes, B. McDougall, L. McBain, and F.L. Barron. Saskatoon: University Extension Press, 2000.

- *Like the Sound of a Drum*. Winnipeg: University of Manitoba Press, 2005.

Laing, R.D. *The Politics of Experience*. New York: Pantheon Books, 1967.

LaRocque, Emma. *Defeathering the Indian*. Agincourt: Book Society of Canada, 1975.

- "White Control of Indian Education." An unpublished "mini"-thesis towards an M.A. in History, University of Manitoba. Submitted to Dr. Jean Friesen, 1978.

- "Stereotypes: The Walls of an Invisible Prison." *Mandate* 16, no. 4 (1985): 36–7.

- "Conversations on Métis Identity." *Prairie Fire* 7, no. 1 (1986): 19–24.

- "Racism/Sexism and Its Effects on Native Women." In *Public Concerns on Human Rights: A Summary of Briefs*, 30–40. Ottawa: Canadian Human Rights Commission, 1989.

- "The Uniform of the Dispossessed." In *Writing the Circle: Native Women of Western Canada*, edited by Jeanne Perrault and Sylvia Vance, 147–8. Edmonton: NeWest, 1993.

— "Three Conventional Approaches to Native People in Society and Literature." In *Survival of the Imagination: The Mary Donaldson Memorial Lectures*, edited by Brett Balon and Peter Resch, eds. Regina: Coteau Books, 1993a.

- "Re-Examining Culturally Appropriate Models in Criminal Justice Applications." In *Aboriginal and Treaty Rights in Canada: Essays on Law, Equality and Respect for Difference*, edited by Michael Asch. UBC, 1997.

- "Native Writers Resisting Colonizing Practices in Canadian Historiography and Literature." Ph.D. dissertation. University of Manitoba, 1999.

- "Teaching Aboriginal Literature: The Discourse of Margins and Mainstreams." In *Creating Community: A Roundtable on Canadian Aboriginal Literature*, edited by Renate Eigenbrod and J. Episkenew. Penticton, BC and Brandon, MB: Theytus and Bearpaw, 2002.

References

287

- "Opening Address." *Studies in Canadian Literature* 31, no. 1 (2006). https://journals.lib.unb.ca/index.php/SCL/article/view/10193
- *When the Other Is Me: Native Resistance Discourse, 1850–1990*. Winnipeg: University of Manitoba Press, 2010.
- "Mennonites and Me: The Way We Were 'the Other'." *Center for Mennonite Writing Journal* 12, no. 4 (2012). https://mennonitewriting.org/journal/4/6/metis-and-mennonites-way-we-were-other/
Laurence, Margaret. *A Jest of God*. Toronto: McClelland and Stewart, 1966.
- *The Stone Angel*. Toronto: McClelland and Stewart, 1968.
- *The Fire-Dwellers*. Toronto: McClelland and Stewart, 1969.
- *A Bird in the House: Stories by Margaret Laurence*. Toronto: Macmillan, 1970.
- *The Diviners*. Toronto: McClelland and Stewart, 1974.
Lee, Alice. "Child's Play." In *Writing the Circle: Native Women of Western Canada*, edited by Jeanne Perrault and Sylvia Vance, 153. Edmonton: NeWest, 1993.
Leggatt, Judith. "Native Writing, Academic Theory: Post-Colonialism Across the Cultural Divide." In *Is Canada Postcolonial? Unsettling Canadian Literature*, edited by Laura Moss. Waterloo: Wilfrid Laurier University Press, 2003.
Levine, Paul. "Frantz Fanon: The Politics of Skin." In *Divisions*. Toronto: Canadian Broadcasting Corporation, 1975.
Lower, Arthur RM. *Great Britain's Woodyard: British America and the Timber Trade, 1763–1867*. McGill-Queen's Press-MQUP, 1973.
Lundgren, Jodi. "Being a 'Halfbreed': Discourses of Race and Cultural Syncreticity in the Works of Three Metis Women Writers." *Canadian Literature* 144 (1995): 62–77.
Lutz, Hartmut. "Native Literatures in Canada Today: An Introduction." *Zeitschrift der Gesellschaft für Kanada-Studien*, 10, no. 17 (1990): 27–47.
- *Contemporary Challenges: Conversations with Canadian Native Authors*. Saskatoon: Fifth House Publishers, 1991.
- "Confronting Cultural Imperialism: First Nations People Are Combating Continued Cultural Theft." In *Multiculturalism in North America and Europe – Social Practices Literary Visions*, edited by Hans Braun and Wolfgang Kloss. Wissenschaftlicher Verlag Trier, 1995.
- "Not 'Neither-Nor' But 'Both, and More?': A Transnational Reading of Chicana and Métis Autobiografictions by Sanda Cisneros and Howard Adams." In *Native Americans and First Nations: A Transnational Challenge*, edited by Waldemar Zacharasiewicz and Christian Feest, 190–208. Paderborn: Ferdinand Schoningh, 2009.
Lutz, Hartmut, Murray Hamilton, and Donna Heimbecker, eds. *Howard Adams: Otapawy!* Saskatoon: Gabriel Dumont Institute, 2005.
MacDonald, David B. *The Sleeping Giant Awakens: Genocide, Indian Residential Schools, and the Challenge of Conciliation*. Toronto: University of Toronto Press, 2019.

Mandelbaum, David G. *The Plains Cree*, Revised ed. Regina: The Canadian Plains Research Centre, 1978.

Manuel, George, and Michael Posluns. *The Fourth World: An Indian Reality*. New York: The Free Press, 1974.

Maracle, Lee. *Bobbi Lee: Indian Rebel – Struggles of a Native Canadian Woman*. Liberation Support Movement Information Centre, 1975.

– *I Am Woman*. Vancouver: Write-On Press, 1988.

– *Sundogs*. Penticton, BC: Theytus Books, 1992.

– *Ravensong*. Vancouver: Press Gang Publishers, 1993.

– *Bent Box*. Penticton: Theytus Books, 2000.

– *Daughters Are Forever*. Penticton: Theytus Books, 2002.

Maracle, Lee, and Sandra Laronde, eds. *My Home as I Remember*. Toronto: Natural Heritage Books, 2000.

Martens, Tony, Brenda Daily, and Maggie Hodgson. *The Spirit Weeps*, Vol. 123. Edmonton: Nechi Institute, 1988.

Masuzumi, Barney, and Susan Quirk. *Exploring Community-Based Research Concerns for Aboriginal Northerners*. Dene Tracking, 1993

McCullum, Hugh, and Karmel Taylor McCullum. *This Land Is Not for Sale: Canada's Original People and Their Land: A Saga of Neglect, Exploitation, and Conflict*. Anglican Book Centre, 1975.

McDonald, Miriam. Lucassie Arragutainaq, and Zach Novalinga. *Voices from the Bay Traditional Ecological Knowledge of Inuit and Cree in the Hudson Bay Bioregion*. Ottawa: Canadian Arctic Resources Committee and Environ-mental Committee of Municipality of Sanikiluaq, 1997.

McKittrick, Katherine. *Demonic Grounds: Black Women and the Cartographies of Struggle*. Minneapolis: University of Minnesota Press, 2006.

McLeod, John. *Beginning Postcolonialism*. Manchester: Manchester University Press, 2000.

McLeod, Neal. "Coming Home through Stories." In *Addressing Our Words: Aboriginal Perspectives on Aboriginal Literatures*, edited by Armand Garnet Ruffo. Penticton: Theytus Books, 2001.

McMaster, Gerald, and Lee-Ann Martin, eds. *Indigena: Contemporary Native Perspectives*. Toronto and Vancouver: Douglas & McIntyre, 1992.

McNaught, Kenneth. *The Pelican History of Canada*. Penguin Books, 1976.

Mealing, S.R. ed. *The Jesuit Relations and Allied Documents: A Selection, 1632–73*. Toronto: McClelland and Stewart, 1965.

Memmi, Albert. *The Colonizer and the Colonized*. Boston: Beacon Press, 1967.

Mercredi, Duncan. *Spirit of the Wolf: Raise Your Voice*. Winnipeg: Pemmican, 1991.

Métis National Council. 2013. Accessed May 6. www.metisnation.ca/index .php/who-are-themetis.

Michelet, Jules. *History of the French Revolution*. Edited by Gordon Wright. Chicago: University of Chicago Press, 1967.

References

Mildon, Drew. "A Bad Connection: First Nations Oral Histories in the Canadian Courts." In *Aboriginal Oral Traditions*, edited by Renée Hulan and Renate Eigenbrod. Halifax: Fernwood Publishing, 2008.

Minnesota History [B.L.H.]. "Artist as Buffalo Hunter: Paul Kane and the Red River Half-Breeds." (1959): 309–14. Accessed August 7, 2014. http://collections.mnhs.org/MNHistoryMagazine/articles/36/v36i08p309-314.pdf.

Missing Women Commission of Inquiry, 2012. Vol. I–IV. https://missingwomen.library.uvic.ca/index.html%3Fp=30.html

Monkman, Leslie. *A Native Heritage: Images of the Indian in English Canadian Literature*. Toronto: University of Toronto Press, 1981.

Monture-Angus, Patricia. 1995. *Thunder in My Soul: A Mohawk Woman Speaks.* Halifax: Fernwood Press, 1981.

Morrison, R. Bruce, and C. Roderick Wilson, eds. *Native Peoples: The Canadian Experience*. Toronto: McClelland & Stewart, 1995.

– eds. *Native Peoples: The Canadian Experience*, 3rd ed. Oxford: Oxford University Press, 2004.

Morrison, Toni. *Playing in the Dark: Whiteness and the Literary Imagination.* Cambridge: Harvard University Press, 1992.

Morton, Desmond. "Cavalry or Police: Keeping the Peace on Two Adjacent Frontiers, 1870–1900." *Journal of Canadian Studies* 12, no. 2 (1977): 27–37. https://doi.org/10.3138/jcs.12.2.27.

Morton, W.L. "The Canadian Metis." *Beaver* (September 1950): 3–7.

Moses, Daniel David, and Terry Goldie, eds. *An Anthology of Canadian Native Literature*. Toronto: Oxford University Press, 1992.

Mosionier, Beatrice. *In Search of April Raintree*. Winnipeg: Pemmican, 1983.

– *Spirit of the White Bison*. Winnipeg: Pemmican, 1985.

– *In Search of April Raintree: Critical Edition*. Edited by Cheryl Suzack. Winnipeg: Portage and Main, 1999.

– *In the Shadow of Evil*. Penticton, BC: Theytus, 2000.

Mosionier,[1] Beatrice. *Come Walk with Me: A Memoir*. Winnipeg: Portage and Main, 2009.

Mowat, William, and Christine, eds. *Native Peoples in Canadian Literature*. Toronto: Macmillan of Canada, 1975.

Mukherjee, Arun. *Oppositional Aesthetics: Readings from a Hyphenated Space.* Toronto: TSAR, 1994.

Nagler, Mark. *Indians in the City: A Study of the Urbanization of Indians in Toronto*. The Canadian Research Centre for Anthropology. Saint Paul University, 1970.

---

1 Previously known as Beatrice Culleton; see also Culleton. Elaine Coburn – editor's note.

Native Women's Association of Canada. *What Their Stories Tell Us: Research Findings from the Sisters in Spirit Initiative*, 2010. https://nwac.ca/assets-knowledge-centre/2010_What_Their_Stories_Tell_Us_Research_Findings_SIS_Initiative-1.pdf.

New, W.H., ed. *Native Writers and Canadian Writing: Canadian Literature Special Issue*. Vancouver: University of British Columbia Press, 1990.

Nichols, John D. "The Composition Sequence of the First Cree Hymnal." *Essays in Algonquian Bibliography in Honour of V.M. Dechene*, edited by H.C. Wolfart, 1–21. Winnipeg: University of Manitoba Press, 1984.

Oakes, Jill, and Rick Riewe. "Communicating Inuit Perspectives in Research." In *Issues in the North*, Vol. I, edited by Jill Oakes and Rick Riewe. Edmonton: Canadian Circumpolar Institute, 1996.

O'Connor, John E. *The Hollywood Indian*. Trenton: New Jersey State Museum, 1980.

Ontario Native Women's Association. *Breaking Free: A Proposal for Change to Aboriginal Family Violence*. Thunder Bay, 1989.

Ouellette, Grace J.M.W. *The Fourth World: An Indigenous Perspective on Feminism and Aboriginal Women's Activism*. Halifax: Fernwood Publishing, 2002.

Overall, Christine. *A Feminist I: Reflections from Academia*. Peterborough: Broadview Press, 1998.

Owen, Louis. *Mixedblood Messages: Literature, Film, Family, Place*. University of Oklahoma Press, 1998.

Pakes, Fraser J. "Seeing with the Stereotypic Eye: The Visual Image of the Plains Indian." *Native Studies Review* 1, no. 2 (1985): 1–31.

Parker, Gilbert. *Pierre and His People: Tales of the Far North*, 2nd ed. Chicago: Stone and Kimball, 1894.

Patterson, E.P. *The Canadian Indian: A History Since 1500*. Collier MacMillan, 1972.

Paul, Daniel N. *We Were Not the Savages*. Halifax: Nimbus Publishing, 1993.

Payne, Brenda. "*A Really Good Brown Girl*: Marilyn Dumont's Poems of Grief and Celebration." Ruffo, *(Ad)dressing*, 135–42.

Pearce, Roy Harvey. *Savagism and Civilization*, Revised ed. Baltimore: Johns Hopkins University Press, 1965 (1953).

Pelletier, Wilfred. "For Every North American Indian That Begins to Disappear I Also Begin to Disappear." In *The School in the Social Setting: Source Readings*, edited by Al Gorr, 257–71. New York: Educational Publication Company, 1971.

Perrault, Jeanne, and Sylvia Vance. *Writing the Circle: Native Women of Western Canada*. NeWest, 1993.

Perreault, Jeanne. *Writing Selves: Contemporary Feminist Autography*. Minneapolis: University of Minnesota Press, 1995.

– "Memory Alive: An Inquiry into the Uses of Memory in Marilyn Dumont, Jeannette Armstrong, Louise Halfe, and Joy Harjo." In Hulan, 1999, 251–70

Peterson, Jacqueline, and Jennifer S.H. Brown, eds. *The New Peoples: Being and Becoming Métis in North America*. Winnipeg: University of Manitoba Press, 1985.

Petrone, Penny. *Native Literature in Canada: From the Oral Tradition to the Present*. Toronto: Oxford University Press, 1990.

Pocklington, Thomas C. *The Government and Politics of the Alberta Metis Settlements*. Regina: Canadian Plains Research, 1991.

Pratt, Mary Louise. *Imperial Eyes: Travel Writing and Transculturation*. London: Routledge, 1992.

Priest, Lisa. *The Conspiracy of Silence*. Toronto: McClelland and Stewart Ltd, 1989.

Proulx-Turner, Sharron. *What the Auntys Say*. Toronto: McGilligan Books, 2002.

Puxley, Peter. "The Colonial Experience." In *Dené Nation – The Colony Within*, edited by M. Watkins. Toronto: University of Toronto Press, 1977.

Rasporich, Beverly. "Native Women Writing: Tracing the Patterns." *Canadian Ethnic Studies* 28, no. 1 (1996).

Ray, Arthur J. "Reflections on Fur Trade Social History and Métis History in Canada." *American Indian Culture and Research Journal* 6, no. 2 (1982): 91–107. https://doi.org/10.17953/aicr.06.2.925273427q34p671

Ray, Arthur, and Donald Freeman. *Give Us Good Measure*. Toronto: University of Toronto Press, 1977.

Razack, Sherene. *Looking White People in the Eye: Gender, Race and Culture in Courtrooms and Classrooms*. Toronto: University of Toronto Press, 1998.

– ed. *Race, Space and the Law: Unmapping a White Settler Society*. Toronto: Between the Lines, 2002.

Redbird, Duke. *We Are Métis: A Métis View of the Development of a Native Canadian People*. Toronto: Ontario Ministry of Culture and Recreation and Willowdale: Ontario Metis and Non Status Indian Association, 1980.

Reeves, W., and Jim Frideres. "Government Policy and Indian Urbanization: The Alberta case." *Canadian Public Policy/Analyse de Politiques* (1981): 584–95. https://doi.org/10.2307/3549488

Reimer, Gwen. "'Community-Based' as a Culturally Appropriate Concept of Development: A Case Study from Pangnirtung, NT." *Culture* 13, no. 2 (1993): 67–74. https://doi.org/10.7202/1083122ar

Rich, Adrienne. *On Lies, Secrets, and Silence: Selected Prose 1966–1978*. W.W. Norton & Company, 1980.

Richardson, Boyce, ed. *Drumbeat: Anger and Renewal in Indian Country*. Toronto: Summerhill Press, Assembly of First Nations, 1989.

Richardson, Major John. *Wacousta*. Toronto: McClelland and Stewart, with an Introduction by Carl F. Klinck, 1967 (1832).

Ridington, Robin. "Technology, World View, and Adaptive Strategy in a Northern Hunting Society." *Canadian Review of Sociology & Anthropology* 19, no. 4 (1982): 469–80. https://doi.org/10.1111/j.1755-618x.1982.tb00875.x

292 References

- "Cultures in Conflict: Problems in Discourse." In *Native Writers and Canadian Writing: Canadian Literature Special Issue*, edited by W.H. New. Vancouver: University of British Columbia Press, 1990.

Robinson, Eden. *Monkey Beach*. Toronto: Alfred A. Knopf, 2000.

Rockhill, Kathleen. "The Chaos of Subjectivity in the Ordered Halls of Academe." *Canadian Woman Studies* 8, no. 4 (1987).

Rogin, Michael Paul. *Fathers and Children*. New York: Knopf, 1975.

Roscoe, William. *Changing Ones: Third and Fourth Genders in Native North America*. New York: St. Martin's Press, 1998.

Royal Canadian Mountain Police. Missing and Murdered Aboriginal Women: A National Operational Overview. Ottawa, 2014. Available here: https://www.rcmp-grc.gc.ca/en/missing-and-murdered-aboriginal-women-national-operational-overview.

- Missing and Murdered Aboriginal Women: 2015 Update to the National Operational Overview. Ottawa, 2015. Available here: https://www.rcmp-grc.gc.ca/en/missing-and-murdered-aboriginal-women-2015-update-national-operational-overview.

Royal Commission on Aboriginal Peoples. "Métis Perspectives." Vol. 4, Chapter 5 (1996): 198–386.

Ruffo, Armand Garnet. "Why Native Literature?" In Hulan, 1999, 109–21.

- ed. *(Ad)dressing Our Words: Aboriginal Perspectives on Aboriginal Literatures*. Penticton: Theytus Books, 2001.

- "Remembering and (Re)Constructing Community: Considering Maria Campbell's *Halfbreed* and Gregory Scofield's *Thunder Through My Veins: Memories of a Métis Childhood*." In *Canada and Decolonization: Images of New Society*, 77–87. Japan: Centre for Interdisciplinary Studies of Science and Culture, Kyoritsu Women's University, 2003.

Ryan, Joan, and Michael Robinson. "Community Participatory Research: Two Views from Arctic Institute Practitioners." *Practising Anthropology* 18, no. 4 (1996): 7–11. https://doi.org/10.17730/praa.18.4.8165n7kw19187181.

Ryan, William. *Blaming the Victim*. Vintage, 1976.

Ryga, George. *Indian*. Vancouver: Talon Books Ltd, 1970.

Said, Edward. *Orientalism*. New York: Vintage Books, 1979.

- *The World, the Text, and the Critic*. Cambridge: Harvard University, 1983.

- *Culture and Imperialism*. New York: First Vintage Books, 1994.

- *Representations of the Intellectual*. New York: Vintage Books, 1996.

Saum, Lewis O. *The Fur Trade and the Indian*. Seattle: The University of Washington Press, 1965.

Sawchuk, Joe. *The Métis of Manitoba: Reformulation of an Ethnic Identity*. Toronto: Peter Martin Associates Limited, 1978.

Sawchuk, Joe, Patricia Sawchuk, Terry Ferguson, and Métis Association of Alberta. *Métis Land Rights in Alberta: A Political History*. Edomonton: Métis Association of Alberta, 1981.

References

Schick, Carol. "Keeping the Ivory Tower White: Discourses of Racial Domination." In *Race, Space, and the Law: Unmapping a White Settler Society*, edited by S. Razack. Toronto: Between the Lines, 2002.

Schick, Carol, and Verna St. Denis. "Troubling National Discourses for Anti-Racist Education." *Journal of Canadian Education* 28, no. 3 (2005): 296–319.

Schwarz, Herbert T. *Tales from the Smokehouse*. Edmonton: Hurtig Press, 1972.

Scofield, Gregory. *The Gathering: Stones for the Medicine Wheel*. Vancouver: Polestar, 1993.

– *Thunder Through My Veins: Memories of a Métis Childhood*. Toronto: HarperCollins, 1999.

– *I Knew Two Métis Women: The Lives of Dorothy Scofield and Georgina Houle Young*. Vancouver: Polestar, 1999a.

– *Singing Home the Bones*. Vancouver: Raincoast, 2005

– *Louis: The Heretic Poems*. Gibsons, BC: Nightwood, 2011.

Scudler, June. "'The Song I am Singing': Gegory Scofield's Interweavings of Métis, Gay, and Jewish Selfhoods." *Studies in Canadian Literature* 31, no. 1 (2006): 129–45

Sealey, Bruce D., and Antoine S. Lussier. *The Métis: Canada's Forgotten People*. Winnipeg: Manitoba Métis Federation Press, 1975.

Sheehy, Gail. *Passages: Predictable Crises of Adult Life*. New York: Bantam Books Inc, 1977.

Shilling, Arthur. *The Ojibway Dream*. Montreal: Tundra Books, 1986.

Shkilnyk, Anastasia M. *A Poison Stronger Than Love: The Destruction of an Ojibwa Community*. New Haven and London: Yale University Press, 1985.

Simpson, Leanne. "The Construction of Traditional Ecological Knowledge: Issues, Implications and Insights." Ph.D. dissertation, University of Manitoba, 1999.

Sinclair, Niigonwedom J. "Resistance and Protest in Indigenous Literatures." *Canadian Dimension* 44, no. 2 (2010): 25–8.

Sinclair, Niigonwedom James. "Tending to Ourselves: Hybridity and Native Literary Criticism." In DePasquale et al., 2010, 239–58.

Sinclair, Niigaanwewidam James, and Warren Cariou, eds. *Manitowapow: Aboriginal Writings from the Land of Water*. Winnipeg: Highwater Press, 2011.

Sing, Pamela V. "Intersections of Memory, Ancestral Language, and Imagination; or, the Textual Production of Michif Voices as Cultural Weaponry." *Studies in Canadian Literature* 31, no. 1 (2006): 95–115.

Sioui, Georges. *For an American Autohistory*. Toronto: McGill-Queens, 1992.

Slipperjack, Ruby. *Honour the Sun*. Pemmican Publications, 1987.

– *Silent Words*. Saskatoon: Fifth House Publishers, 1992.

– *Weesquachak and the Lost Ones*. Penticton: Theytus Books, 2000.

– *Little Voice*. Regina: Coteau Books, 2001.

– *Dog Tracks*. Saskatoon: Fifth House, 2008.

Smith, Graham Hingangaroa. "Maori Education: Revolution and Transformative Action." *Canadian Journal of Native Education* 24, no. 1 (2000): 57–72.

Smith, Linda Tuhiwai. *Decolonizing Methodologies: Research and Indigenous Peoples*. London: Zed Books, 1999.

Speck, Dara Culhane. *An Error of Judgement: The Politics of Medical Care in an Indian/White Community*. Vancouver: Talonbooks.

Sprague, Douglas N. "Government Lawlessness in the Administration of Manitoba Land Claims, 1876–1887." *Manitoba Law Journal* 10 (1980): 415–41.

– *Canada and the Métis, 1869–1885*. Waterloo: Wilfried Laurier University Press, 1988.

Stacey-Moore, Gail. "In Our Own Voice: Aboriginal Women Demand Justice." *Herizons*, 6, no. 4 (1993): 21–3.

Stalker, Jacqueline, and Susan Prentice, eds. *The Illusion of Inclusion: Women in Post-Secondary Education*. Halifax: Fernwood Publishing, 1998.

Standing Bear, Luther. *Land of the Spotted Eagle*. Lincoln: University of Nebraska Press, 1978 (1933).

Stanley, George F. *The Birth of Western Canada: A History of the Riel Rebellions*. Toronto, London and New York: Longmans, Green, 1936.

Starblanket, Tamara. *Suffer the Little Children: Genocide, Indigenous Nations and the Canadian State*. Atlanta: Clarity Press, 2018.

Steinbeck, John. *Travels with Charley in Search of America*. New York: The Viking Press, 1962.

Sterling, Shirley. *My Name Is Seepeetza*. Toronto: House of Anansi Press, 1992.

Stevenson, M. "In Search of Inuit Ecological Knowledge: A Protocol for Its Collection, Interpretation and Use." Paper for Dept. of Renewable Resources, GNWT, Qikiqtaaluk Wildlife Board, and Parks Canada, 1992.

Stevenson, Winona, et al. "Peekiskwetan." *Commentaries/Commentaires Canadian Journal of Women and the Law/Revue Femmes et Droit* 6 (1993).

Stocking Jr., George W. "Franz Boas and the Culture Concept in Historical Perspective 1." *American Anthropologist* 68, no. 4 (1966): 867–82. https://doi.org/10.1525/aa.1966.68.4.02a00010.

Stoler, Laura A. *Carnal Knowledge and Imperial Power: Race and the Intimate in Colonial Rule*. Berkeley: University of California Press, 2002.

Stump, Sarain. *There Is My People Sleeping*. Sidney, BC: Grays, 1970.

Sullivan, Harry Stack. *The Interpersonal Theory of Psychiatry*. London: Routledge, 1955.

Taylor, Drew H. "Pretty Like a White Boy: The Adventures of a Blue-Eyed Ojibway." In *An Anthology of Canadian Native Literature in English*, edited by D.D. Moses and T. Goldie, 327–30. Toronto: Oxford University Press Moses and Goldie, 1992.

Thwaites, Reuben Gold, ed. The Jesuit Relations and Allied Documents: Travels and Explorations of the Jesuit Missionaries in New France, 1610–1791. The Original French, Latin, and Italian Texts, with English Translations and Notes. 73 volumes. Cleveland: Burrows Brothers, 1896–1901.

References 295

Tilton, Robert S. *Pocahontas: The Evolution of an American Narrative*. Cambridge: Cambridge University Press, 1994.

Tully, James, Michael Asch, and John Borrows, eds. *Resurgence and Reconciliation: Indigenous-Settler Relations and Earth Teachings*. Toronto: University of Toronto Press, 2018.

Underhill, Ruth Murray. *Red Man's America: A History of Indians in the United States*. Chicago: University of Chicago Press, 1971.

Ursmiani, Renate, ed. *Kelusultiek: Original Women's Voices of Atlantic Canada*. Halifax: Institute for the Study of Women, Mount St. Vincent University, 1996.

Valaskakis, Gail Guthrie. *Indian Country: Essays on Contemporary Native Culture*. Waterloo: Wilfrid Laurier University Press, 2005.

Van Kirk, Sylvia. *'Many Tender Ties': Women in Fur Trade Society 1670–1870*. Norman: University of Oklahoma Press, 1983 (1980).

Vermette, Katherena. *North End Love Songs*. Winnipeg: The Muses Company, 2012.

Wagamese, Richard. *Quality of Light*. Toronto: Doubleday Canada, 1997.

Walker, Alice. *The Color Purple*. New York: Pocket Books, 1982.

Walker, James St. G. "The Indian in Canadian Historical Writing." *Canadian Historical Association Report* 22 (1971): 21–51. https://doi.org/10.7202/030455ar.

Walter, Maggie, and Chris Andersen. *Indigenous Statistics: A Quantitative Research Methodology*. Walnut Creek: Left Coast Press, 2013.

Warrior, Emma Lee. "Compatriots." In *An Anthology of Canadian Native Literature in English*, edited by D.D. Moses and T. Goldie, 160–7. Toronto: Oxford University Press, 1992.

Warry, Wayne. "Doing Unto Others: Applied Anthropology, Collaborative Research and Native Self-Determination." *Culture* 10, no. 1 (1990): 61–73. https://doi.org/10.7202/1080935ar

Watkins, Mel, ed. *Dene Nation: The Colony Within*. Toronto: University of Toronto Press, 1977.

Waubageshig, ed. *The Only Good Indian: Essays by Canadian Indians*. New Press, 1970.

Weatherford, Jack. *Indian Givers: How the Indians of the Americas Trans formed the World*. New York: Ballantine Books, 1988.

– *The Indians Enriched America*. New York: Fawcett Books, 1991.

Weaver, Jace, Craig S. Womack, and Robert Warrior. *American Indian Literary Nationalism*. Albuquerque: University of New Mexico Press, 2006.

Weinstein, John. *Quiet Revolution West: The Rebirth of Métis Nationalism*. Saskatoon: Fifth House, 2007.

Wiebe, Rudy. *Peace Shall Destroy Many*. Toronto: McClelland and Stewart, 1962.

– *The Scorched-Wood People: A Novel*. Toronto: McClelland and Stewart, 1977.

Williams, David. *The Burning Wood*. Toronto: Anansi, 1975.

Williamson, Janice. *Sounding Differences: Conversations with Seventeen Canadian Women Writers*. Toronto: University of Toronto Press, 1993.

Willis, Jane. *Geneish: An Indian Girlhood*. Toronto: New Press, 1973.

Wilson, Betty. *André Tom Macgregor*. Toronto: Macmillan of Canada, 1976.

Woodcock, George. "Prairie Writers and the Metis: Rudy Wiebe and Margaret Laurence." *Canadian Ethnic Studies* 14, no. 1 (1982): 9–22.

Wright, Ronald. *Stolen Continents: The "New World" Through Indian Eyes*. Toronto: Penguin Books, 1993.

X, Malcolm. *Malcolm X Speaks: Selected Speeches and Statements*, ed. George Breitman. New York: Grove Press, 1965.

York, Geoffrey. *The Dispossessed: Life and Death in Native Canada*. 1989. London: Vintage, 1990 (1989).

Young, Robert C. *Colonial Desire: Hybridity in Theory, Culture and Race*. New York: Routledge, 1995.

Young, Robert J.C. *Postcolonialism: A Very Short Introduction*. Oxford: Oxford University Press, 2003.

Young, T.K. *Health Care and Cultural Change*. Toronto, ON. University of Toronto Press, 1988.

Index

Acoose, Janice: critical appraisal of Maria Campbell's *Halfbreed*, 245; on writing in English, 187

Adams, Howard: allegations of bias against, 195n15; *Prison of Grass*, 71–2, 188, 239, 266; the White ideal and internalization of racism, 49, 71–2, 128, 188, 239, 266

Adams, John Quincy, 129

Ama (mother): Emma LaRocque's, xxvin2; cultural heritage from, 263; death, 53; knowledge and skills, 3, 58–9; depiction of knowledge as prehistoric, 58–9; discipline, 145; dissonance in Hollywood portrayal of "Indians" and, 123; Emma LaRocque's separation from, 50–1; experiences of racism, xxix, 252; gendered division of labour and, 49, 147; patriarchy and, 146; poverty, 146; storytelling, 4, 138, 262. *See also* family

Apeetowgusanuk. See Métis

appropriation: cultural, 31–3, 87n15, 130, 163, 171; of English by Indigenous people, 184; of Métis identity, 90n2, 107, 159. *See also* Métis identity

Armstrong, Jeannette: *Looking at the Words of Our People*, 192–3; on poetry, 168, 181; *Slash*, 166–7, 174; *Whispering in the Shadows*, 168

Arnott, Joanne, 242

assimilation policies: cultural hierarchy and, 7; difference from adaptation, 48–9, 103, 112, 114, 131, 133, 176, 226; English and, 33; negative socioeconomic consequences of, 20; public school system and, 33, 49, 102, 270; residential school system and, xxiii, 51; segregation as contradiction to, 256. *See also* English

authenticity: in Maria Campbell's *Halfbreed*, 12–13; White demands for, 27, 28, 30–1, 130–1. *See also* stereotypes

Bapa (father): domestic labour and, 147; experience of healing tent, 58; land-based and wage labour, 49–50, 100–1, 144; relationship to land, 100, 144, 208–9; relationship to public school, 3–4, 48–50, 186, 252–3; storytelling, 4, 48. *See also* family

298   Index

bias: accusations of Indigenous, 22, 25, 26, 84–5, 118, 194–5, 199, 271; gender, 146, 152; in the justice system, 76, 128; urban-centric, 143, 176; in Western scholarship, 16, 58, 84–6, 162, 164, 169, 198–9. *See also* ethnocentrism

Bill C-31. *See Indian Act*

Blaut, J.M.: *The Colonizer's Model of the World*, 171, 216–17, 247; tradition, 218n7

Bouvier, Rita, 242–3

Brébeuf, Jean de, 191

Buffalo Bill. *See* Wild West Show

Campbell, Maria: *The Book of Jessica*, 239; *Halfbreed*, 12–13, 103, 165, 173–4, 207, 238–9; influence on Emma LaRocque, 12–13; literary criticism about, 245; *Stories of the Road Allowance People*, 174, 239

Cardinal, Harold: influence on Emma LaRocque, 55–6, 228, 256; *The Rebirth of Canada's Indians*, 269; *The Unjust Society*, 55–6, 191–2, 228, 238, 256

Cariou, Warren, 243

Catholicism. *See* Christianity, priests

childhood: disease and, 48, 53–4, 145; -Emma LaRocque's – Catholicism and, 48, 53; English literacy, 261–3; first experience at school, 3–4; flexible gender roles during, 152; gender taboos during, 146; growing up Métis, xxix, 48–55, 112–13; living off the land, 49, 214; Mennonites and, 56; poverty and, 3–4, 145; racism in Town, 52–5; separation from family during, 50–1, 55; storytelling, 138, 186, 261; violence, 48, 53. *See also* schooling

Christianity: Catechism at school, 254; cultural hierarchy and, 6, 15, 17; elements in Métis religion, 53, 103, 106, 262, 146; Martyr's shrine, 201–2; missionary work, 24, 70; patriarchy and, xxxii, 70, 151. *See also* priests

civ/sav dichotomy: dehumanization and, 172, 266–7; fictional Métis as "mixed" representatives of, 10–11; in Flanagan, Tom's *First Nations, Second Thoughts*, 203; in history books, 6–9, 14–17, 123, 162, 170, 171n9, 191; in Hollywood movies, 16; terra nullius claims and, 219, 267; Wild West and, 123. *See also* cowboys and Indians; ethnocentrism; Hollywood movies

Clutesi, George: on avoiding documentation, 185–7

colonialism: gendered experiences of, 153; justification for, 203; lived experience of, 251–8, 267; modernization as a form of, 102, 217; patriarchy and, 70–1, 153; as progress, 217. *See also* civ/sav dichotomy

Connor, Ralph (also known as Charles William Gordon), 9

contrapuntal reading, 198; of Canadian history, 267–8; Emma LaRocque's distinct use of. *See also* Said, Edward

Cook-Lynn, Elizabeth, 209n7

cowboys and Indians, 16, 30, 32, 121–35; Emma LaRocque's childhood experience of, 54, 122–3, 261–2; as hate literature, 32, 121–35. *See also* Hollywood movies

Cree language: Emma LaRocque's mother tongue, 4, 28, 29, 33, 52, 54, 63, 94n6, 100, 122, 138, 161, 201,

212–14, 248–9, 261–3, 272; Greg
Scofield relationship to, 241; Métis
people and, 24, 98–9, 100–1, 103,
106, 122, 143–6, 159, 161, 233, 265–6;
no standard English spelling
of, 28; poets, 188, 196, 243, 249;
scholarly inquiry and, 187, 194,
196, 271; as sign of authenticity, 27;
suppression in public school, 4, 33,
252, 270; syllabics, 233, 262; voice,
196, 271. *See also* Métis, voice

Culleton, Beatrice: *In Search of April
Raintree*, 25–6, 166, 239–40; *Spirit of
the White Bison*, 25, 166

Defeathering the Indian, 57, 182–3,
267; Armando Ruffo's encounter
with, vii; excerpt, "A Personal
Lesson on Poverty from", 3–5

Dickason, Olive: *Canada's First
Nations*, 191; dehumanization of
Indigenous peoples, 127; Métis
identity and mixed ancestry, 106

dispossession, xxvi–viii, 8, 20, 51, 56,
59n9, 70, 83, 95–7, 101–4, 165, 177,
210, 213, 256, 258; consequences
for Emma LaRocque's family,
146; depiction in Graham Green's
novel *Clearcut*, 125; legitimized by
nomad stereotype, 128–9, 208, 219;
schooling as, 144. *See also* scrip

Dumont, Gabriel: exile, 232; literary
representation of, 11, 12; Maria
Campbell as descendant of, 238;
writing in Michif, 234

Dumont, Marilyn: *A Really Good
Brown Girl*, 241–2, 248; (poem)
"not just a platform for my dance"
211; (short story) "The Gift" 207–8

education. *See* public schools;
residential schools

English: Emma LaRocque's
relationship to, 28, 29, 33,
52, 54, 63, 249, 261–3; family
relationship to, 52, 54, 59, 249n16,
252; Indigenous contributions
to literature, 26, 137, 178, 239,
269, 271; Indigenous dialectical
relationship to, 28, 33–4, 48n2,
116, 138, 184, 186–8, 221; Métis in
literature, 6–13; Nelson, George's
problematic translations into, 18;
political nature of, 85–6. *See also*
assimilation; childhood
ethnocentrism, 6–7, 14–18, 58.
See also civ / sav dichotomy

family: disease, 145; -Emma
LaRocque's -xxviin2; gender
differences in, 146–7; land-based
living, 3–4, 104, 112, 144n4; pain
at dehumanization, 180, 200;
public school and relationship
to, 3–4, 48–50, 153, 186, 201, 211,
252–4; storytelling, 4, 103, 122, 178,
250, 261–2; violence suffered by
women in, 61, 146. *See also Ama*
(mother), *Bapa* (father), childhood,
public school

feminism, 139–57, 270; definition of,
142–3; negative reactions to, 143.
See also gender, sexism

Flanagan, Tom, 97n8, 203

Forer, Mort, 10–11

gender: "balance" 141; colonial roles
and, 84n8, 142, 150–3, 165, 174;
in Indigenous communities, 146,
153, 154, 156, 163; Métis divisions
of labour and, 50, 50n4, 152, 174;
taboos and, 146. *See also* feminism;
stereotypes

genocide, xxiv; intellectual, 226

300 Index

George, Chief Dan, 47
Green, Joyce: critique of Flanagan, Tom, 203; on Indigenous feminism, 88, 139–40; on Native Studies, 218; on the Western canon, 215

Harper, John Joseph "J.J", 60
hate literature, xxxiii, 17, 20, 31–2, 85, 85n10
heterosexism: traditionalism and, 150, 152, 155
history and historians: denial of Canadian racism and, 22, 73–4, 155; Indigenous history missing or distorted, 7–8, 14–18, 19–20, 29, 31, 33, 58, 60, 82, 84, 115, 170–1, 182, 217, 234, 256, 270; political nature of, 86, 118, 145, 164, 197–8, 217–18. *See also* civ/sav dichotomy; hate literature; Vanishing Indian, stereotypes
Hollywood films: *Billyjack*, 209; *Clearcut*, 125; *Legend of the Falls*, 124–5; *Pocahontas*, 84, 125; racism in, 16, 32, 54, 60, 124–8, 202, 219, 220n10. *See also* cowboys and Indians, stereotypes
hooks, bell, 142

Idle No More, xxiii
Ignoble Savage, 122, 128–34, 188. *See also* Noble Savage, stereotypes
Indian Act (1876), xxvin1, 95–7, 165; amendment in, 1880, xxii; Bill C-31, 97, 235n6; Métis exclusion from, xxv, 96, 99, 159–60, 161, 165; residential schools and, 50n5, 213n3, 235n6; sexism in, 88, 96, 143
Indian Princess, 63, 88, 132, 165. *See also* Pocahontas, stereotype

Indigenous literature (Native literature), 23–37; contemporary Métis, 231–50; diversity of, 35, 87; Emma LaRocque's experience of and importance to, viii, 137; as expression of cultural continuity, 170–80; feminist, 149; flourishing of, 227–8; ghettoization of, 26, 27; literary criticism of, 87, 110, 137–8; power politics in, 24–5; as protest literature, 25–6; relationship to English, 28, 33; as resistance literature, 183–200, 224, 268; voice in, 29, 34, 193–204; White audiences, 24–7, 30; by women, 36–7, 86–7, 158, 164–81. *See also* appropriation, oral tradition, voice
Indigenous studies (Native studies): challenges from Indigenous and White students in, 118, 149; charges of bias against, 83–4, 227, 271; community ideological and political control over, 115–17, 149, 228–9, 272; contributions to challenging racism and stereotypes, 59, 217; diversity within and interdisciplinary nature of, 221–2, 268; Emma LaRocque developing and teaching in, 57, 58, 83, 137, 193, 214–15, 222, 267, 271; ethical impulse in, 212, 217–18, 221–2; foregrounding Indigenous knowledges, 115, 215–16, 269; as form of ghettoization, 26, 115, 119; stereotypes in, 118; traditional ecological knowledge and, 115–17; universities and, 119, 218, 271. *See also* bias – accusations of Indigenous, resistance writing
Indigenous writers. *See* Indigenous literature

Index

Jannetta, Armando (E. Armando), 244–5

Johnson, Pauline: absence from school curriculum, 252; *Flint and Feather*, 165; Indian princess persona, 132

Keeshig-Tobias, Lenore: on cultural appropriation, 32; (poem) "Trickster Beyond, 1992: Our Relationship", 178

King, Thomas, 223

Kulchyski, Peter: ethical impulse, 212, 222; literacy, 184n3; Native Studies and, 215–16

land: central to decolonization, 190; city life and, 180; as home, 205–11, 265–6; Jeanette Armstrong's depiction of, 168; knowledge based in, 109–20, 186–7, 215–16; Maria Campbell's depiction of, 173–4; Métis legal claims, 105, 107–8, 128, 160, 210, 213; Métis life based on, 47n1, 48–9, 58, 59n9, 85, 100–1, 104, 122, 138, 141, 143, 159, 162–3, 173–6, 205–11; research on occupied Indigenous, 197; Ruby Slipperjack's depiction of, 175. *See also* dispossession, scrip, traditional ecological knowledge

Laurence, Margaret: Métis representation in *The Diviners*, 12, 206, 209

Longfellow, Henry Wadsworth: Emma LaRocque's childhood encounter with Hiawatha, 48, 129; Hiawatha as "authentic" Indian, xxxv, 130, 131; *The Song of Hiawatha*, 262. *See also* stereotypes

MacDonald, Johan A.: assimilationist attitudes to Métis, 236–7

Mandelbaum, David G. 58

Manitoba Act: Métis dispossession, rights and, 104, 107, 232, 266

Maracle, Lee: *Bobbi Lee: Indian Rebel – Struggles of a Native Canadian Woman*, 166; *Daughters are Forever*, 179; *I am Woman*, 192; *Ravensong*, 177–8

media: failures to report on anti-Indigenous racism, 19–22, 256–7; Indigenous people missing or distorted, 31–2, 59, 73, 105, 123–4, 162, 170–1, 188, 222, 224, 117, 246n12; media attention to *Defeathering the Indian*, 57. *See also* Hollywood movies; stereotypes

Memmi, Albert, 85n2; on the colonized and colonizer, 27, 225; on internalized racism, xxxiii; on literacy, 184–5

Métis National Council: definition of Métis people, 107; distinguish Métis from "mixed" métis persons, 91, 235

Métis: *Apeetowgusanuk* ("half-sons"), 144, 146, 161; Canadian Constitution (1982) recognition of, 104; denial of distinct peoplehood, 89n1, 95–7, 248; difference from métis of "mixed" ancestry, 91–2, 106; Halfbreed, relationship to, 89–95; identity, 89–108; literature, 205–11, 231–50; *Nehiyawewak* ("Cree speaking people"), 33, 159, 196, 249; *Otehpayimsuak* ("the independent and self-reliant ones" or "the people who own themselves"), 89–108, 161; *Sagaweenuak* ("bush people"), 100, 102, 104. *See also* Gabriel Dumont, Métis National Council, Red River Resistance, Louis Riel,

302   Index

Road Allowance people, Royal
Commission on Aboriginal
Peoples, stereotypes
Michif: diversity of, 106; Emma
LaRocque and family's
relationship to, 100, 143, 214,
248–9, 261–3; in Maria Campbell's
writing, 239; in Rita Bouvier's
writing, 243; spoken by Métis
people, 93–4, 98–9, 103, 143, 233–4;
suppression of, 252; written,
233n2, 234. *See also* Métis
Missing and Murdered Indigenous
Women and Girls Inquiry, xxiv, 270
Mosionier, Beatrice Culleton. *See*
Beatrice Culleton
mother. *See Ama*

native literature. *See* Indigenous
literature
native studies. *See* Indigenous
studies
Nelson, George, 14–18
Noble Savage, 15, 124, 125, 128–34,
188. *See also* Hollywood movies;
Ignoble Savage; stereotypes

objectivity: Hollywood films
mistaken for, 124–5; in
scholarship, 15, 28, 29, 197–8, 216,
271; Western scholarly claims to,
22, 29, 83–4, 84n9, 86n14, 115, 118,
195, 197, 203, 216, 271. *See also*
bias, Hollywood films
Obomsawin, Alanis: Indigenous
voice in film, 34, 200
oral tradition: denigration and
suppression of, 23–4, 186; Emma
LaRocque's experience of, 29, 145,
198, 205, 249, 261–3; Indigenous
knowledges and, 23–4, 109–10,
112, 138, 164, 171, 233, 262; written

expression, knowledge and, 28,
33, 35, 85, 161, 171, 184–7, 198n18,
239, 262, 271
Osborne, Betty Helen, 60
Otehpayimsuak people. *See* Métis

Parker, Gilbert, 10
Pochahontas, 88, 125; stereotype
in Disney film, 84, 125. *See also*
Indian Princess, stereotypes
poverty, 228n13, 269; colonialization as
cause of, 55–6, 104, 139; depicted by
Howard Adams, 239; depicted by
Lee Maracle, 166, 167; depicted
by Greg Scofield, 240; depicted by
Maria Campbell, 165, 238; Emma
LaRocque and family experience of,
3–5, 144–8, 266–7; Métis experience
of, 213; violence against Indigenous
women and, 76
priests, 36; control in Métis
communities, 53, 56; sexual abuse
and, 26, 53, 61. *See also* Christianity
Proulx-Turner, Sharron, 242
public school: Beatrice Culleton's
depiction of, 240; - Emma
LaRocque's experience of -
alienation from family and culture
because of, 3–4, 48, 54–5, 99, 100–1,
144–5, 174, 186, 213–14, 251–2, 255;
erasure of Indigenous knowledges
and languages in, 24, 33; failures
to teach Indigenous children in,
144–5, 153, 184n4, 213–14; kind
teacher in, 214, 254; land based
life and, 49–50, 52, 100–1; Métis
in, 50, 50n5; racism in, 3–4, 49,
50–1, 54, 56, 122–3, 201–3, 252–3,
266; racism in curriculum and
textbooks, 20, 54, 122–3, 170–1,
201; stereotypes in curriculum,
131, 170–1, 182, 261–2, 266;

survivor, 270; violence in, 213, 252, 254, 270. *See also* childhood, civ/sav dichotomy, stereotypes

racism, 19–22, 71–3, 83, 126; internalized, 128, 155, 188, 195, 202–3, 239, 248, 251, 255–8, 266, 271. *See also* civ/sav dichotomy, Hollywood films, Howard Adams -White ideal, public school, stereotypes
reconciliation, 257, 258, 268. *See also* Truth and Reconciliation
Red River Resistance, xxvi, 7–8, 95, 239, 265. *See also* Gabriel Dumont, Métis, Louis Riel
re-settler (also resettler), 189, 195, 202, 217–18, 236–7; definition of, 220–2
residential schools, 24, 36, 51, 101, 112, 151, 166, 167, 177, 270; Métis exempt from, 50n5, 99, 100, 213, 249n16, 254
resistance writing, 85, 86, 138, 164, 164n5, 165, 177, 212–30. *See also* voice
Riel, Louis: absence from curriculum, 252; depicted by Maria Campbell, 238–9; depicted by Beatrice Culleton, 240; depicted by Greg Scofield, 241; depicted by Rudy Wiebe, 11–12; execution of, 232; as leader and symbol of Métis resistance, xxvi, 7–8, 90–1, 94–5, 100, 135, 205–6; urbanized, 98; writings of, 189, 234, 245, 250. *See also* Red River Resistance
Road Allowance people, xxvii–iii, 98, 99, 165, 208, 210, 237; *Stories of the Road Allowance People*, 174, 239. *See also* Maria Campbell, Métis
Robinson, Eden, 178

romanticization: of colonialism, 8, 30; in Indigenous communities and literature, xxiv–v, 30, 35, 199; of the land, xxxiv, 175; of the Métis, 11, 90, 206, 233, 245; misleading, of Indigenous peoples, xxvii, xxix, 11, 113, 125, 129–35, 152–3, 162, 219n8, 224. *See also* Indian Princess, Noble Savage, Vanishing Indian, stereotypes
Royal Commission on Aboriginal Peoples (1991–6): definition of Métis in, 89, 91, 92, 107; Emma LaRocque's contribution to, 69–77; on Métis constitutional rights, 96n7, 104, 105, 213n4, 237n9; on Métis cultural loss, 103, 104; on Métis diversity, 91, 106, 160n3; on Métis population numbers, 104n13; on Métis self-determination, 99; on Michif, 94n6; on oral traditions, 185

Said, Edward, 197–8; contrapuntal reading and, xxivn5; *Orientalism*, 197; on the master narrative, 225; on the role of the intellectual, 200, 226–7, 229, 230, 273; *The World, The Text, and the Critic*, 200. *See also* contrapuntal reading
Scofield, Greg: *The Gathering: Stories for the Medicine Wheel*, 240; *I Knew Two Métis Women*, 241; *Louis: The Heretic Poems*, 241; *Singing Home the Bones*, 241; *Thunder Through My Veins*, 208, 240–1
scrip, 8n1, 91, 91n4, 97–100, 144–6, 165, 210, 236–7; Half-Breed Scrip Commission, 132. *See also* dispossession
settlers. *See* re-settler

304 Index

sexism, 57, 60, 147n6, 149; blamed on Indigenous cultures, 74; in the English language, 28; exacerbated under colonialism, 83, 83n3, 88, 227; feminism challenging, 143, 153; feminist as struggle to end, 142; in Indigenous communities, 71–3, 83n3, 88, 88n17; against Indigenous girls and women, 60, 74–5, 83; in Indigenous societies, 88, 88n17; racism and, 28, 60, 71–3, 139, 155, 227, 248, 251, 255; relationship to racism and violence against Indigenous women and girls, 61, 71, 155; sexual violence and, 71–3, 76; tolerated, 60–1, 147n6; as universal, 76, 153; violence and, 83. *See also* feminism, gender, Indian Princess, Pocahontas, squaw

Shakespeare, William: contemporary relevance of, 226; in school curriculum, 24, 252, 26; as universal heritage, 225

Sinclair, Brian, 257

Sinclair, Niigonwedom James (also Niigaanwiwedam), 223–4

Slipperjack, Ruby: *Honour the Sun*, 26, 167, 175; *Weesquachak and the Lost Ones*, 168

spirituality, 110, 114, 115; Catholic Church and, 53; women and, 36. *See also* Christianity

squaw, 28, 52, 242, 266; reclaiming word, 221; sexual violence and, 60, 71, 73, 84, 251. *See also* stereotypes

stereotypes, 62, 90, 127–8, 132–4, 217, 221, 224; cultural, 20–1, 27, 154, 174–5, 225–6; gender and heterosexist, 152; in Hollywood films, 219; Indigenous literature reproducing, 33; Indigenous literature challenging, 179, 222, 245; of Indigenous people as primitive, 103; of Indigenous people as voiceless, 23; Indigenous scholarship challenging, 114, 183, 222, 268; internalization of, 35, 60, 72, 177, 188, 199, 245, 266; legitimating violence, 59–60, 71–2, 75–6, 84; in mass media, 227; of Métis people, 209–10; racist, 255, 266–7, 271; sexist, 75–6, 84, 88, 139, 150, 154–5, 241; in textbooks, 182; traditionalism and, 88, 110, 115, 118, 131, 150, 172, 172n10, 177. *See also* civ/sav dichotomy, Hollywood films, Ignoble Savage, Indian Princess, Noble Savage, Pocahontas, squaw; Urban Cowboy, Urban Indian, Vanishing Indian

Stump, Sarain, 35; poem "There is My People Sleeping", 204

traditional ecological knowledge (TEK), 109–120, 213–15. *See also* land

Trickster, 18, 63n14, 168, 178, 261, 263. *See also* Wehsakehcha

Truth and Reconciliation Commission, xxiii, 256. *See also* reconciliation

university: community control over Indigenous knowledge in, 115–17; culture of criticism in, 229; distorted representation of Indigenous peoples in, 55, 203; Emma LaRocque in, 57, 137, 193, 194–5, 198, 203, 214, 228, 255–6, 263, 265, 267, 267n2, 271; ghettoization of Indigenous knowledges in, 26; Indigenous pedagogy in, 117–19, 215, 271; Indigenous women's writings in, 181; traditional ecological knowledge (TEK) and, 109–20. *See also* civ/sav, White

Urban Cowboy, 133. *See also* stereotypes; urbanism

Urban Indian, 133. *See also* stereotypes; urbanism

urbanism: academic study of, 222; bias from, 143; colonialism and, 95, 101–2, 107, 144–5, 165, 177, 208, 169; contemporary Indigenous, 106, 116, 176, 213, 233; Indigenous women, 148; literary representations of, 166, 168, 176; Louis Riel's, 98; tension with land-based life, 47n1, 187, 161. *See also* Urban Cowboy, Urban Indian

Vanishing Indian, xxiii, 111, 130, 131, 220n10, 226

Vine Deloria Jr.: vii

violence, 48, 49, 54, 145–8, 177, 190, 269–70; in Cowboy and Indian films, 134; against Indigenous men by women, 153; against Indigenous women, 36, 60, 61–2, 69–77, 83–4, 88, 139, 142, 145–9, 222, 270; depicted by Beatrice Culleton, 166; depicted by Lee Maracle, 167; depicted by Maria Campbell, 238; Indigenous gendered experience of, 84n8; institutional, 19. *See also* genocide, John Joseph Harper, Missing and Murdered Indigenous Women and Girls, Helen Betty Osborne, Brian Sinclair

voice: -Emma LaRocque's, 29, 63, 85, 114–15, 182, 182n1, 196, 198–9, 222, 272; Indigenous women's, 23–37, 150; in Métis storytelling, 239; Obomsawin, Alanis Obomsawin and, 34, 200; post-colonial, 86; as resistance writing, 179, 193–8, 237, 249; silencing of Indigenous, 22, 24, 27, 31, 33; in scholarship, 222, 230; White, 195. *See also* resistance writing

Wehsakehcha (also Wihsakehcha), 63, 225, 261–3, 272; in contemporary Indigenous culture, 176; Cree legend about ducks, 63n14; not in school curriculum, 24; storytelling in Emma LaRocque's childhood, 138, 225. *See also* Trickster

White: appropriation, 32–3; authority, 22, 24, 31–2; backlash against Indigenous people, 21–2, 24–5; claims to superiority, 6–7, 15–16, 18–22; claims to universality, 27; Métis as half, 10, 12; trash, 11. *See also* Howard Adams – White ideal, appropriation, civ/sav dichotomy, racism, stereotypes

Wiebe, Rudy: *The Scorched Wood People*, 11–12

Wihsakehcha. *See* Wehsakehha

Wild West Show, 124, 125, 134

Willis, Jane, 165–6

Wilson, Elizabeth "Betty", 11

DAVID LIPNOWSKI (www.davidlipnowski.com)

DR. EMMA LAROCQUE is a scholar, author, poet, and a professor in the Department of Indigenous Studies at the University of Manitoba, where she has been teaching since 1976. LaRocque is originally from a Cree/Michif-speaking and land-based Métis family and community from northeastern Alberta.

Overcoming obstacles of marginalization and poverty, LaRocque acquired a Bachelor of Arts degree in English/Communications (1973) from Goshen College, Indiana; a Master of Arts in Peace Studies (1976) from the Associated Mennonite Seminaries, Elkhart, Indiana (for which she received a Rockefeller Fellowship); and an MA in History (1980) as well as a doctorate in Interdisciplinary Studies in History/English (1999) from the University of Manitoba. Her dissertation on Aboriginal resistance literature (1999) was nominated for the Distinguished Dissertation Award, University of Manitoba.

Her prolific career includes numerous publications in areas of colonization/decolonization, Canadian historiography, racism, violence against women, and First Nation and Métis literatures and identities. Her poems are widely anthologized in prestigious collections and journals. She has appeared as a consultant on Métis identity in the NFB film *Women in the Shadows*.

A role model for Indigenous scholars and students, Dr. LaRocque has been a significant, if not leading, figure in the growth and development of Native (now Indigenous) Studies as a teaching discipline and an intellectual field of study. Her work has focussed on the deconstruction of colonial misrepresentation and on the advancement of an Indigenous-based critical resistance theory in scholarship, and she is one of the most recognized and respected Indigenous Studies scholars today.

Dr. LaRocque is frequently cited in a wide variety of places, including scholarly books, anthologies, and creative and learned journals. She has received national and international recognition and has presented papers and poetry in Australia, England, Hawaii, Italy, and throughout North America.

In 2005 Dr. LaRocque received the National Aboriginal Achievement Award. In 2019 she received the Indigenous Excellence-Trailblazer Award from the University of Manitoba. Also at the University of Manitoba she received the World's Teacher's Day award from the Arts Student Body Council in 2021. She is author of *Defeathering the Indian* (1975), which is about stereotypes in the school system; and more recently, author of *When the Other Is Me: Native Resistance Discourse 1850–1990* (2010), which won the Alexander Kennedy Isbister Award for Non-Fiction. She has written numerous articles, many of which are included in this collection of her works.

Her Alberta family's history, culture, and genealogy are rooted in the Red River Métis. She has maintained her family connections and has been a strong advocate for gender equality and for Métis land, resources, and human rights. Believing in the social purpose of knowledge, Dr. LaRocque has taught and published in the hopes of transforming mainstream Canadian perceptions and policies about Indigenous peoples.

Printed and bound by CPI Group (UK) Ltd, Croydon, CR0 4YY

31/07/2025

14712040-0002